About the Author

**Photo copyright ©
Shane Van Boxtel.**

Nick Redfern works full time as an author, lecturer, and journalist. He writes about a wide range of unsolved mysteries, including Bigfoot, UFOs, the Loch Ness Monster, alien encounters, and government conspiracies. His many books include *The Zombie Book* (co-written with Brad Steiger); *Close Encounters of the Fatal Kind*; and *Monster Diary*. He writes regularly for *Cryptomundo.com*, the *Mutual UFO Network Journal* and *Mysterious Universe*. He has appeared on numerous television shows, including Fox News; History Channel's *Ancient Aliens*, *Monster Quest*, and *UFO Hunters*; VH1's *Legend Hunters*; National Geographic Channel's *The Truth about UFOs* and *Paranatural*; BBC's *Out of This World*; MSNBC's *Countdown*; and SyFy Channel's *Proof Positive*. Nick lives just a few miles from Dallas, Texas' infamous Grassy Knoll and can be contacted at his blog: *http://nickredfernfortean.blogspot.com*.

ALSO FROM VISIBLE INK PRESS

Alien Mysteries, Conspiracies, and Cover-Ups
by Kevin D. Randle
ISBN: 978-1-57859-418-4

Conspiracies and Secret Societies: The Complete Dossier, 2nd edition
by Brad Steiger and Sherry Hansen Steiger
ISBN: 978-1-57859-368-2

The Government UFO Files
by Kevin D. Randle
ISBN: 978-1-57859-477-1

Hidden Realms, Lost Civilizations, and Beings from Other Worlds
by Jerome Clark
ISBN: 978-1-57859-175-6

Real Aliens, Space Beings, and Creatures from Other Worlds
by Brad Steiger and Sherry Hansen Steiger
ISBN: 978-1-57859-333-0

Real Encounters, Different Dimensions, and Otherworldly Beings
by Brad Steiger and Sherry Hansen Steiger
ISBN: 978-1-57859-455-9

Real Ghosts, Restless Spirits, and Haunted Places, 2nd edition
by Brad Steiger
ISBN: 978-1-57859-401-6

Real Miracles, Divine Intervention, and Feats of Incredible Survival
by Brad Steiger and Sherry Hansen Steiger
ISBN: 978-1-57859-214-2

Unexplained! Strange Sightings, Incredible Occurrences, and Puzzling Physical Phenomena, 3rd edition
by Jerome Clark
ISBN: 978-1-57859-344-6

The Zombie Book: The Encyclopedia of the Living Dead
by Nick Redfern and Brad Steiger
ISBN: 978-1-57859-504-4

Please visit us at www.visibleinkpress.com.

SECRET HISTORY

CONSPIRACIES FROM ANCIENT ALIENS TO THE NEW WORLD ORDER

Nick Redfern

Visible Ink Press

Detroit

SECRET HISTORY: CONSPIRACIES FROM ANCIENT ALIENS TO THE NEW WORLD ORDER

Visible Ink Press®
43311 Joy Rd., #414
Canton, MI 48187-2075

Visible Ink Press is a registered trademark of Visible Ink Press LLC.

Most Visible Ink Press books are available at special quantity discounts when purchased in bulk by corporations, organizations, or groups. Customized printings, special imprints, messages, and excerpts can be produced to meet your needs. For more information, contact Special Markets Director, Visible Ink Press, www.visibleinkpress.com, or 734-667-3211.

Managing Editor: Kevin S. Hile
Art Director: Mary Claire Krzewinski
Typesetting: Marco Di Vita
Proofreaders: Larry Baker and Dorothy Scott
Indexer: Shoshana Hurwitz

Front cover images: Stonehenge (Shutterstock), security camera (Shutterstock), Mason symbol (Shutterstock), 9/11 image (Robert J. Fisch), Quetzalcoatl (public domain).

Back cover images: President John F. Kennedy motorcade (Victor Hugo King), Edward Snowden (Wikileaks), crop circles (public domain).

Library of Congress Cataloging-in-Publication Data

Redfern, Nicholas, 1964-
  Secret history : conspiracies from ancient aliens to the new world order / by Nick Redfern.
       pages cm
  Includes bibliographical references.
  ISBN 978-1-57859-479-5 (pbk. : alk. paper)
  1. Conspiracies—United States. 2. Civilization, Ancient—Extraterrestrial influences. 3. Human-alien encounters. I. Title.
  HV6275.R45 2015
  001.9—dc23   2014046946

Printed in the United States of America

10 9 8 7 6 5 4 3 2

CONTENTS

Contents

NEW WORLD ORDER

Acknowledgments

I would like to offer my very sincere thanks to my tireless agent, Lisa Hagan; everyone at Visible Ink Press, and particularly Roger Jänecke and Kevin Hile; and good friends Micah Hanks and Greg Bishop.

Photo Credits

Airliners.net: p. 260.

Biblical illustrations by Jim Padgett, courtesy of Sweet Publishing, Ft. Worth, TX, and Gospel Light, Ventura, CA: p. 70.

Gary Blakeley: p. 359.

Das Bundesarchiv: pp. 133, 135, 143.

Cadiomals: p. 313.

California Department of Corrections: p. 211.

John Cavanagh: p. 296.

Central Intelligence Agency: pp. 154, 258.

Colegota: p. 76.

Nick Cooper: p. 356.

Cyberspaceorbit: p. 44.

Dallas Police: p. 198.

DavGreg: p. 203.

Bill de Blasio: p. 362.

Gustave Doré pp. 20, 51.

Dudeanatortron: p. 261.

eurok: p. 157.

Tim Evanson: p. 213.

Farm Security Administration/ Office of War Information: p. 129.

Farragutful: p. 220.

Federal Bureau of Investigation: p. 223.

Federal Emergency Management Agency: p. 291.

Nicolas Genin: p. 333.

Juergen Graf: p. 191.

Billy Hathorn: p. 299.

Andrew Heneen: p. 394.

Christian Jansky: p. 288.

The Jewish Museum, New York: p. 4.

Frederic Jueneman: p. 32.

Roy Kerwood: p. 237.

J.G. Klein: p. 193.

Lapavaestacaliente: p. 45.

Library of Congress: p. 196.

MacMax: p. 317.

Mary Evans Picture Library: pp. 6, 9, 84, 88, 106, 164, 227, 284.

McMarcoP: p. 91.

Finlay McWalter: p. 257.

Michael73072: p. 28.

NASA: pp. 33, 93, 96, 168, 232, 242, 243, 245, 396.

National Institutes of Health: p. 378.

National Park Service: pp. 31, 170, 173.

National Security Agency: p. 390.

The Nobel Foundation: p. 176.

ONAR: p. 13.

Oxfam East Africa: p. 360.

Pan American Coffee Bureau: p. 130.

Geoff Pick: p. 280.

Plazak: p. 82.

pop culture geek: p. 22.

Joaquín Alvarez Riera: p. 304.

Row17: p. 99.

Palimp Sesto: p. 61.

David Shankbone: p. 236.

Sternrenette: p. 369.

Olaf Tausch: p. 15.

Francis Tyers: p. 351.

Unukorno: pp. 77, 78.

UpstateNYer: p. 310.

U.S. Agency for International Development: p. 364.

U.S. Air Force: pp. 253, 282.

U.S. Army: pp. 325, 327, 342, 385.

U.S. Department of Defense: pp. 73, 127, 134, 287, 320.

U.S. Department of Energy: pp. 37, 140, 263.

U.S. Department of Justice: p. 205

U.S. Department of State: p. 337.

U.S. Marine Corps: pp. 39, 48.

U.S. National Archives and Records Administration: pp. 111, 217.

Caio do Valle: p. 239.

Erik van Wees: p. 295.

Jim Wallace (Smithsonian Institution): p. 218.

The White House: p. 190, 207, 331, 382.

Martin Whitely: p. 302.

Roque Wicker: p. 381.

The Wiki Leaks Channel: p. 388.

Public domain: pp. 14, 16, 19, 21, 26, 36, 40, 53, 55, 58, 63, 66, 103, 110, 115, 116, 118, 122, 146, 148, 179, 181, 186, 199, 219, 268, 273, 319, 324, 332, 338, 367, 374.

INTRODUCTION

The title of this book, as you will already have observed, is *Secret History*. It is a title that begs a number of important questions: What, precisely, *is* history? How does it impact us, both as individuals and as the collective human race? What can we learn from studying our history, both recent and ancient? Can historical events be manipulated in ways that we can scarcely begin to imagine? With those questions in mind, let's take a look at a few choice, wise words from a variety of noted individuals.

> Julian Barnes, the author of the best-selling *The Sense of an Ending*, said: "History is that certainty produced at the point where the imperfections of memory meet the inadequacies of documentation."

> In his classic novel *Ulysses*, James Joyce wrote: "History ... is a nightmare from which I am trying to awake."

> Aldous Huxley remarked: "That men do not learn very much from the lessons of history is the most important of all the lessons that history has to teach."

> George Orwell warned us: "The most effective way to destroy people is to deny and obliterate their own understanding of their history."

> "If you don't know history, then you don't know anything. You are a leaf that doesn't know it is part of a tree," wrote Michael Crichton of *Jurassic Park* fame.

> "History will be kind to me for I intend to write it," bragged British Prime Minister Sir Winston Churchill.

All of the above words, in their own, unique fashion, are important ones to remember and ponder. They are also words that are central to the themes of this book: (a) the ways by which certain, significant portions of history have been lost; (b) the ease with which entire swathes of our history have been erased; (c) the reasons why history has been suppressed and hidden and by whom; and (d) the secret, near-maniacal satisfaction on the part of powerful figures who have created deceptive histories that so many accept while barely asking a single question.

In the pages that follow you will come to appreciate—although, you will most certainly not approve of—the means by which history has been mauled, manipulated, and buried for reasons that are disturbing, mysterious, sinister, outrageous, unforgivable, and downright deadly.

You will understand how, even going back to the very dawn of civilization, humankind has been a slave to those who wish to present history as they wish it presented, rather than how it actually was and is. It's a situation that, even after thousands of years of manipulation, shows no signs of stopping.

From the sagas of the Old Testament to 9/11, from Jack the Ripper to the Roswell UFO crash, from the assassination of President John F. Kennedy to the mysterious 2014 disappearance of Malaysian Airlines flight MH370, and much more, *Secret History* demonstrates that what we *think* we know is not all that we *should* know or *can* know.

Both modern and millennia-old history, in their real, untouched form, are in danger of going the same way as the dinosaurs: down the road sign-posted towards extinction. Unless we pull ourselves back from the brink and recognize who we are and what we are, and why the good, the bad, and even the downright ugly parts of our history should be made available to us—however unpalatable they might be—we will remain blind to the truth. Opening our minds and lifting the shades of deception are particularly important if we are to progress as a species, rather than descend into a nightmarish realm that is part George Orwell's *1984* and part Aldous Huxley's *Brave New World*, combined with an "ignorance is bliss" attitude.

ANCIENT
ALIENS

THE TEN COMMANDMENTS: ALIEN PARALLELS

There can be very few people—regardless of their religious persuasions or otherwise—who have not heard of the Ten Commandments. Also referred to as the Decalogue, they are, essentially, purported to be strict laws prepared by the Christian god; laws designed to ensure that humanity follows a good and righteous path. They were laid down on a pair of stone tablets that were given to Moses at Mount Sinai—Moses being an Egyptian prince who turned prophet and religious leader.

It's notable that midway through the twentieth century, a number of people who claimed contact with very human-like extraterrestrials had experiences that eerily paralleled the story of Moses receiving the commandments at Mount Sinai. Before we get to the matter of ancient aliens, however, let's take a look at the story behind the Ten Commandments.

The story of the Ten Commandments appears twice in the pages of the Bible, in Deuteronomy and Exodus. It commences with the Israelites (variously referred to as the Sons of Israel or the Children of Israel) reaching Mount Sinai. Also known as Mount Horeb, Mount Sinai stands at approximately 7,500 feet in Egypt's Sinai Peninsula, which is located between the Red Sea and the Mediterranean Sea. There is, however, much debate on whether or not this particular Mount Sinai and the Mount Sinai of the Old Testament are one and the same.

It's to Exodus 19 we have to turn our specific attentions, since this is when, for all intents and purposes, the story begins. Approximately seventy-two hours after Moses and the Israelites arrived at the foot of the legendary mount, something strange and extraordinary occurred. The air was filled with huge flashings of lightning, and thunder crashed loudly and wildly. What was described as a "thick cloud" descended upon Mount Sinai, and the "voice of the trumpet" echoed throughout the vicinity. The people gathered together, wondering what might happen next.

We are told that "the Lord came down upon Mount Sinai," after which Moses had a short communication with God. On his return to the base of the mount, Moses told the Israelites that something amazing would soon happen. As far as the people were concerned, however, it was terror, rather than amazement, that took hold of their minds. That much became evident when, as if in unison, they moved far away from Mount Sinai, fearful of what might happen. Moses, seeing dissent amongst the people, quickly reassured them that all was well. "Fear not," were his famous words to the multitude. The Old Testament states that following his reassurances, Moses walked towards that somewhat ominous "thick cloud"—or "thick darkness," as it was also termed—and listened carefully as the voice of God boomed and proceeded to lay down the law.

The following morning, Moses, along with Aaron—the high priest of Israel—and his sons, Nadab and Abihu, climbed Mount Sinai. They "saw the God of Israel" hovering above what was described as a "paved work" of sapphire. God bellowed, as only a god surely can: "Come up to me into the mount, and be there … I will give thee tablets of stone, and a law, and commandments which I have written; that thou mayest teach them."

For no less than six days, so the story goes, Mount Sinai was covered by that mysterious "thick cloud." Then, on day number seven, Moses entered the cloud and remained "in the mount forty days and forty nights" (Exodus 24:18).

A turn-of-the-twentieth-century artwork by James Jacques Joseph Tissot illustrates the familiar biblical scene in which Moses descends Mount Sinai with the Ten Commandments.

While Moses was gone, the children of Israel reportedly decided to take matters into their own hands, which basically meant that Aaron created a deity, in the form of a golden calf and "built an altar before it" (Exodus 32:5). Wild partying, orgies, the drinking of lots of alcohol, and worshiping the golden calf were the name of the game. At least until Moses returned, at which point all hell broke loose—if you will pardon the pun. Moses had brought with him a pair of stone tablets that contained the Ten Commandments. Such was his anger at the way in which the Israelites had rebelled in his absence that Moses smashed the tablets on the ground.

God, fortunately, saw that Moses's actions were aimed at his people, not at God himself. The result, God ordered Moses: "Hew thee two tablets of stone like unto the first: and I will write upon these tablets the words that were in the first tablets, which thou brakest."

The Old Testament states of this: "And he wrote on the tablets, according to the first writing, the Ten Commandments, which the LORD spake unto you in the mount out of the midst of the fire in the day of the assembly: and the LORD gave them unto me" (Deut 10:4).

The golden calf was destroyed, the Ten Commandments became the law of the land, the two tablets found their way into the Ark of the Covenant (about which, there will be more very soon), and the rest—as the saying goes—is history. And with that all said, it's now time to look at the Ten Commandments. They are as follows:

1. Thou shalt have no other gods before me.

2. Thou shalt not make unto thee any graven image, or any likeness of any thing that is in heaven above, or that is in the earth beneath, or that is in the water under the earth: Thou shalt not bow down thyself to them, nor serve them: for I the LORD thy God am a jealous God, visiting the iniquity of the fathers upon the children unto the third and fourth generation of them that hate me; And shewing mercy unto thousands of them that love me, and keep my commandments.

3. Thou shalt not take the name of the LORD thy God in vain; for the LORD will not hold him guiltless that taketh his name in vain.

4. Remember the sabbath day, to keep it holy. Six days shalt thou labour, and do all thy work: But the seventh day is the sabbath of the LORD thy God: in it thou shalt not do any work, thou, nor thy son, nor thy daughter, thy manservant, nor thy maidservant, nor thy cattle, nor thy stranger that is within thy gates: For in six days the LORD made heaven and earth, the sea, and all that in them is, and rested the seventh day: wherefore the LORD blessed the sabbath day, and hallowed it.

5. Honour thy father and thy mother: that thy days may be long upon the land which the LORD thy God giveth thee.

6. Thou shalt not kill.

7. Thou shalt not commit adultery.

8. Thou shalt not steal.

9. Thou shalt not bear false witness against thy neighbour.

10. Thou shalt not covet thy neighbour's house, thou shalt not covet thy neighbour's wife, nor his manservant, nor his maidservant, nor his ox, nor his ass, nor any thing that is thy neighbour's.

The story of the Ten Commandments is one that millions of people believe to be the gospel truth. There is, however, an issue that needs to be addressed and that places the story of the Ten Commandments into a very different context; namely, the context of the UFO controversy.

The matter of the flashing and booming in the sky, that curious "thick cloud" (or "thick darkness") that suddenly appeared, as if out of nowhere, and the disembodied voice of God, have all led to theories that what Moses actually encountered were extraterrestrials, aboard a huge, dark-colored spacecraft, that wished to try and civilize the human race by indoctrinating it with a rigid, alien system of rules, regulations, and laws.

While many people of a deeply religious persuasion might be angered at such a scenario even being suggested, the fact is that more than a few UFO encounters have uncannily similar parallels with the biblical version of what happened across that forty-day period at Mount Sinai.

We will start with the man who absolutely typified the UFO scene in 1950s America: George Adamski (1891–1965). Born in Poland, Adamski moved to the United States, with his parents, when he was just a child. He spent four years in the military—at the height of the First World War—then spent time working variously, in a flour mill and at Yellowstone National Park. It was during the 1930s, however, that Adamski began to gravitate towards the world of the unknown, of the paranormal, and, finally, of the flying saucer. Adamski received significant publicity in early 1934, when the *Los Angeles Times* newspaper profiled him in its pages. The article told of Adamski's relocation to California. Interestingly, the newspaper took particular note of Adamski's words that revolved around a trek he made to the Himalayas. Rather notably, Adamski—while high in the mountains—had an experience that mirrored Moses's moment of enlightenment on Mount Sinai.

The *Los Angeles Times's* article noted:

> The ten-foot trumpets of far away Lhasa, perched among perpetual snows in the Himalayan Mountains in Tibet, will shortly have their echo on the sedate hills of Southern California's Laguna Beach. Already the Royal Order of Tibet has acquired acreage on the placid hills that bathe their Sunkist feet in the purling Pacific and before long, the walls, temples, turrets and dungeons of a Lama monastery will serrate the skyline. It will be the first Tibetan monastery in America and in course of time, the trained disciples of the cult will filter through its glittering gates to spread "the ancient truths" among all who care to listen. [The] central figure in the new movement is Prof. George Adamski.

The Polish-born George Adamski made a name for himself as a ufologist who declared that he had managed to take photographs of real alien spaceships.

Perhaps echoing the kind of transformation Moses went through, Adamski told the newspaper:

> I learned great truths up there on the roof of the world, or, rather, the trick of applying age old knowledge to daily life, to cure the body and the mind and to win mastery over self and soul. I do not bring to Laguna the weird rites and bestial superstition in which the old Lamaism is steeped, but the scientific portions of the religion.

Adamski wasn't long for Laguna Beach, however. He soon had another base of operations: Palomar Gardens, located near California's Palomar Mountain. As for the important matter of earning money, Adamski established the Palomar Gardens Café. It was in 1946 that Adamski and the intelligences behind the UFO phenomenon crossed paths in legendary fashion. In early October of that year, Adamski and several of his friends and followers encountered a gigantic, unidentified flying object in the skies near the mountain, one that was long and pencil-shaped. A similar craft—or, perhaps the very same one—appeared in the following year, 1947, and yet again at the site of the huge mountain. It was 1952, however, that really thrust Adamski into the ufological big time.

Greg Bishop, who has carefully studied the life and ufological claims of Adamski, tells the story of what happened, in an article titled "Tracks in the Desert," which appears in a 2000 book, *Wake Up Down There!*:

> … Adamski left his Palomar mountain retreat at 1.00 A.M. on Thursday November 20, 1952 along with his lifetime secretary Lucy McGinnis and Alice Wells—the owner of the property where Adamski gave lectures on Universal Law and the café where he flipped burgers to pay the rent. At about 8.00 A.M. they met with Al Bailey and his wife Betty, and George Hunt Williamson [a fellow Contactee and about who more imminently] and his wife, Betty, in Blythe, [California] just west of the Arizona / California border.

The group then suddenly turned back, on what was described as a "hunch." They retraced their steps, taking a small highway eleven miles northeast towards the town of Parker, Arizona, where they stopped. After breakfast, the group scanned the skies for saucers. Passing motorists slowed down, they wondered what was going on. When, around noon, an aircraft flew over the group, it provoked brief excitement. The main event was still to come, however. In fact, it was only moments away: a huge, silver-colored, cigar-shaped UFO suddenly loomed into view.

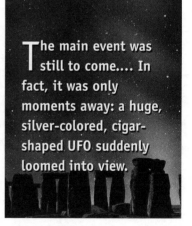

The main event was still to come…. In fact, it was only moments away: a huge, silver-colored, cigar-shaped UFO suddenly loomed into view.

Bishop said: "Williamson understatedly asked: 'Is that a space ship?', as Betty Bailey tried to set up a movie camera, but couldn't because 'she was so excited.' According to Adamski, they were anxious not to attract attention to the object, so they didn't point at it and alert other passing cars to this event."

"Someone take me down the road, quick! That ship has come looking for me and I don't want to keep them waiting!" Adamski yelled, as he jumped into the car with McGinnis and Mr. Bailey. About a half-mile down the road, with the craft shadowing them, Adamski told McGinnis to turn off the road. He then instructed the two to "go back to the others as quickly as possible … and watch for anything that might take place"—from the safe viewing distance of half a mile or more away. After this first craft was chased away by interceptor jets, another "beautiful small craft" arrived and landed behind the crest of a mountain about half a mile away.

Adamski soon saw a figure waving to him and walked towards it. Adamski said of this experience, "I fully realized I was in the presence of a man from space— a human being from another world!" The entity identified himself as Orthon and claimed to come from the planet Venus. After some warnings about atomic weapons and wars, and a refusal to be photographed, Orthon returned to his ship and sailed away.

Bishop added: "Adamski waved to his companions to approach, which they did soon after. Conveniently enough, Williamson had brought along some plaster-of-paris and proceeded to make casts of the footprints the Venusian had left in the desert floor. According to Williamson … he was

> … the first to arrive at the footprints after the contact had been made. I could see where the space being had scraped away the topsoil in order to get more moist sand that would take the impressions from the carvings on the bottom of his shoes. The carvings on the shoes must have been finely done for the impressions in the sand were clear cut. Either Orthon had a weight problem on Earth, or someone had taken extra care in making the impressions.

Bishop then notes something that, again, has a parallel with the saga of the Ten Commandments. He said that Adamski

> … goes on to state his interpretation of what meaning the symbols hold for those who "fail to obey the laws of the Infinite Father." Williamson also stresses that the designs are not "alien," since the Earth is "part of the Great Totality" and ancient symbols of Earth are the symbols of the space beings as well.… After this event Williamson seemed to have found his calling, and concentrated on turning out his own brand of Contactee literature—most of it "channeled"—leaving clear the nuts-and-bolts domain to his friend and inspiration, the other George—Adamski.

That Adamski had set up his organization on a mountain, that he had several profound UFO encounters on that very same mountain, and that all of this culminated in a statement that offered warnings to those who failed to "obey the laws of the Infinite Father" is a clear demonstration of the undeniable parallels between the story of the Ten Commandments and the saga of the most famous, so-called "Contactee" of all. Adamski's Moses-like experiences were not alone, however. There were others which experienced deeply similar encounters.

Truman Bethurum was a Californian, born in 1898, who spent many of his early years working jobs that never seemed to last. His first marriage both began and crumbled during the Second World War. He entered into a second marriage only several months after the war ended and ultimately wound up working out in the harsh, hot deserts of Nevada—specifically in the highway construction game. It was while Bethurum was out in the desert, in 1952, and while his second wife, Mary, was stuck at home in Santa Barbara, that Bethurum claimed he had an extremely close encounter with extraterrestrials on Mormon Mesa, a near-2,000-foot-high mount in Nevada's Moapa Valley.

On the fateful night in question, and after the working day was over, Bethurum climbed the mountain, primarily to search for shells, something that Mary particularly enjoyed collecting. The story goes that Bethurum was rendered into a strange, altered state of mind, during which advanced aliens suddenly manifested before him, having arrived in a huge, gleaming, flying saucer. Although only around five feet in height, the aliens were eerily human-looking and claimed to come from a faraway planet called Clarion. Not only that, their leader was one Captain Aura Rhanes, a shapely, Pamela Anderson-type who Bethurum described as being "tops in shapeliness and beauty." All thoughts of Mary—back in Santa Barbara—were suddenly gone from Bethurum's mind.

Not only did the Clarionites impart a great deal of data about their home world, their religion, and their belief in an all-powerful deity, they did something else too, something that those of a Christian persuasion will find all too familiar: they provided Bethurum with a gold plate that outlined the laws of the space people. Yet again, we have a prime example of someone taking a walk into the mountains, communing with superior entities, and being given a priceless artifact that detailed the rules and regulations of those same, superior beings. In that sense, there is very little difference between Moses's trek up Mount Sinai—where he communed with God and received the Ten Commandments, inscribed on two stone tablets—and Truman Bethurum heading up Mormon Mesa and being given a golden platter, courtesy of human-looking extraterrestrials who wished to share their laws with the human race.

There was another parallel too: in the same way that the God of the Old Testament is portrayed very much as a ruthless, cold-hearted deity, so the Clarionites were described as somewhat fascist, bullying types who insisted that Bethurum help them spread their word—or else. The wrath of God vs. the wrath of extraterrestrials: there's really not that much difference.

Then there was a certain George Van Tassel, who claimed interaction with aliens out in the harsh, roasting desert near Joshua Tree, California, in the early 1950s. Just like the extraterrestrials that both George Adamski and Truman Berthurum claimed to have encountered in the very same time frame, Van Tassel's visitors from the stars were: (a) extremely human-like and (b) highly demanding, when it came to getting across their space-laws and regulations. At the time of the encounters Van Tassel was living in the desert region of a small town called Landers—actually in a large, converted cave beneath a gigantic rock that, locally and unsurprisingly, was given the name Giant Rock.

Van Tassel claimed the aliens told him that the human race had been molded, guided, and manipulated for thousands of years—by extraterrestrials that posed as gods. In that sense, God was nothing more than a fabrication, one that was created to ensure the people of Earth ad-

A drawing of the space vehicle Truman Bethurum said he saw in the Nevada desert in 1952. (Mary Evans)

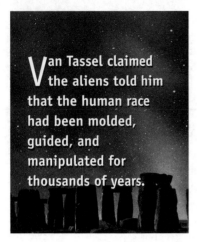

Van Tassel claimed the aliens told him that the human race had been molded, guided, and manipulated for thousands of years.

hered to the word of the space-aliens. Such was the fascination that the public had with his claims, Van Tassel was prompted to establish a yearly UFO conference at Giant Rock that—at its height, in the mid-1950s—attracted audiences in excess of *ten thousand*. The "word" was spreading. It even reached the FBI.

Documentation declassified by the FBI demonstrates that Van Tassel was of keen interest to J. Edgar Hoover and his G-Men, as were Van Tassel's statements concerning ancient aliens and the saga of the Ten Commandments. An FBI report on a lecture Van Tassel gave in Denver, Colorado, in 1960—titled "Unidentified Flying Objects" and prepared by an FBI agent on April 26, 1960—states the following:

> The major part of his lecture was devoted to explaining the occurrences in the Bible as they related to the space people.

He said that the only mention of God in the Bible is in the beginning when the universe was being made. He said that after that all references are to "out of the sky" or "out of heaven."

He said that this is due to the fact that man, space people, was made by God [sic] and that in the beginning of the world the space people came to the earth and left animals here. These were the prehistoric animals which existed at a body temperature of 105 degrees; however, a polar tilt occurred whereby the poles shifted and the tropical climates became covered with ice and vice versa.

After the polar tilt the temperature to sustain life was 98.6 degrees, which was suitable for space people, so they established a colony and left only males here, intending to bring females at a later date on supply ships. This is reflected in Adam not having a wife. He said that Adam was not an individual but a race of men.

[Van Tassel] said that this race then intermarried with "intelligent, upright walking animals," which race was EVE [sic]. Then when the space people came back in the supply ships they saw what had happened and did not land, but ever since, due to the origin of ADAM, they have watched over the people on Earth.

He said that this is in the Bible many times, such as MOSES receiving the Ten Commandments. He said the Ten Commandments are the laws of the space people and men on earth only give them lip service [Note from the author: Italics mine]. Also, the *manna* from heaven was bread supplied by the space people.

He also stated that this can be seen from the native stories, such as the Indians in America saying that corn and potatoes, unknown in Europe, were brought here by a "flaming canoe." He said that this can be shown also by the old stories of Winged Chariots and Winged White Horses, which came out of the sky.

He said that JESUS was born of MARY, who was a space person sent here already pregnant in order to show the earth people the proper way to live. He said the space people have watched over us through the years and have tried to help us. He said they have sent their agents to the earth and they appear just as we do; however, they have the power to know your thoughts just as JESUS did. He said this is their means of communication and many of the space people are mute, but they train a certain number of them to speak earth languages.

While those who interpret the Bible literally will doubtless balk at the claims of George Van Tassel, Truman Bethurum, and George Adamski, the fact is that all three men told stories that paralleled the biblical saga of the events at Mount Sinai to near-identical degrees.

Someone, or something, has for thousands of years attempted to enforce its rules and regulations on the human race. Whether it was *a* god, or all-powerful aliens from a far-off star-system very much depends on one's personal belief system—which is the way things have always been, and, likely, always will be.

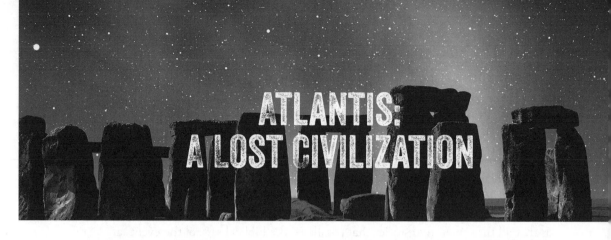

ATLANTIS: A LOST CIVILIZATION

They were a mighty race of people who, millennia ago, allegedly held sway over entire swathes of the planet. They were, in many ways, far more advanced than our own civilization. Such was the level of renown that surrounded this ancient and majestic culture. Their legend, even today, continues to live on. More correctly, for *some* it does. For others, the entire matter is one that should be relegated to the world of folklore and mythology. In all likelihood, the truth can be found in a hazy, foggy, combination of the two. We are talking about the story of the ill-fated land, and inhabitants, of Atlantis.

Although countless words and numerous books have been written on the rise and fall of Atlantis, they can almost all be traced back to the work of none other than Plato, the famous Greek philosopher who was born around 420 B.C.E. It was Plato's *Critias* that introduced people to the world of Atlantis. Plato's story told of an unsuccessful attempt by the Atlanteans to invade and conquer the people of Athens, the capital of Greece. Although *Critias* is presented as fiction, many researchers of the Atlantis enigma are of the opinion that Plato had acquired his information from archaic, secret texts that told the truth of the astoundingly advanced society that existed long before our own.

So the story goes, the ancient gods of Greece—or space aliens, one can take one's pick—elected to apportion various parts of the planet to equally various gods. Atlantis's lord and master was the god Poseidon. Like so many other gods that came before and after him, Poseidon lusted after human, mortal women—one young woman in particular, named Cleito. Demonstrating that the gods were actually as flesh and blood as the rest of us, Poseidon and Cleito had a number of children, the first being a character named Atlas—a man who had a lengthy reign over Atlantis, eventually ceding rule to his firstborn.

According to Plato, for a long time the relationship between the gods and the Atlanteans was a positive one. *Critias* records that for many generations, and ... as long as the divine nature lasted in them, they were obedient to the laws and well-affectioned towards the god whose seed they were; for they possessed true and in every way great spirits, uniting gentleness with wisdom in the various chances of life and in their intercourse with one another. They despised everything but virtue, caring little for their present state of life, and thinking lightly of the possession of gold and other property, which seemed only a burden to them; neither were they intoxicated by luxury; nor did wealth deprive them of their self-control; but they were sober, and saw clearly that all these goods are increased by virtue and friendship with one another, whereas by too great regard and respect for them, they are lost and friendship with them.

Sadly, the state of harmony did not last, as Plato recorded, also in the pages of *Critias*:

> When the divine portion began to fade away, and became diluted too often and too much with the mortal admixture, and the human nature got the upper hand, they then, being unable to bear their fortune, behaved unseemly, and to him who had an eye to see grew visibly debased, for they were losing the fairest of their precious gifts; but to those who had no eye to see the true happiness, they appeared glorious and blessed at the very time when they were full of avarice and unrighteous power.

A definitive wrath of god-style punishment followed, one in which Atlantean cities fell, people died in multitudes, landscapes shifted, volcanoes spewed forth, and finally, the land of renown sunk beneath the waves—taking its secrets with it—somewhere in the Atlantic Ocean. But was the story of Atlantis really just that—a story—after all? Or, could it have had a basis in reality?

The Greek philosopher Plato wrote about the world of Atlantis in his work *Critias*.

Such was the fascination with Plato's detailed and thought-provoking saga. It ensured that entire generations of Atlantis-seekers sought to find the remains of the legendary land and its people. In the domain of fiction, Plato's *Critias* clearly inspired Thomas More's *Utopia*—written in 1516—and Sir Francis Bacon's circa 1626 novel, *The New Atlantis*. Whereas neither More nor Bacon perceived Plato's work as being anything but fiction, others were of a very different view. The one man who was largely responsible for bringing the story of Atlantis to a new and wide audience—and for promoting the idea that Plato's story was based on an ancient reality—was nineteenth-century writer and a U.S. congressman from Minnesota who also served as that state's lieutenant governor) Ignatius L. Donnelly (1831–1901). He wrote, in *Atlantis: The Antediluvian World*:

> The fact that the story of Atlantis was for thousands of years regarded as a fable, proves nothing. There is an unbelief that grows out of ignorance, as well as a skepticism which is born of intelligence. The people nearest to the past are not always those who are best informed concerning the past.

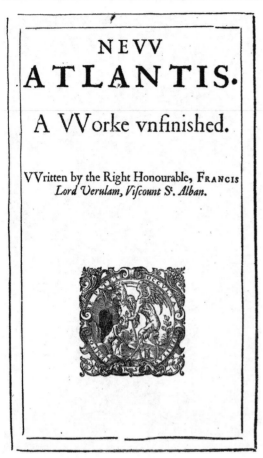

NEVV
ATLANTIS.

A VVorke vnfinished.

VVritten by the Right Honourable, Francis
Lord *Verulam*, *Vifcount* S⁺. *Alban*.

The New Atlantis is an incomplete utopian novel by Sir Francis Bacon that expressed his hopes for a world dedicated to science, dignity, community, and enlightenment.

In Donnelly's world, Atlantis was the inspiration for the biblical Garden of Eden and for Asgard, the Norse realm of the Scandinavian gods, such as Thor and Loki. As for its location, Donnelly suggested somewhere in the Mediterranean Sea. He, too, came to believe that the Atlanteans met a terrible and almost complete destruction. I say "almost" because Donnelly also believed that a few ragged bands of survivors made their way to what, today, is Egypt, and laid the foundations for the civilization that ultimately surfaced under the rule of the pharaohs.

Like Plato, Donnelly told of Atlantis being overwhelmed by gargantuan waves, something that, Donnelly concluded, had inspired the tales of the Great Flood, as presented in the pages of the Bible. In turn, Donnelly's work prompted other seekers of Atlantis to seek out the truth, including James Bramwell (*Lost Atlantis*, 1938), Edgar Cayce (who, in 1959, wrote *Earth Changes*), and Charles Berlitz (author of the 1969 book, *The Mystery of Atlantis*).

One problem, more than any other, has hindered the quest to resolve the conundrum that is Atlantis: its location.

Many investigators of the Atlantis legend have followed the leads of Plato and Donnelly by suggesting Atlantis was somewhere in the Atlantic Ocean or the Mediterranean Sea. Cyprus, Crete, Malta, and Sardinia have all been offered as viable locations. The Crete theory is a particularly engaging one: history has demonstrated that around 1500 B.C.E. the Minoan culture, on the island of Crete, was nearly obliterated by a powerful tsunami. Logically, Crete is a good candidate. There is, however, one big problem: the more that researchers, adventurers, authors, and scholars looked into the Atlantean tales, the more the time frame was pushed back, and back … and back.

For example, in his 1969 book, *Atlantis: The Truth behind the Legend*, Angelos Georgiou Galanopoulos suggested that the stories of Atlantis were distorted accounts of a cataclysmic event that occurred more than 9,000 years ago. It was a theory that took hold of the minds and opinions of many Atlantis-seekers. The result: nearly half a century later, the idea that Atlantis existed in the very remote past—rather than the relatively recent past—still holds firm sway.

That Atlantis may have been swallowed up millennia upon millennia ago has given rise to other theories for its final resting place. Rand and Rose Flem-Ath, for example—the authors of *Atlantis Beneath the Ice*—offer the controversial theory that Atlantis was, in reality, what today we call Antarctica. The Flem-Aths push the origins of the story back even further: to 9600 B.C.E.

And the list of potential sites for Atlantis doesn't end there: Turkey, northern Africa, Ireland, the Canary Islands, India, and the Andes—the vast South American mountain range—have all been offered. In other words, despite all the research and all the books, we're really none the wiser.

In terms of the theory that the Atlanteans possessed astonishing technologies that might very well have rivaled—and even surpassed—our own, it's necessary to focus on the work of a controversial man whose following is as devoted today as it was decades ago: Edgar Cayce (1877–1945). A product of the latter part of the nineteenth-century, Cayce, a prodigious author on all manner of esoteric topics, had a deep obsession with Atlantis and its people. Despite having died in 1945—the final year of the Second World War—Cayce's words on Atlantis are still influencing today's seekers of the legendary land.

Like Ignatius L. Donnelly, Cayce believed that the remnants of the Atlantean society seeded what ultimately became the Egyptian empire. Cayce's the-

Ruins of the city of Chania in Crete are evidence of the Minoan civilization that was destroyed by a tsunami around 1500 B.C.E.

ories didn't come from in the field, archaeological-style probing, however. Quite the contrary: Cayce asserted he was nothing less than a reincarnated Egyptian priest, one Ra Ta, who oversaw the running of a sacred Egyptian construction called the Temple of Sacrifice.

While many of a skeptical nature dismissed Cayce's claims, there is one particularly notable story that deserves telling. According to Cayce, a vast "hall of records," one that contained the full and unexpurgated story of the rise and fall of Atlantis, existed in a chamber buried below the carved, right paw of the Sphinx, at Giza, Egypt. Decades later, Robert Schoch, a renowned Sphinx authority, found, in his own words, what he described as "clear evidence of a cavity or chamber under the left paw of the Sphinx." That, at the time, Schoch was unaware of Cayce's assertions on this matter makes things even more remarkable.

In light of the above, it might be very wise to pay far more attention to Edgar Cayce's work, including his statements relative to what it was, exactly, that destroyed the Atlanteans. According to Cayce, Atlantis was not a small island—as many assume—but a vast area of land that bordered upon the size of Europe. The Atlanteans, he maintained, were highly advanced people, possessed of fantastic crystals that provided a near-unique power source, one that could be used to provide heat and electricity, and that could heal numerous ailments and disease.

A photo of Edgar Cayce from 1910. Cayce believed that survivors from Atlantis founded the ancient Egyptian empire.

Cayce said that as the years passed by, the Atlanteans—once a proud and upstanding culture—became filled with what he called "greed and lust" and inadvertently destroyed themselves via reckless use of their high-energy crystals.

And the story is still not over. Cayce famously predicted that, in either 1968 or 1969, Atlantis would finally rise from the waters and show itself to one and all. Well, it didn't quite happen like that. What *did* happen, however, is that in September 1968, and near North Bimini Island in the Bahamas, something known as the "Bimini Road" was found. It shows all the signs of being a half-mile-long "road," one that was intelligently constructed in the very distant past. While arguments, counter-arguments, and counter-counter arguments have been made with regard to whether or not the "road" is man-made or a curious product of Mother Nature, that it was discovered in the same time frame that Edgar Cayce predicted evidence of Atlantis would, at last, be found, is—at the very least—thought-provoking.

We would be wise to consider the possibility that one day, tens of thousands of years from now, tales of our civilization may be perceived as nothing more than the ravings of lunatics, born out of folklore and mythology.

A perfect example of how this has happened in the world of fiction is the ending of the original *Planet of the Apes* movie—made in 1968 and starring Charlton Heston. Throughout the movie, Heston's character—an astronaut named Taylor—believes he has crash-landed on an insane world ruled by talking apes. It is only at the end of *Planet of the Apes* that Taylor realizes he has traveled into the far future, at a time when the human race is no more. Worldwide nuclear war was our downfall. How does Taylor know? He finds the semi-buried remains of a shattered Statue of Liberty protruding out of the sands of a new, battle-scarred landscape—the Forbidden Zone, as the apes refer to it.

Maybe, one day, we will finally find the remnants of the Atlanteans. If we do, it will provoke a stark and stunning revelation: *we were not the first.*

THE ARK OF THE COVENANT: A DEADLY WEAPON

Beyond any shadow of doubt, the Ark of the Covenant is one of the most legendary and revered artifacts described in the pages of the Old Testament. It's also one of the most mysterious biblical artifacts, too. In fact, so mysterious is the Ark, and the attendant story that surrounds it, that a number of widely differing theories have been presented to try and explain both its origins and purpose. Each and every one of the theories has something in common: they are all highly sensational and deeply inflammatory.

There is the theory that the Ark was a two-way communication device, one that allowed the user to speak with none other than God himself. Or, as some researchers conclude, with devious extraterrestrials posing as deities and whose sinister agenda was to manipulate and control the human race. Another scenario has the Ark as a powerful weapon, one designed to provoke deadly electric shocks in those who dared to get too close to, or meddle with, it. Then there is the controversial possibility of the Ark being nothing less than radioactive. Other theorists suggest that the Ark had the power to transform sound itself into a deadly and devastating weapon of war. That there are so many wildly differing theories demonstrates only one thing for sure: thousands of years after it first surfaced, the Ark of the Covenant remains the definitive and undeniable mystery that it was to so many of the ancients themselves.

We learn of the Ark in the pages of the Exodus, in which it is presented as a highly decorated chest. It was designed to house the sacred stone tablets on which the Ten Commandments were written, having been provided to Moses while on Mount Sinai. Some biblical scholars believe that Mount Sinai is located in what, today, is Egypt's Sinai Peninsula. Others suggest somewhere in Saudi Arabia, or in the region of the ancient city of Petra, in the Kingdom of Jordan.

But how did the Ark of the Covenant, itself, come to exist? The answer is that we don't know—at least, not for sure. We are solely reliant upon ancient texts that have been written, rewritten, censored, and translated across thousands of years by multiple people with equally multiple agendas. The version accepted by those who adhere to the teachings of the Christian God is that around a year after the Israelites left Egypt behind them and embarked upon what has become known as the Exodus, God provided Moses with the necessary information to construct the mighty Ark, while the latter was at the base of Mount Sinai. It was a creation that instilled awe in all of those who encountered it. In others, it instilled death—and particularly so when touched.

In a 2006 article, titled "Re-Engineering the Ark," and penned for *Fortean Times* magazine, researchers Michael Blackburn and Mark Bennett note that:

> In verses 10–21 [of the Exodus], the instructions for the Ark are given; it is a lidless rectangular box construction, made of Shittim wood, measuring two and a half cubits long by one and half cubits wide and high. It is covered in gold over the inner and outer surfaces, with a gold crown or border around the top. Four gold rings are then added to each corner, for the carrying poles. These are to be made of the same gold-covered wood, and it is specifically ordered that they should never be removed.

The Ark of the Covenant is brought to the Temple in Jerusalem in this 1894 illustration by Henry Davenport Northrop that appeared in *Treasures of the Bible.*

Given that the Ark of the Covenant was, essentially, just a chest or box, how is it possible that—as the Old Testament states—it apparently played a major role in the legendary parting of the Red Sea, something that allowed the fleeing Israelites to escape the clutches of the pursuing Egyptian army? And how, also according to the Old Testament, was the Ark able to provoke the catastrophic fall of the walls of Jericho, when the Israelites began their conquest of Canaan? The answer is simple and confounding at the same time: the Ark wasn't just a chest or box. It was a great deal more.

That the walls of Jericho were, reportedly, brought down in part as a result of the presence of the Ark of the Covenant, and that the waters of the Red Sea were directly parted by the mysterious powers of the Ark, has led to an amazing and thought-provoking theory. It's one that posits the ancients possessed a long forgotten, and now long lost, technology. It was a technology based around the manipulation of acoustics, possibly to near-effortlessly move through the air the massive stones that were used in the construction of the Pyramids of Egypt, the similar Pyramids of South America, and England's famous Stonehenge. The technology, still very much at a theoretical level in today's world, has become known as acoustic levitation.

In their 2009 book, *The Resonance Key*, investigators Marie D. Jones and Larry Flaxman describe acoustic levitation as a means to introduce "two opposing sound frequencies with interfering sound waves, thus creating a resonant zone that allows the levitation to occur. Theoretically, to move a levitating object, simply change or alter the two sound waves and tweak accordingly."

The walls of Jericho tumble down in this illustration by Gustave Doré. According to the Book of Joshua, the power of the Ark was used by the Levites, who carried it around the city seven times, trumpets blaring.

In this process, it would also be theoretically feasible to use such sound waves as a sonic weapon (to flatten the walls of a city, such as Jericho), and as a means to manipulate and alter the flow of water (which is precisely what is alleged to have occurred at the Red Sea).

The idea that the Ark of the Covenant was an acoustic weapon of deadly proportions is a notable one. It's an idea that has a number of rivals, however, all of them eagerly vying for the top spot.

"I have never bashed the Bible for its accuracy or inaccuracy but only for its legitimacy as God's word," said Ark investigator Paul Schroeder, in a 2010 article, "Ancient Aliens and the Ark of the Covenant." He takes the view that it was ancient aliens, rather than an ancient god, that engineered the Ark of the Covenant: "There is overwhelming biblical evidence that the Ark of the Covenant was structurally designed to act as both an alien transmitter-capacitor/weapon. The Ark, lethal if touched, was used to communicate with aliens posing as God and it aided Israelites when it was carried into battles." He concluded: "This machine/ weapon technological artifice was an alien designed three-in-one communication device set, religious receptacle and weapon of mass destruction."

Roger Isaacs, in his book *Talking with God*, offers the astounding theory that the Ark of the Covenant was nothing less than radioactive. Isaacs said that while studying the stories of the Ark and its unique properties, he uncovered a "startling" use for something that appears on a number of occasions in the Old Testament: incense.

Isaacs said in his book:

Throughout history consumers of incense have used the sweet, smoky fragrance for mystical rites—but not the ancient Israelites. For them incense had a very practical, protective function relative to the Ark of the Testimony. The Israelite priests were trained to manufacture and use the Lord's specified mixture, not to propitiate the gods, not to make a nice smell, not to drive away demons or please kings and pharaohs.

No, the reason was very different, Isaacs maintains: "Incense was used to protect the priests and people from radiation burn. The resinous material had to be burned to become activated. It was the protective smoke, not the fragrance, that made incense effective."

Others suggest that electricity is the key to understanding the mysterious—and very often lethal—properties of the Ark of the Covenant. They just might be right.

Michael Blackburn and Mark Bennett, who have deeply studied the many and varied legends linked to the Ark, say that "the biblical Ark of Moses, the lost golden treasure that once stood in the Tabernacle in the wilderness of Sinai," and "the same Ark that led Moses and his followers into the Promised Land and stood in the legendary Temple of Solomon," was nothing less than "a Leyden Jar, a device capable of producing thousands of volts of static electricity!"

And what, precisely, is a Leyden jar? In simple terminology, it is a device that is able to retain static electricity via two pairs of electrodes, one positioned on the outside of, and the other on the inside of, a glass jar. In that sense, the Ark of the Covenant may have been a powerful early capacitor, one created by ancient man, long before electricity was on anyone else's radar. Such a controversial theory may one day prove to be not quite so controversial after all.

Researcher David Meyer stated in "Ark of the Covenant: Lost Technology": "For centuries, the Ark was viewed as a mystical object from God, beyond the knowledge of man. However, that changed on September 9, 1915, when the famous scientist Nikola Tesla published an article entitled *The Wonder World to be Created by Electricity*."

Within the pages of his article, Tesla, an undeniable genius, and a man way ahead of his time, brought up the matter of the controversy surrounding the Ark of the Covenant:

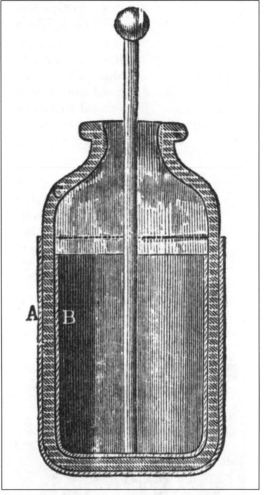

A Leyden jar is a glass jar lined on the outside (A) and inside (B) with metal foil. The top of the jar has no foil so as to prevent the release of electrical charge generated by the metal electrode inserted into it. It was invented in the eighteenth century, but some speculate that the Ark was actually a type of Leyden jar.

Moses was undoubtedly a practical and skillful electrician far in advance of his time. The Bible describes precisely and minutely arrangements constituting a machine in which electricity was generated by friction of air against silk curtains and stored in a box constructed like a condenser. It is very plausible to assume that the sons of Aaron were killed by a high tension discharge.

But, how—and when—could the ancients have developed electricity, or at least a degree of understanding of it and its life-threatening effects? Let's take a look at what has become known as the Baghdad Battery, an amazing artifact that appears to demonstrate the ancients had far more than a passing knowledge of electricity.

"The enigmatic vessel," said author Mark Pilkington, of the Baghdad Battery, in a 2004 paper, "Ancient Electricity":

> was unearthed by the German archaeologist Wilhelm Koenig in the late 1930s, either in the National Museum or in a grave at Khujut Rabu, a Parthian (224 B.C.E.–226 C.E.) site near Baghdad (accounts differ). The corroded earthenware jar contained a copper cylinder, which itself encased an iron rod, all sealed with asphalt. Koenig recognized it as a battery and identified several more specimens from fragments found in the region.

Koenig was almost certainly not wrong, as Pilkington demonstrates in his paper:

> Following the war, fresh analysis revealed signs of corrosion by an acidic substance, perhaps vinegar or wine. An American engineer, Willard Gray, filled a replica jar with grape juice and was able to produce 1.5–2 volts of power. Then, in the late 1970s, a German team used a string of replica batteries successfully to electroplate a thin layer of silver—electroplating being a process that utilizes an electric current to coat the surface of one kind of metal with another.

Somewhere, in this tangled mass of theories, the truth of the Ark of the Covenant might very well lurk. The biggest problem in solving the riddle is that, today, the Ark cannot be found—anywhere.

This movie prop of the Ark of the Covenant was used in the 1951 film *David and Bathsheba*. Similar to the one used in the more recent *Raiders of the Lost Ark* it was designed based on biblical accounts of the Ark.

The Lumba people of South Africa believe that the Ark is hidden deep inside an ancient cave, somewhere in South Africa's Dumghe Mountains. On a similar path, biblical scholars point to an undiscovered cave on Jordan's Mount Nebo. Ireland's Hill of Tara—where numerous ancient artifacts have been found, many dating back to the beginnings of the Iron Age, 1200 B.C.E.—has also been suggested as a candidate. A place of secret safekeeping, somewhere in the Ethiopian city of Axum, has also been suggested, one where the Ark is guarded with a near paranoid zeal by elements of the Ethiopian Orthodox Church. On the conspiratorial front, there's the idea that the Ark sits in a heavily guarded vault within the likes of Fort Knox or Area 51. In that sense, the final scenes of the 1981 Indiana Jones movie, *Raiders of the Lost Ark*, might not have been too wide of the mark when they showed the Ark locked away by the U.S. government in a secret warehouse.

The unfortunate reality is that until, or unless, the Ark of the Covenant finally surfaces, we will never really know if the enigmatic, legendary device was the work of God, extraterrestrials, or just regular people with far more scientific and technical savvy than we currently credit them possessing.

EZEKIEL'S WHEEL: A CLOSE ENCOUNTER WITH E.T.

In the final, memorable scenes of Steven Spielberg's acclaimed 1977 movie, *Close Encounters of the Third Kind*, a huge spacecraft descends to earth, in a remote location, where humans and aliens meet in just about the most direct way possible—hence the movie's unforgettable title. As astonishing as it may sound, just such a thing may have happened in the real world, albeit thousands of years ago. Even more astonishing, it's to the pages of none other than the Bible we have to turn to learn about this extraordinary and controversial incident. The story revolves around a man named Ezekiel and his close encounter with what sounds eerily like a classic flying saucer.

Before we get to the potentially other-world event itself, let's take a look at the life of the man in question. What we know of Ezekiel is fairly limited, but it does provide us with valuable insight. The data comes from the Book of Ezekiel, which is written in the author's very own, astounding words. Ezekiel, the Old Testament tells us, was the son of a man named Buzi and someone born into an upper-class, Jewish family in a place referred to as Anathoth. While there is a fair amount of significant dispute amongst biblical scholars about the actual location of Anathoth, some have suggested that it is an ancient name for what, today, is Abu Ghosh, a town situated in Israel, around six miles outside the city of Jerusalem.

> [W]hen Ezekiel was thirty, ... he had a profound, life-changing experience. It might just have been an encounter with beings born on another world, in another galaxy even.

Nebuchadnezzar II was the king of what, at the time of Ezekiel's encounter, was called the Neo-Babylonian Empire. It came to the fore in 626 B.C.E. and lasted until 539 B.C.E. As the ruler of Babylonia, in 597 B.C.E. Nebuchadnezzar ordered his armies to banish into exile no less than 3,000 Jews, all of the Kingdom of Judah. That included Ezekiel, at the time, around twenty-five years of age, as well as his wife—both of whom were sent to Babylon. Unfortunately, Ezekiel's wife was not long for this world—she was dead less than a decade after their period of time in exile began. It was roughly half way through the exile, when Ezekiel was thirty, that he had a profound, life-changing experience. It might just have been an encounter with beings born on another world, in another galaxy even.

Ezekiel's words make it very clear that he perceived the experience to be nothing less than a close encounter with God, himself. Others take a far different stance, saying it had far less to do with a literal deity and far more to do with highly advanced entities from a faraway world. Let's see what Ezekiel had to say. In both Chapters 1 and 10 of his book, he describes his encounter with something incredible, in graphic terms. Since it's important to have a full understanding of what Ezekiel encountered, the text of his experience is related in full:

> And I looked, and, behold, a whirlwind came out of the north, a great cloud, and a fire infolding itself, and a brightness was about it, and out of the midst thereof as the colour of amber, out of the midst of the fire.

> Also out of the midst thereof came the likeness of four living creatures. And this was their appearance; they had the likeness of a man.

> And every one had four faces, and every one had four wings.

> And their feet were straight feet; and the sole of their feet was like the sole of a calf's foot: and they sparkled like the colour of burnished brass.

> And they had the hands of a man under their wings on their four sides; and they four had their faces and their wings.

> Their wings were joined one to another; they turned not when they went; they went every one straight forward.

> As for the likeness of their faces, they four had the face of a man, and the face of a lion, on the right side: and they four had the face of an ox on the left side; they four also had the face of an eagle.

> Thus were their faces: and their wings were stretched upward; two wings of every one were joined one to another, and two covered their bodies.

> And they went every one straight forward: whither the spirit was to go, they went; and they turned not when they went.

> As for the likeness of the living creatures, their appearance was like burning coals of fire, and like the appearance of lamps: it went up and down among the living creatures; and the fire was bright, and out of the fire went forth lightning.

> And the living creatures ran and returned as the appearance of a flash of lightning.

> Now as I beheld the living creatures, behold one wheel upon the earth by the living creatures, with his four faces.

> The appearance of the wheels and their work was like unto the colour of a beryl: and they four had one likeness: and their appearance and their work was as it were a wheel in the middle of a wheel.

> When they went, they went upon their four sides: and they turned not when they went.

> As for their rings, they were so high that they were dreadful; and their rings were full of eyes round about them four.

> And when the living creatures went, the wheels went by them: and when the living creatures were lifted up from the earth, the wheels were lifted up.

Whithersoever the spirit was to go, they went, thither was their spirit to go; and the wheels were lifted up over against them: for the spirit of the living creature was in the wheels.

When those went, these went; and when those stood, these stood; and when those were lifted up from the earth, the wheels were lifted up over against them: for the spirit of the living creature was in the wheels.

And the likeness of the firmament upon the heads of the living creature was as the colour of the terrible crystal, stretched forth over their heads above.

And under the firmament were their wings straight, the one toward the other: every one had two, which covered on this side, and every one had two, which covered on that side, their bodies.

And when they went, I heard the noise of their wings, like the noise of great waters, as the voice of the Almighty, the voice of speech, as the noise of an host: when they stood, they let down their wings. (Ezekiel 1:4–24)

As far back as 1964, the UFO research community was beginning to realize that what Ezekiel was reporting may not have been an encounter with God, after all. W. Raymond Drake (1913–1989) stated: "The Book of Ezekiel abounds with references to chariots from heaven and to Extraterrestrials, whom we would class as Spacemen."

The late Robert Dione (1922–1966) was someone who was fascinated by the story of Ezekiel. A paratrooper in the Second World War, and a graduate of the University of Maine, he penned two books: *God Drives a Flying Saucer* and *Is God Super-Natural?* Of Ezekiel's close encounter, Dione said—in the pages of *God Drives a Flying Saucer*—that he, Ezekiel, provided "a remarkably accurate description of a flying saucer which visited him as an agent of God … he describes a device very similar to a device which has been described thousands of times in recent years by flying saucer observers."

The description of the prophet Ezekiel's vision from the Bible sounds remarkably like an encounter with alien beings.

Dione makes a valuable point in his book: "Had Ezekiel used the same language to describe a submarine or an airplane, not a single reader would doubt that he had seen it … but because it is a flying saucer that he describes, many of us prefer to stick our heads in the sand and dismiss the whole incident."

He also had significant things to say about Ezekiel's description of the "cloud" and its apparent occupants. On the matter of the "wheel" and "the work of them was like the appearance of the sea," Dione said: " … is not Ezekiel telling us that the device hovered, rocked and yawed…?"

Dione also comments on the following from Ezekiel: "When they went, they went by their four parts: and they turned not when they went." Dione observed: "They could fly sideways, forward and back without turning; this is a typical flying saucer characteristic." Then there was the issue of these words from Ezekiel: "... the whole body was full of eyes round about all the four." This led Dione to note, and not without considerable justification: "Many flying saucers are reported to have lights around the rims which to Ezekiel might have appeared as eyes."

And as Dione concluded: "So we see that Ezekiel describes a craft which came down from the sky with voluble, or rotating, wheels; it shines like amber and makes a noise like that of rushing waters. It yaws and hovers and has lights around its rims. Surely he's describing nothing else than a flying saucer."

Robert Dione was not the only one to come to such a conclusion about Ezekiel's famous close encounter.

Ancient astronaut authority, Zecharia Sitchin made a notable contribution to the Ezekiel controversy. He explained that the Book of Ezekiel doesn't just cover Ezekiel's close encounter, but also visionary—or holographic—events, in which extraterrestrials may have revealed to him their future plans.

In his book *Divine Encounters*, Sitchin explained:

Ezekiel was not only miraculously transported (twice) from Mesopotamia to the Land of Israel. The second time he was shown, in what nowadays we would call a 'Virtual Reality' technology, scene by scene, details of something that did not yet exist—the *future* temple; the House of Yahweh that was to be built according to the architectural details revealed to Ezekiel in this *Twilight Zone* vision.

He further noted in his book:

Visitors to science museums are often fascinated by the holographic displays in which two beams project images that when combined seem to enable one to see an actual, three dimensional image floating in the air. Were these kinds of techniques, undoubtedly far more advanced, used to enable Ezekiel to see, visit, and even enter things that were not really there, in physical, 3-D form?

Frank E. Carlisle, who has studied the story of Ezekiel very closely, notes that in terms of what is reported within the pages of the Old Testament, the story of Ezekiel does not stand alone. There are other cases that parallel, and which are very similar to, that of Ezekiel.

Carlisle said, in a 2004 report, "Solving the Riddle of Ezekiel's Wheels":

The Old Testament abounds with texts that speak of how angels came to the earth in ancient times riding in heavenly vehicles that are represented metaphorically as "horses" and "chariots" of God. Psalm 68:17 is probably the most definitive example of the Old Testament "angelic chariot" texts. This Psalm addresses the chronology of the Jewish Exodus from captivity in Egypt, their encampment at Mount Sinai, and the events that transpired at that time. "The chariots of God are twenty thousand, even thousands multiplied: the Lord was among them at Sinai, in the [heavenly] Temple/Sanctuary."

A long-retired test stand for the Saturn V rocket at the Marshall Space Flight Center, where Josef Blumrich worked as an engineer. Blumrich was convinced Ezekiel had seen an alien ship.

Of all the people who looked deeply into the saga of Ezekiel, certainly no one highlighted the UFO connections more than a man named Josef Blumrich (1913–2002), an engineer who worked at NASA's Marshall Space Flight Center in Alabama—where the initial research on the Saturn launch vehicles for the *Apollo* project began. The reason why Blumrich came to take such an interest in the story of Ezekiel—which led him, in 1974, to write an entire book on the subject, *The Spaceships of Ezekiel*—has been told by Nephilim authority Scott Alan Roberts. It's a story filled with irony, as Roberts notes, in the following words from his book, *The Rise and Fall of the Nephilim*:

> NASA spacecraft engineer Josef F. Blumrich had read Erich von Däniken's *Chariots of the Gods*. In the book, von Däniken described Ezekiel's vision as none other than a "flying disk." Blumrich immediately set about to disprove von Däniken's theory, but upon further investigation found that the vision in Ezekiel was nearly identical to a proposed craft that he had invented.

It's hardly surprising, then, that Blumrich became fascinated—nearly to the point of obsession—with trying to figure out what it was that Ezekiel encountered; even to the extent that, as a result of his engineering background, Blumrich constructed scale-models, based upon Ezekiel's description of the phenomenon before him.

Ezekiel researcher Jim Aho noted in his 2014 article, "Ezekiel's Wheel," that what Blumrich found, "after an extensive amount of research from an engineering point of view," was not what he had expected to find:

> He went from an extreme skeptic to becoming convinced that the book of Ezekiel was a real accurate and detailed account of an encounter with extraterrestrial visitors. Very interesting coming from a person who is not a religious zealot by any means and is about as far as you can get from a gullible person who might be prone to jump to conclusions.

Blumrich's research uncovered something notable in the extreme: Ezekiel's famous encounter was not a solitary event. Ezekiel, said Blumrich, had no less than four experiences of the other world type. Of the second event, Blumrich said, it was "brief and fragmentary." The third event, however, was something else entirely, as Blumrich demonstrated in a 1974 paper, "The Spaceships of the Prophet Ezekiel":

> In his account of the third experience one year after the first Ezekiel narrates a fascinating event culminating in what seems to be a maintenance

or repair operation on the spacecraft. A mechanical arm reaches from a helicopter unit toward the red-hot area at the lower tip of the main body and hands a "hot" part of some kind to a member of the crew on the ground who had been ordered to take a position near one of the helicopters. The crewman carries away the hot pan. A comparison of the temple Ezekiel describes with a plan of Solomon's Temple (still standing at that time) shows that Ezekiel's description is of another temple, but where?

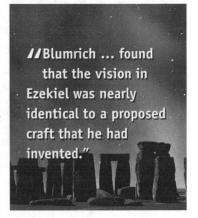

//Blumrich ... found that the vision in Ezekiel was nearly identical to a proposed craft that he had invented."

As for Ezekiel's fourth and final experience, Blumrich stated:

Ezekiel's arrival at a large complex of buildings proves to have been scheduled because he is awaited by a man wearing clothing similar to that of the ship's commander and who takes the prophet on an extended tour through the temple. The report of this encounter, as well as the Book of Ezekiel, ends abruptly and must be considered as a fragment.

In finality, Blumrich had to admit:

With these conclusions, I had to declare defeat; I wrote to Erich von Daniken, explaining that my attempt to refute his theory had resulted in a structural and analytical conformation of a major part of his hypothesis. Determining the form, dimensions and functional capabilities of what Ezekiel saw makes understandable a number of passages in his text that are otherwise meaningless; it also aids considerably in separating the prophetic or visionary parts of Ezekiel's book from those concerning encounters with spaceships.

Did Ezekiel, thousands of years ago, experience something that, today, we would consider to be nothing less than a full-blown extraterrestrial encounter of the third—and deeply, profound—kind? The problem, of course, and the matter of why the entire issue remains one of such controversy, is very simple: those who adhere to the teachings of the Bible insist that we should take its words as they are written and not reinterpret them, ad infinitum.

On the other hand, UFO researchers have suggested that reinterpreting the words of Ezekiel is essential, since—given the time frame when the incident(s) occurred—the man himself would hardly have been in a position to understand the concept of what an alien spacecraft really was, or still is. Like so many other biblical mysteries, conspiracies, and secrets—and those events that fall into all three categories—the story of Ezekiel continues to mystify mankind, very much as it did the man himself, all those centuries ago.

ANCIENT NUCLEAR WAR: A TIME BEFORE OURS

On July 16, 1945, at 5.30 A.M., history was made at Alamogordo, New Mexico. The specific location was an innocuous stretch of desert on the White Sands Missile Range (at the time, called the White Sands Proving Ground). That same stretch of desert was not destined to remain innocuous, however. Today, it is downright historic. Code-named *"Trinity,"* it was the site of the very first atomic bomb test, and was the culmination of years of highly classified work to perfect the ultimate weapon of mass destruction. The program itself, the Manhattan Project, was overseen by a brilliant physicist, J. Robert Oppenheimer (1904–1967), and employed thousands of personnel. The destructive power of the atomic bomb shocked even those working on the program—who, it transpires, were far from sure what the precise effects would be when the bomb was detonated. They soon found out.

A crater, no less than 340 feet across, was carved into the desert floor. The desert sand melted, turning it into a radioactive, green colored glass that was dubbed trinitite. The blast—which was the equivalent of 19 tons of TNT detonating at once—was felt more than 200 miles away, while the accompanying flash that lit up the early morning sky was visible across much of New Mexico. To protect the secrecy surrounding the detonation of the device, a cover story was put out by the military, one that assured the press and the local populace that "a remotely located ammunitions magazine containing a considerable amount of high explosives and pyrotechnics exploded," adding that "there was no loss of life or limb to anyone."

With the test having succeeded beyond the wildest dreams of the project team, the next step was to use the threat of the awesome power of the bomb as a means to end the Second World War. The fighting in Europe had come to its closure on May 8, 1945. Problematic, however, was that in the Pacific Theater the conflict still raged wildly. Seeing there was a distinct possibility that battling the Japanese in conventional fashion would be very costly in terms of Allied casualties, the U.S. military elected to do something else: on July 26, 1945, Japan was warned, in no uncertain terms, that if it did not surrender it would face "prompt and utter destruction."

They were ominous words, ones that the Japanese—to their cost—failed to heed. When Japanese forces continued to wage war and summarily ignored the threat, a plan was put into operation that brought the war to an end in shuddering, pummeling, fashion. On August 6, 1945, the Japanese city of Hiroshima was destroyed by an atomic weapon dubbed *Little Boy*. Three days later, the city of Nagasaki was equally flattened—by an identical device known as *Fat Man*. Faced with the prospect of seeing its nation systematically wiped off the face of the planet, Japan surrendered. The death-count was huge: the combined fatalities in both cities were estimated to have been in excess of a quarter of a million.

It is a testament to the power, and the devastating effects, of the atomic bomb—not to mention the fear that such weapons generate—that it has never again been used during warfare. But, is it possible that atomic weapons might have been used *before* the Trinity test and the attacks on Japan? Incredibly, is it possible that such weapons were used millennia ago, by highly advanced civilizations that, today, are perceived as nothing more than the stuff of legend, mythology, and folklore?

The website *Message to Eagle* notes in a report entitled "Physical Evidence of Ancient Atomic Wars Can Be Found World-Wide" that, in the early 1950s,

> … archaeologists conducting excavations in Israel discovered a layer of fused green glass. The layer was a quarter of an inch thick and covered an area of several hundred square feet. It was made of fused quartz sand with

A V-2 rocket facility at White Sands Missile Range in New Mexico. It was at White Sands where the first nuclear tests were conducted during World War II.

Immanuel Velikovsky was an independent, Russian scholar who wrote books such as *Worlds in Collision* that reinterpreted history in controversial ways.

green discoloration, similar in appearance to the layers of vitrified sand left after atomic tests in Nevada in the 1950s. Five years earlier a thin layer of the same glass was dug up below the Neolithic, Sumerian and Babylonian strata in southern Iraq. To the south, the western Arabian desert is covered with black rocks that show evidence of having been subjected to intense radiation. These broken and burned stones are called "harras" that are strewn over an area of 7,000 square miles.

Of these anomalies, Immanuel Velikovsky (1895–1975), the author of such books as *Worlds in Collision* (1950) and *Earth in Upheaval* (1955), noted they were very similar to those found at the Trinity site, New Mexico, in 1945. He wrote in *Earth in Upheaval:*

> Some single fields are one hundred miles in diameter and occupy an area of six or seven thousand square miles, stone lying next to stone so densely packed that passage through the field is almost impossible. The stones are sharp-edged and scorched black. No volcanic eruption would have cast scorched stones over fields as large as the harras. Neither would the stones from volcanos have been so evenly spread. The absence in most cases of lava (the stones lie free) also speaks against a volcanic origin for the stones....

Similarly, researcher Leonardo Vintini said, in a 2103 article, "Desert Glass Formed By Ancient Atomic Bombs?":

> In December 1932, Patrick Clayton, a surveyor from the Egyptian Geological Survey, drove between the dunes of the Great Sand Sea, close to the Saad Plateau in Egypt, when he heard crunching under the wheels. When he examined what was causing the sound, he found great chunks of glass in the sand.

Vintini continued:

> The find caught the attention of geologists around the world and planted the seed for one of the biggest modern scientific enigmas. What phenomenon could be capable of raising the temperature of desert sand to at least 3,300 degrees Fahrenheit, casting it into great sheets of solid yellow-green glass?

David Icke (1952–), who has studied reports of ancient atomic warfare in the Pakistan/India area, states in *Children of the Matrix* that the stories are supported by an amazing find found in the prehistoric Indian cities of Mohenjo-daro and Harappa. On the street level were discovered skeletons, appearing to be fleeing, but death came too quick. They were found to be highly radioactive, on a level comparable to Hiroshima and Nagasaki. Yet there are absolutely no indications of volcanic activity, and it appears that both cities were destroyed at virtually the same time.

In an article titled "The Ancient Nukes Question: Were There WMDs in Prehistoric Times?" Micah Hanks, a noted authority on claims of ancient nuclear warfare, said of

places like Mohenjo-daro, a once prosperous ancient city in modern day Pakistan … [that they appear to] bear trace evidence of some kind of cataclysmic event in its historic past that, even by today's standards, remains difficult to explain. Granted, if we are to utilize modern conventions available to us in the present day, a number of the peculiarities about this particular location can (and do) bear remarkable similarity to the aftermath of a nuclear explosion.

Hanks continues,

The problem, of course, is to attempt to reconcile with the anomalies of places like Mohenjo-daro by asserting that nuclear explosions—the likes of which have been seen previously only at places like Hiroshima and Nagasaki during WWII—could have occurred *thousands* of years ago.

Hanks adds to his observations:

While I'm hesitant, as many probably should be, to say there is definitive proof of nuclear weapons being used in ancient or even prehistoric times, I don't think it can be argued that nuclear *events* of some variety—perhaps even naturally occurring—did occur in Earth's distant past.

Still, on the matter of India, ancient anomalies researcher David Hatcher-Childress said:

Another curious sign of an ancient nuclear war in India is a giant crater near Bombay. The nearly circular 2,154-metre-diameter Lonar crater, located 400 kilometers northeast of Bombay and aged at less than 50,000 years old, could be related to nuclear warfare of antiquity.

No trace of any meteoric material, etc., has been found at the site or in the vicinity, and this is the world's only known "impact" crater in basalt. Indications of great shock (from a pressure exceeding 600,000 atmospheres) and

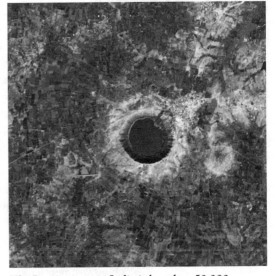

The Lonar crater in India is less than 50,000 years old. Researcher David Hatcher-Childress (1957–), in his 2014 report, "Giant Unexplained Crater Near Bombay," speculates it could be evidence of an ancient nuclear war.

intense, abrupt heat (indicated by basalt glass spherules) can be ascertained from the site.

During the course of his research, Micah Hanks uncovered further examples of what might amount to prime examples of ancient, atomic warfare:

One interesting example of this is an article that was penned by researchers Richard B. Firestone and William Topping, titled *Terrestrial Evidence of a Nuclear Catastrophy in Paleoindian Times*. The article appeared in *Mammoth Trumpet Magazine's* March 2001 issue, and recounted curiously high levels of radiocarbon data gathered from the Great Lakes Region of the United States.

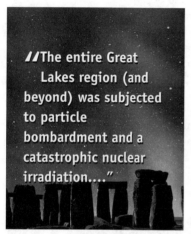

//The entire Great Lakes region (and beyond) was subjected to particle bombardment and a catastrophic nuclear irradiation...."

Indeed, Firestone and Topping made interesting observations in their 2001 article: "The entire Great Lakes region (and beyond) was subjected to particle bombardment and a catastrophic nuclear irradiation that produced secondary thermal neutrons from cosmic ray interactions."

Concerning this, Hanks notes that "it was a wide scale nuclear event dating back to Paleo-Indian times, and though the authors speculate that a supernovae *might* have been the cause for the event in question, it remains uncertain exactly what else could account for such an anomaly."

The late Philip Coppens (1971–2012) asked: "In the search for an advanced ancient civilization, what would be this 'best evidence?'" He answered his own question with the following, extracted from his 2005 article, "Ancient Atomic Wars: Best Evidence."

One possible item that would classify as "best evidence" exists within the Indus River Valley, where towns such as Harappa and Mohenjo Daro flourished in 3000 B.C.E. The question is why these cities were abandoned. And one answer that has been put forward is that the ancient cities might have been irradiated by an atomic blast.

If true, it would be impossible to ignore the conclusion that ancient civilization possessed high technology.

Coppens noted further:

The story begins when a layer of radioactive ash was found in Rajasthan, India. It covered a three-square mile area, ten miles west of Jodhpur. The research occurred after a very high rate of birth defects and cancer was discovered in the area.

The levels of radiation registered so high on investigators' gauges that the Indian government cordoned off the region. Scientists then apparently unearthed an ancient city where they found evidence of an atomic blast dating back thousands of years: from 8,000 to 12,000 years.

Now, we come to what is without doubt the most fascinating, and disturbing, body of evidence relative to what may very well be a description of atomic war in the distant past. An ancient Sanskrit text of an undetermined age, the *Mahabharata*, along with the *Ramayana*, is an epic saga of life, strife, adventure, and war in ancient India—some suggest extremely ancient India. Suggestions range from 6000 B.C.E. to, perhaps, even tens of thousands of years prior to that, as incredible as such a thing might sound. The relevant portion of the *Mahabharata*—which, many theorists believe, describes an atomic war, at the height of the Kurukshetra War that took place in northern India—reads:

> … (it was) a single projectile
> Charged with all the power of the Universe.
> An incandescent column of smoke and flame
> As bright as the thousand suns
> Rose in all its splendour…
> …it was an unknown weapon,
> An iron thunderbolt,
> A gigantic messenger of death,
> Which reduced to ashes
> The entire race of the Vrishnis and the Andhakas.
> …The corpses were so burned
> As to be unrecognizable.
> The hair and nails fell out;
> Pottery broke without apparent cause,
> And the birds turned white.
> After a few hours
> All foodstuffs were infected…
> ….to escape from this fire
> The soldiers threw themselves in streams
> To wash themselves and their equipment.

A further extract from the ancient text reads:

> Gurkha, flying in his swift and powerful Vimana hurled against the three cities of the Vrishnis and Andhakas a single projectile charged with all the power of the Universe. An incandescent column of smoke and fire, as brilliant as ten thousand suns, rose in all its splendour. It was the unknown weapon, the iron Thunderbolt, a gigantic messenger of death.

And what, you may ask, were Vimanas? They were fantastic craft, possessed of devastating weapons that could take to the skies and destroy entire cities. On the matter of the people of ancient India possessing such incredible technology, Colonel Henry S. Olcott, the cofounder with Helena Blavatsky and William Quan Judge of the Theosophical Society said, in an 1881 lecture in Allahabad:

> Ancient Hindus could navigate the air, and not only navigate it, but fight battles in it like so many war-eagles combating for the domination of the clouds. To be so perfect in aeronautics, they must have known all the arts and sciences related to the science, including the strata and currents of the atmosphere, the relative temperature, humidity, density and specific gravity of the various gases.

An 1888 photo of Helena Blavatsky and Colonel Henry S. Olcott, two of the founders of the Theosophical Society. They believed that ancient Hindus had mastered flight.

Professor Ramchandra Dikshitar of Madras University echoed this (in "Hindu Wisdom— Vimanas"):

> No question can be more interesting in the present circumstances of the world than India's contribution to the science of aeronautics. There are numerous illustrations in our vast Puranic and epic literature to show how well and wonderfully the ancient Indians conquered the air.

We may never know for sure if, in the distant past, a civilization not unlike ours—or, perhaps, more likely not a worldwide civilization, but one composed of localized, advanced people— developed atomic energy, weaponized it, and then largely wiped themselves out, to the extent that they became the stuff of nothing more than legend and folklore. There is, however, one uncanny and unsettling factor that links all of these tales from the distant past with the events at the Trinity site, Alamogordo, New Mexico, in the summer of 1945.

It turned out that none other than J. Robert Oppenheimer had a near-obsession with those very same ancient texts that seem to eerily parallel the events that brought the Second World War to a tumultuous closing. Only two days before the Trinity test was conducted, Oppenheimer was compelled to read the following from the the *Bhagavad-Gita*, which is a significant portion of the text of the *Mahabharata*. The key section in question reads: "In battle, in the forest, at the precipice in the mountains, on the dark great sea, in the midst of javelins and arrows, in sleep, in confusion, in the depths of shame, the good deeds a man has done before defend him."

In the wake of both the test and the dropping of the atomic bombs on Hiroshima and Nagasaki, Oppenheimer came to view his creation as a definitive nightmare. He said (in film-footage that can be viewed at the Atomicarchive website):

> We knew the world would not be the same. A few people laughed, a few people cried, most people were silent. I remembered the line from the Hindu scripture, the *Bhagavad-Gita*. Vishnu is trying to persuade the Prince that he should do his duty and to impress him takes on his multiarmed form and said, "Now, I am become Death, the destroyer of worlds." I suppose we all thought that one way or another.

Interestingly, Isidor Rabi—who was an associate of Oppenheimer—offered the opinion that he was "overeducated in those fields which lie outside the scientific tradition, such as his interest in religion, in the Hindu religion in particular, which resulted in a feeling of mystery of the universe that surrounded him like a fog."

Now we come to the most fascinating part of the story; it's something that occurred in 1952. Micah Hanks takes up the story, in a 2012 paper, "Secrets of the Past: Early Evidence of Nuclear Weapons?": "... during a seminar Oppenheimer was giving at Rochester University on the development of nuclear weapons, a college student asked if the blast at Alamogordo had been the first of its kind. Oppenheimer replied rather strangely by saying, 'Well, yes, in modern times.'"

Micah Hanks makes an extremely valuable observation on this issue:

> This statement is troubling for a number of reasons. For one, Oppenheimer seems to be intimating that there had been other nuclear explosions in the past that he knew about. Even if this were indeed found to be the case, where could any such blast have occurred, and who would have been responsible for it? Since Oppenheimer specifically referenced "modern times," it would seem that something akin to the blasts at Alamogordo, Hiroshima, and Nagasaki had once transpired at some point earlier in Earth's history.

Dr. Robert Oppenheimer, whose work was key to the development of the atomic bomb during World War II, believed that the *Bhagavad-Gita* text revealed how ancient Indian civilization wiped itself out with atomic bombs.

Hank's research has also shown that not only was Oppenheimer deeply fascinated by the *Bhagavad-Gita*, but that he was very keen to share its contents with friends and colleagues—to the extent that he would give them a gift of it on birthdays and at holidays. He also quoted from it at the funeral of none other than U.S. President Franklin D. Roosevelt.

Since Hanks has, perhaps, done more research into this particular, and particularly controversial, field than anyone else, it is to him we shall leave the last word:

> Perhaps, as Oppenheimer watched "trinity" erupted at Alamogordo in 1945, he had known all along that he was observing a re-telling of a story so ancient it has been long-forgotten by most today ... and yet, strangely, it served as the very impetus for something hellish and devastating; and a creation he would be best remembered for.

SECRETS OF THE MUSEUM: ANCIENT IMMORTALITY

In terms of American history, 2003 will be remembered as the year in which the controversial war in Iraq commenced. While most of the world's media focused its attention on the hostilities themselves, something else was going on, something very intriguing and, ultimately, something saturated in conspiracy theories. It was the widespread pillaging of the National Museum of Iraq, which is situated in the city of Baghdad. It's a huge facility, one that is home to countless, unique items of archaeological, religious, and historical importance—and many of which date back to 3000 to 4000 B.C.E. Collectively, they help paint a picture of life and culture in the Middle East thousands of years ago.

It's intriguing to note that when it became clear that a United States-driven assault on Iraq was in the cards, the American Council for Cultural Policy (ACCP) requested that something—*anything*—be done to ensure that those very same items of antiquity didn't end up in the wrong hands or, worse still, destroyed. It transpires that the ACCP's concerns were well-placed; very well-placed, to the extent that staff may have known that someone was about to target the museum for their own secret reasons. Their nightmares came true when, during the second week of April 2003, and over approximately a forty-eight-hour period, the museum was in chaos: looters overwhelmed the staff and thousands of items were stolen. But, were the raids entirely the work of random actions, or was something else going on? And if so: what and why, exactly?

There was both dismay and surprise when the ACCP's request that the U.S. government help to secure the National Museum of Iraq was rejected, because of claims that, at the height of battle, *nothing* could be guaranteed. Of course, that all makes perfect sense: after all, when lives were in danger, very few would be focusing their attentions on preserving millennia-old pots and carvings. Nevertheless, this situation gave rise to an interesting scenario on the part of conspiracy theorists: they concluded that the lack of protection for the museum was part of a secret plot to raid it of certain archaic items of astonishing proportions.

It was only, and specifically, after the raids of April 2003 that the sheer and shocking scale of the looting became apparent. It was thanks to the efforts of the U.S. Marine Corps' Colonel Matthew Bogdanos that the seriousness of the situation became clear. Colonel Bogdanos was the man with the extensive, and even daunting task of trying to figure out what had been taken. By the turn of 2004, Bogdanos's team had been able to say with certainty that several dozen important items had been taken from the museum's publicly open areas. Far more intriguing, however, was what was taken from those parts of the museum that were *not* open to the public.

They totaled, somewhat shockingly, in excess of 2,500 artifacts—all of historical and archeological importance. While many were ultimately recovered—thanks to good intelligence data and the U.S. military's dedication to the task at hand—a large number was not. It was not without a great deal of significance when Colonel Bogdanos said (see "A Conversation with Matthew F. Bogdanos"): "It is inconceivable to me that the basement was breached and the items stolen without an intimate insider's knowledge of the museum. From there about 10,000 pieces were taken. We've only recovered 650, approximately."

U.S. Marine Colonel Matthew Bogdanos was assigned the task of figuring out just what had been pillaged from the National Museum of Iraq in 2003.

Staff at the museum said that the missing items included,

> … the Warka Vase, a Sumerian alabaster piece more than 5,000 years old; a bronze Uruk statue from the Akkadian period, also 5,000 years old, which weighs 660 pounds; and the headless statue of Entemena. The Harp of Ur was torn apart by looters who removed its gold inlay.

Museum employees continued: "The Entemena statue, which is estimated to be 4,400 years old, is the first significant artifact returned from the United States and by far the most important piece found outside Iraq. American officials declined to discuss how they recovered the statue."

So, what might those thousands of items, that never resurfaced, have been? To answer that question, it's necessary to take a look at the history of the National Museum of Iraq.

It's notable that, even from its very earliest of years, the National Museum of Iraq was steeped in matters relative to secrecy, intrigue, and government activity. It was largely all thanks to a woman named Gertrude Bell. As well as being a noted archaeologist, Bell worked in the secret field of espionage with British Intelligence during the First World War. Bell, the author of the book *Persian Pictures*, did not wish to see the growing collection of ancient artifacts that were being found all across Iraq end up spread all across the planet, and so, she took matters into her own hands.

As a result, in 1922, Bell handed just about all that she could over to the Iraqi government. The collection of items—most of which dated back thousands

The National Museum of Iraq in Baghdad was damaged and raided during the 2003 war. Many ancient national treasures were looted. Researcher Jim Marrs speculated one of the items taken might have been the mysterious *white powder gold* mentioned as *manna* in the Bible.

of years—was relocated to an official facility of the Iraqi government; that is until 1926, when what was titled the Baghdad Antiquities Museum was created. Exactly forty years later, the museum was renamed the National Museum of Iraq and given a brand new location, east of the Tigris River. Thus was born the place that, in 2003, was subjected to widespread looting of just about everything that had been collected since the time of Gertrude Bell.

But, if the looting of the museum was steeped in matters of a conspiratorial nature, rather than simply because of the chaos and turmoil of warfare, what might the thieves have been looking for? It's possible that the operation may have been designed to try and find the secret for the one thing that each and every one of us, at some time or another, has surely craved: immortality. It's a theory that has been promoted by Jim Marrs, noted for his research and writings in a wide variety of fields, including 9/11, the JFK assassination, and UFOs.

Jim Marrs has suggested that someone within the U.S. government had a secret agenda in place when the war on Iraq began. It was an agenda that had at its heart a quest to find *white powder gold*. As for what, precisely, *white powder gold* is, or may be, Marrs muses on the possibility that it's the legendary *manna* from Heaven.

Exodus 16: 1–15 stated:

And they took their journey from Elim, and all the congregation of the children of Israel came unto the wilderness of Sin, which is between Elim and Sinai, on the fifteenth day of the second month after their departing out of the land of Egypt.

And the whole congregation of the children of Israel murmured against Moses and Aaron in the wilderness:

And the children of Israel said unto them, Would to God we had died by the hand of the LORD in the land of Egypt, when we sat by the flesh pots, and when we did eat bread to the full; for ye have brought us forth into this wilderness, to kill this whole assembly with hunger.

Then said the LORD unto Moses, Behold, I will rain bread from heaven for you; and the people shall go out and gather a certain rate every day, that I may prove them, whether they will walk in my law, or no.

And it shall come to pass, that on the sixth day they shall prepare that which they bring in; and it shall be twice as much as they gather daily.

And Moses and Aaron said unto all the children of Israel, At even, then ye shall know that the LORD hath brought you out from the land of Egypt:

And in the morning, then ye shall see the glory of the LORD; for that he heareth your murmurings against the LORD: and what are we, that ye murmur against us?

And Moses said, This shall be, when the LORD shall give you in the evening flesh to eat, and in the morning bread to the full; for that the LORD heareth your murmurings which ye murmur against him: and what are we? your murmurings are not against us, but against the LORD.

And Moses spake unto Aaron, Say unto all the congregation of the children of Israel, Come near before the LORD: for he hath heard your murmurings.

And it came to pass, as Aaron spake unto the whole congregation of the children of Israel, that they looked toward the wilderness, and, behold, the glory of the LORD appeared in the cloud.

And the LORD spake unto Moses, saying,

I have heard the murmurings of the children of Israel: speak unto them, saying, At even ye shall eat flesh, and in the morning ye shall be filled with bread; and ye shall know that I am the LORD your God.

And it came to pass, that at even the quails came up, and covered the camp: and in the morning the dew lay round about the host.

And when the dew that lay was gone up, behold, upon the face of the wilderness there lay a small round thing, as small as the hoar frost on the ground.

And when the children of Israel saw it, they said one to another, It is *manna*: for they wist not what it was. And Moses said unto them, This is the bread which the LORD hath given you to eat.

Manna may also have been the legendary *amrita*, which was a life-extending form of nectar that was first referred to in the pages of the *Rig Veda*, a collection of hymns dating back to the second millennium B.C.E. In 2009, the Ambrosia Society noted in an article at its website, "Ambrosia & Nectar": "In the Rig Veda Hymns, Soma, Amrita and Nectar are found as descriptive terms for the same 'plant/God/drink' so the Soma or 'pressed' drink was Amrita or 'without death' and it was also the nectar or 'death overcoming.'"

Then there is *ambrosia*, described by the Ambrosia Society like this: "*ambrosia*" is derived from the Greek ambrotos, where a- means "not" and *mbrotos* is "mortal." The literal translation of *ambrotos* into English would be the word "a-mortal in which *a-* means "not" and *mortal* means "death." In Greek mythology *ambrosia* is sometimes the food, sometimes the drink, of the gods, often depicted as conferring ageless immortality upon whomever consumes it.

If at least a part of the mission in Iraq *was* to find the legendary *manna*, it clearly wouldn't have been just to provide food, as described in *Exodus 16*. Legend suggests that *manna*—also known as the "bread of presence"—may have possessed life-extending properties, which might have allowed for the extension of human life to incredible ages. They might well have been ages reached by the ancient, mighty men of the Old Testament, such as Methuselah and Noah, both of whom reputedly lived for close to a thousand years.

> Legend suggests that *manna* ... may have possessed life-extending properties, which might have allowed for the extension of human life to incredible ages.

Should that prove to be too difficult for many to swallow, consider the following: only months before the dawning of the twenty-first century, digging outside of the city of Baghdad revealed numerous artifacts that dated back to the time of King Gilgamesh, who reigned from around 2500 B.C.E. What is particularly notable about Gilgamesh is not so much *where* he reigned in Iraq, but for how long: in excess of 120 years.

If the legends are true, and Gilgamesh really did reign for such a long period (something that does not take into account how long he lived *before* he was crowned), then anyone with a vested interest in trying to understand the secrets of immortality would likely take a deep interest in those items excavated in 1999. They very possibly did exactly that: when the stash of artifacts from the reign of Gilgamesh was found it was taken to—of course—the National Museum of Baghdad. Certain key items from that very same excavation went missing in 2003, never to be seen again, despite all the efforts of the U.S. military team that investigated the lootings.

Is a secret, elite, body of powerful individuals doing its utmost to unravel the mysteries of why we age? Incredibly, might they have solved the riddle, not by digging into today's fringe science, but by unearthing—quite literally—the secrets of the past? The events at the Baghdad-based National Museum of Iraq in 2003 suggest the answers to both questions might be: "Yes."

THE ANUNNAKI: THE REAL ANCIENT ALIENS

Within the history and lore of ancient Mesopotamia—which comprised parts of what, today, are Syria, Iran, Kuwait, Iraq, and Turkey—the most legendary, revered, unearthly beings were known as the Anunnaki. They were entities that, over the last few decades, have collectively become an integral part of "ancient astronaut" research. This is hardly surprising, since the word "Anunnaki" literally translates into English as "those who from the heavens came to earth," and is taken from the name of an ancient god of the skies, Anu. On top of that, Mesopotamia is acknowledged as being one of the key places on the planet where human civilization began.

This has all given rise to the idea that, far from being the literal deities that many take them to have been, the Anunnaki were visiting astronauts, from a faraway world—ones who tried to bring stability and culture to the previously primitive people of Earth—although specifically for *their* benefit, rather than for ours.

Although the Anunnaki have been depicted as definitively reptilian-like in appearance, there is also a widely held belief that they were very human-like in appearance, but much taller, and perhaps even in the region of eight to twelve feet tall. It is this belief that has led to suggestions that the Anunnaki, and their half-human offspring, were the legendary "giants" of the Old Testament.

It has also been suggested that the Anunnaki were very much a chthonic body of entities—that's to say they were the denizens of a dark underworld. But, whether they were gods, visitors from a faraway solar system, or a highly advanced race of humans that dwelled deep underground, no one can deny that they left a profound mark on the people of Mesopotamia.

Researcher Lawrence Gardner said of the Anunnaki (in 1999's *Genesis of the Grail Kings*):

> Every item of written and pictorial attestation confirms that the ancient Sumerians were absolutely sincere about the existence of the Anunnaki, and those such as Enki, Enlil, Nin-khursag and Inanna fulfilled earthly functions with designated community duties. They were patrons and founders; they were teachers and justices; they were technologists and kingmakers. They were jointly and severally venerated as archons and masters, but there were certainly not idols of religious worship as the rit-

ualistic gods of subsequent cultures became. In fact, the word which was eventually translated to become "worship" was *avod*, which meant quite simply, "work." The Anunnaki presence may baffle historians, their language may confuse linguists and their advanced techniques may bewilder scientists, but to dismiss them is foolish. The Sumerians have themselves told us precisely who the Anunnaki were, and neither history nor science can prove otherwise.

There can be no doubt at all that the dominating player in the development of the theory that the Anunnaki were ancient extraterrestrials was the late Zecharia Sitchin (1920–2010). Over the course of several decades and numerous books, Sitchin formulated a startling scenario in relation to these legendary beings from afar. He concluded that the Anunnaki were the inhabitants of a vast, faraway planet that has been referred to as both Nibiru and Planet X. Sitchin believed—rather controversially, it must be stressed—that Nibiru is actually a resident of our very own solar-system. Its orbit around the Sun is so near-infinitely gigantic, however, that it is only viewable every few thousand years, he concluded. Sitchin also believed he had discovered the exact time-cycle, as he noted in his book, *The 12th Planet*:

> The Mesopotamian and biblical sources present strong evidence that the orbital period of the 12th Planet is 3,600 years. The number 3,600 was written in Sumerian as a large circle. The epithet for the planet, shar, also meant "a perfect circle" or "a completed cycle." It also meant the number 3,600. The identity of the three terms—planet/orbit/3,600—could not be a mere coincidence. The reign periods (a Sumerian text) are also perfect multiples of the 3,600 year shar. The conclusion that suggests itself is that these shars of rulership were related to the orbital period shar, 3,600 years.

Sitchin portrayed Nibiru as a planet very much on its last legs, one whose atmosphere was degrading—something that could have spelled the end for the Anunnaki, had they not chosen to take certain actions that had major implications for us, the human race. The Anunnaki elected to hold off their demise by using and exploiting the Earth and its people to ensure their survival. It was gold—specifically *our* gold—that the Anunnaki needed to stabilize their fraught situation. The plan was to flood their planet's atmosphere with gold dust, thus keeping deadly ultra-violet rays at bay.

This image reproduced from ancient Mesopotamian wall art shows what looks like flying aircraft.

While on Earth, said Sitchin, the Anunnaki chose to do two things in particular: (a) they embarked on a program to turn what amounted to the human race into a subservient, slave-like species; and (b) they began to genetically manipulate us. In part, this was done via sophisticated science and technology—perhaps not unlike so-called gene-splicing techniques that we are now developing. Then, there was the tried and tested way that has worked since time

The late Zecharia Sitchin believed that the Mesopotamians encountered the Anunnaki, who were aliens from a planet in our solar system who wished to enslave humanity.

immemorial: sex. That male Anunnaki were supposedly able to mate—successfully—with human women suggests a common, and even more ancient, lineage and connection between the two species.

As for when all of this took place, the time frame is somewhat confusing. Sitchin took the view that the initial Anunnaki journey to our world occurred more than 400,000 years ago and resulted in the Anunnaki landing in certain parts of both Africa and the Middle East. With outposts constructed, the Anunnaki set about their controversial process of mutating early Homo Erectus into what, today, is us: Homo Sapiens. The long-term plan to create millions of human slaves—all under the extraterrestrial thumb of their masters—was well underway. There was, however, one problem.

Perhaps unforeseen by the Anunnaki, their tinkering with the human race and their attempts to upgrade us, and turn us into robust, unquestioning slaves, had a side-effect: the human race grew quickly and spread far and wide, to the point where we were eventually seen as troublesome entities, in danger of becoming unmanageable to the Anunnaki. The Anunnaki saw an answer to the problem of the growing human infestation, however. Around 10,500 B.C.E., concluded

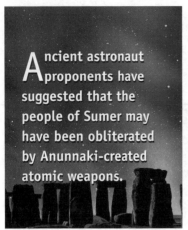

Ancient astronaut proponents have suggested that the people of Sumer may have been obliterated by Anunnaki-created atomic weapons.

Sitchin, Nibiru passed perilously close to the Earth. Its huge, gravitational pull had an overwhelmingly disastrous effect on our planet, to the extent that it led to a huge, worldwide flood, as described in numerous ancient texts, such as the *Bible* and the *Quran*. It also killed millions of those humans that the Anunnaki were becoming increasingly concerned about. Those spared the massive destruction were then used, in slavish style, to help create the vast, stone structures of the Middle East, South America, Central America, Mexico, India, and Pakistan, and also to mine for the gold that their bullying alien masters demanded.

It was Sitchin's belief that, in the post-flood era, the Anunnaki decided that their main base of operations would be Sumer, which is situated in Mesopotamia's southern regions, and dominated by both the Euphrates and Tigris rivers. Although conventional archaeology suggests that Sumer was inhabited—and well on its way to becoming one of the earliest, truly civilized places on the planet—several thousand years ago, Sitchin suggested the Sumer people may have been introduced to the area by the Anunnaki long before that—or, at the very least, used and even genetically manipulated to allow them to technologically progress with phenomenal speed. And, then, said Sitchin, with their work done, and their gold harvested, the Anunnaki left. That's not quite the whole story, however. The civilization of Sumer came to its end as mysteriously as it flourished.

Ancient astronaut proponents have suggested that the people of Sumer may have been obliterated by Anunnaki-created atomic weapons. As for why, perhaps to further keep the human race in check now that the Anunnaki had secured all they needed from our world. Or, it may have been that the conflict was provoked by warring factions of the Anunnaki, ones who had gone from exploiting the human race to fighting each other.

The official website of Zecharia Sitchin states, in a paper from Sitchin, titled *The Evil Wind*:

> At the end of the third millennium B.C.E. the great Sumerian civilization came to an abrupt end. Its sudden demise was bewailed in numerous lamentation texts that have been discovered by archeologists. The texts ascribed the calamity to an Evil Wind that came blowing from the west (from the direction of the Mediterranean Sea)—a deathly cloud that caused excruciating death to all living beings, people and animals alike, that withered plants and poisoned the waters.

> In *The Wars of Gods and Men* (third book of *The Earth Chronicles* series), Zecharia Sitchin saw an explanation of the sudden death in a long text known to scholars as The Erra Epos, that described a chain of events that ultimately led to the use of "Weapons of Terror" in a conflict between opposing clans of the Anunnaki....

> Zecharia Sitchin concluded that the Weapons of Terror were nuclear weapons. Used to obliterate the spaceport that then existed in the Sinai

Peninsula (and some "sinning cities" such as Sodom and Gomorrah), the nuclear cloud then was carried by the prevailing winds eastward, causing death and desolation in the Lands Between the Rivers (Mesopotamia)—the empire of Sumer and Akkad.

Besides claiming that nuclear weapons were first used on Earth not in the 1940's in Hiroshima but thousands of years earlier in the Near East, Zecharia also pinpointed the date: 2024 B.C.E.!

Millennia-old texts tell of a massive and sudden event that occurred just west of Sumer and that may have wiped out the people and their culture. From today's context, it sounds eerily like an out of the blue, nuclear strike. Translated into English, it reads like this:

On the land [Sumer] fell a calamity, one unknown to man;
one that had never been seen before,
one which could not be withstood.
A great storm from heaven …
A land-annihilating storm …
An evil wind, like a rushing torrent …
A battling storm joined by a scorching heat …
By day it deprived the land of the bright sun, in the evening the stars did
    not shine …
The people, terrified, could hardly breathe;
the evil wind clutched them, does not grant them another day …
Mouths were drenched with blood, heads wallowed in blood …
The face was made pale by the Evil Wind.
It caused cities to be desolated, houses to become desolate;
stalls to become desolate, the sheepfolds to be emptied …
Sumer's rivers it made flow with water that is bitter;
its cultivated fields grow weeds, its pastures grow withering plants.

So much for the story of the Anunnaki in the *distant* past; it's now time to take a trip forward into time to the *very recent* past.

In 2003, when the Iraqi war began—significant portions of which were fought in what was once Mesopotamia—a controversial story surfaced that suggested the saga of the Anunnaki was not over, after all. It was a story that came from a UFO researcher and author named Michael Salla. He claimed to have uncovered the strands of a fantastic secret: part of the reason why the war on Iraq went ahead, said Salla, was because there were people working under President George W. Bush who had stumbled upon stories suggesting that, somewhere in Iraq, there existed an ancient Anunnaki device called a star-gate.

In essence, it was a highly advanced piece of technology that would allow the user to travel, near-instantaneously, from one part of the universe to another—in fact, to just about anywhere and everywhere. If the technology could be understood, it would surely allow the user to eventually, and probably with astonishing speed, dominate the entire planet. So, the race was on to try and find the star-gate—albeit under the ingenious guise of a mission to topple Saddam Hussein.

U.S. Marines enter Saddam Hussein's palace at the end of the U.S. war with Iraq. Some speculate that the reason for invading Iraq had nothing to do with "weapons of mass destruction," but, rather, with something else much more important hidden in that ancient land.

Prior to the downfall and death of Hussein, Salla said: "From the perspective of the Bush administration, control of the Sumerian star-gate would enable clandestine government organizations to continue their global campaign of non-disclosure of the ET presence."

He continued:

On the part of Hussein Regime, control of the star-gate would allow him to activate it and to fulfill prophesy by facilitating the return of an advanced race of ETs, the elite Anunnaki. President Hussein probably imagines that in return for his loyalty to the elite Anunnaki, he would be rewarded with a position of great global authority. Perhaps he would even see himself as some kind of human savior facilitating the return of the gods who would solve all of humanity's problems, and end the rule of clandestine government organizations perpetuating non-disclosure of the ET presence.

Of course, such a thing never happened and, as history has shown us, Saddam Hussein was thankfully soon no more. Was the story true? Was a real, ancient, Anunnaki-created star-gate found by U.S. military personnel at the height of the Iraq war? Could this, rather than the overthrow of Saddam Hussein, have been the primary reason for the invasion? If the answers are yes, this begs an even bigger, and far more serious, question: What if, one day, the Anunnaki return and decide to take back that incredible piece of technology…?

GOLIATH: A DESCENDENT OF THE SPACE GODS

As was noted in the previous chapter, it has been suggested that the legendary "giants" of the Old Testament were, in reality, either the extraterrestrial Anunnaki or, at the very least, their half-human and half-E.T. offspring. On this particular issue, researcher Angela Sangster said in a 2010 paper, "Who Were the Anunnaki?":

Were the giants spoken of in Genesis actually aliens from another planet? The *Enuma Elish* (the creation story according to the ancient Babylonians) has many parallels with the Christian bible. The Book of Genesis speaks of these giants (also called Nefilim) who were taught by the Church as having been angels who came to Earth and cohabitated with the daughters of Man (Genesis chapter six). The Book of Enoch, which was removed from the Christian Bible, speaks of the resulting hybrids of humans and these giants, or "watchers."

Zecharia Sitchin, not surprisingly, had things to say on this matter, too. He told *Connecting Link* magazine:

Who were the Nefilim, that are mentioned in Genesis, Chapter six, as the sons of the gods who married the daughters of Man in the days before the great flood, the Deluge? The word Nefilim is commonly, or used to be, translated "giants."

He continued:

I questioned this interpretation as a child at school, and I was reprimanded for it because the teacher said "you don't question the Bible." But I did not question the Bible. I questioned an interpretation that seemed inaccurate, because the word, Nefilim, the name by which those extraordinary beings, "the sons of the gods" were known, means literally, "Those who have come down to earth from the heavens."

Further evidence of ancient giants absolutely abounds in the pages of the Bible, as the website *Beginning and End* clearly shows:

When Moses sent his spies to scout the Promised Land so the children of Israel could enter it, the spies reported seeing beings there who were giants. The Bible makes it abundantly clear that there were races of people at that time who were so large, that regular sized men appeared as "grasshoppers" before them.... And we see that when the great servant of the Lord,

Joshua, was sent to conquer the Promised Land that God commands him to kill all of the men, women and children of these giant races. They were to be wiped as if any remnant of their kind would post a great danger.

The words of Numbers 13:31 confirm this particular story:

But the men that went up with him said, We be not able to go up against the people; for they are stronger than we. And they brought up an evil report of the land which they had searched unto the children of Israel, saying, The land, through which we have gone to search it, is a land that eateth up the inhabitants thereof; and all the people that we saw in it are men of a great stature. And there we saw the giants, the sons of Anak, which come of the giants: and we were in our own sight as grasshoppers, and so we were in their sight.

Moving on, there is Genesis 6:2–4, the words of which point in the direction of cross-breeding between the giant, alien men, and human women:

That the sons of God saw the daughters of men that they were fair; and they took them wives of all which they chose. There were giants in the earth in those days; and also after that, when the sons of God came in unto the daughters of men, and they bare children to them, the same became mighty men which were of old, men of renown.

All of this raises an important question: is it possible that the legendary giant, Goliath—perhaps *the* definitive giant of all time—was an extraterrestrial, one of the Anunnaki? Certainly, the question is a controversial one. That does not mean, however, that we should outright dismiss it.

The Old Testament story of Goliath's death, at the hands of David (who ultimately went on to become the second king of the United Kingdom of Israel and Judah), is a well-known and thought-provoking one. It can be found in Samuel 1, chapter seventeen. It tells of a violent confrontation between Philistine forces and those of the Israelites—at the Valley of Elah, which is located on Palestine's West Bank, near the city of Hebron.

So the story goes, for no less than forty days, the most feared soldier of the Philistines, Goliath, taunts, goads, and dares the Israelites to send a solider to try and defeat him. Goliath asserts that whoever wins—he or the chosen Israelite—will also decide the outcome of the entire battle. The stakes, then, are high in the extreme. David is the only one who dares to take

Many people are familiar with the biblical story of how David slew the giant Goliath, but is it more than a story? Could there really have been giants living with ordinary humans?

on the mighty giant. And he does so in a decidedly alternative fashion: whereas Goliath is heavily armored and equipped with a large shield and a powerful, razor-sharp sword, David elects to arm himself with nothing more than a sling and a handful of stones.

As told in 1 Samuel 17:38–50:

And Saul armed David with his armour, and he put an helmet of brass upon his head; also he armed him with a coat of mail.

And David girded his sword upon his armour, and he assayed to go; for he had not proved it. And David said unto Saul, I cannot go with these; for I have not proved them. And David put them off him.

And he took his staff in his hand, and chose him five smooth stones out of the brook, and put them in a shepherd's bag which he had, even in a scrip; and his sling was in his hand: and he drew near to the Philistine.

And the Philistine came on and drew near unto David; and the man that bare the shield went before him.

And when the Philistine looked about, and saw David, he disdained him: for he was but a youth, and ruddy, and of a fair countenance.

And the Philistine said unto David, Am I a dog, that thou comest to me with staves? And the Philistine cursed David by his gods.

And the Philistine said to David, Come to me, and I will give thy flesh unto the fowls of the air, and to the beasts of the field.

Then said David to the Philistine, Thou comest to me with a sword, and with a spear, and with a shield: but I come to thee in the name of the LORD of hosts, the God of the armies of Israel, whom thou hast defied.

This day will the LORD deliver thee into mine hand; and I will smite thee, and take thine head from thee; and I will give the carcases of the host of the Philistines this day unto the fowls of the air, and to the wild beasts of the earth; that all the earth may know that there is a God in Israel.

And all this assembly shall know that the LORD saveth not with sword and spear: for the battle is the LORD's, and he will give you into our hands.

And it came to pass, when the Philistine arose, and came and drew nigh to meet David, that David hasted, and ran toward the army to meet the Philistine.

And David put his hand in his bag, and took thence a stone, and slang it, and smote the Philistine in his forehead, that the stone sunk into his forehead; and he fell upon his face to the earth.

So David prevailed over the Philistine with a sling and with a stone, and smote the Philistine, and slew him; but there was no sword in the hand of David.

Those who accept the Bible precisely and unswervingly might be inclined to suggest that Goliath was simply a tall man; a giant possessed of such incredible fighting skills and appearance that they made him feared throughout the land. There are, however, reasons why we should conclude that Goliath's reputation was based around much more than that. Although the Dead Sea Scrolls provide a height for Goliath of six feet and nine inches, additional ancient texts state that his height was just a few inches short of an astonishing ten feet. Six feet nine is not at all unheard of in today's world—check out the average basketball team. Ten feet, however, most assuredly is.

The tallest, and undisputed, man on record is Robert Wadlow. A disorder of the pituitary gland caused Wadlow of Alton, Illinois, to grow to a height of eight feet eleven inches. The disorder also took his life at just twenty-two years old, in 1940. Moreover, Wadlow's height and weight had major, adverse effects on his legs— which had to be supported by braces at all times, causing him to slowly shuffle as he walked. In addition, Wadlow was plagued by infections in his legs, feet, and ankles. In other words, for the average human, really immense heights result in major problems. In short, we are not genetically programmed to reach such heights. And, when and if we do, the results are never positive.

Robert Wadlow had a pituitary disorder that caused him to grow to a height of nearly nine feet. Many physical ailments came with his height, demonstrating that being that large is not practical for human beings.

All of this is in sharp contrast to Goliath, who, we are told, was a powerful, skilled warrior. In addition, his immense size did not appear to have been caused by a disorder— of the pituitary gland or, indeed, of anything else. The description of Goliath is simply that of an immense, well-proportioned giant, one who was around a foot taller than anyone else in the entirety of recorded history. In view of that, we might want to give careful consideration to the possibility that when David ended the life of Goliath, he also took the life of someone who was not entirely human.

FROM BABYLONIA TO THE DEPARTMENT OF DEFENSE: ALIEN DEMONS

In November 1991, a Nebraskan priest named Ray Boeche had a clandestine meeting with a pair of physicists working on a top secret program for the U.S. Department of Defense. Both men were deeply worried and were looking for advice and guidance from Boeche on the project in which they were immersed. The classified operation revolved around attempts by the DoD to contact what were termed "Non-Human Entities," or NHEs. Most people might call them extraterrestrials, aliens, or in terms of the field of Ufology and popular culture—"the Grays." For a while, the DoD referred to them in those terms, too. But not for long: as Ray Boeche listened carefully and concerned by what his Deep Throat sources told him, he came to realize that the Pentagon was dabbling in decidedly dangerous areas.

The scientists explained to Boeche that the contact with the NHEs was not achieved on a face-to-face basis but, rather, in mind-to-mind fashion. Telepathy, ESP, and channeling were the primary ways by which interaction occurred. But, as the program progressed, something ominous occurred: it was as if a dark cloud descended on all those tied to the program. Bad luck, illness, and even death blighted the members of the team. Such was the extent of the negativity that surrounded the operation that the DoD had come to a startling and disturbing conclusion.

Although the DoD had initially assumed the entities they were dealing with were extraterrestrial, over time that view changed significantly and dramatically. Indeed, within seven or eight months of the commencement of the project, the scientists on board came to believe that they were not dealing with aliens from faraway galaxies, but with highly dangerous, deceptive, manipulative demons—as in literal demons from a literal Hell.

The UFO presence on our planet, the Pentagon group believed, was designed to seduce us into believing aliens were amongst us, when the reality—as they saw it—was that we were being led to accept that belief as a means to allow Satan's minions to get his claws into us. Such was the concern on the part of the DoD about their actions—namely opening a door or a portal to something monstrous and malignant—that it began digging deep into the ancient past for the answers to the UFO puzzle. It was ancient demons, rather than ancient aliens, that tasked the finest minds of the Pentagon.

As incredible as it might sound, those attached to the Pentagon program consulted numerous early texts and books that addressed the field of demonology, chiefly to try and figure out the extent to which the UFO phenomenon—*some* of it or, perhaps, even *all* of it—was the result of demonic activity and attendant satanic deception. A great deal of time was spent studying numerous books on ancient and modern demonology, including John Deacon and John Walker's 1601 work, *Dialogical Discourses of Spirits and Devils*, Reginald C. Thompson's *Devils and Evil Spirits of Babylonia*, and Edward Langton's *Essentials of Demonology*.

The Deacon and Walker book presented to its readers a long and complicated history of demonology, the means by which demons could get their grips into easily manipulated people, and the deceptive nature of these unholy creatures—all of that was unsettlingly familiar to the Department of Defense team.

As for Reginald C. Thompson's book, this was the one title, more than any other, which deeply influenced the mindset of the Pentagon project. Thompson had an intriguing background: as a nineteenth-century archaeologist, he spent a great deal of time excavating the remains of the ancient city of Nineveh, which features prominently in the Old Testament story of Jonah and the whale—about which there will be more in a later chapter. Thompson also excavated at Carchemish, where, in 605 B.C.E., the soldiers of the Egyptian pharaoh Necho II were destroyed by the troops of Babylonia's Nebuchadnezzar II. In terms of all things demonic, it was in the direction of ancient Babylonia that most of Thompson's research headed.

Of particular fascination to Thompson were the stories he collected of predatory, supernatural entities that invaded the bedrooms of the Babylonians. Thompson noted that practically all cultures had their own equivalents, most famously the incubus and the succubus: malevolent entities that can take on male or female form, they sexually violate their victims in the dead of night. For the Pentagon, this was very familiar territory: they saw deep parallels between the ancient Babylonian incubi encounters and today's so-called alien abductions, which also predominantly occur in the middle of the night, and which have major sexual components, too. Today's allegedly intergalactic abductors, the DoD concluded, were really the incubi of old, remodeled and camouflaged for a new era, but with the same agenda: to use, abuse, deceive, and manipulate the human race.

The Department of Defense team also spent countless hours reviewing Emil Schneweis's *Angels and Demons According to Lactantius*. The Lactantius of the title was a Christian writer who was born around 230 to 240 C.E. in Africa. He firmly believed that the whole purpose of this bizarre and disturbing interaction with the people of Earth had just one goal: the enslavement of the human soul.

An image of Lactantius from an old frescoe. Lactantius was a Christian writer who lived during the third century C.E. and believed incubi were trying to enslave human souls.

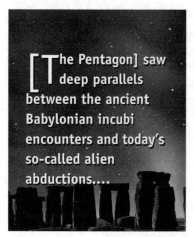

[The Pentagon] saw deep parallels between the ancient Babylonian incubi encounters and today's so-called alien abductions....

The Pentagon also took great note of the books of Dr. Merrill F. Unger. A prestigious writer of dozens of books—and someone who obtained A.B. and Ph.D. degrees at Johns Hopkins University and his Th.M. and Th.D. degrees at Dallas Theological Seminary—one title of Unger's that the Department of Defense team studied in detail was his 1971 book, *Demons in the World Today*. In the pages of his book, Unger recorded:

> Believers can be hindered, bound, and oppressed by Satan and even indwelt by one or more demons, who may derange the mind and afflict the body. One woman, who excelled in the gift of intercessory prayer, was nevertheless constantly the center of a disturbance because of lack of tact and wisdom, due apparently to some alien spirit indwelling her. The writer remembers well the occasion of a prayer meeting when this woman was delivered from this evil spirit, as she and a group of us were on our knees in intercession. All of a sudden, as she quietly prayed, the demon in her gave an unearthly yell that could be heard for a block and came out of her, frightening the group almost out of their wits. After falling into an unconscious state for a minute or two, the woman regained consciousness and rose to her feet, joyfully confident that she had been set free from an evil power.

Six years later, Unger penned *What Demons Can Do to Saints*. It stated, in part:

> Clinical evidence abounds that a Christian can be demon-possessed as a carry-over from pre-conversion days, or can fall under Satan's power after conversion and become progressively demonized, even seriously. If such a person blatantly lives in scandalous sin, subscribes to and embraces heresy, engages in occultism, or gives himself to rebellion and lawlessness against God's Word and will, he may expect a demon invasion in his life.

The Pentagon team nodded knowingly—and with growing concern, too.

One particular section of Dr. John Warwick Montgomery's *Principalities and Powers* was highlighted by the Pentagon:

> There is a definite correlation between negative occult activity and madness. European psychiatrist L. Szondi has shown a high correlation between involvement in spiritualism and occultism on the one hand, and schizophrenia on the other. Kurt Koch's detailed case studies have confirmed this judgment. Being a genuine Christian believer is no guarantee of exemption from the consequences of sorcery and black magic.... The tragedy of most sorcery, invocation of demons, and related practices is that those who carry on these activities refuse to face the fact that they always turn out for the worst. What is received through this Faustian pact never satisfies and one pays with one's soul in the end anyway.

Then there was Neil T. Anderson, author of *Victory over the Darkness* and an engineer with NASA. The Pentagon noted that encounters with supposed aliens and those with what were perceived as demons weren't just interconnected because of the sexual components of the experiences, but because of something else too: strange marks on the skin. UFO researchers suggest this is because of aliens extracting cells, DNA, blood, and so on. Demonologists suggest otherwise. Of great interest to the DoD, Anderson had, himself, experienced this, as his book notes:

> I was prepared to speak in chapel on the topic of deliverance and evangelism, in which I would expose some of the strategies of Satan in these areas. Early that morning I rose and showered before my wife and children were awake. When I stepped out of the shower I found several strange symbols traced on the fogged-up mirror. I didn't do it, and Joanne, Heidi, and Karl were still asleep; they hadn't done it either.
>
> I wiped the markings off the mirror, suspicious that someone was flinging darts at me to dissuade me from my chapel message. I went down to eat breakfast alone, and as I was sitting in the kitchen, suddenly I felt a slight pain on my hand that made me flinch. I looked down and saw what appeared to be two little bite-marks on my hand. "Is that your best shot?" I said aloud to the powers of darkness attacking me. "Do you think symbols on the mirror and a little bite are going to keep me from giving my message in chapel today? Get out of here." The nuisance left and my message in [the] chapel went off without a hitch.

The Pentagon noted that encounters with supposed aliens and those with what were perceived as demons weren't just interconnected because of the sexual components of the experiences, but because of … strange marks on the skin.

One of the most fascinating theories of the Pentagon was that from the days of ancient Babylonia to the present day, the violent, predatory, and intrusive attacks on people in the dead of night did not occur in what we would call reality. Rather, the events were projected into the human mind—something that made them part-manipulated dream and part-hologram. Of deep relevance to the work of the DoD was a book titled *Unmasking the Enemy*.

Its authors were Dr. Nelson Pacheco—a Principal Scientist with the Supreme Headquarters, Allied Powers, Europe (SHAPE), Technical Center—and Tommy Blann, of the U.S. Air Force. They wrote in their book:

> … we propose that the "reality" behind the UFO phenomenon … is due to a manifestation of non-human preternatural consciousness—for the purpose of deception—that can interact with our physical environment and with our human consciousness to produce visual, physical, and psychological effects. The artificial construct created by this consciousness mimics our three-dimensional objects and systems and even our religious imagery—the purpose being to slowly condition our minds through subtle deception to accept a false belief, while undermining our rational thought processes and our human spirit.

Nicole Malone's *The Bible, Physics, and the Abilities of Fallen Angels* also captured the attention of the DoD. This is hardly surprising when one considers Malone's words:

An incubus would invade human homes in the dead of night, according to old European folklore, sexually violating them for an evil purpose.

It is important to note that sometimes fallen angels do cause abductees to see "humans" during the apparition; however, these are not real humans, but instead are part of the vision caused by the fallen angel.... In many cases in which fallen angels cause visions of humans, the humans are military personnel, and advanced technology appears to be present. These kinds of abductions are called "Milabs," for military abductions.

Except in rare cases of actual government investigation of abductions and interviews with abductees [which is the precise path followed by the Collins Elite], these Milabs are caused by fallen angels, and are just one variety of abduction experiences. The entire experience, like other mental attack visions, is a vision, including the military personnel and advanced technology the person sees. Remember, these experiences are real to the bodily senses, and the perception of time passage seems normal to the abductee during the experience.

Joe Jordan, a safety specialist at NASA's Kennedy Space Center, said of this same theory, in an interview with me in 2010:

> The people don't get taken to a ship; they are physically still in bed. I have a couple of cases where people had the abduction experience while in the presence of a witness who was awake. They didn't go anywhere. They almost went into an unconscious state. This was only for a few minutes, but they came out of it totally exhausted and could talk about what had happened to them, and it would take hours for them to tell it all. But it was just minutes—like a time-displacement. I'm not sure I would call it a hallucination, maybe more of an apparition, something along the lines of a hologram, but it's still in the mind. These entities can create this experience in our minds and we can interact with it, and it can leave physical manifestations from the experience. And that's why this is so confusing.

> The purpose of all this is to deny the reality of Christianity. And, they have probably the best propaganda machine I've ever seen or read about. I believe that's the purpose behind this whole experience. Look at the stories of old of gnomes, fairies, and elves: we wouldn't believe that today. So they come in the emperor's new clothes. And they come in a guise that we will accept. But their purpose is to defeat us and to delude us, so that we will take our focus off the one true God.

Reportedly, the Pentagon's secret team—dedicated to unraveling the dark and disturbing truth about the connection between ancient demons and modern day aliens—continues its work to this day.

ANCIENT X-FILES: THE GOVERNMENT'S SECRETS

Any mention of secret, government interest in such issues as UFOs and alien visitations, invariably provokes imagery relative to such things as the Roswell UFO crash of 1947 and tales of cosmic conspiracies coming out of Area 51. It is, however, a little known fact that U.S. government agencies have taken a great deal of interest in the UFO-themed mysteries of not just recent history, but of the distant past, too, and particularly those with a connection to the issue of ancient extraterrestrials.

Of keen interest to the government, and since at least the 1950s, is the riddle that surrounds the means by which the Pyramids of Egypt—as well as numerous other ancient structures—were built. Of even greater interest to officialdom is the theory that those same structures were built via levitation technology.

It is a fact that when we examine the stories and legends of how the ancients managed to move and manipulate gigantic, multi-ton stones, we find that levitation appears to play a significant role in the saga. In the 900s, for example, a Baghdad-born writer named Abu al-Hasan Ali al-Mas'udi described how stories had reached him, suggesting that the pyramids of Egypt were built in decidedly unconventional fashion. According to al-Mas'udi the massive blocks would almost magically rise into the air when tapped by a mysterious metal pole. Depending on how the stones were struck, they could be made to travel horizontally or vertically, with virtually no manpower needed at all.

This ties in with stories coming out of the ancient Americas, as researcher Richard Mooney noted, in his 1974 book, *Colony Earth*:

> There is a tradition that appears in the mythology of the Americas that the priests "made the stones light," so that they were moved easily. Mooney added this was directly connected to "the legend of levitation," which he described as an "actual technique or device, long since forgotten."

A similar story surrounds the construction of the city of Troy. We are told that "the God of Music seated himself nearby and played such inspiring tunes that the stones moved into place of their own accord." We are also told that the Greek city of Thebes was built in near-identical fashion: Amphion, the son of Zeus, reportedly plucked a lyre to effortlessly raise the huge stones of the city. Then there is the Mayan city of Uxmal. Now largely in ruins, it is said to have been built around 500 C.E. by a mysterious race of dwarves that had the ability to move gigantic stones by whistling at them. Rather intriguingly, Stonehenge has a similar story attached to it. It is the story of the Giants' Dance, in which the mighty stone pillars are moved by music.

Of course, we should not take these stories literally, in terms of lyres, whistles, and music. They do, however, all have one thing in common: they tell of the moving of massive stones via sound. This is acutely similar to something that, today, is very much in its infancy, but which the U.S. government has secretly investigated for decades. It is called acoustic levitation.

Researchers Marie Jones and Larry Flaxman describe acoustic levitation in their book *The Resonance Key* as "two opposing sound frequencies with interfering sound waves, thus creating a resonant zone that allows the levitation to occur. Theoretically, to move a levitating object, simply change or alter the two sound waves and tweak accordingly."

Although the U.S. military has succeeded in moving small objects via acoustic levitation, the ability to raise multi-ton stones still eludes them. Other avenues have been explored to try and resolve the matter, however. As the Freedom of Information Act has shown, in the 1950s and 1960s files were secretly opened on two authors who were aggressively following the notion of the ancients possessing levitation technology. They were an American named Morris Jessup

The ancient Mayan city of Uxmal is said to have been built by a mysterious race of dwarves.

(the author of *The Case for the UFO*), and a New Zealand pilot, Bruce Cathie. Both men wrote extensively on what we might call the concept of anti-gravity and the ancients.

Whether the product of highly advanced, ancient extraterrestrials, or a long-lost technology of millennia-old human civilizations, we don't know. But, just maybe, some secret element of the U.S. government *does* know.

Still on the matter of things relative to the Egyptian Pyramids, we have to turn our attention to their nearest ancient neighbor: the Sphinx. A huge construction—it is 65 feet high and 240 feet long long. The general consensus on the part of mainstream archaeology is that the Sphinx was built around 2550 B.C.E. It has, however, been suggested that this particular date is not just wide of the mark, but *very* wide of the mark.

Schoch takes the view that the Sphinx may date back more than 7,000 years and possibly even further.

Making absolutely no bones about his belief that the Sphinx dates back much further into antiquity is Robert Schoch, a Ph.D., and an associate professor of natural science at the College of General Studies, Boston University. Schoch takes the view that the Sphinx may date back more than 7,000 years and possibly even further. It's a point of view dictated by the fact there is strong evidence the Sphinx, at some point, was significantly weathered by massive amounts of rainfall. That such heavy rain certainly did not fall any time around, or after, the conventional time frame in which the Sphinx was allegedly built is a good pointer that convention has it wrong. There's another aspect to the mystery of the Sphinx: the interest that none other than the CIA has taken in the mighty structure.

The late and renowned psychic Edgar Cayce made the controversial claim that he had been reincarnated from an Egyptian priest—named Ra Ta—who managed the construction of a magical and sacred locale that Cayce termed the Temple of Sacrifice. While in a hypnotic state, Cayce channeled the spirit of Ra Ta, who maintained that inside the right, front paw of the Sphinx a vast treasure existed: ancient records on the truth of the legendary land of Atlantis.

The Freedom of Information Act has demonstrated—although, admittedly, to a very limited degree—that, in the early 1960s, the CIA quietly opened a file on Cayce's work. As part of its study of Cayce's claims pertaining to the Sphinx—and the ancient mysteries it may well hide—in 1974, CIA remote-viewers (psychic spies, in simple terminology) tried to use their mind-powers to penetrate the Sphinx and psychically uncover what it was that the Sphinx was so jealously guarding. To date, those findings remain classified.

Also on the matter of the CIA, there is the strange saga of its involvement in the saga of none other than Noah's Ark. The biblical story of the huge, worldwide flood that allegedly wiped out practically all of the human race reads as follows in Genesis 6:12–20:

And God looked upon the earth, and, behold, it was corrupt; for all flesh had corrupted his way upon the earth.

And God said unto Noah, The end of all flesh is come before me; for the earth is filled with violence through them; and, behold, I will destroy them with the earth.

Make thee an ark of gopher wood; rooms shalt thou make in the ark, and shalt pitch it within and without with pitch.

And this is the fashion which thou shalt make it of: The length of the ark shall be three hundred cubits, the breadth of it fifty cubits, and the height of it thirty cubits.

A window shalt thou make to the ark, and in a cubit shalt thou finish it above; and the door of the ark shalt thou set in the side thereof;with lower, second, and third stories shalt thou make it.

And, behold, I, even I, do bring a flood of waters upon the earth, to destroy all flesh, wherein is the breath of life, from under heaven; and every thing that is in the earth shall die.

But with thee will I establish my covenant; and thou shalt come into the ark, thou, and thy sons, and thy wife, and thy sons' wives with thee.

And of every living thing of all flesh, two of every sort shalt thou bring into the ark, to keep them alive with thee; they shall be male and female.

Of fowls after their kind, and of cattle after their kind, of every creeping thing of the earth after his kind, two of every sort shall come unto thee, to keep them alive.

We are told that, after the waters receded, Noah's Ark came to rest on what many believe, today, to have been Mt. Ararat, Turkey.

It just so happens that the CIA holds an extensive file on the claims that Mt. Ararat was the final resting place for Noah's Ark. Or, as it is referred to within the CIA, and by the Pentagon, too: the "Ararat Anomaly." It is a reference to a large object first spotted in 1949 by the crew of a U.S. Air Force spy plane. Whatever the strange object is, no one doubts it exists. For some it's nothing stranger than a weirdly shaped, rocky outcrop that vaguely resembles a boat. For others, it is nothing less than Noah's Ark itself. For more than a few, it's an ancient, wrecked UFO, one that crash-landed on Mt. Ararat thousands of years ago, and which led to the development of the Ark legend—because of the assertions that the UFO had numerous examples of terrestrial animals aboard.

It has long been surmised that Noah's Ark rested atop Mt. Ararat (in modern-day Turkey) after the flood waters receded.

Whatever the truth of the matter, there's no denying that the CIA's interest in the Ararat Anomaly dates back to the late 1940s. Then, in the 1950s, U-2 spy planes were flown over the area to secure high-quality photographs. In 1973, spy satellites were vectored over Turkey—once again, as part of a concerted effort to try and figure out the true nature of the anomaly. The official story is that no firm conclusion has been reached, chiefly because of (a) the inhospitable, icy, snowy environment at the top of Mt. Ararat; and (b) the reluctance of the Turkish government to permit people to examine it in person.

The off-the-record story, however, is that at some point in 1975, a Delta Force-type team secretly parachuted into the area and made its way to the Ararat Anomaly and found not a huge rock or even the remains of a rotting, old, wooden boat. No, the story is that what was discovered was nothing less than the rusted remains of a huge metal craft, one estimated to have become embedded in both the ice and the mountain thousands of years ago. Was it an ancient equivalent of the famous Roswell UFO crash of July 1947? Just perhaps, that's exactly what it was. And, also just perhaps, the CIA knows that the story of Noah's Ark was prompted not by acts of God, but by the actions of extraterrestrials that visited our world and died in the process.

QUETZALCOATL: A TEACHER FROM THE STARS

Within the realms of Ufology, the paranormal, the folkloric, and conspiracy theories, there is quite possibly no phenomenon guaranteed to provoke more controversy, debate, and unbridled paranoia than that concerning the Reptilians.

Diabolical and ominous shape-shifting entities from faraway star systems and twilight dimensions beyond our own, the Reptilians are cold-hearted, ruthless entities that have played formative roles in the development and manipulation of human history, folklore, mythology, and culture. They are the secret rulers of the planet, exerting powerful, Machiavellian influence over each and every one of us.

Seven to twelve feet tall, green-skinned, scaled, and monstrous, the Reptilians are the real masters of the world. Using their shape-shifting skills, they have infiltrated and enslaved government, industry, society, royalty, and even the world of Hollywood. In fact, just about no one is free of the terrifying presence and wrath of the dreaded Reptilians.

They are creatures whose existence and presence on our world has nurtured legends of dragons, aliens, and demons. Even the biblical story of the talking snake that tempted Adam and Eve to eat from the Tree of Knowledge in the Garden of Eden can be traced back to Reptilian presence and control.

The Reptilians are the masterminds behind alien abductions. They greedily feast upon the thousands of people who, every year, vanish without trace. They surround us at all times, disguised and camouflaged, using and abusing us as the mood and the need takes them. They can even count Queen Elizabeth II and Prince Charles amongst their vile flesh-eating and blood-drinking numbers. And their mightiest of all figures secretly inhabit vast underground caverns that exist far below our surface world.

So, we are told by the conspiracy minded, at least.

Perhaps the most famous of all the Reptilians was Quetzalcoatl, a god of Mesoamerican lore—Mesoamerican meaning central to the cultures and people of Mexico, Belize, Nicaragua, Costa Rica, El Salvador, Guatemala, and Honduras. According to predominantly Aztec legend, Quetzalcoatl was a highly advanced entity, with near-magical skills and possessed of highly advanced sciences who tried to bring civilization, technology, and a new world to the Mesoamericans. His name

A drawing from the sixteenth-century Codex Magliabechiano shows a man dressed as Quetzalcoatl. Notice the reptilian appearance of this mask.

translates as "feathered serpent," hence the potential connection to the controversy surrounding the so-called Reptilians of UFO lore.

Nicoletta Maestri said of Quetzalcoatl that he is

> ... represented in many different ways according to different epochs and Mesoamerican cultures. He is both represented in his non-human form, as a feathered serpent, with plumage along its body and around the head, as well as in his human form, especially among the Aztecs and in Colonial codices. In his human aspect, he is often depicted in dark color with a red beak, symbol of Ehecatl, the wind god, and with a cut shell as a pendant, symbol of Venus. In many images he is depicted wearing a plumed headdress and holding a plumed shield.

So far as can currently be determined, the worship of this enigmatic deity began at some point between 100 B.C.E. and 100 C.E. It should be noted, however, that devotion to serpent-like gods in Mesoamerica, in general, began much earlier. Evidence of such worship can be found at Tabasco, Mexico, which is estimated to have dated back to at least 900 B.C.E., when it was embraced by the Olmec people.

As evidence of the influence that serpent gods had over Mesoamericans, one only has to take a look at the Temple of the Feathered Serpent, which is situated at Teotihuacan, around thirty miles outside of Mexico City, and which was constructed around 100 B.C.E. Classic imagery of feathery serpents, or war serpents, adorns the huge step pyramid, as it is known, and which is also termed the Temple of Quetzalcoatl, even though it pre-dates widespread worship of Quetzalcoatl. Such was the reverence with which the people viewed their serpent god, human sacrifice to them was both widespread and commonplace.

Interpretations on what, or who, Quetzalcoatl was, are as many as they are varied.

Within Mormon lore, we are told:

The story of the life of the Mexican divinity, Quetzalcoatl, closely resembles that of the Savior; so closely, indeed, that we can come to no other conclusion than that Quetzalcoatl and Christ are the same being. But the history of the former has been handed down to us through an impure Lamanitish source, which has sadly disfigured and perverted the original incidents and teachings of the Savior's life and ministry.

Karl Andreas Taube is an archaeologist who has studied the stories of Quetzalcoatl and states that, in his opinion, the god symbolized fertility. He also said (and is quoted in "The Ideology of the Absent: The Feathered Serpent and Classic Maya Rulership" by Lucero and Panganiban): "It is possible that the alternating serpent heads, Quetzalcoatl and the War Serpent, refer to dual aspects of rulership, the feathered serpent with fertility and the interior affairs of the state, and the War Serpent with military conquest and empire."

David Carrasco, a noted historian, has suggested Quetzalcoatl is a deity that represents culture and civilization. And, now, we come to the most controversial theory of all: that Quetzalcoatl was an ancient astronaut, one who was determined to bring culture and science to what he perceived as a decidedly primitive body of people.

On this matter, it is intriguing to note that throughout Mesoamerica Quetzalcoatl was associated with the planet Venus. Alberto Mendo's paper, "Quetzalcoatl: Beyond the Feathered Serpent," notes that "the date of birth of Quetzalcoatl and the day when Venus reappears on the same position in the eastern horizon once every eight years" is the same.

> **//Ancient Aliens have been suspected to have helped create many wonders we see today including the massive Temples found through Central America and the Yucatan Peninsula."**

Author Vicky Anderson (in "Goddess, the Divine Feminine") said: "To the ancient Maya and the Aztecs, the god Xolotl was the evening star and his brother Quetzalcoatl was the morning star. The Maya and the Aztecs prophecy that, one day, the god Quetzalcoatl will return to the Earth from Venus."

John Major Jenkins (cited by Sandra Weaver in "Quetzalcoatl Is Deeper Than Just a Mayan Story or Myth") offers the opinion that "the Toltec pantheon that represented the Zenith Cosmology was Quetzalcoatl, whose earliest astronomical association is with the Pleiades.... The Pleiades were known as the serpent's rattle, and the flight of the Pleiades into alignment with the zenith sun evoked the image of a flying serpent."

That Quetzalcoatl was so inextricably tied to the heavens above makes it relatively easy to understand why suggestions have been made that he was an extraterrestrial entity.

Quetzalcoatl researcher Rick Popko has a scenario for the nature of the legend that is definitively extraterrestrial-themed, but in a different way. He offers the following, in 2010's "Mythology/quetzalcoatl":

> The theory I have is that Q was actually a very large UFO. As the craft entered Earth's atmosphere, it broke into flames and began its long descent, flaming, smoking and spiraling out of control. If this thing was multiple football fields in size, from the ground, it could very well look like a flaming serpent head, and the spiral smoke trails could be interpreted as feathers. Of course a ship of this size is going to make a big impact when it crashes and probably take out a lot of innocent people in the process. Keep in mind most of these people have probably never seen anything like this in their lives, let alone watch it crash into their society and kill

a bunch of people. Heck if I were there at the time, I'd probably bow down to as my god as well.

The website *Arcturi* noted, in its "Retilians and Aztec" article:

Ancient Aliens have been suspected to have helped create many wonders we see today including the massive Temples found through Central America and the Yucatan Peninsula. Like other great American civilizations, Reptilians have been an integral part in the Aztec civilization which cultivated a belief system around the alien we now know as the Reptilians.

Writer Paul Dale Roberts said of the Quetzalcoatl saga, in his "In Search of Quetzalcoatl" that:

What is also interesting is that there is a reptilian influence.... The reptilian influence is saturated throughout Egypt, East Asia, India and the list goes on and on.

I believe the reptilian influence represents ancient astronauts that resembled reptiles. The reptile influence can even be found in our own bible as it was the serpent that influenced Eve to bite from the forbidden fruit.

Could it be that ancient astronauts long ago were living amongst our advanced cultures like the Phoenicians, Egyptians and bringing their knowledge of science, math, and astronomy to cultures like the Olmecs, Toltecs, and Mayans?

Roberts provides us with a notable statement to ponder on: "As the pieces of the puzzle come together, it appears that Erich Anton Paul von Däniken may have been right all along."

THE PLAGUES OF EGYPT: UNLEASHING EXTRATERRESTRIAL VIRUSES

The Old Testament is filled to the brim with tales demonstrating that God's almighty, homicidal wrath was not something that any sane person would want to incur. Without doubt one of the prime examples of how God could turn his hand to widespread slaughter—even of babies, no less—can be found in the Book of Exodus. It's a book that tells the story of how God threatens Pharaoh by warning him that unless he frees the Israelites from the shackles of slavery, he, God, will unleash a series of deadly and devastating plagues upon Pharaoh and his people. Pharaoh—for a while, at least—ignores God's warnings, something that Pharaoh ultimately comes to majorly regret. When, essentially, Pharaoh said to God: "Do your worst," that's exactly what God does. No less than ten plagues devastate the land.

The first turns the water of the River Nile into blood. As noted in Exodus 7:20:

And Moses and Aaron did so, as the LORD commanded; and he lifted up the rod, and smote the waters that *were* in the river, in the sight of Pharaoh, and in the sight of his servants; and all the waters that *were* in the river were turned to blood.

That was soon followed by a plague of frogs, as described in Exodus 8:1–4:

And the LORD spake unto Moses, Go unto Pharaoh, and say unto him, Thus saith the LORD, Let my people go, that they may serve me.

And if thou refuse to let *them* go, behold, I will smite all thy borders with frogs:

And the river shall bring forth frogs abundantly, which shall go up and come into thine house, and into thy bedchamber, and upon thy bed, and into the house of thy servants, and upon thy people, and into thine ovens, and into thy kneadingtroughs:

And the frogs shall come up both on thee, and upon thy people, and upon all thy servants.

The frogs were followed by lice, which, in turn, gave way to another plague, this time of flies:

… and there came a grievous swarm *of flies* into the house of Pharaoh, and *into* his servants' houses, and into all the land of Egypt: the land was corrupted by reason of the swarm *of flies*. (Exodus 8:24)

The second plague set upon Egypt was countless frogs. Why frogs? Well, in Egypt frogs were considered sacred because the goddess Heket had the head of a frog. Therefore, the Egyptians could not rid themselves of the amphibians.

When all of that failed to move Pharaoh, God turned his attentions to the animals:

For if thou refuse to let *them* go, and wilt hold them still,

Behold, the hand of the LORD is upon thy cattle which *is* in the field, upon the horses, upon the asses, upon the camels, upon the oxen, and upon the sheep: *there shall be* a very grievous murrain.

And the LORD shall sever between the cattle of Israel and the cattle of Egypt: and there shall nothing die of all *that is* the children's of Israel. (Exodus 9:2–4)

Next on the list was an outbreak of terrible disease amongst the human population, one that caused the eruption of horrific boils on the skin of the infected. God didn't let up with that. He continued to make each plague worse than the previous one. In thunderous tones, he warned Pharaoh:

As yet exaltest thou thyself against my people, that thou wilt not let them go?

Behold, to morrow about this time I will cause it to rain a very grievous hail, such as hath not been in Egypt since the foundation thereof even until now.

Send therefore now, and gather thy cattle, and all that thou hast in the field; for upon every man and beast which shall be found in the field, and shall not be brought home, the hail shall come down upon them, and they shall die. (Exodus 9:17–20)

The storm gave way to a veritable invasion by locusts. Once again, Pharaoh was warned in advance:

And Moses and Aaron came in unto Pharaoh, and said unto him, Thus saith the LORD God of the Hebrews, How long wilt thou refuse to humble thyself before me? let my people go, that they may serve me.

Else, if thou refuse to let my people go, behold, to morrow will I bring the locusts into thy coast:

And they shall cover the face of the earth, that one cannot be able to see the earth: and they shall eat the residue of that which is escaped, which remaineth unto you from the hail, and shall eat every tree which groweth for you out of the field:

And they shall fill thy houses, and the houses of all thy servants, and the houses of all the Egyptians; which neither thy fathers, nor thy fathers' fathers have seen, since the day that they were upon the earth unto this day. And he turned himself, and went out from Pharaoh. (Exodus 10:3–6)

Perhaps the eeriest of all the plagues that God dispatched was darkness. It was a darkness quite unlike any other, one that was so dark it effectively left the people of Egypt in a state of blindness; such was its intensity. It lasted for three days. Then there came the most devastating plague of all.

As Exodus 11:4–6 related:

And Moses said, Thus saith the LORD, About midnight will I go out into the midst of Egypt:

And all the firstborn in the land of Egypt shall die, from the firstborn of Pharaoh that sitteth upon his throne, even unto the firstborn of the maid-servant that is behind the mill; and all the firstborn of beasts.

And there shall be a great cry throughout all the land of Egypt, such as there was none like it, nor shall be like it any more.

Prior to this mass execution of Egypt's children, God warned Moses that he and his people needed to take a specific step to ensure they did not fall victim to the deadly plague. The only way to survive it was to smear the blood of a lamb on the door of the family home. Moses instructed his followers to do exactly that. It was an act that ensured the survival of their first-born. Pharaoh's people, however, did not do likewise and, as a result, an untold number of first-born Egyptians died overnight. It was this act that finally caused Pharaoh to relent and release the Israelites from their bondage.

There is a distinct possibility that the ten plagues of Israel were provoked not by an angry, homicidal God, but by the work of technologically advanced extraterrestrials....

Although Christians are happy to accept the story in literal terms, there is a distinct possibility that the ten plagues of Israel were provoked not by an angry, homicidal God, but by the work of technologically advanced extraterrestrials, using a combination of weather-control technology and the unleashing of deadly, alien viruses on the human and animal population.

It was revealed in the British *Observer* newspaper on March 5, 2006, that on July 25, 2001, "blood-red rain" fell over the Kerala district of western India, and continued for the next two months. All along the coast it rained crimson, turning local people's clothes pink, burning leaves on trees and falling as scarlet sheets at some points. It must be said this sounds *astonishingly* like the claims that the Nile was turned blood red. Researchers, however, did not conclude that the Indian events were due to the work of a deity, but possibly some form of "alien bacteria."

Godfrey Louis, a physicist at Mahatma Gandhi University in Kottayam, stated to the authors of the *Observer* article, Amelia Gentleman and Robin McKie: "If you look at these particles under a microscope, you can see they are not dust, they have a clear biological appearance." Instead, Louis decided that the rain was made up of bacteria-like material that had been swept to Earth from "a passing comet."

Milton Wainwright, a microbiologist at Sheffield, tested samples of Kerala's "red rain." He said: "It is too early to say what's in the phial. But it is certainly not dust. Nor is there any DNA there, but then alien bacteria would not necessarily contain DNA."

Louis added:

If anybody hears a theory like this, that it is from a comet, they dismiss it as an unbelievable kind of conclusion. Unless people understand our arguments—people will just rule it out as an impossible thing, that extra-terrestrial biology is responsible for this red rain.

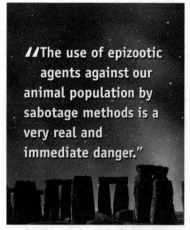

//The use of epizootic agents against our animal population by sabotage methods is a very real and immediate danger."

Moving on from matters relative to red rain and alien viruses and how they might, potentially, affect people, there is that matter of God allegedly delivering devastating disease to wipe out the animal population. This brings us to something else that has secretly worried the world of officialdom. Prepared by the U.S. government's Committee on Biological Warfare—at the request of the Research and Development Board—is a now-declassified fifty-page file that dates from March 1947 through to the latter part of 1948. It can be read at the National Archives in Maryland and makes for disturbing reading. Interestingly, the files cover two issues relative to the Old Testament wrath of God, and which are described in the files as "exotic diseases and insect pests.

The Committee said on this very point:

Within the last few years there have been several outbreaks of exotic diseases and insect pests which are believed to have been introduced accidentally but which could have been introduced intentionally had someone wished to do so. The use of epizootic agents against our animal population by sabotage methods is a very real and immediate danger. Foot-and-mouth disease and rinderpest are among those which would spread rapidly, and unless effective counter-measures were immediately applied, would seriously affect the food supply of animal origin.

Worse still is the following:

Since foot-and-mouth is now present in Mexico, it would be relatively easy for saboteurs to introduce the disease into the United States and have this introduction appear as natural spread from Mexico. Since rinderpest and foot-and-mouth disease are not present in the United States, our animal population is extremely vulnerable to these diseases.

Alarmingly, the papers reveal, the United States was in no position to prevent a large-scale biological attack on the animal population had it indeed occurred:

The United States is particularly vulnerable to this type of attack. It is believed generally that espionage agents of foreign countries which are potential enemies of the United States are present already in this country. There appears to be no great barrier to prevent additional espionage agents from becoming established here and there is no control over the movements of people within the United States.

And, stressing even further the extraterrestrial connection to all this, in 1949, a doctor from Indiana believed that he had solved the riddle of the alien presence on our planet. Moreover, he took great steps to try and warn the world of officialdom of what was taking place: nothing less than a covert extraterrestrial attack on human beings via biological warfare. Documentation contained within the same file housed at the National Archives reveals that the doctor's claims were scrutinized deeply by the Federal Bureau of Investigation; the Aero Medical Laboratory at Wright-Patterson Air Force Base, Ohio; the Atomic Energy Commission; and the Air Force's Office of Special Investigations.

Staff at the FBI's Office in Indianapolis informed Bureau director J. Edgar Hoover that the doctor, whose name is deleted from the now-declassified papers,

> found himself in the midst of a polio epidemic and that as a result he had read as much literature as possible with respect to polio, its symptoms, diagnosis, etc. Dr. [Deleted] told that in his opinion, the cases which were thought to be polio in the vicinity of Decatur, Indiana, were not polio, but possibly the result of uranium poisoning and that he felt the presence of flying saucers had direct bearing on the polio epidemic.

Hoover was further informed:

> [The Doctor] pointed out that flying saucers were observed in the Carolinas in 1948 and there was a polio epidemic in the vicinity at that time. Dr. [Deleted] stated he had consulted one of the physicians at the Benjamin Harrison Air Base and had also checked the records with reference to allegations concerning the sighting of flying saucers and had done a little research with respect to correlating the presence of flying saucers and any polio epidemic.

As for that violent, killer storm that God unleashed, again there is a distinct possibility that it was technology, rather than anything supernatural that provoked the storm to specifically target Egypt. April 28, 1997, was the date on which a startling statement was made by William S. Cohen, who, at the time, was the U.S. secretary of defense under the Clinton administration. The location was the University of Georgia, which was playing host to the Conference on Terrorism, Weapons of Mass Destruction, and U.S. Strategy. As a captivated audience listened intently, Cohen revealed something that was as remarkable as it was controversial.

Hostile groups—that Cohen, whether by design or not, did not name—were actively "engaging in an eco-type of terrorism whereby they can alter the climate, set off earthquakes, volcanos remotely through the use of Electro-Magnetic waves."

Those of a religious mindset will continue to believe that the plagues of Israel were unleashed by an angry God—and, of course, it is their right to believe that. On the other hand, as the above data demonstrates, there is a distinct possibility that what devastated Egypt and finally forced Pharaoh to back down was the combined unleashing of alien viruses, biological weapons (that affected both people and animals), and weather-modification technology of the type described in 1997 by Secretary of Defense Cohen.

THE NAZCA LINES: SIGNS FROM THE STARS

They can be found in the hot Nazca desert areas of southern Peru. They were constructed around 500 C.E. Their specific location is a huge plateau, situated about twenty miles from Peru's capital city of Lima. More than 1,500 years after their creation they continue to provoke awe, wonder, and a sense of deep mystery. They have also provoked theories that they were either built by, or with the assistance of, highly advanced extraterrestrials. They have become famously known as the Nazca Lines. Regardless of who, or what, made them, it's important to note that the Nazca Lines are not just straight lines in the sand. Indeed, they are more than that; *much* more, in fact. The literally hundreds of creations—of what are known as geoglyphs—include intricate portrayals of a variety of animals, birds, insects, and fish, as well as a wide variety of flora.

The process by which the Nazca Lines—some of which extend for hundreds of feet—were created is actually quite simple and down to earth. The natural color of the Nazca desert's ferrous oxide-containing pebbles is a combination of red, brown, and orange. However, one only has to dig down a few inches to find that the soil below is of a very different color: a slightly discolored, yellowish-white. Thus, the stark contrast between the topsoil pebbles and the earth below makes for an excellent medium in which to create huge, intricate imagery that can be easily viewed, which is exactly what the Nazca Lines are noted for. The big questions then are who created the lines and why?

The general consensus—even among those who adhere to the idea that there is an extraterrestrial component to the mystery—is that the lines were the work of the Nazca people; they made their homes on the land surrounding Peru's Ica River and a large body of valleys on the southern coast of the country. Although the Nazcas rose to prominence around 100 B.C.E., they were not destined to last. By around the ninth century C.E. their culture had fragmented, splintered, and split into various other groups. Without doubt, however, the Nazca Lines remain the most famous, lasting legacy of their existence and culture. The sheer extent to which the lines have gained such historical significance can be demonstrated by the fact that the United Nations Educational, Scientific and Cultural

//The credit for the discovery of the lines goes to Peruvian archaeologist Toribio Mejia Xesspe who spotted them when hiking through the foothills in 1927."

This example of one of the Nazca Lines looks like a spider, but can only be seen as such from the air.

Organization (UNESCO) officially designated the Nazca Lines as a World Heritage Site.

UNESCO describes a World Heritage Site as one that "is an outstanding example of a type of building, architectural or technological ensemble or landscape which illustrates [a] significant stage[s] in human history"; that bears "a unique or at least exceptional testimony to a cultural tradition or to a civilization which is living or which has disappeared," that "represents a masterpiece of human creative genius"; which "exhibits an important interchange of human values, over a span of time, or within a cultural area of the world, on developments in architecture or technology, monumental arts, town-planning, or landscape design," and that "is directly or tangibly associated with events or living traditions, with ideas, or with beliefs, with artistic and literary works of outstanding universal significance."

Clearly, *all* of those categories easily apply to the Nazca Lines.

As for when the Nazca Lines first came to prominence—outside of their very own culture, of course—the earliest example can be found in a sixteenth-century book penned by a Spanish conquistador named Piedra Cieza de Leon. Its title translates into English as *The Chronicle of Peru*. The book describes de Leon's journeying around Peru, and in which he refers to the Nazca Lines as "signs," "paths," and "signals."

It was in the 1920s that their existence became more widely known. Katherine Reece, a noted authority on the Nazca Lines, said: "The credit for the discovery of the lines goes to Peruvian archaeologist Toribio Mejia Xesspe who spotted them when hiking through the foothills in 1927."

The man who really got the ball rolling, however, was Paul August Kosok, a professor of history, whose interest in, and fascination with, the lines began in 1939—and all thanks to a flight he made over the area, which brought them to his attention. Kosok's primary interest was in the intricate canals and irrigation systems that the ancient Peruvians had constructed. Kosok thought—as he peered out of the aircraft window—that the Nazca Lines just might have played a role in the old canal constructions. He quickly realized, however, that their shallow depth meant this simply could not be the case. Instead, he came to the conclusion that the lines represented something else entirely: a still-existing, near-unique aspect of ancient Nazca culture.

At the dawning of the 1940s, Kosok connected with, and worked closely with for years, a woman named Maria Reiche. It was Reiche—of Dresden, Germany—perhaps more than anyone else, who demonstrated that some of the Nazca Lines had links to astronomical events, such as the summer solstice and the winter solstice.

Bonnie Hamre (the author of "Nazca Lines, Peru: Who Drew the Lines in the Sand? How?") noted:

> Maria Reiche developed the theory that the ancient Peruvians drew the lines to please the gods and secure their good will. She called the desert an astronomical calendar to remind the gods that the desert was dry and needed water; that crops needed blessings; that the seas needed fish. There are theories that the figures correspond to constellations and the annual change of the seasons. Other theories contend that the figures represent a pantheon of gods and goddesses and were the site of religious ceremonies.

Such was the interest in Reiche's research and theories that she succeeded in having the Peruvian Air Force use its aircraft to carefully map the lines. In 1949, Reiche's book on the lines, titled *The Mystery of the Desert*, was published. Its theories, on the astronomical angle, were met with both support and derision. Reiche's theories were downright tame compared to those that began to surface a couple of decades later, however.

It has been suggested that the Nazca people may have possessed fairly sophisticated technology when it came to the matter of how they were able to make such massive patterns and designs—ones that, chiefly, can only really be appreciated by viewing them from above.

Sacred Destinations noted in its "Nazca Lines, Peru" feature:

In 1977, Jim Woodman accepted that the Nazca people made the lines themselves, but puzzled over why they would make them so big that they couldn't even see them. He hypothesized that the Nazca people used hot-air balloons for "ceremonial flights" to view their creations.

Woodman attempted to demonstrate the validity of his theory by constructing a hot-air balloon out of the materials that would have been available to the Nazca. Using cloth, rope and reeds, Woodman and his colleagues assembled the balloon then risked their lives on a balloon ride that reached a height of 300 feet. The balloon soon descended rapidly; the balloonists bailed out 10 feet above the desert before it crashed some distance away.

In his full-length book on the subject, *Nazca: Journey to the Sun*, Woodman said:

Another Nazca Line looks like a hummingbird. Did ancient Peruvians create the lines to please their gods?

From the ground, Nazca is totally incomprehensible, yet from the air one gasps with astonishment—and that is what most fascinates modern man. The riddle of Nazca asks why this colossal puzzle was created over two thousand years ago if no one could have seen it? To appreciate Nazca one must be airborne above the plains.

Woodman added that, of his balloon theory, "It is totally unreasonable that Nazca was a prehistoric spaceport for extraterrestrial visitors. Far more acceptable is the idea that the obviously indigenous men of Nazca had learned to fly there long, long ago."

Not everyone was in agreement. Author Joe Nickell ("The Nazca Lines Revisited: Creation of a Full-Sized Duplicate") referred to the balloon theory as "merely a flight of fancy."

Katherine Reece, who penned "Grounding the Nasca Balloon," said that: "the 'evidence' that Woodman put forward to support his theory" was "flawed." She also said: "It is incorrect to say that the lines cannot be seen from the ground. They are visible from atop the surrounding foothills.... The Nasca lines have nothing to do with balloons."

But, might they have had something to do with visiting, ancient astronauts?

In 1968, Erich von von Däniken's famous and controversial book *Chariots of the Gods* was published. In the pages of his best-selling book, von Däniken offered the controversial scenario that the Nazca Lines had an extraterrestrial component to them. The website *Peru Facts* noted, in 2008, in its "Chariots of the Gods" feature:

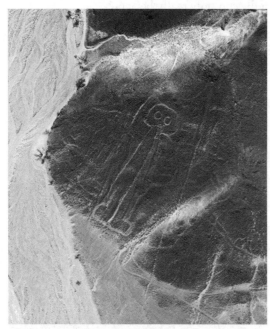

This Nazca Line looks remarkably like a modern-day astronaut. Might it be true that alien astronauts visited that part of Earth long ago?

> Erich Von Däniken believed that the Nazca lines of Peru were the remains of an alien lifeform that had used the markings as a guide for a landing base in Peru. He believed that the markings and lines were from the aliens that had used the airport to visit earth....
>
> With some of the lines being over six miles in length it is hard to believe that the people of Nazca had the ability to create these lines as they would not have been able to view the work they were creating as it is unlikely that they would of been able to build a flying vessel to monitor the construction of the lines they were creating. Therefore the theory of Erich Von Däniken could be a fitting reason on how the Nazca lines were created.

Jacques Bergier, a noted proponent of the theory that ancient astronauts—from faraway galaxies—visited the Earth in the distant past, said of the Nazca Lines in his 1974 book, *Mysteries of the Earth*: "The design is made up of straight lines and large surfaces in trapezoid form, rather resembling one of our airports as seen from an airplane. Also to be seen are giant spirals analogous to what telescopes show us of the spiral nebula. There are also large-sized nonhuman figures, or figures of gods or extraterrestrial beings; take your pick."

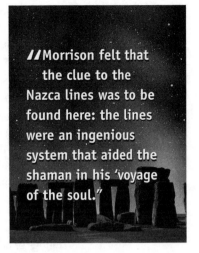

//Morrison felt that the clue to the Nazca lines was to be found here: the lines were an ingenious system that aided the shaman in his 'voyage of the soul."

Bergier suggested that the Nazca Lines may have been made by the local populace, which was "following the orders, if not of the Intelligences, at least of some higher race representing them." And how might such a thing successfully be achieved? Bergier had a few ideas:

> After a number of miracles, a voice is heard, the people assemble, and each worker receives exact instructions as to what he must do. The entire maneuver is directed from a helicopter, balloon, or some other machine capable of hovering—one that we still have not invented. The work lasts for years, even decades and, when it is finally done, the Intelligences or their representatives go away.

The reason, suggested Bergier, was "to build a sort of astroport, where the recorders collecting data about the earth could be brought for retrieval by relatively simple, optically self-guiding machines."

The late Philip Coppens was the author of a number of books, including *The Ancient Alien Question* and *The Lost Civilization Enigma*. And, until his untimely passing in late 2012, he was a regular on the History Channel's *Ancient Aliens* series. Coppens had a fascinating theory about of the Nazca Lines. Commenting on the nature and beliefs of Nazca people, Coppens said, in 1999's "Nazca: Airport of the Gods?":

> Shamanic cultures use "shamans" [priests] to seek contact with the gods, the ancestors, the dead. These are local in a different dimension; they are not physical beings, but "spiritual entities," often the souls of the tribal ancestors, as well as creator deities. The land of the dead was similar to Earth, but was found in another dimension—here, yet invisible to our eyes.

Commenting on the research of Tony Morrison (who wrote the 1987 book *The Mystery of the Nazca Lines*), Coppens said: "Morrison felt that the clue to the Nazca lines was to be found here: the lines were an ingenious system that aided the shaman in his 'voyage of the soul.' He argued that the lines often converged in certain nodes, from which they continued. On these nodes and at regular intervals along the lines, small altars could be found, sometimes little more than a small heap of stones and earth.

> Von Däniken was right, [offered Copens] when he suggested that the animals and lines had to be seen from the sky. They were seen during the shamanic flight, on his voyage to the Otherworld. Shamanic theory states that the shaman leaves his body and "floats" or "soars" through the

sky, where often the eagle or another animal is his totem animal—the animal mimics or symbolizes the flight of the soul. If these lines were an airstrip, they were an airstrip for the soul—to take off to and return from the Otherworld.

This was something expanded upon by Grahame Johnston, who said in "Nazca Lines and the Nazca Culture":

Using experimental archaeology the British explorer, Tony Morrison, observed that the old folk customs of the Andes Mountain people demonstrated an unusual and pertinent tradition. His research discovered that the mountain people would travel from shrine to shrine in direct straight paths praying as they walked. A straight, direct path, similar to the patterns found at Nazca, linked each shrine, which could be nothing more than a carefully grouped pile of stones or more elaborate structures. Morrison has concluded that the Nazca lines could have been used during religious or ceremonial occasions.

And the theories don't end there, as Lee Krystek noted in "The Lines of Nazca Peru":

Two researchers, David Johnson and Steve Mabee, have advanced a theory that the geoglyphs may be related to water. The Nazca plain is one of the driest places on Earth, getting less than one inch of rain a year. Johnson, while looking for sources of water in the region, noticed that ancient aqueducts, called puquios, seemed to be connected with some of the lines.

Johnson thinks that the shapes may be a giant map of the underground water sources traced on the land. Mabee is working to gather evidence that might confirm this theory.

Today, countless centuries after they were first lain down on the desert floor of southern Peru, we still don't have a definitive answer for what it was that made ancient man construct such vast, intricate patterns that could only be appreciated from a significant height—whether from in the sky itself or from the high, surrounding hills. Whether the work of ancient extraterrestrials, equally ancient humans inspired by ETs, balloon-flying Nazcas, or shamanic figures engaging in out-of-body experiences, of just one thing we can be sure: the atmosphere of intrigue, mystery, and fascination that surrounds the Nazca Lines is unlikely to fade away anytime soon—or, for that matter, anytime later, too.

NATIVE AMERICAN LEGENDS: BIGFOOT AND UFOS

Although the term "Bigfoot" was not coined until the late 1950s, it is a fact that reports of giant, hairy, humanoid creatures inhabiting the wilder, mountainous, and forested areas of the United States date back to the earliest years of Native American culture. Loren Coleman, one of the world's leading authorities on Bigfoot, said:

> When Europeans colonized from the East to the West, their initial encounters were with the rare, eastern Bigfoot, which the native they met spoke about. The first Americans acknowledged these hairy races, and their tales come down to us in the records that ethnographers, folklorists, and anthropologists have preserved in overlooked essaid on hairy-giant legends and myths.

There is, however, something very intriguing about the Native American beliefs in Bigfoot. They suggest the creatures are far more than they appear to be. That's to say that they do not just represent an undiscovered kind of North American ape, but something directly linked to the UFO phenomenon. Given the fact that reports exist of Bigfoot from centuries ago, as astonishing as it may sound Bigfoot may be nothing less than an ancient alien.

In a 2012 report—"Native American Bigfoot Figures of Myth and Legend"—the *Native Languages* website stated:

> The Bigfoot figure is common to the folklore of most Northwest Native American tribes. Native American Bigfoot legends usually describe the creatures as around 6–9 feet tall, very strong, hairy, uncivilized, and often foul-smelling, usually living in the woods and often foraging at night.... In some Native stories, Bigfoot may have minor supernatural powers— the ability to turn invisible, for example—but they are always considered physical creatures of the forest, not spirits or ghosts.

> That is where the intertribal Bigfoot similarities end, however. In the Bigfoot myths of some tribes, Sasquatch and his relatives are generally shy and benign figures—they may take things that do not belong to them or even kidnap a human wife, but do not harm people and may even come to their aid. Sometimes Bigfoot is considered a guardian of nature in these tribes. These more benevolent Bigfeet usually appear alone or in a small family unit, and may exchange gifts or use sign language to communicate with Native American communities. But Bigfoot legends from other tribes

describe them as malevolent creatures who attack humans, play dangerous tricks on them, or steal children; they may even eat people. These more dangerous Bigfoot monsters, known as Stick Indians or Bush Indians, are sometimes found in large groups or even villages, which engage in warfare with neighboring Indian tribes.

One of the most fascinating cases of relevancy came from James C. Wyatt of Memphis, Tennessee, who shared with paranormal expert Brad Steiger a copy of his—Wyatt's—grandfather's journal from 1888. Steiger told the story in his 2011 book, *Real Monsters, Gruesome Critters, and Beasts from the Darkside*. It described the old man's exposure to the Bigfoot phenomenon. The location was the Humboldt Meridian, in northwestern California. It was while in the area, on one particular day, that Wyatt's grandfather encountered a tribesman carrying a plate of raw meat. Puzzled, he asked what it was for. After pondering on things for a while the man motioned Wyatt Sr. to follow. On arriving at a cave built into a cliff face, he was shocked to see a huge, hair-covered, man-like beast. It was, however, quite docile and enthusiastically ate the meat provided for him.

It was then that Wyatt's grandfather got the full story. The beast—nicknamed "Crazy Bear"—had supposedly been brought to the forests "from the stars." Nothing less than a "small moon" had descended, ejecting both the creature and several others of its kind. The "moon" was reportedly piloted by very human-looking entities that always waved at the Indians as they dumped the hairy beasts on their land.

A wooden carving of a Bigfoot has become an attraction to travelers on highway 504 in Washington State.

James C. Wyatt asked Brad Steiger: "Who is to say the Crazy Bears weren't exiled to our planet for some crime or other infraction of the laws of another planet?"

On a very similar path, the respected investigator Lon Strickler, in "The Bigfoot Paradox," said:

> Researcher and author Kewaunee Lapseritis maintains that the Bigfoot race was brought to Earth by the "Star People," long before human civilization even existed. His evidence is the creature's use of telepathic communications, alleged hundreds of joint Bigfoot-UFO sightings going back over a hundred years and theoretical physics. He also stated that conventional Bigfoot investigators have not found the creature because they are limited in their belief that Bigfoot is "simply a relic hominid that never became extinct."

"That really may be true," Lapseritis said in an interview, as Lon Strickler chronicles in his "The Bigfoot Paradox" article: "But in addition to that, (Bigfoot) may literally be, as I've discovered, a paraphysical, interdimensional native people that have told me and other people telepathically that they were brought here millions of years ago by their friends, the Star People."

Strickler added:

The beast—nicknamed "Crazy Bear"—had supposedly been brought to the forests "from the stars."

I recently received a telephone call from a woman in British Columbia who said she was the daughter of a Kootenai shaman. She stated that most Native tribes seem to believe Sasquatch is a non-physical creature. Some tribal elders mention that they have seen the creature shapeshift into a wolf. She said her father thought that the creatures lived in another dimension from our physical plane, but can come here as it wishes.

Micah Hanks, who wrote "Curious Cryptohominids: A Link Between Aliens and Bigfoot?" and who is one of the world's leading authorities on a wide and varied body of paranormal mysteries, said of this controversial issue:

Researchers such as John Keel and Stan Gordon have noted the apparent parallels between sightings of anthropomorphic ape-like creatures and UFO encounters. In a few smaller Fortean circles, this sort of research has even occasionally led to the belief that Bigfoot creatures might represent some form of an alien being themselves. Various websites online have even gone so far as to denote Bigfoot-type creatures under the extraterrestrial classification of "Sasquans" and similar names, likening the beasts to being an extraterrestrial race exiled (whether or not it's a self-imposed exile) here on Earth. Other bizarre speculation along similar lines suggests that Bigfoot creatures are actually pets which, similar to an irresponsible dog or cat owner taking an animal off to a remote location and release it, have been turned loose on this planet by their extraterrestrial owners.

Now, it's time to move across the Atlantic.

Regardless of what people may personally feel or conclude about the ancient Bigfoot-UFO connection—or, more correctly, the theoretical connection—when we go looking for places in Britain where both enigmas have been seen and encountered, there's certainly no shortage of stories to address. Back in 1879 sightings began of a strange, "ape-man-like" creature known as the Man-Monkey that haunted England's Shropshire Union Canal and the nearby village of Ranton. It so happens that, back in the 1950s, Ranton was the site of a famous—but now largely forgotten—UFO encounter.

Researcher Gavin Gibbons wrote (in his 1957 book, *They Rode in Space Ships*) that one October evening in 1954, a Dutchman living in England named Tony Roestenberg returned home to find his wife, Jessie, "in a terrified state." According to Jessie: earlier that day nothing less than a flying saucer hovered over their isolated farmhouse in Ranton. In addition, Jessie could see peering down from the craft two very "Nordic"-like men.

A number of researchers have drawn connections between sightings of Bigfoot and UFOs. This illustration depicts a 1972 sighting in Missouri. (mary evans)

Their foreheads were high, their hair was long and fair, and they seemed to have "pitiful" looks on their faces. The strange craft reportedly circled the family's home twice, before streaking away. Curiously, on the following Sunday, Tony Roestenberg had a "hunch" that if he climbed on the roof of his house "he would see something unusual," which he most certainly did. It was a high-flying, cigar-shaped object that vanished into the clouds.

Gavin Gibbons, who investigated the case personally, stated: "When I visited the Roestenberg's house almost three weeks after the sighting … Jessie Roestenberg appeared. She seemed highly strained and nervous and her husband, coming in later, was also very strained. It was evident that something most unusual had occurred."

Then there is the ape-like Shug Monkey of Rendlesham Forest, Suffolk, England—which also happens to be the site of what is undeniably Britain's most famous UFO encounter: that of December 1980 and most vividly described in the book *Left at East Gate* by Larry Warren and Peter Robbins. And, to illustrate still further the UFO-hairy man connection, just down the road, so to speak, from Rendlesham Forest is the town of Orford—home to a legendary wild man caught in the seas off the coast of Orford centuries ago.

Returning to the United States, there is Stan Gordon's book, *Silent Invasion*, which details a wave of Bigfoot-UFO activity in Pennsylvania in the early 1970s. Gordon's book is a swirling cauldron filled with dark and ominous woods; glowing-eyed beast-men prowling the countryside by night; strange lights in the sky; UFO landings; neighborhoods gripped by terror and fear; and much, much more, too. And, it's thanks to Gordon's research, as well as his in-depth files prepared back when all the dark drama was going on, that we're now able to appreciate the curious chaos and calamity that collectively hit the unsuspecting folk of Pennsylvania all those years ago.

But, that's not all: macabre Men in Black, paranormal activity, psychic possession, secret government interest in Bigfoot, and prophetic visions of a dark and foreboding future all come to the fore in a book that is guaranteed to make you think twice about the true nature of Bigfoot.

As to how the Bigfoot beasts might access our environment, we have to turn to a man named Ronan Coghlan, who has developed an intriguing theory that explains the "here one minute, gone the next minute" aspect of the Bigfoot controversy, and which may also help explain the nature of the old Native American legends.

Coghlan told me in 2012:

It's now becoming acceptable in physics to say there are alternative universes. The main pioneer of this is Professor Michio Kaku, of the City College of New York. He has suggested that not only are there alternate universes, but when ours is about to go out in a couple of billion years, we might have the science to migrate to a more congenial one that isn't going to go out. I think he expects science to keep improving for countless millennia, which is very optimistic of him, but whatever one thinks about that, the idea of alternative universes is now gaining an acceptance among physicists, and he's the name to cite in this area.

The subject is far from one lacking in mysteries and questions, however, as Coghlan acknowledged:

Now, how do you get into, or out of, alternative universes? Well, the answer is quite simple: You have heard of wormholes, I'm sure? No-one has ever seen a worm-hole, I hasten to add. They are hypothetical, but mainstream physicists say they could be there, and there's one particular type called the Lorentzian Traversable Wormhole.

Physicists admit there is a possibility that this exists, and it would be like a short-cut, from one universe to another. Thus, for example, it's rather like a portal: Something from the other universe would come through it. Or, something from another planet could come through it.

> **// If there are any of these worm-holes on Earth, it would be quite easy for anything to come through, and it's quite possible any number of anomalous creatures could find their way through from time to time."**

Turning his attentions towards the links between worm-holes and bizarre beasts, Coghlan commented that:

If there are any of these worm-holes on Earth, it would be quite easy for anything to come through, and it's quite possible any number of anomalous creatures could find their way through from time to time. You remember John Keel and his window-areas? That would tend to indicate there's a worm-hole in the vicinity; such as Point Pleasant, West Virginia, where the Mothman was seen.

I have the distinct suspicion we are dealing with window-areas that either contact some other planet, or they contact another universe. My money is on the other universe, rather than the other planet, to be honest with you. Either a short-cut through time, or a short-cut through space, is recognized as possible these days. This is kind of cutting-edge physics, as it were.

Now, the other one isn't cutting-edge physics at all. It's my own little theory. I think, looking at a great many legends, folk-tales, and things of that nature, it is possible to vibrate at different rates. And if you vibrate at a different rate, you are not seen. You are not tangible. And, then, when your vibration changes, you are seen, and you are tangible; maybe that this has something to do with Bigfoot appearing and disappearing in a strange fashion.

And, finally, on the question of UFOs: Quite a large number of Bigfoot-type creatures have been seen in the vicinity of UFOs. I'm not saying there's necessarily a connection between the two, but they do—quite often—turn up in the same areas. Now, if UFOs travel by worm-holes, and if Bigfoot does the same, that might allow for a connection between the two. They might not be mutually exclusive.

Based on a careful study of Ronan Coghlan's words, we may well be justified in saying that the ancient Native American tribes knew far more about the real nature of Bigfoot than we do today.

THE GREEN CHILDREN OF WOOLPIT: VISITORS FROM BEYOND

Within the field of Ufology, the term "little green men" turns up with deep regularity—usually in a disparaging, fun-poking, debunking fashion. And, although it's a term that has very much become ingrained within popular culture, it's a fact that reports of little green men are not uncommon in UFO research. Certainly, one of the most famous—or, perhaps, infamous—examples can be found in a certain saga that occurred on the night of August 21, 1955.

The location was a farmhouse situated between the towns of Kelly and Hopkinsville, Kentucky. What began with sightings of strange lights in the sky soon expanded into a definitive shoot-out with a group of little, green-colored men. The farmhouse belonged to the Sutton family, who wasted no time trying to blast the diminutive things into oblivion. It's a case that remains a ufological favorite. The association between aliens and small, green humanoids isn't exclusively tied to the Kelly-Hopkinsville case, however.

A researcher of folklore named Chris Aubeck has been able to determine that those three, now-famous, words—little green men—date back to the final years of the nineteenth century. In 1899, for example, the *Atlanta Constitution* newspaper published a story written by Charles Battell Loomis, and titled "Green Boy from Hurrah"—the *Hurrah* of the title being a reference to another world. The renowned fantasy novelist Edgar Rice Burroughs wrote of the "green men of Mars" in his 1906 story, *A Princess of Mars*.

On May 22, 1947, just one month before the term "flying saucer" was coined (following the sighting of a squadron of UFOs seen over Mount Rainier, Washington, by a pilot named Kenneth Arnold) a reference to "little green men" was made in a Harrisburg, Illinois, newspaper, the *Daily Register*. Although the small article was on a medical condition that can cause the skin to turn green, it demonstrates that the terminology was in popular use before UFOs were, themselves, a part of our culture. Four years later, in 1951, a sci-fi novel, Mack Reynolds's *The Case of the Little Green Men*, was published. The subject matter was alien entities infiltrating the human race.

We may never know, for sure, when the "LGM" term was specifically created; however, when it comes to the matter of potential, ancient aliens, we find a linkage between the phenomenon and those now widely used three words. It's

Kenneth Arnold posed in front of the airplane he was flying in 1947, when he reportedly saw UFOs near the Cascade Mountains.

a story that takes us to the east coast of England and centuries back in time.

So the tale goes, back in the twelfth century, a young girl and boy, of strangely green-hued skin, appeared in the English village of Woolpit, which is situated between the towns of Bury St. Edmunds and Stowmarket. The children claimed to have come from a magical place called St. Martin's Land, which existed in an atmosphere of permanent twilight, and where the people lived underground, on nothing but green beans. While the story has been relegated by many to the realms of mere myth and folklore, it may not be just that. It might, actually, be much more.

According to the old legend, the two children remained in Woolpit and were ultimately baptized by the villagers, who accepted them as their very own. And although the boy ultimately grew sickly and eventually died, the girl did not. She thrived and finally lost her green-tinged skin to normal colored skin of healthy appearance. She also, somewhat in defiance of the disapproving attitudes of certain members of the village, became, as it was amusingly termed back then, according to the legend, "rather loose and wanton in her conduct."

Today, the story shows no signs of going away anytime soon. In fact, the people of the village of Woolpit still embrace the story to this very day, as the following extract from an article titled "Welcome to Woolpit Village," which can be found at the the village's official website, demonstrates:

> In 1016 Ulfketel, Earl of East Anglia, granted the church and manor of Wlfpeta to the Abbey of St Edmunds. The monks received ten marks yearly from this grant, but the King appropriated the revenues for the benefit of one of his officials. A monk named Sampson determined to put matters right and in 1159 travelled to Rome to obtain a charter from Pope Alexander III. Despite being captured and robbed by his enemies in the course of his journey, Sampson managed to preserve the Popes precious letter directing the reversion of Woolpit and its church to the monks, and returned to England after three years. The monks were once again able to enjoy the income, and Sampson was later appointed Abbot.

> One prominent feature of the village sign is two small children. They depict a story that goes back to the 12th century and tells the legend of "The Green Children of Woolpit." This curious tale is recorded as taking place at about the same time as Sampson's journey to Rome. Very briefly, reapers were astonished at the discovery of a boy and a girl in a hole in the ground.

The children were green, and spoke no recognizable language. The boy, who was sickly, soon died, but the girl grew up in Woolpit, and is said to have married a man from King's Lynn. This story has been re-enacted on many occasions and has appeared on childrens' television.

Ralph of Coggeshall, a thirteenth-century monk, wrote specifically of the strange girl, who fortunately survived and thrived in Woolpit all those centuries ago:

> Being frequently asked about the people of her country, she asserted that the inhabitants, and all they had in that country, were of a green colour; and that they saw no sun, but enjoyed a degree of light like what is after sunset.

> Being asked how she came into this country with the aforesaid boy, she replied, that as they were following their flocks, they came to a certain cavern, on entering which they heard a delightful sound of bells; ravished by whose sweetness, they went for a long time wandering on through the cavern, until they came to its mouth.

> When they came out of it, they were struck senseless by the excessive light of the sun, and the unusual temperature of the air; and they thus lay for a long time. Being terrified by the noise of those who came on them, they wished to fly, but they could not find the entrance of the cavern before they were caught.

That both wild children were reportedly green-skinned and lived underground in a mysterious locale has led many to disregard the tale out of hand as one of fairy-based, mythological proportions and nothing else whatsoever. That may not actually have been the case, however.

The pair may have been suffering from a condition called hypochromic anemia, in which the sufferer—as a result of a very poor diet that, in part, affects the color of the red blood cells—can develop skin of a noticeably green shade. In support of this scenario, hypochromic anemia was once known as chlorosis, a word formulated in the early 1600s by a Montpellier professor of medicine named Jean Varandal. And why did Varandal choose such a name? Simple: It came from the Greek word *chloris*, meaning greenish-yellow or pale green.

[R]eapers were astonished at the discovery of a boy and a girl in a hole in the ground. The children were green, and spoke no recognizable language.

Therefore, we might very well, and quite justifiably even, conclude that the strange children of Woolpit were definitively wild in nature. And given their state of poor health, they may certainly have lived poor and strange lives, very possibly deep underground. Or, perhaps, permanently under a thick canopy of dense forest of the type that dominated England at that time—with others of their kind, in and around Suffolk, just as they had claimed to the villagers of Woolpit; and, all the while struggling to survive on the meager supplies of food available to them that were ultimately responsible for their green-yellow hue.

There is another possibility, however; these little green children may not have been of this world. They may have been ancient extraterrestrials.

Dr. Karl Shuker, an authority on the mysteries of our world, has spent a great deal of time investigating the saga of the green children of Woolpit. In his 2012 paper, "The Green Children of Woolpit: Investigating a Medieval Mystery," Shuker said:

> A very different and far more dramatic explanation was proffered by Harold T. Wilkins, an investigator of unexplained anomalies. In his book *Mysteries: Solved and Unsolved* (1959), Wilkins boldly proposed that the green children may have entered our world from a parallel version (existing in a separate dimensional plane but directly alongside our own), by accidentally passing through some form of interdimensional "window" bridging the two. Another dramatic proposal is that the green children are extraterrestrials. As long ago as 1651, Robert Burton opined in his tome *Anatomy of Melancholy* that they may have come from Venus or Mars.

On a similar path, Tristan Eldritch noted, in "The Green Children of Woolpit:" "To a modern reader, the children might suggest stranded extraterrestrials of some kind, and this interpretation of the tale goes back much further than you would imagine." Indeed, as Eldritch also reveals, "the story found its way into Francis Goodwin's fancy *The Man in the Moone* (1638), a work sometimes regarded as the very earliest example of science fiction."

Researcher Melanie Koslovic said in "Green Children of Woolpit":

[T]hese little green children may not have been of this world. They may have been ancient extraterrestrials.

> It has also been suggested that the children may have been aliens, or inhabitants of a world beneath the Earth. In 1996 an article was published in the magazine *Analog* concerning this mystery; astronomer Duncan Lunan hypothesized that the children were accidentally sent to Woolpit from their home planet due to a malfunction in their "matter transmitter."
>
> Lunan thinks that the planet from which the children originated may be trapped in a synchronous orbit around its sun, presenting the conditions for life only in a narrow twilight zone between a fiercely hot surface and a frozen dark side. He believes the children's green color is a side effect of consuming genetically modified alien plants eaten on their planet.

Hubpages notes of Lunan's theory (in "Green Children of Woolpit: Mysterious Visitors from an Unknown Land") that:

> encouraged by the introduction of this element of science fiction to the proceedings, another unusual hypothesis has surfaced. The foundation of this theory is based on the belief that the children came from another dimension. Proponents of this reasoning believe that the pair inadvertently discovered a cave opening which was a portal between their dimension, and our own. Evidently, the portal was not a two-way access point; or

once the children were through, it vanished: as no one was ever able to pinpoint such an opening near the wolf pit where the two were discovered.

Duncan Lunan, himself, said (in an interview with Michael S. Collins) that the green girl ultimately became the wife of one

> … Richard Barre, one of Henry II's senior ambassadors, which rather puts paid to the "runaways from some primitive tribe" class of explanations. Her first, illegitimate child may have been fathered by Henry himself. I've traced her descendants to the present—one of them was deputy head of the House of Lords under Margaret Thatcher, and he thinks it's a hoot: "I knew my ancestors were colorful, but not that colorful." It looks as if the children grew up in a human colony on a planet with a trapped rotation and were returned to Earth in a matter-transmitter accident, one of a number which happened while the Earth's magnetic field was disturbed by the most violent solar activity since the Bronze Age.

Before you write off Lunan's theory as being far too fanciful, it's worth noting that he attended Marr College and Glasgow University. He has a master's, with honors, in English and philosophy, with physics, astronomy, and French as supporting subjects, and has a postgraduate diploma in education.

Author of *Children from the Sky,* Duncan Lunan believes that the strange children of Woolpit were sent there accidentally by an alien race.

Such is the age of the curious tale of Woolpit's centuries-old saga of the village's eerie, green-skinned children, that we'll likely never know if they really were ancient aliens or of far more down-to-earth origins. But, whatever the truth, of one thing we can be sure: the enchanting nature of the story ensures that, with every new generation that comes along, it gathers more momentum and provokes increased fascination.

THE FACE ON MARS: MEGA-BUILDING IN THE DISTANT PAST

Situated in a specific section of the planet Mars called Cydonia is a vast, sprawling structure that appears to resemble nothing less than a carving into the rock of an extremely human-looking face. Its dimensions are impressive: it is around three kilometers in length and around half that size in width. It first gained attention on July 25, 1976, when the face was photographed by NASA's *Viking 1* probe that, at the time, was orbiting Mars. To some, it's nothing but a large mesa that *looks* like a face. To others, it *is* a face—one constructed, possibly hundreds of thousands of years ago, by ancient Martians.

One person who dug very deeply into the many and varied areas of controversy that surround what has become known—to skeptics and believers, alike—as the "Face on Mars," was the late Mac Tonnies, who penned an entire book on the subject, in 2004, titled *After the Martian Apocalypse*. Before his death in 2009 at the age of thirty-four, Tonnies shared his thoughts with me on this curious, otherworldly structure. It was an interview that covered just about each and every facet of the Face on Mars controversy.

Tonnies began:

I've always had an innate interest in the prospect of extraterrestrial life. When I realized that there was an actual scientific inquiry regarding the Face and associated formations, I realized that this was a potential chance to lift SETI [Search for Extraterrestrial Intelligence] from the theoretical arena; it's within our ability to visit Mars in person. This was incredibly exciting, and it inspired an interest in Mars itself—its geological history, climate, et cetera.

I have a BA in Creative Writing. So of course, there are those who will happily disregard my book because I'm not "qualified." I suppose my question is "Who *is* qualified to address potential extraterrestrial artifacts?" Certainly not NASA's Jet Propulsion Laboratory, whose Mars exploration timetable is entirely geology-driven.

Tonnies noted to me how the controversy first surfaced:

NASA itself discovered the Face and even showed it at a press conference, after it had been photographed by the Viking mission in the 1970s. Of course, it was written off as a curiosity. Scientific analysis would have to await independent researchers. The first two objects to attract atten-

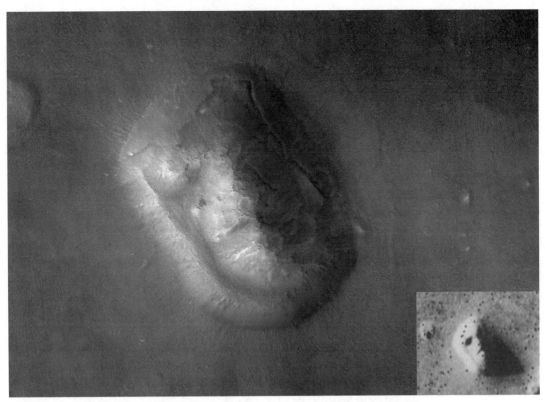

**The Mars Reconnaissance Orbiter took this 2007 photo of the famous "Face on Mars"
that shows a much-less distinctive human appearance than the photo captured earlier
(inset) by the *Viking 1 Orbiter* in 1976.**

tion were the Face and what has become known as the "D&M Pyramid."
Both unearthed by digital imaging specialists Vincent DiPietro and Gregory Molenaar. Their research was published in *Unusual Martian Surface
Features*; shortly after, Face researcher Richard Hoagland pointed out a
collection of features [some, eerily pyramid-like] near the Face which he
termed the "City."

When asked by me how the controversy was ignited, Tonnies replied:

When NASA dismissed the Face as a "trick of light," they cited a second,
discomfirming photo allegedly taken at a different sun-angle. This photo
never existed. DiPietro and Molenaar had to dig through NASA archives
to find a second image of the Face—and, far from disputing the face-like
appearance, it strengthened the argument that the Face remained face-
like from multiple viewing angles.

Tonnies continued with his comments and observation in regards to the
NASA–Face on Mars issue:

The prevailing alternative to NASA's geological explanation—that the
Face and other formations are natural landforms—is that we're seeing ex-

tremely ancient artificial structures built by an unknown civilization. NASA chooses to ignore that there is a controversy, or at least a controversy in the scientific sense.

Since making the Face public in the 1970s, NASA has made vague allusions to humans' ability to "see faces" (e.g. the "Man in the Moon") and has made lofty dismissals, but it has yet to launch any sort of methodical study of the objects under investigation. Collectively, NASA frowns on the whole endeavor. Mainstream SETI theorists are equally hostile.

Tonnies made valuable observations to me relative to the controversy:

Basically, the Face—if artificial—doesn't fall into academically palatable models of how extraterrestrial intelligence will reveal itself, if it is in fact "out there." Searching for radio signals is well and good, but scanning the surface of a neighboring planet for signs of prior occupation is met with a very carefully cultivated institutionalized scorn. And of course it doesn't help that some of the proponents of the Face have indulged in more than a little baseless "investigation."

As for Tonnies's own thoughts, they were as intriguing as they were notable:

I think some of the objects in the Cydonia region of Mars are probably artificial. And I think the only way this controversy will end is to send a manned mission. The features under investigation are extremely old and warrant on-site archaeological analysis. We've learned—painfully—that images from orbiting satellites won't answer the fundamental questions raised by the Artificiality Hypothesis.

When asked by me: "Do you believe all the perceived anomalous structures are indeed that or do you feel some are of natural origin while some are of unnatural origin?" Tonnies replied:

I suspect that we're seeing a fusion of natural geology and mega scale engineering. For example, the Face is likely a modified natural mesa, not entirely unlike some rock sculptures on Earth but on a vastly larger and more technically challenging scale.

I then asked a couple of questions of a very controversial nature: "Is there a relationship between the face and the pyramids on Mars and similar ones at Egypt? What does the research community think of this perceived connection?" Tonnies responded thus:

There's a superficial similarity between some of the alleged pyramids in the vicinity of the Face and the better-known ones here on Earth. This has become the stuff of endless arcane theorizing, and I agree with esoteric researchers that some sort of link between intelligence on Mars and Earth deserves to be taken seriously. But the formations on Mars are much, much larger than terrestrial architecture. This suggests a significantly different purpose, assuming they're intelligently designed. Richard Hoagland, to my knowledge, was the first to propose that the features in Cydonia might be "arcologies"—architectural ecologies—built to house a civilization that might have retreated underground for environmental reasons.

"If these things are artificial, who built them—Martians? Someone visiting Mars? Ancient earth civilizations now forgotten or lost to history?" I asked. He replied:

It's just possible that the complex in Cydonia (and potential edifices elsewhere on Mars) were constructed by indigenous Martians.... Mars was once extremely Earth-like. We know it had liquid water. It's perfectly conceivable that a civilization arose on Mars and managed to build structures within our ability to investigate. Or the anomalies might be evidence of interstellar visitation—perhaps the remains of a colony of some sort. But why a humanoid face?

That's the disquieting aspect of the whole inquiry; it suggests that the human race has something to do with Mars, that our history is woefully incomplete, that our understanding of biology and evolution might be in store for a violent upheaval. In retrospect, I regret not spending more time in the book addressing the possibility that the Face was built by a vanished terrestrial civilization that had achieved spaceflight. That was a tough notion to swallow, even as speculation, as it raises as many questions as it answers.

Was there any way to determine when the Face and the surrounding structures were built, if they were built? He said:

We need to bring archaeological tools to bear on this enigma. When that is done, we can begin reconstructing Martian history. Until we visit in person, all we can do is take better pictures and continue to speculate.

I wanted to know what Tonnies's theories were as to how Mars—if it once was home to intelligent life—was transformed into a dead world. He had a few eye-opening ideas:

Astronomer Tom Van Flandern has proposed that Mars was once the moon of a tenth planet that literally exploded in the distant past. If so, then the explosion would have had severe effects on Mars, probably rendering it uninhabitable. That's one rather apocalyptic scenario. Another is that Mars's atmosphere was destroyed by the impact that produced the immense Hellas Basin [a 7,152-meter-deep basin located in Mars's southern hemisphere]. Both ideas are fairly heretical by current standards; mainstream planetary science is much more comfortable with Mars dying a slow, prolonged death. Pyrotechnic collisions simply aren't intellectually fashionable—despite evidence that such things are much more commonplace than we'd prefer.

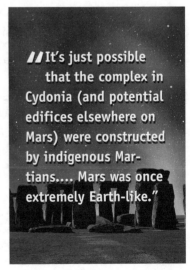

// It's just possible that the complex in Cydonia (and potential edifices elsewhere on Mars) were constructed by indigenous Martians.... Mars was once extremely Earth-like."

I asked Tonnies what it was that had stimulated him not just to investigate the controversy surrounding the Face on Mars, but to write an entire book on the subject, too. It was, he said, all down to one thing: "Anger."

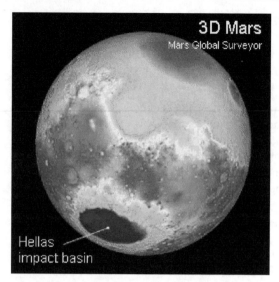

3D Mars
Mars Global Surveyor

Hellas
impact basin

The Hellas Basin on Mars's southern hemisphere is an immense crater that might have been caused by a huge impact that destroyed the planet's atmosphere.

He explained:

I was, frankly, fed up with bringing the subject of the Face on Mars up in on-line discussion and finding myself transformed into a straw man for self-professed experts. It was ludicrous. The book is a thought experiment, a mosaic of questions. We don't have all of the answers, but the answers are within our reach. Frustratingly, this has become very much an "us vs. them" issue, and I blame both sides. The debunkers have ignored solid research that would undermine their assessment, and believers are typically quite pompous that NASA et al. are simply wrong or, worse, actively covering up.

On this latter point, of whether or not NASA was engaged in a conspiracy to hide the truth of the Face on Mars, Tonnies had some interesting thoughts that he wished to share:

When NASA/JPL released the first Mars Global Surveyor image of the Face in 1998, they chose to subject the image to a high-pass filter that made the Face look hopelessly vague. This was almost certainly done as a deliberate attempt to nullify public interest in a feature that the space agency is determined to ignore. So yes, there is a cover-up of sorts. But it's in plain view for anyone who cares to look into the matter objectively. I could speculate endlessly on the forms a more nefarious cover-up might take—and I come pretty close in the book—but the fact remains that the Surveyor continues to return high-resolution images. Speculation and even some healthy paranoia are useful tools. But we need to stay within the bounds of verifiable fact lest we become the very conspiracy-mongering caricatures painted by the mainstream media.

Tonnies also wanted to point out that the Face on Mars and the surrounding pyramid-like structures were not the only anomalies on Mars:

The Mars Global Surveyor has taken images of anomalous branching objects that look, for all the world, like organic phenomena. Arthur C. Clarke [the late, acclaimed science-fiction author, who died in 2008] for one, is sold on the prospect of large forms of life on Mars, and has been highly critical of JPL's silence. Clarke's most impressive candidates are what he has termed "banyan trees" near the planet's south pole. And he collaborated with Mars researcher Greg Orme in a study of similar features NASA has termed "black spiders"—root-like formations that suggest tenacious macroscopic life.

My final question for Tonnies was: "What do you hope your book *After the Martian Apocalypse* will achieve?"

He said:

Our attitudes toward the form extraterrestrial intelligence will take are painfully narrow. This is exciting intellectual territory, and too many of us have allowed ourselves to be told what to expect by an academically palatable elite. I find this massively frustrating.

I hope *After the Martian Apocalypse* will loosen the conceptual restraints that have blinkered radio-based SETI by showing that the Face on Mars is more than collective delusion or wishful thinking. This is a perfectly valid scientific inquiry and demands to be treated as such.

More than a decade since Tonnies's book was published, the controversy surrounding the Face on Mars still stands—as does that eerie, mysterious, visage itself.

CIRCLES OF STONE AND STRANGE SECRETS

In the same way that ancient Native American lore suggests the United States' Bigfoot has unearthly origins, very much the same can be said of reports of such creatures seen in the United Kingdom. While the U.K. has a surprisingly large number of Bigfoot reports for such a small nation, it's a fact that the sightings are not made at random. Rather, the vast majority occur in and around some of the U.K.'s most ancient and sacred stone circles. Why that may be is a question that will be answered at the very end of this chapter. First, however, let's take a look at a number of the stand-out cases on record.

Tucked away on the fringes of an old English village called Long Compton is a roughly circular formation of stones called the Rollright Stones. For just about everyone who visits the stones, the effect is very much the same: a sense of being deep in the heart of a magical realm, one saturated by matters paranormal and supernatural. It's not surprising, then, that the Rollright Stones have attracted numerous legends to explain their presence. There's no doubting their point of origin: the Bronze Age. As for their purpose, that's quite another matter.

That the Rollright Stones are made up of a circle referred to as the King's Men and a burial area that the locals call the Whispering Knights has led to the creation of an engaging legend. It's a legend that dates back to the first decade of the seventeenth century. So the enduring story goes, an evil witch—one Mother Shipton—did not take kindly to the king and his knights intruding upon her land. As a result, she cast powerful spell and turned the entire party into blocks of stone. In that scenario, the Rollright Stones are the petrified remains of a long-gone army that was defeated not by bows and arrows, swords, and spears, but by a malevolent hex.

Now we come to the matter of monsters. Paul Devereux is a noted expert on British-based stone circles and areas of archaeological significance, and the author of many books, including *Stone Age Soundtracks: The Acoustic Archaeology of Ancient Sites*. In 1977, Devereux created an ambitious program to study numerous standing stone formations in the U.K., ones that seemed to be surrounded by an excess of ultrasonic and magnetic phenomena. At the height of the investigation at the Rollright Stones, one of Devereux's team caught a very brief view of a large, *upright*, shaggy-haired animal lurking near the stones. In an instant, it was gone—something that prevented the witness from getting a good look at it. Nevertheless, he was sure it was no normal wild animal of the types that roam around the U.K., such as a fox or a deer.

Moving on to the English county of Devon, and specifically the wilds of Dartmoor—where Sir Arthur Conan Doyle set his Sherlock Holmes novel *The Hound of the Baskervilles*—there are the thought-provoking words of a woman named Theo Brown, a noted historian, author, and devotee of Devon legend and lore. Back in the 1940s, a colleague of Brown encountered something very strange at the site of an ancient, Neolithic stone circle on Dartmoor called Lustleigh Cleave, which is estimated to have been constructed around 580 C.E.

The story provided to Brown was that the person in question stumbled upon "a family of 'cave men,' either naked and covered in hair or wrapped in the shaggy pelts of some wild animal, shambling around the stone circle at the top of the cleave."

A particularly notable account of an encounter with a bizarre beast near the site of a stone circle comes from the files of investigative author Merrily Harpur. In fact, the site was not just near *a* stone circle, but close to *the* definitive stone circle of all: Stonehenge. It was in the fall of 2002 when a man named George Price—at the time serving with the British Army—had a bizarre encounter on a huge expanse of English wilderness called Salisbury Plain, which is also home to Stonehenge.

Near the village of Long Compton, England, stand the Rollright Stones. Legend has it that the stones are what remain of the king's knights who were turned to stone by a witch.

It was on the plain that Price, taking part in Army training maneuvers at the time, caught sight of an immense creature of apelike proportions and appearance that was sporting a hairy coat similar to that of an orangutan. As the military closed in, the beast wasted no time in exiting the area at high speed and vanishing into the undergrowth. That the monster should have been encountered near one of the world's most famous, sacred sites—one that dates back to approximately 3,100 B.C.E.—is surely no coincidence.

Then there is the curious tale of a man named W. E. Thorner. Late one night, on the remote Scottish island of Hoy in the early 1940s, Thorner was stunned by a bizarre sight: a band of hairy people engaged in a wild dance near the edge of a large cliff. Thorner said:

> These creatures were small in stature, but they did not have long noses nor did they appear kindly in demeanour. They possessed round faces, sallow in

> **//** These creatures were small in stature, but they did not have long noses nor did they appear kindly in demeanour. They possessed round faces, sallow in complexion, with long, dark, bedraggled hair."

complexion, with long, dark, bedraggled hair. As they danced about, seeming to throw themselves over the cliff edge, I felt that I was a witness to some ritual dance of a tribe of primitive men. It is difficult to describe in a few words my feelings at this juncture or my bewilderment. The whole sequence could have lasted about three minutes until I was able to leave the cliff edge.

Still on the topic of unknown, hairy, humanoid animals seen in the U.K.—and ones seen in the direct vicinity of ancient, historical sites—cryptozoologist Neil Arnold told me the following, in a January 2012 interview:

I've always wondered what type of manifestation these U.K. "wild men" could be. In the autumn of 2011 a psychic lady who I know as a friend and who I trust—I don't often have any interests in psychics—accompanied me to Blue Bell Hill, which is a very haunted village in Kent, a few miles short of the town of Maidstone. I knew of several obscure "man-beast" reports in the area which she knew nothing about. I took her to one particular spot, near some ancient stones, hoping she'd pick up a ghostly presence and she said she felt nothing whatsoever, but she did state quite categorically that a few years previous, around 2003 she'd had a bizarre encounter in the area one night.

Arnold continued:

She had visited Kit's Coty House—a set of stones—with a group of fellow psychics. Her friends were over on one side of the field which harbours the stones and she was in another area when she noticed someone walking towards her a few hundred yards away. The figure seemed to be striding rather aggressively and was coming from the direction of a thicket which runs alongside the field.

The woman, whose name is Corriene, said Arnold,

… stated that from a distance the figure appeared huge in build and covered in hair and she sensed it was not "real" but gave off an air of malevolence. The figure marched towards her and she could see it had long hair and a beard, covering most of its face. The hulking figure was taller than six feet and appeared to have a loin cloth around its waist and furred boots. No-one else saw this figure, but I was intrigued as I knew that in the past several witnesses had come forward to say they'd seen similar figures in woods within miles of Blue Bell Hill.

Arnold told me this set him on an intriguing and alternative pathway:

I began to wonder if people had seen, from a distance, some type of ghostly primitive man—long hair, bearded, muscular, animal fur around the waist—who, from several hundred yards away, or in ill light, may have looked as if he was covered in hair. Blue Bell Hill and much of Kent is steeped in history—so maybe people were seeing some type of Neolithic hunter. Corriene was intrigued by what I said and then, rather startled, mentioned that on another occasion whilst in the area of the stones she'd seen several of these people who she felt were not aggressive, and although armed with spears were simply guarding the area and stooping low in the bushes, curious as to what they were seeing.

All of this brings us to an important question: why, in the U.K., do so many ancient sites play host to nightmarish, hairy animals of unknown origin and type? Linda Godfrey, who has penned a number of excellent books on unknown animals, such as *The Beast of Bray Road* and *The Michigan Dogman*, has formulated a theory in her home country of the United States that might just as easily apply to what is afoot in the U.K. It revolves around a creature both feared and revered by Native Americans: the Skinwalker.

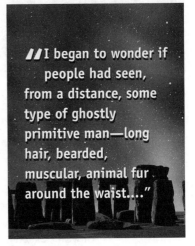

//I began to wonder if people had seen, from a distance, some type of ghostly primitive man—long hair, bearded, muscular, animal fur around the waist...."

Godfrey refers to them, in her 2012 book, *Real Wolfmen*, as "entities created by magic ritual that look like animals but are really spirit doubles of the shaman that either go out from the physical body or envelope it like a supernatural costume." Godfrey adds that Skinwalkers are akin to Tibetan beliefs in what are known as Tulpas, or thought-forms: creations of the human mind that have the ability to leap out of the brain and take on a degree of reality. In essence, a Tulpa is a creation of the human mind, but one that can be projected externally and given a semblance of quasi-independent life in our 3-D world.

Godfrey also said: "I can tell you that Native Americans from various locations have indicated to me that these things absolutely exist, as do zoomorphic (animal-shaped) spirit guardians made to watch over sacred grounds."

"Animal-shaped spirit guardians," brought into our world to protect areas deemed sacred to the ancients: does this not sound very familiar? It should: while Godfrey's words are directed at paranormal hotspots in the United States, based on what we just have seen they could easily apply to the U.K. and its famous stone circles and their accompanying monsters.

JONAH AND THE WHALE: ABDUCTED BY E.T.

Beyond any shadow of doubt, it's one of the strangest of all the stories that appear in the pages of the Old Testament. It's the controversial saga of a man named Jonah, who allegedly spent no less than three days immersed in the water-filled belly of a whale. Biblical scholars and believers are content to accept the story in wholly literal terms. Many of those who adhere to the theory that the tales in the Old Testament are born out of distorted accounts of alien visitation have suggested that Jonah was not swallowed by a whale but abducted by the extraterrestrial crew of a UFO. Before we get to the alien angle, however, let us first address the matter of what, exactly, the Bible said about Jonah's underwater exploits.

Jonah, the son of Amittai, was a prophet from Gath Hepher, Israel, who, according to the book of Jonah in the Bible, was instructed by God to go to Nineveh (a Mesopotamian city on the east side of the Tigris River, which flows through Turkey and Iraq) and preach the Gospel.

By all accounts, Jonah was not one to take orders—from anyone, and that even included an all-powerful deity. As a result, he outright ignored God's command and elected to head for Joppa, a seaport, and make his way by ship to Tarshish.

Given that we are specifically talking about the Old Testament, God's response was hardly surprising: it was one filled with wrath and dire punishment for Jonah. God conjured up an appropriately almighty storm, the huge waves of which, when coupled with violent thunder and lightning, almost battered the ship to the point of complete destruction. The crew, it becomes clear, was a suspicious bunch and drew lots to determine whose wrongdoing had incurred the backlash of God. Jonah came up short and was quickly tossed overboard by the frightened crew. Suddenly, however, something remarkable happened.

The pounding waves became calm, the skies cleared, and the storm was gone—in pretty much an instant. Then something even more astounding occurred: a mighty whale surfaced from the depths and swallowed Jonah, who, up until that point, had been doing his best to stay afloat in the churning waters. As he sat in the fishy, watery belly for a full three days, Jonah came to realize his error and soon repented for not following God's orders to preach to the people of Nineveh. A satisfied God arranged for Jonah to be deposited back on dry land in a most curious fashion: the whale, rather unceremoniously, vomited him up.

In the biblical story, Jonah is swallowed up by a whale—or large fish of some kind— while voyaging to Joppa. Perhaps, though, the "fish" was not a fish at all, but an Unidentified Submerged Object, or USO.

There was, however, something very strange about the newly returned Jonah: the three days in the belly of the whale had bleached his skin and clothes white, giving him a decidedly unsettling, eerie appearance. This may well have had some bearing on why, exactly, the people of Nineveh listened to Jonah when he ordered them to give up their evil, wanton ways, lest God destroy the city. They not only listened, they also did as Jonah had insisted: they changed their behavior, fasted, and repented. God, seeing that the people of Nineveh had indeed changed, forgave them and the city was spared destruction.

That is the Old Testament version of the story of Jonah and the mysterious whale in which he was inexplicably able to live for three full days. The idea that a person could survive, for around seventy-two hours, in the belly of a whale, deep within the waters of a churning ocean, is, however, ridiculous. We are, therefore, required to look in other directions for potential answers to what really lay at the heart of the story.

Michel M. Deschamps, of Northern Ontario UFO Research & Study (NOUFORS), said in his article "My Personal Belief System (and How It's Been Affected UFOs):"

I did some research and found that it was impossible for a man to be inside of a whale for three days because there is no species of whale that can

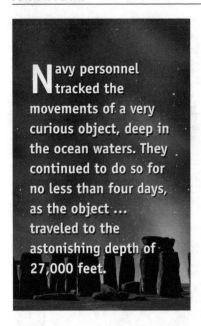

Navy personnel tracked the movements of a very curious object, deep in the ocean waters. They continued to do so for no less than four days, as the object ... traveled to the astonishing depth of 27,000 feet.

actually swallow a man whole, and then spit him out. The largest whales only eat plankton, which is microscopic in size compared to that of a man.

I kept thinking that maybe Jonah had been taken aboard a vessel of some type ... which then brought him to shore, a few days later.

I had read many reports of these black silhouettes that were seen floating on the surface of the ocean during the 1950s and 1960s. Some thought that maybe, they were dealing with Soviet submarines. But whatever they were, they always managed to disappear without a trace, leaving the authorities dumbfounded.

It is a known fact amongst UFOlogists that USOs (Unidentified Submerged Objects) do exist, and they are of a non-terrestrial origin. They're actually UFOs that have the ability to submerge themselves in our world's oceans and lakes.

So it would not be too surprising for me to find out that this is what lies behind the story of "Jonah and the whale."

That the field of ufology is rife with sightings of so-called USOs is not in doubt. The late author and anomalies research Ivan T. Sanderson wrote an entire book on the subject of unidentified craft seen in the world's oceans. Its title: *Invisible Residents*. While it would be impossible to summarize all of Sanderson's bulging case-files, one will suffice.

From military sources, Sanderson learned of a fascinating case that occurred off the coast of Puerto Rico in 1963. U.S. Navy personnel were taking part in a military exercise: aircraft, ships, and submarines played significant roles in the operation.

At some point in the exercise, Navy personnel tracked the movements of a very curious object, deep in the ocean waters. They continued to do so for no less than four days, as the object—which was clearly under intelligent control—traveled to the astonishing depth of 27,000 feet. Whatever the nature of the USO, it remained unidentified.

In his 2013 paper, "The Story of Jonah," researcher John Black makes good observations on the story of Jonah:

Let us travel back thousands of years to a time when there was no technology and ask ourselves how an advanced, modern vehicle would have been perceived and described using the limited terms and references the civilization had. Is it not obvious that an airplane would have been perceived as a shiny, metallic bird, or perhaps a chariot of fire?

Similarly, isn't it possible that a submarine would have been perceived as a whale, since whales, even then, were the largest mammals in the sea? A prime example of such a limitation is how we still use the term "flying disc" for unknown vehicles simply because they remain, to us, unknown disc-like shaped objects that fly. If we had this kind of technology then the term we use would be completely different.

Black concluded:

This story makes you wonder whether this "God" could have just been a supreme being with knowledge and power beyond the author's comprehension, along with a fleet of vehicles at his disposal to force the faith and obedience of his subjects.

It's interesting to note that within alien abduction lore, there are many accounts of people reportedly taken on-board UFOs and submerged into liquids, or gels. They sound eerily like the accounts of Jonah while he was caught in the water-filled belly of a whale. An extract from one such report—taken from an online article, "A True Account of Alien Abduction"—reads thus:

I woke up again, this time naked in a funnel shaped pool filled with a greenish black gel type liquid. The pool had to be 20 yards wide all around. And pretty deep. The pool was made of some kind of shiny metal. With the gel it made the surface very slippery and you would slip under the gel if you tried to get out. I then realized something very odd at that time. I wasn't alone.

There were at least 15 other humans with me. All of them screaming and panicking. This is what scared me. I didn't know what they were screaming about. I thought they knew something I didn't, so I got scared. Some were under the gel moving around I could see. Most were trying to escape.

A second account, from the iwasabducted.com website's post, "Abducted at night from bedroom," reads:

I found myself inside a clear glass cylinder, totally submerged in some kind of warm fluid, thicker than water, thinner than oil. To my surprise, I was able to breathe this warm fluid without discomfort. I could also open my eyes without a problem. The solution was clear, of a greenish color and the container was softly lit. I remember, still fully submerged in this solution, that I slowly began to recall the abduction that had taken me away from my bedroom, minutes, maybe hours before. (impossible to tell). Then I made the connection with the place I was now in and real fear took hold of me. I remember desperately trying to get out of the container but I could not move a muscle except for my eyelids.

Finally, and all at once by sheer force of will, I was able to regain movement of my limbs. I jumped out of the glass container faster than a spring. Apparently, what I had been breathing while submerged was very different than air because I felt the urgent need to take a big breath of air as soon as I came out.

I was naked and dripping this fluid/solution that was sort of a slimy gel. The place was dark, very steamy with a strange, unpleasant smell.

Researcher Helmut Lammer—in "New Evidence of Military Involvement in Abductions"—tells the story of an abductee he calls "Lisa." In Lammer's own words:

UFO authority Stanton Friedman suggested that a person could survive g forces and long travel in a spacecraft better if submerged in fluids.

Lisa … was kidnapped and brought to a military underground facility, where she saw naked humans floating in tubes. Lisa claims that she was forced by humans into some type of pool filled with a golden yellow bubbly fluid, while other humans looked at her. Lisa has traumatic recollections that her kidnappers tried to make her and other victims able to breathe in the liquid. In two of the before mentioned cases the abductee was forced to breathe the liquid like Lisa. The hypnosis transcripts reveal that the liquid breathing experiences were traumatic for the abductees. Both abductees where totally immersed in the liquid and both reported that they could breathe the fluid.

UFO authority Stanton Friedman made a notable observation in "UFO Propulsion Systems":

The amount of acceleration a person can stand depends on many factors; the three most important depends on the duration of acceleration (the greater the force, the shorter the time it can be tolerated), the direction of the force in relation to the body (back to front acceleration is much easier to handle then head to foot acceleration, and for this reason Apollo astronauts have their backs perpendicular to the direction of the thrust, rather than along it as in an elevator), and body environment is important (*a person immersed in fluid can withstand greater acceleration than one not so immersed*).

In light of Friedman's words, we might wish to consider the possibility that Jonah's time spent within the belly was actually time spent immersed in fluids that allowed for his body to cope with the rigors of travel in a craft not normally designed to transport humans. It may well have been a liquid that had an unfortunate side-effect: it bleached Jonah's skin as white as a ghost.

Perhaps the story of Jonah is, in reality, one of the earliest accounts on record of an alien abduction.

CONSPIRACIES

ABRAHAM LINCOLN: ASSASSINATION, COVER-UP, AND THE MASONS

Any mention of presidential assassinations that changed the face of the United States will, probably first and foremost, conjure up imagery relative to the November 22, 1963, assassination of President John F. Kennedy, at Dealey Plaza, Dallas, Texas. Long before JFK was killed, however (whether by Lee Harvey Oswald, the Cubans, the Mafia, or the KGB), there was the murder of President Abraham Lincoln, on April 15, 1865.

Unlike so many presidents of the twentieth century, Lincoln was not born into a rich, powerful family. It was exactly the opposite: Lincoln was very much a self-made man, one who was brought up in near-poverty in Hardin County, Kentucky. Lincoln was determined to make a significant life for himself, however, and he achieved exactly that—and much more, besides. Prior to his election to the position of president of the United States in March 1861, Lincoln had worked as both a state legislator and a lawyer, and, in 1846, was elected to the House of Representatives. From there, it was a case of the sky being the limit; until, that is, a man named John Wilkes Booth put paid to all of that. There are, however, widely held beliefs that Booth did not act alone when he shot and killed Lincoln. Powerful bankers, the Confederates, the Jesuits, or possibly even high-ranking Masons, it has been suggested, may have been in on the deadly act.

To understand the conventional theory that John Wilkes Booth was the culprit we have to go back to the dawning of the 1860s. In the presidential election of 1860, Lincoln gained a great deal of support from those who demanded an end to slavery—as did Lincoln himself. There were, however, significant numbers who were vehemently against the abolition of slavery. They were the people of Georgia, Mississippi, Texas, South Carolina, Louisiana, Alabama, and Florida. So vehemently anti-abolition were they, they created what became known as the Confederate States of America. Tensions began to mount between north and south, to the point when, on April 12, 1861, civil war broke out. It continued until May 9, 1865, and saw the South soundly defeated. Slavery was no more, and the Confederate States of America was gone, too. It was a decisive victory for the president, who celebrated a new beginning for the United States and its people. Unfortunately, Lincoln would not have long to celebrate. Someone was planning a quick demise for the nation's victorious leader.

Actor John Wilkes Booth is shown assassinating President Abraham Lincoln at Ford's Theatre in Washington, D.C.

It's ironic that John Wilkes Booth was so anti-Lincoln, and for this particular reason—despite his hatred of the president—Booth chose never to enlist with the Confederate military and do in-the-field battle with the North. That's not to say he was a coward, though. Rather, Booth forged deep and intriguing links to the world of espionage, acting for the Confederates in decidedly "James Bond, 007"-style. Demonstrating his loathing for the president, more than a year before Lincoln was killed, Booth had secretly devised an operation to have the president kidnapped and held until such a time that he authorized the release of a large number of Southern soldiers. Things really reached their peak in early April 1865, however. That was when Booth, outraged by Lincoln's plans to allow black people to vote, decided that kidnapping wasn't enough for Lincoln: nothing less than the president's death would satisfy Booth.

The date on which America was changed was April 14, 1865. It was Good Friday—albeit a very *bad* Friday for Lincoln. The location was the Washington, D.C., Ford's Theatre, where Lincoln and his wife, Mary, were due to watch Tom Taylor's play *Our American Cousin*. It was during an interval that disaster struck. Lincoln's main bodyguard was a man named John Parker. During the interval, Parker left the president and headed for a drink or two at the *Star Saloon*, which stood adjacent to the theater. It was the perfect moment for Booth to strike—and strike he did. It was shortly before 10:15 P.M. when Booth stealthily made his way to the balcony seats in which Lincoln and Mary were sitting and fired a bullet at the president's head.

Pandemonium broke out. Booth was almost apprehended by Major Henry Rathbone, but he managed to escape by plunging a knife into the major. As for the president, his hours were numbered. It turns out that sitting hardly any distance from the president was Dr. Charles Leale, who raced over to the rapidly fading Lincoln. Despite frantic attempts to save his life, Lincoln died, after plunging into a coma for more than eight hours. As for Booth, he fled the theater and outwitted and out-maneuvered his military pursuers for almost two weeks. A stand-off occurred at a Virginia farm, where Booth was shot to death by Sergeant Boston Corbett.

When it comes to the conspiracy theories concerning the death of President Abraham Lincoln, they differ significantly from the killing of President John F. Kennedy in November 1963. Whereas most conspiracy researchers of the JFK affair suggest Lee Harvey Oswald was nothing but a convenient patsy who never fired even a single bullet, when it comes to the killing of Lincoln,

Mary Surratt, Lewis Powell, David Herold, and George Atzerodt were executed by hanging on July 7, 1865, for conspiring to kill President Lincoln.

most investigators are convinced Booth was the gunman. A big question, however, exists: Was Booth the brains behind the operation, or was someone else pulling the strings? To try and answer that question, let's start with the Masonic theory.

Researcher John Daniel lays the blame squarely on the tentacles of British-based Masonry. He suggested that the reason why powerful figures in the British establishment wanted President Lincoln gone were two-fold. First, by having Lincoln assassinated, it would splinter the United States into two, less than powerful sections, both of which could easily be conquered much easier than could one unified nation. Daniel also argued that the Brits wished to create a central bank under their control.

Such a bank would likely have been established under the powerful Rothschilds, who history has shown did offer the Lincoln government a loan—one with an extremely high interest rate. The Rothschilds were convinced that Lincoln would have no choice but to accept the loan to help get the United States back on its feet. Lincoln chose not to, however. The Rothschilds were soundly rebuffed.

Daniel said, in "Scarlet and the Beast":

Had it not been for Abraham Lincoln, English Freemasonry would have succeeded. When Lincoln restored the Union, the British Brotherhood, out of revenge, plotted his assassination. The Knights of the Golden Circle, bankrolled by British Masonic interests, selected John Wilkes Booth, a 33rd degree Mason and member of Mazzini's Young America, for the task.

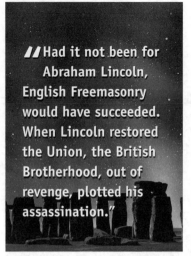

// Had it not been for Abraham Lincoln, English Freemasonry would have succeeded. When Lincoln restored the Union, the British Brotherhood, out of revenge, plotted his assassination."

As for how the crime was hidden, Daniel concludes that Edwin Stanton—both a Freemason and the secretary of war during the Lincoln administration—coordinated the effort to bury the truth. He said that it was Stanton who ordered the blocking of all the roads out of Washington, D.C., aside from the one from which John Wilkes Booth was able to escape and make his way to Virginia. On top of that, Daniel does not believe that Booth died at the Virginia farm that the history books assure us he did:

> Stanton then arranged for a drunk man to be found, similar in build and appearance to Booth. This man was to be murdered and his body burned in a barn adjacent to the only road not guarded by the military. Stanton just happened to be on that road when he "found" the murdered man, certifying that the charred body was the remains of John Wilkes Booth. The real John Wilkes Booth escaped.

Moving on, we have the Jesuit-based conspiracy theory.

The idea that President Lincoln's assassination was orchestrated by Jesuits has its origins in events that occurred in 1856, in Urbana, Illinois. In that year, while employed as a lawyer, Lincoln successfully offered defense to a Canadian Catholic priest named Charles Chiniquy. The case revolved around the claim that Chiniquy had slandered Bishop Anthony O'Regan, of the Roman Catholic Church. When Peter Spink, a Catholic from Illinois, filed suit against Chiniquy, Lincoln was the man who came to the rescue. And although the court's decision did not rule totally in favor of Chiniquy, an agreement was, at least and at last, reached.

Rather intriguingly, when the trial was over, Chiniquy developed deep concerns that the Jesuits—better known as the Society of Jesus, or as they are sometimes called, "God's Marines"—would take revenge on Lincoln for humiliating Spink and, as a result, the entire Catholic Church. More disturbingly, Chiniquy learned of an association between the Jesuits and John Wilkes Booth. It was a discovery that, in 1906, prompted Chiniquy to go public with his conclusion that the Jesuits were indeed guilty of killing the president—via the deadly actions of Booth.

An equally controversial theory suggests that none other than Lincoln's vice president, Andrew Johnson, ran the operation to have Lincoln permanently removed from office—or that, at the very least, Johnson knew of the planned killing and deliberately did nothing to stop it from occurring. The latter was a theory that even Lincoln's wife, Mary, came to believe. As unbelievable or as unlikely as such a theory might sound, it is a fact that Booth and Johnson crossed paths in February 1864, when Booth—who worked as an actor—performed at the Wood's Theatre in Nashville. Even more damning, in terms of establishing a connection, two years earlier, in 1862, both men shared a mistress.

On top of that, although Johnson and Lincoln amounted to a political pair, they were certainly not friends. Johnson did not share Lincoln's views when it came to the issue of the abolition of slavery. Johnson wasn't even Lincoln's first choice for a running mate: that went to Hannibal Hamlin a Republican. After serving as Lincoln's first-term vice president, Hamlin was dropped in favor of Johnson, when it was decided that by choosing Johnson—as a southerner—it would send a message to the people that Lincoln was doing his utmost to reunite the country.

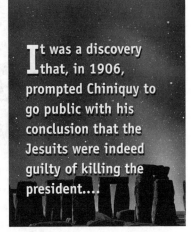

It was a discovery that, in 1906, prompted Chiniquy to go public with his conclusion that the Jesuits were indeed guilty of killing the president....

Such was the extent to which the finger-pointing in Johnson's direction extended that a Congressional Assassination Committee was created to address the claims of Johnson's complicity in the killing of the president. It found no evidence of guilt on the part of Johnson.

Almost 150 years have now passed since President Abraham Lincoln was assassinated by John Wilkes Booth at Washington, D.C.'s Ford's Theatre. It's doubtful that Booth was a wholly innocent patsy—as has been suggested in the case of Lee Harvey Oswald of roughly a century later. As for the possibility that Booth was the main man in a deep, dark conspiracy, however, that the theories continue to circulate after such a large passage of time suggests that the killing of the president was not just the work of one crazed man, after all.

JACK THE RIPPER: THEORIES AND SUSPECTS

In the latter part of 1888, a deadly figure roamed the shadowy and foggy back-streets of Whitechapel, London, England, by night, violently slaughtering prostitutes and provoking terror throughout the entire capital. He quickly became—and still remains to this very day—the world's most notorious serial killer. He was, in case you haven't by now guessed, Jack the Ripper. But, what makes the Ripper so infamous, more than a century after his terrible crimes were committed, is that his identity still remains a mystery. And everyone loves a mystery.

So, who might Jack have been? The theories are almost endless. Indeed, no less than thirty potential suspects have been identified. They include a powerful Freemason, a surgeon, a doctor, a poet, and even a member of the British royal family. What follows is a list of those individuals who have had more fingers pointed at them than any others.

Without doubt, the most controversial theory for whom, exactly, Jack the Ripper might have been, is that he was a member of the British Royal Family, specifically Prince Albert Victor, the Duke of Clarence. It was a theory that first surfaced in the early 1960s, specifically in the pages of a book by French author, Philippe Julian. In the 1967 English language version, Julian wrote:

> Before he died, poor Clarence was a great anxiety to his family. He was quite characterless and would soon have fallen a prey to some intriguer or group of roués, of which his regiment was full. They indulged in every form of debauchery, and on one occasion the police discovered the Duke in a *maison de recontre* of a particularly equivocal nature during a raid. The young man's evil reputation soon spread. The rumor gained ground that he was Jack the Ripper.

Additional rumors suggested that Albert had caught syphilis from a London prostitute and, in a deranged state of mind caused by the increasing effects of his condition, roamed the Whitechapel district of London in search of prostitutes, upon whom he could take out his rage and revenge. Nothing concrete, however, has surfaced—so far, at least—to suggest the prince was Jack. That hasn't stopped the theory from thriving, however.

A variation on the theory that the Duke of Clarence was Jack the Ripper is that he was not the killer, but was connected to him in a roundabout fashion.

The duke, theorists suggest, secretly married a woman who was a Catholic. This was too much for Queen Victoria, and so a dark plan was put into place. Sir William Withey Gull, the first baronet of Brook Street and a noted physician and Freemason, took on the grim task of killing the friends of the young woman in question who knew of the secret marriage. Gull, then, trying to protect the royals from scandal, was the man behind the Ripper legend. And to ensure that the killings were not traceable back to the highest levels of the British royal family, the legend of the serial killer Jack the Ripper was created as a convenient cover and diversion. Maybe.

As early as the 1890s, American newspapers were reporting on the rumor that Jack was actually a prominent figure in London medicine, one who, according to the man's wife, had displayed violent characteristics at the height of the killings. Supposedly, the story got back to the man's co-workers. They quickly visited the family home and found a number of undisclosed items that strongly suggested the man was indeed Jack the Ripper. He was reportedly hospitalized for his own good and died soon after. Perhaps of

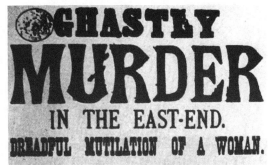

GHASTLY MURDER IN THE EAST-END. DREADFUL MUTILATION OF A WOMAN.

Capture : Leather Apron

Another murder of a character even more diabolical than that perpetrated in Back's Row, on Friday week, was discovered in the same neighbourhood, on Saturday morning. At about six o'clock a woman was found lying in a back yard at the foot of a passage leading to a lodging-house in a Old Brown's Lane, Spitalfields. The house is occupied by a Mrs. Richardson, who lets it out to lodgers, and the door which admits to this passage, at the foot of which lies the yard where the body was found, is always open for the convenience of lodgers. A lodger named Davis was going down to work at the time mentioned and found the woman lying on her back close to the flight of steps leading into the yard. Her throat was cut in a fearful manner. The woman's body had been completely ripped open and the heart and other organs laying about the place, and portions of the entrails round the victim's neck. An excited crowd gathered in front of Mrs. Richardson's house and also round the mortuary in old Montague Street, whither the body was quickly conveyed. As the body lies in the rough coffin in which it has been placed in the mortuary - the same coffin in which the unfortunate Mrs. Nicholls was first placed · it presents a fearful sight. The body is that of a woman about 45 years of age. The height is exactly five feet. The complexion is fair, with wavy brown hair; the eyes are blue, and two lower teeth have been knocked out. The nose is rather large and prominent.

A newspaper story from September 1888 describes the horrific murder of Annie Chapman. Not all the details are correct here; for example, it was not true that the victim's heart was removed.

some significance, Gull—who famously coined the term anorexia nervosa—died in 1890, and just two years after the Ripper murders took place.

In 1970, the late English physician Thomas Edmund Alexander Stowell stated that Gull was not the Ripper, but was the killer's doctor. Although Stowell did not come straight to the point and name Jack, his words and description of the man make it clear that he was talking about the Duke of Clarence.

Six years later, in 1976, the Gull theory was advanced at length in the pages of Stephen Knight's book *Jack the Ripper: The Final Solution*. The work was lauded at the time, but the story he told—of Gull, of a huge Masonic conspiracy, and of terrible murders that were linked to the British monarchy—has since been denounced, even by leading figures in the Jack the Ripper research community.

John Hamill, of the Freemasons' United Grand Lodge of England, said (and is quoted in David Peabody's article, "Exploding the Ripper Masonic Link"):

> The Stephen Knight thesis is based upon the claim that the main protagonists, the Prime Minister Lord Salisbury, Sir Charles Warren, Sir James Anderson and Sir William Gull were all high-ranking Freemasons. Knight knew his claim to be false for, in 1973, I received a phone call from him in the Library, in which he asked for confirmation of their mem-

One theory is that the physician Sir William Withey Gull murdered women who knew of the Duke of Clarence's marriage to a Catholic; he then created the story of Jack the Ripper to cover up the plot.

bership. After a lengthy search I informed him that only Sir Charles Warren had been a Freemason. Regrettably, he chose to ignore this answer as it ruined his story.

One person who often pops up in Ripper research is John Pizer, an admittedly unsavory Polish Jew who worked in Whitechapel as a bootmaker, and who was known locally as "Leather Apron." Strongly suspected of having assaulted a number of prostitutes in the area, and with a conviction for stabbing already on record, Pizer was arrested by Police Sergeant William Thicke in September 1888—perhaps with much justification, it might be argued.

Unfortunately for Thicke, Pizer had alibis for two of the murders. One of them was one hundred percent cast-iron. At the time of Jack the Ripper's second killing, Pizer was speaking with none other than a police officer. The two of them were watching a huge fire as it engulfed the London docks. Nevertheless, the investigation of Pizer continued, something that revealed there had been bad blood between Pizer and Thicke for years.

Despite having the perfect alibi, elements of the London press openly named him as Jack the Ripper. Pizer had his revenge, however—a bit of legal wrangling ensured monetary compensation for the controversial boot maker. And, in a strange bit of irony that no doubt pleased Pizer—and as British Home Office papers of 1889 reveal—Sergeant Thicke was himself once accused of being the Ripper.

A doctor who specialized in abortions (which, for the numerous prostitutes of Whitechapel in the late 1800s, would have been many), Thomas Cream was someone who often surfaces in those domains in which Ripper investigators dwell. In 1881 Cream was jailed for poisoning in Illinois. Upon his release in 1891, however, he moved to London, where his murders continued. He was hung by the neck at Newgate Prison in 1892. Legend said that Cream was literally halfway through admitting to be the Ripper when the rope snapped his neck, although it's a claim that has yet to be vindicated.

There is a problem here: Cream was in jail in the United States in 1888, the year in which the Ripper murders occurred. Or was he? Some Ripper-researchers suggest Cream bribed his way out of his U.S. prison years earlier and was secretly replaced by a lookalike. Was it all too good to be true? As with just about every suspect in the Ripper affair, the jury remains steadfastly out.

On New Year's Eve 1888, the body of Montague John Druitt was hauled out of the River Thames. A barrister, one who also doubled as an assistant, schoolmaster, and someone who was born in Dorsett, England, Druitt was suspected by Assistant Chief Constable Sir Melville Macnaghten of being Jack the Ripper. Macnaghten was no fool: he rose to the position of assistant commissioner of the London Metropolitan Police.

That the Ripper murders ceased after Druitt's suicide only served to amplify the theory that he was the killer.

It is a fact that mental illness ran through the Druitt family: both his mother and grandmother were deranged souls. There was also talk that Druitt had taken his life for fear that word might get out that he was homosexual. That the Ripper murders ceased after Druitt's suicide only served to amplify the theory that he was the killer. For example, in his 1906 book, *The Mysteries of Modern London*, poet and novelist George Robert Sims wrote that the Ripper had avoided the gallows by throwing himself into the Thames just after the Ripper murders ended—which is exactly what Druitt did. A near-identical statement was made by Sir John Moylan, the Home Office's under-secretary of state. If Druitt was Jack the Ripper, then he took with him to the grave the secrets of his homicidal, double life.

William Henry Bury, originally from London's East End, might be considered the ideal candidate for Jack the Ripper. Shortly after the horrific murders occurred, he moved to live in the city of Dundee, Scotland. It was while living there that Bury killed his wife, Ellen. Notably, Ellen was a former prostitute and was the victim of vicious cuts to her stomach. That Jack the Ripper solely targeted prostitutes and took a great deal of glee in slicing and dicing his victims did not pass by unnoticed.

Bury freely admitted to having killed his wife. And, after having done so, he was quickly found guilty of her murder and soon thereafter hanged for his crime. Interestingly, the hangman himself, a character named James Berry, told just about anyone who cared to ask about Bury that he, Bury, was Jack the Ripper. Had Bury made a secret confession to the man who ended his life? It's difficult to say for sure, but Berry was sufficiently sure in his own mind. He told the story in 1927, in the pages of *Thomson's Weekly News*.

One of the biggest problems facing the police in the Ripper affair was that the killer always acted in an elusive fashion. But one man claimed to have actually gotten a good look at him—as in up close and personal. That man was George Hutchinson, a laborer. Hutchinson's story revolved around the life and death of Jack the Ripper's final victim, Mary Kelly.

According to Hutchinson's somewhat unlikely claim made to the police, at around 2.00 A.M., just a few hours before Kelly's death, he had seen her with a suspicious-looking character. As Kelly and Hutchinson crossed paths, and as the former walked towards Thrawl Street, she was approached by a man. It was a man, wearing a hat, who was determined to ensure that Hutchinson didn't get a good look at his face. Oddly, Hutchinson then contradicted himself by asserting that

A newspaper sketch of William Henry Bury, who was suspected of being Ripper because he had killed his wife, a former prostitute.

the man was in his mid-thirties, wore a long coat, had a "stern" look on his face, and sported a thin moustache, slightly curled at the ends.

Allegedly somewhat concerned for Kelly's safety, Hutchinson decided to keep careful watch on Kelly's rented room, to where she took the man, and where she was violently torn to pieces only hours later. Despite hanging around for a while, Hutchinson never saw Kelly or the man leave the room. The astonishingly detailed nature of Hutchinson's report led some in London's police force to wonder if he, himself, was the Ripper, trying to cover his tracks by providing a detailed, false description of the killer.

Between April and October 1888, Joseph "Danny" Barnett was in a relationship with Jack's final victim, Mary Kelly. At the time, Barnett was working at Billingsgate Fish Market. And with money coming in, there was no more need for Mary to walk the streets. Unfortunately, when, in October, Barnett lost his job, Kelly had to return to selling herself for pennies. And, after a violent quarrel, the two split up. Nevertheless, Barnett—after the initial drama had calmed down—continued to give Mary money, when he had some to spare. As a result, intriguing theories have been suggested concerning Barnett's possible role as Jack the Ripper. First, there is the scenario of Barnett killing Kelly's prostitute friends as a means to scare Kelly out of earning her living on the streets of London. Although, it must be said, this is taking persuasion to its absolute extreme. A second theory suggests that during their violent argument, Barnett killed Mary—whether by accident or design is unknown. But, to try and avoid suspicions that he was the killer, Barnett chose to hideously mutilate her body in a fashion befitting the Ripper, as a means to camouflage his own actions. Since the Ripper was on everyone's minds, Barnett would fall under the radar—if the story is true, of course.

One of the strangest stories concerning the identity of Jack the Ripper revolves around a man named Alexander Pedachenko, a Russian doctor. It's a story that has conspiratorial overtones to it since Pedachenko, as well as being a doctor, was a member of the Okhrana. It was, essentially, a "secret police" unit—one that was focused on fighting terrorists and revolutionary types.

The story that links Pedachenko to Jack the Ripper's murderous spree in Whitehall sounds unlikely, but is nonetheless thought-provoking. Supposedly, Pedachenko, working secretly with two colleagues, went on homicidal rampages around London's East End.

According to the strange and controversial story, Pedachenko embarked on the mad killing spree with one specific goal in mind: make the finest minds of Scotland Yard to look foolish so they lacked in credibility. That the story was supposed to have surfaced from Rasputin—the famous healer, mystic, and "Mad Monk" who had an unrelenting hold on the Russian royal family—only made matters even more controversial.

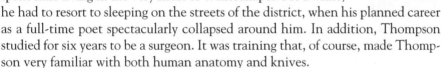

Pedachenko embarked on the mad killing spree with one specific goal in mind: make the finest minds of Scotland Yard to look foolish....

In 1889, just one year after Jack the Ripper brought overwhelming fear to Whitechapel, a man named Francis Thompson penned a short story titled *The End Crowns the Work*. It told of a poet who sacrificed young women to ancient gods, as a means to ensure he became successful in his career in the field of poetry. Thompson was a keen poet himself, one who also spent time living in the very heart of Whitechapel. For a while, he had to resort to sleeping on the streets of the district, when his planned career as a full-time poet spectacularly collapsed around him. In addition, Thompson studied for six years to be a surgeon. It was training that, of course, made Thompson very familiar with both human anatomy and knives.

Ripper theorists have suggested that Thompson's story—of young girls and sacrificial rites—might very well have been based upon Thompson's own, warped and deranged attempts to achieve literary success by killing—and, in his crazed mind, sacrificing—London's East End prostitutes. Interestingly, while down and destitute in London, Thompson actually lived with a prostitute for a short period. She was a prostitute who, soon thereafter, disappeared.

Beyond any shadow of doubt, the most important development in decades—maybe even *ever*—in the saga of Jack the Ripper surfaced in September 2014. It all revolved around a man named Aaron Kosminski. Born in 1865, in the Polish town of Klodawa, Kosminski moved to England with his family in the 1880s, at the age of sixteen.

There are several notable things about Kosminski: (a) he lived in Whitechapel when the Ripper murders occurred; (b) he suffered from acute mental illness and was placed in an insane asylum; and (c) the police had suspected him of being Jack the Ripper. He was plagued—night and day—by voices in his head. He had a fear of eating food prepared by anyone but himself and had an even bigger terror of bathing. Because of his psychological state, Kosminski spent time in two institutions: Colney Hatch Lunatic Asylum and Leavesden Asylum, the latter being the place where he died at the age of fifty-three, chiefly because of the effects of severe malnutrition provoked by anorexia.

In terms of the Jack the Ripper connections, in 1894, Sir Melville Macnaghten, who at the time was the assistant chief constable of the London Metropolitan Police, recorded in a memo that Kosminski was considered a suspect. Far more telling, Macnaghten described Kosminski as someone who had a "great hatred of women" and who had "strong homicidal tendencies."

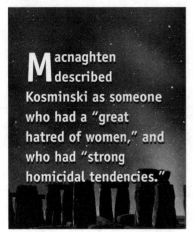

Macnaghten described Kosminski as someone who had a "great hatred of women," and who had "strong homicidal tendencies."

In September 2014, Britain's *Daily Mail* newspaper revealed the results of a mitochondrial DNA analysis, which demonstrated the presence of Kosminski's semen on a shawl owned by one of the Ripper's victims, Catherine Eddowes. Critics, however, have pointed out that the shawl was "in the same room" as two of Eddowes' descendents in 2007, something that could have contaminated the shawl with the DNA then, rather than back in 1888.

That is all well and good, but then there is the matter of the semen. Writer Tom Head noted in his article "5 Reasons Aaron Kosminski Might Not Have Been Jack the Ripper":

> Finding Kosminski's mtDNA in a semen stain on the shawl is *much* more impressive, and is much harder to explain. Contrary to Ripperologist Richard Cobb's claim that the stain could be explained by Kosminski's history with prostitutes in the area, the likelihood that Kosminski's mtDNA just *happened* to end up on a shawl that had already been described as an artifact of the murder scene seems prohibitively remote to me.

It was thanks to Russell Edwards, the author of the book *Naming Jack the Ripper*, that the shawl surfaced: he purchased it at an auction, which ultimately led it to be tested for DNA evidence. Edwards said, in a *Guardian* article titled "Jack the Ripper was Polish immigrant, Aaron Kosminski, book claims:" "I've got the only piece of forensic evidence in the whole history of the case. I've spent fourteen years working on it, and we have definitively solved the mystery of who Jack the Ripper was. Only non-believers that want to perpetuate the myth will doubt. This is it now—we have unmasked him."

TUNGUSKA: AN EARLY ROSWELL?

June 30, 1908, is a date that has gone down in history, chiefly because it is shrouded in mystery, controversy, and conspiracy. It was just as dawn was breaking that an unknown, and unearthly, entity entered the Earth's skies. Whatever it was, it exploded spectacularly and violently over Tunguska, Russia, at a height of around four to six miles. The precise location was an area of heavily forested hills near Siberia's Lake Baikal. By all accounts the object was huge: somewhere in the vicinity of 200 to 600 feet in length. Such was its pummelling force—the unknown intruder flattened entire swathes of the landscape for miles and miles. Trees were laid down like matchsticks, the sky lit up in ominous fashion, and the terrifying sound of a deafening explosion filled the ears of those unfortunate enough to have been caught up in the cataclysmic event. Such was the scale of the incident that the explosion was seismically recorded in both the United States and the United Kingdom. To put things into a perspective that can be readily appreciated today, the blast was the equivalent of around *ten to thirty megatons* of TNT.

Not surprisingly, the Soviet media was quick to report on the almost apocalyptic affair. The *Sibir* newspaper was one of the first to have its reporters hot on the trail. Two days after the calamitous events, staff at the *Sibir* reported:

> In the N Karelinski village the peasants saw to the North-West, rather high above the horizon, some strangely bright bluish-white heavenly body, which for 10 minutes moved downwards. The body appeared as a "pipe," i.e. a cylinder. The sky was cloudless, only a small dark cloud was observed in the general direction of the bright body. It was hot and dry. As the body neared the ground, the bright body seemed to smudge, and then turned into a giant billow of black smoke, and a loud knocking was heard, as if large stones were falling, or artillery was fired. All buildings shook. At the same time the cloud began emitting flames of uncertain shapes. All villagers were stricken with panic and took to the streets, women cried, thinking it was the end of the world.

Another newspaper, *Krasnoyaretz*, offered the following on July 13, 1908:

> At 7:43 the noise akin to a strong wind was heard. Immediately afterwards a horrific thump sounded, followed by an earthquake which literally shook the buildings. The first thump was followed by a second, and then a third. Then the interval between the first and the third thumps

This photo of fallen trees was taken by an expedition led by Leonid Kulik almost fifteen years after the event in Tunguska.

were accompanied by an unusual underground rattle, similar to a railway upon which dozens of trains are travelling at the same time.

Afterwards for 5 to 6 minutes an exact likeness of artillery fire was heard: 50 to 60 salvoes in short, equal intervals, which got progressively weaker. After 1.5–2 minutes after one of the "barrages" six more thumps were heard, like cannon firing, but individual, loud, and accompanied by tremors. The sky, at the first sight, appeared to be clear. There was no wind and no clouds. However, upon closer inspection to the north, where most of the thumps were heard, a kind of an ashen cloud was seen near the horizon which kept getting smaller and more transparent and possibly by around 2–3.00 P.M. completely disappeared.

Although the event was big news at the time it occurred—which is hardly surprising—it's somewhat curious to note that the story died very quickly, to the extent that it was pretty much forgotten by one and all. There was, however, one person who never forgot—a man who intended to find out what it was that caused such massive damage to, thankfully, a very sparsely populated area of Russia. That man was Leonid Kulik, a mineralogist who was funded by the Soviet Academy of Sciences to check out the area—in 1921, some thirteen years after the incident took place.

Despite the passing of almost a decade and a half by the time Kulik arrived on the scene, widespread devastation was still very much the order of the day:

thousands of flattened trees, a scorched landscape, and evidence of some terrible and violent event having occurred chilled Kulik to the bone. Kulik's visit was just a brief one; nevertheless it gave him the opportunity to formulate a theory that the cause of the destruciton was a huge meteorite.

Such was the interest that Kulik's trek to Tunguska provoked that six years later he was back. This time, the expedition was a far more ambitious one. It turns out that the Soviet government's decision to financially back Kulik was not because of any particular overriding desire to solve the riddle of the aerial anomaly. No—it was because the Soviets dearly wished to recover the massive amount of fragmented iron that Kulik suspected had been deeply deposited in the ground when the meteorite exploded. It was matters of an economical, rather than an astronomical, nature that dominated the Soviet mind.

It was during this particular visit that Kulik was finally able to gauge the full and shocking scale of the incident: the area of complete devastation was no less than 50 kilometers wide. Kulik was also able to speak with a man who witnessed the apocalyptic event unfold. It was a man named Semen Semenov, who told Kulik, in 1927:

> At breakfast time I was sitting by the house at Vanavara Factory, facing north. I suddenly saw that directly to the north, over Onkoul's Tunguska road, the sky split in two and fire appeared high and wide over the forest. The split in the sky grew larger, and the entire northern side was covered with fire. At that moment I became so hot that I couldn't bear it, as if my shirt was on fire. From the northern side, where the fire was, came strong heat. I wanted to tear off my shirt and throw it down, but then the sky shut closed, and a strong thump sounded, and I was thrown a few yards. I lost my senses for a moment, but then my wife ran out and led me to the house.

> After that such noise came, as if rocks were falling or cannons were firing, the earth shook, and when I was on the ground, I pressed my head down, fearing rocks would smash it. When the sky opened up, hot wind raced between the houses, like from cannons, which left traces in the ground like pathways, and it damaged some crops. Later we saw that many windows were shattered....

Another witness, identified only as Chuchan, came forward and said:

> We had a hut by the river with my brother Chekaren. We were sleeping. Suddenly we both woke up at the same time. Somebody shoved us. We heard whistling and felt strong wind. Chekaren said, "Can you hear all those birds flying overhead?" We were both in the hut, couldn't see what was going on outside. Suddenly, I got shoved again, this time so hard I fell into the fire. I got scared. Chekaren got scared too. We started crying out for father, mother, brother, but no one answered.

> There was noise beyond the hut, we could hear trees falling down. Chekaren and I got out of our sleeping bags and wanted to run out, but then the thunder struck. This was the first thunder. The Earth began to move and rock, wind hit our hut and knocked it over. My body was

pushed down by sticks, but my head was in the clear. Then I saw a wonder: trees were falling, the branches were on fire, it became mighty bright, how can I say this, as if there was a second sun, my eyes were hurting, I even closed them. It was like what the Russians call lightning. And immediately there was a loud thunderclap. This was the second thunder. The morning was sunny, there were no clouds, our Sun was shining brightly as usual, and suddenly there came a second one!

Chekaren and I had some difficulty getting out from under the remains of our hut. Then we saw that above, but in a different place, there was another flash, and loud thunder came. This was the third thunder strike. Wind came again, knocked us off our feet, struck against the fallen trees.

We looked at the fallen trees, watched the tree tops get snapped off, watched the fires. Suddenly Chekaren yelled "Look up" and pointed with his hand. I looked there and saw another flash, and it made another thunder. But the noise was less than before. This was the fourth strike, like normal thunder.

Now I remember well there was also one more thunder strike, but it was small, and somewhere far away, where the Sun goes to sleep.

Post-Kulik, Tunguska once again fell off the radar of many—until the period from the mid 1950s to the mid 1960s, when further investigations at the site uncovered evidence of massive quantities of iridium and nickel—both of which are characteristic of a meteorite. It should be noted, however, that the meteorite theory was not the only one that was gaining favor. As the sixties became the seventies, the theories became more and more controversial and exotic. They included a small comet, a black hole and even a collision between matter and anti-matter. Without a doubt, however, the most controversial theory was the one that suggested an alien spacecraft, which possibly suffered some form of disastrous and fatal on-board malfunction, exploded high above Tunguska, and in the process, forever scarred massive amounts of the landscape.

"Then I saw a wonder: trees were falling, the branches were on fire, it became mighty bright ... as if there was a second sun, my eyes were hurting, I even closed them."

"According to [Alexei] Zolotov [a Soviet scientist]," said writer David Darling (in "Tunguska Phenomenon"), "a spaceship controlled by 'beings from other worlds' may have caused the 1908 explosion. He imagined a nuclear-propelled craft that exploded accidentally because of a malfunction."

Zolotov was not alone. Without doubt the major flag-fliers of the "alien accident" angle were John Baxter and Thomas Atkins, who penned an entire book on the case: *The Fire Came By*. Researchers Matthew Wittnebel and Andrew Mann noted in their article, "The Tunguska Event," that Baxter and Atkins

… say the Earth's magnetic field was disturbed at the time of the explosion, as it would have been by a nuclear blast. Secondly, the pattern of destruction in the shattered forest is more consistent with the shock waves produced by an atomic bomb than with those of a conventional explosion.

Other clues were the extreme intensity of the light, and a later discovery of numerous tiny green globules of melted dust, called trinitites, which are characteristic of an atomic blast.

The E.T. angle also received support from Vladimir V. Rubtsov, Ph.D. He said, in a 2001 article "The Unknown Tunguska—What We Know and What We Do Not Know about the Great Explosion of 1908":

> The hypothesis of a thermal explosion, according to which the Tunguska space body was a meteorite or the core of a small comet that exploded as a result of the rapid deceleration in the lower atmosphere, met with difficulties.

> A rare mutation among the human natives of the region also arose in the 1910s in one of the settlements near the epicenter. According to Dr. N. V. Vasilyev, medico-ecological examination of the state of health of the native inhabitants reveals population genetic effects similar to those observed in the regions affected by nuclear weapon tests. These facts (as well as the local magnetic storm that started after the explosion) count in favor of the nuclear character of the Tunguska explosion. Maybe we are even dealing in this instance with a novel type of nuclear reaction.

Then there is the matter of the brilliant, maverick scientist, Nikola Tesla. In 1995, Oliver Nicholsen said of the Tunguska-Tesla connection, in his paper, "Tesla's Wireless Power Transmitter":

> Associating Tesla with the Tunguska event comes close to putting the inventor's power transmission idea in the same speculative category as ancient astronauts. However, historical facts point to the possibility that this event was caused by a test firing of Tesla's energy weapon.

> In 1907 and 1908, Tesla wrote about the destructive effects of his energy transmitter....

> Then, in 1915, he stated bluntly: "It is perfectly practical to transmit electrical energy without wires and produce destructive effects at a distance. I have already constructed a wireless transmitter which makes this possible.... But when unavoidable [it] may be used to destroy property and life. The art is already so far developed that the great destructive effects can be produced at any point on the globe, defined beforehand with great accuracy...."

> The nature of the Tunguska event, also, is consistent with what would happen during the sudden release of wireless power. No fiery object was reported in the skies at that time by professional or amateur astronomers as would be expected when a 200,000,000 pound object enters the atmosphere at tens of thousands miles an hour.

//He imagined a nuclear-propelled craft that exploded accidentally because of a malfunction."

Today, we are still very much in the dark with regard to the Tunguska affair. Comet, meteorite, black hole, anti-matter, UFO, or the fringe-science of Nikola Tesla: the theories are almost as near-endless as is that massive area of flattened, burned, earth.

PEARL HARBOR: ALLOWING THE ATTACK TO HAPPEN

Although the Second World War broke out in September 1939, it was in December 1941 that the United States was brought into the conflict, as a direct result of the terrible attack on Pearl Harbor, Hawaii, on December 7, 1941. When Japanese forces launched a surprise attack on the U.S. naval base, it resulted in death on a scale near-unimaginable. More than 350 Japanese aircraft—comprised of bombers, fighters, and planes equipped with torpedoes—targeted Pearl Harbor. It was an attack that killed 2,403 American citizens and residents. Nearly 200 American military planes were destroyed. Each and every battle ship was severely damaged, of which four sunk. As for the Japanese, their losses were the exact opposite: less than thirty aircraft, a handful of small submarines, and not even seventy personnel.

The primary reason for the attack was to try and prevent U.S. naval forces from impacting on Japan's plans to hit the southeastern Asia interests of the Allies. Such was the nationwide outrage that immediately erupted that just twenty-four hours after the attack the U.S. government declared outright war on Japan. From there, matters escalated quickly: on December 11, both Germany and Italy declared war on the United States. Full-scale, worldwide conflict was now pretty much the name of the game. Had the United States not entered the Second World War, there is a very strong possibility that the Nazi hordes of Adolf Hitler would have overrun Europe, claiming it as their own.

In all of this carnage, chaos, and conflict, a disturbing rumor began to circulate—one that continues to circulate to this very day. It suggests that there were those in the governments of the United States and the United Kingdom who had secret, advance warning of the Pearl Harbor attack, but specifically stayed quiet and allowed the terrible events to occur, thus justifying bringing America into the war. In far more recent times, similar claims have been made in relation to the 9/11 attacks—namely, that they too were allowed to happen to justify a large scale invasion of the Middle East. We will return to 9/11 later. But, for now, we will focus on certain events that preceded and followed the shocking attack of December 7, 1941.

It is a seldom discussed fact that such is the ongoing endurance of the allegations that there was advance knowledge of the attack on Pearl Harbor that the U.S. government has initiated *ten* separate, official inquiries to try and get to the bottom of the rumors. Of those ten, nine were undertaken in the 1940s, while the most recent was in 1995.

To many it might seem inconceivable that the Japanese could launch an attack on Pearl Harbor—using no less than 350 aircraft—and no one, at all, would have had advance notice, or even have heard a whisper, of what was afoot. Nevertheless, that was, essentially, the combined conclusion of all the reports. Rather than Pearl Harbor having been deliberately allowed to occur as a result of high-level conspiracies, fingers were pointed in the direction of errors in communication, a catastrophically mistaken belief that Pearl Harbor was invulnerable, and the way in which adequate intelligence-gathering was sorely absent at the time.

Within conspiracy circles, the theory that someone, deep within officialdom, knew the attack was going to occur and allowed precisely that to happen, still very much endures. One significant part of the theory revolves around the matter of code breaking. American code breakers had, specifically *prior* to the attacks on Pearl Harbor, successfully cracked a significant number of the ciphers that the Japanese military used. Certainly, the U.S. Navy's Office of Naval Intelligence (ONI) had teams of people working day and night to crack the Japanese's codes. The Army's Signal Intelligence Service (SIS) was doing likewise. That at least some of the codes were broken is an established fact.

Much of the controversy surrounds *97-shiki Obun inji*-ki—or what the U.S. government code-named "Purple." It was a secure, diplomatic code used at the highest level of the Japanese government. Those who adhere to the conspiracy

The USS *Shaw* explodes during the Japanese attack on Pearl Harbor on December 7, 1941. But was it *really* a surprise attack?

Those who adhere to the conspiracy theories argue that since the attacks on Pearl Harbor were clearly planned in advance....

theories argue that since the attacks on Pearl Harbor were clearly planned in advance, and would have been steeped in overwhelming secrecy, why is it that nothing of relevance was picked up from the widespread penetration of Purple? Their argument is that relevant data was obtained and decoded, but— as per the conspiracy theory—was ignored, in favor of the attack being permitted to happen. And it wasn't just a few dozen people working to crack Japan's codes, something that might have led to crucial material being overlooked. Collectively, it was in excess of seven hundred—and not a single, solitary word relevant to the Pearl Harbor attacks was ever found and decoded?

A second area of concern revolves around the activities of a certain ship, the SS *Lurline*, a huge liner that had the capacity to hold more than seven hundred people and that was launched in 1932. As one enduring story goes, as the SS *Lurline* was traveling from San Francisco to Hawaii it picked up very unusual communications using a form of Morse code. Contrary to popular assumption, there is not just one kind of Morse code. In fact, there are more than a few. One is a Japanese variation. When the SS *Lurline*'s chief expert in the field of Morse code, Leslie Grogan, heard the messages, he concluded they were Japanese. They were also, reportedly, emanating from the east.

The Japanese denied they engaged in any kind of chatter or communication during the flight towards Pearl Harbor. Japanese military papers of 1942, now in the public domain and available for study at the National Archives, noted:

> In order to keep strict radio silence, steps such as taking off fuses in the circuit, and holding and sealing the keys were taken. During the operation, the strict radio silence was perfectly carried out. The Kido Butai used the radio instruments for the first time on the day of the attack since they had been fixed at the base approximately twenty days before and proved they worked well. Paper flaps had been inserted between key points of some transmitters on board Akagi to keep the strictest radio silence.

Of course, the entire matter could be resolved by carefully studying the documentation and data that had been prepared by Leslie Grogan and which was provided to the 14th Naval District, Honolulu. Unfortunately, that same documentation and data cannot be found—*anywhere*.

Another bone of contention is that relative to a statement made by Vice Admiral Frank E. Beatty—a statement in which he strongly suggested there was a desire for war between Japan and the United States. The statement can be found in a *Before It's News* article titled "When Was Pearl Harbor, December 7, 1941, a Day That Will Live in Infamy!"

> Prior to December 7, it was evident even to me that we were pushing Japan into a corner. I believed that it was the desire of President Roosevelt and Prime Minister Churchill that we get into the war, as they felt the Allies could not win without us and all our efforts to cause the Germans to declare

war on us failed; the conditions we imposed upon Japan—to get out of China, for example—were so severe that we knew that nation could not accept them. We were forcing her so severely that we could have known that she would react toward the United States. All her preparations in a military way—and we knew their over-all import—pointed that way.

On a similar path, on October 7, 1940, a document was prepared by ONI operative Lieutenant Commander Arthur H. McCollum. He listed a number of theoretical issues and scenarios that might provoke the Japanese military into attacking the United States. McCollum also said: "If by these means Japan could be led to commit an overt act of war, so much the better."

Even more telling are the words of a man named Jonathan Daniels. At the time the Pearl Harbor attack occurred, he was President Roosevelt's administrative assistant. Daniels said of the events of December 7, 1941, and of Roosevelt's reaction to it: "The blow was heavier than he had hoped it would necessarily be. But the risks paid off; even the loss was worth the price."

Then there are the words of Congressman Martin Dies. He wrote:

Early in 1941 the Dies Committee came into possession of a strategic map which gave clear proof of the intentions of the Japanese to make an assault

on Pearl Harbor. The strategic map was prepared by the Japanese Imperial Military Intelligence Department. As soon as I received the document I telephoned Secretary of State Cordell Hull and told him what I had. Secretary Hull directed me not to let anyone know about the map and stated that he would call me as soon as he talked to President Roosevelt. In about an hour he telephoned to say that he had talked to Roosevelt and they agreed that it would be very serious if any information concerning this map reached the news services. I told him it was a grave responsibility to withhold such vital information from the public. The Secretary assured me that he and Roosevelt considered it essential to national defense.

Writer James Perloff noted in 2013, in "Pearl Harbor: Hawaii Was Surprised; FDR Was Not," that, as the deadly date got closer and closer:

In Java, in early December, the Dutch Army decoded a dispatch from Tokyo to its Bangkok embassy, forecasting attacks on four sites including Hawaii. The Dutch passed the information to Brigadier General Elliot Thorpe, the U.S. military observer. Thorpe

President Franklin D. Roosevelt is pictured here signing the declaration of war against Japan on December 8, 1941. It is believed by some that the president and England's Winston Churchill wanted the war to happen.

sent Washington a total of four warnings. The last went to General Marshall's intelligence chief. Thorpe was ordered to send no further messages concerning the matter. The Dutch also had their Washington military attaché, Colonel Weijerman, personally warn General Marshall.

Then there are the allegations that the British government—under the command of Sir Winston Churchill—knew what was afoot. Journalist Paul Lashmar noted of the Churchill-based conspiracy theories in a 1998 article, "Pearl Harbor Conspiracy Is Bunk":

> There are two versions of the great Pearl Harbor conspiracy theory. In the first, Churchill informed Roosevelt of Japan's intent but the two leaders agreed to sit on the information. The second version—that Churchill knew of the Japanese plan but did not tell Roosevelt—was most forcefully advanced by the British authors James Rusbridger and Eric Nave in their 1991 book *Betrayal at Pearl Harbor*. They claimed that the British had broken the codes of the Japanese Fleet and knew that the Japanese would steam east and attack the American base.

> This version was given credence because Captain Nave had broken the Japanese naval cipher JN-25 in 1939. James Rusbridger was a former MI6 courier who had become a self-styled expert on intelligence matters. He was also the cousin of MI5's Peter Wright of *Spycatcher* fame. According to conspiracy theorists, Churchill was desperate to get Americans into the war to help the beleaguered British.

And, finally, there is the saga of a man named Edward R. Murrow. On December 7, 1941, Murrow—a noted journalist with CBS—had a dinner date with President and Mrs. Roosevelt at the White House. The events of earlier that day, needless to say, should have taken precedence over dinner—for the president, at least. Nevertheless, the dinner continued for Murrow. At one point, Murrow caught sight of Roosevelt and his staff, deep in discussion about Pearl Harbor. Murrow, mindful of the fact that rumors were circulating that Roosevelt had advance notice of the Japanese attack, later said (and whose words are cited in A.M. Sperber's 1998 book, *Murrow: His Life and Times*):

Famed CBS journalist Edward R. Murrow was with the Roosevelts and several important staff and military personnel the evening of Pearl Harbor attack. He would later say that these people seemed genuinely surprised by the Japanese attack.

> There was ample opportunity to observe at close range the bearing and expression of Mr. Stimson, Colonel Knox, and Secretary Hull. If they were not surprised by the news from Pearl Harbor, then that group of elderly men were putting on a performance which would have excited the admiration of any experienced actor. It may be that the degree of the disaster

had appalled them and that they had known for some time. But I could not believe it then and I cannot do so now. There was amazement and anger written large on most of the faces.

In later years, the journalist, correspondent, and author John Gunther (who penned the acclaimed 1949 book *Death Be Not Proud*) asked Murrow about that fateful night, to which he replied the "full story" of what really happened at Pearl Harbor, and why, would pay enough to put his son through college, but added, guardedly: "If you think I'm going to give it to you, you're out of your mind."

ADOLF HITLER: A SECRET SURVIVOR OF WWII

Is it possible that, going completely against what the history books assure us, Adolf Hitler did not commit suicide in 1945, as the Second World War spiraled down to its end? Was his death actually, and ingeniously, staged to allow him to escape from Nazi Germany and start a new life on the other side of the world? To many, it must sound like the stuff of a big bucks Hollywood movie or of a page-turning thriller. Incredibly, it may not be. It just might be the absolute, astonishing truth.

Born in Austria in 1889, Hitler fought during the First World War with the Bavarian Army and, in 1919, one year after the hostilities were over, became a member of the German Workers' Party, later known as the Nationalsozialistische Deutsche Arbeiterpartei—or, in English, the National Socialist German Workers Party. As an ominous sign of what was soon to surface, Hitler was responsible for coming up with the idea of using the swastika as the sign of the NSGWP.

It was evident that, even at this stage, and long before the Second World War broke out, Hitler was someone filled with a maniacal lust for power. In 1923, in what was called the Beer Hall Putsch, Hitler sought to stage a coup in Munich, the intention being to ultimately take on, and overthrow, Germany's Weimar Republic government, which had been created in 1919. The coup failed and Hitler was jailed. Although his sentence was five years, he only served a fraction of it, during which he wrote *Mein Kampf*.

On his release, Hitler campaigned vigorously for a new Germany, one that, in his crazed, deranged eyes, would take the nation to a whole new level of power and even world domination. Incredibly, Hitler's tactics—fueled by propaganda and claims that he would make Germany strong again—almost worked. The Nazi Party rose to stratospheric proportions, which saw Hitler elected to the position of chancellor in 1933. The Weimar Republic was, essentially, transformed—into what eventually became the notorious Third Reich.

It was Hitler's solid determination to make Germany a major world player, and the dominant force in Europe, that led to the eruption of the Second World War. Only days after Hitler's hordes invaded Poland, on September 1, 1939, Germany was at war with both Britain and France. Two years later, America joined the war, after the devastating attack by Japanese forces on Pearl Harbor. The war

Adolf Hitler is seen here at a 1930 meeting of the early Nazi party.

raged until 1945 when, finally, and thankfully, the Nazi war-machine crumbled about itself. Seeing that the end was in sight, Hitler took the cowardly way out and committed suicide. Or did he?

The problem with the story of Hitler's suicide is that there is no precise consensus on what really happened. A great deal is down to nothing more than rumor, hearsay, and legend. What is known for certain is that in January 1945, the Soviet Union launched what was called the Berlin Strategic Offensive Operation. It was the last, large-scale confrontation of the 1939–1945 hostilities in Europe. The Soviets utterly overwhelmed Berlin, something that reportedly prompted drastic action on the part of Hitler. It is a fact that, with the end in sight, Hitler and his lover, Eva Braun, married. It was, quite possibly, one of the shortest marriages in history: only forty hours after tying the knot, both of them were dead—allegedly.

With the Nazi regime falling all around him, Hitler decided to take a bullet. Braun ended her life via a fatal amount of cyanide. The location of the deaths was Hitler's *Führerbunker*, which was part of a large, underground network of rooms and tunnels constructed below Berlin, and which was expanded in size and scope as the war raged, and as the need for ever-growing protection for Hitler grew. The date was April 30, 1945. Hitler had laid down certain plans in the event that Nazi Germany was defeated. One was that both his and Braun's bodies should be taken

EXTRA THE STARS AND STRIPES **EXTRA**

HITLER DEAD

Fuehrer Fell at CP, German Radio Says;
Doenitz at Helm, Vows War Will Continue

Churchill
Hints Peace
Is at Hand

An issue of *Stars and Stripes* announces that Hitler is dead. His body and that of his wife, Eva, were burned beyond recognition, however.

to the garden area of the Reich Chancellery and torched. Reportedly, that is exactly what happened: rather appropriately in a bomb crater.

The story continues that when the Soviets overran Berlin they took possession of Hitler's burned remains—as well as those of Braun, Hitler's dogs, and the Nazis' propaganda minister, Joseph Goebbels, and his family. The Soviets reportedly buried the remains, dug them up, reburied them, and repeated the process on numerous occasions and in numerous locations. We are told that in 1970, the KGB took a decision to lay the matter to rest, once and for all: whatever was left of the bodies was burned, pulverized, and dumped in the Biederitz River.

That is the accepted story of the death of the most notorious, evil, and despicable man of the twentieth century. It is, however, a story with a few problems attached to it.

First, there are conflicting stories of what really happened in the *Führerbunker*. Reportedly, a gunshot was heard coming from the bunker around 3.30 P.M. As a result, Heinz Linge, who served as Hitler's valet, entered the study room, from which the gunshot came. It was clear that both the Führer and Braun were dead on a couch: blood was dripping from Hitler's temple and his jaw. The odor of almonds told Linge that Braun had opted for cyanide. Another of Hitler's cronies, SS-Sturmbannführer Otto Günsche, said he saw the bodies, claiming that Hitler's head-wound left a significant stain on the couch. And, now, the problems start.

While the accepted version of events is that Hitler shot himself in the temple, others maintain he took a bullet in the mouth. Linge claimed to have seen blood coming from both the temple *and* the mouth, yet only one gunshot was heard. Further claims, some coming out of the KGB, suggested that Hitler, like Braun, had also taken cyanide. That, however, was disputed by Linge, who said only Braun had taken cyanide. Moving on, there is the matter of Hitler's skull.

When the Soviets overran Berlin in 1945, and secured the burned remains of Hitler, very little was reportedly left to recover. Most intact of all were the skull and portions of the jaw. For decades, the Soviet government believed that a particular skull in its possession was that of Hitler, having been recovered from devastated Berlin. Not so—in 2009, DNA analysis showed that, in reality, the skull was that of a woman, one probably in her twenties or thirties. And, no, it was not Eva Braun.

Now it's time to turn our attention towards the FBI.

It's a little known fact that the FBI, in the post-war era, began to quietly compile what ultimately turned out to be a large dossier of material on claims that Hitler had survived the Second World War and secretly fled to South America. It's a dossier that has now been declassified and can be accessed at the FBI's website, The Vault.

As one might expect to be the case, many of the claims are scant in data, second- and third-hand in nature, or written by individuals with more time on their hands than sense in their heads. That said, however, one section of the file is particularly intriguing and noteworthy. Incredibly, it suggests that none other than Allan Dulles—who, in the Second World War, made his mark in the Office of Strategic Services, and served as director of the CIA from 1953 to 1961—was complicit in a top secret program to have Hitler secretly shipped out to South America, when the Nazis were defeated.

The files in question refer to stories coming out of Los Angeles, California, and which reached the eyes and ears of the L.A. office of the FBI. According to

Eva Braun and Adolf Hitler—shown here in 1942—were reportedly seen, alive and well, in Argentina after the war.

what the FBI was told, two Nazi-controlled submarines made their stealthy way to the Argentinean coastline, where they covertly deposited high-ranking Nazis that had escaped the wrath of the United States, the United Kingdom, and the Soviet Union. One of the most astounding rumors concerning this story was that it was not just high-rankers who were making new lives for themselves on the other side of the world. It was *the* most high-ranking Nazi, too—Adolf Hitler—who allegedly was by now hunkered down somewhere in the heart of the Andes.

The big question is: who was the FBI's informant? Unfortunately, we don't know, since his name is excised from the relevant, released documents. Nevertheless, he had a great deal of data to impart, something that definitely made the FBI sit up and take careful notice. It must be noted that the bureau's source, himself a former Nazi, offered the information—with a promise of more to come—in return for safe haven in the United States. As to how the person claimed to know that Hitler had survived the war, it was, if true, sensational. The man said he had been personally present when the submarines in question reached the coastline of Argentina. Aboard one of them were Adolf Hitler and Eva Braun—neither displaying *any* evidence of bullet wounds or the effects of cyanide. Quite the opposite—they were vibrant, healthy, and very much alive.

If the story was simply that—a tall tale told to try and secure asylum in the United States—the man had certainly crafted an elaborate story. The FBI's source provided details of the specific villages that Hitler, and the rest of the straggling remnants of "The Master Race," passed through on their way to safe haven, somewhere in Argentina.

Adding further credence to this, additional files—also declassified under Freedom of Information legislation—revealed that amongst staff of the U.S. Naval Attaché in Buenos Aires, rumors were circulating that Hitler did not die in Berlin, but was now hiding out in Argentina.

In 2014 there was a dramatic new development in the saga of whether or not Adolf Hitler died in Berlin, Germany, in 1945, or secretly made a new life for himself in South America—first in Paraguay and then in Brazil. The new data came from Simoni Renee Guerreiro Dias, the author of a book entitled *Hitler in Brazil—His Life and His Death*. Dias's research suggests that Hitler changed his name to Adolf Leipzig, living out his life in Nossa Senhora do Livramento, a small village approximately thirty miles from the Brazilian town of Cuiaba. Supposedly, to the villagers, Hitler was known as the "Old German."

As to how Dias found out this information, the story is a thought-provoking one: during the course of her research, Dias found an old, fading photograph of Adolf Leipzig and then compared it to photos of Hitler. The suggestion is they were one and the same. Additional confirmation came from a nun who had seen Hitler, when he was in his eighties, hospitalized in Cuiaba. Attempts to have Hitler removed from the hospital were denied, amid rumors that Vatican officials had the last word on the matter—and the last word, apparently, was that Hitler should remain where he was: out of sight and protected.

At the time of writing, the story is progressing in dramatic fashion: the body of Leipzig has been secured and permission has been given for DNA to be extracted from it. And, to ensure there is comparative material, a relative of Hitler, now living in Israel, has offered to provide a sample of DNA to determine if the two match.

The story is not as unlikely as many might assume. As *Liberty Voice* noted, when the Leipzig-Hitler story surfaced in early 2014:

> Thousands of Nazis escaped Germany after the war, including Adolf Eichmann and Josef Mengele. Eichmann and Mengele, two of Hitler's most trusted henchman, both lived in Argentina in the 1940s. The Argentine President, Juan Domingo Perón, did everything that could be done to get the Nazis to South America's second largest country. Argentine agents were sent to Europe to make passage easy by providing falsified travel documents and, in many instances, travel expenses were covered. Even Nazis accused of the most horrific crimes, such as Mengele and Eichmann, were welcomed.

PAPERCLIP: A FAUSTIAN PACT

Immediately after the Second World War came to an end in July 1945, certain elements of the American military and intelligence community clandestinely sought to bring some of the most brilliant figures within the German medical and scientific communities into the United States to continue research—and at times highly controversial research—they had undertaken at the height of the war. It was research that included studies of human anatomy and physiology in relation to aerospace medicine, high-altitude exposure, and what was then termed "space biology." The startling fact that some of these scientists were ardent Nazis, and even members of the notorious and feared SS, proved not a problem at all to the government of the time. Thus was born the notorious Operation Paperclip, so named because the recruit's papers were paper-clipped to regular American immigration forms.

In January 1994, President Bill Clinton appointed an Advisory Committee on Human Radiation Experiments (ACHRE) that was tasked with investigating unethical medical experimentation undertaken on human beings from the mid-1940s onward. The ACHRE was quick to realize that Paperclip personnel played a considerable role in post-war human experimentation on American soil. The ACHRE files on Operation Paperclip have now been declassified under the terms of the Freedom of Information Act, thus allowing each and every one of us to access the controversial material. According to a declassified April 5, 1995, memorandum from the Advisory Committee Staff (ACS) to the members of the ACHRE:

> The Air Force's School of Aviation Medicine (SAM) at Brooks Air Force Base in Texas conducted dozens of human radiation experiments during the Cold War, among them flash blindness studies in connection with atomic weapons tests, and data gathering for total-body irradiation studies conducted in Houston. Because of the extensive postwar recruiting of German scientists for the SAM and other US defense installations, and in light of the central importance of the Nuremberg prosecutions to the Advisory Committee's work, members of the staff have collected documentary evidence about Project Paperclip from the National Archives and Department of Defense records.

> The experiments for which Nazi investigators were tried included many related to aviation research. These were mainly high-altitude exposure studies, oxygen deprivation experiments, and cold studies related to air-

sea rescue operations. This information about air crew hazards was important to both sides, and, of course, continued to be important to military organizations in the Cold War.

The ACHRE memorandum then detailed the background and scope of the project:

Project Paperclip was a postwar and Cold War operation carried out by the Joint Objectives Inelligence Agency (JOIA) [Author's Note: the JOIA was a special intelligence office that reported to the Director of Intelligence in the War Department, comparable to the intelligence chief of today's Joint Chiefs of Staff.] Paperclip had two aims: to exploit German scientists for American research, and to deny these intellectual resources to the Soviet Union. At least 1,600 scientists and their dependents were recruited and brought to the United States by Paperclip and its successor projects through the early 1970s.

ACHRE continued:

In recent years, it has been alleged that many of these individuals were brought to the United States in violation of American government policy not to permit the entrance of "ardent Nazis" into the country, that many were security risks, and that at least some were implicated in Holocaust-related activities.

"At the time of its inception," said ACHRE, "Paperclip was a matter of controversy in the War Department, as demonstrated by a November 27, 1946 memorandum from General [Leslie] Groves, director of the Manhattan Project, relating to the bringing to the United States of the eminent physicist Otto Hahn. Groves wrote that the Manhattan Project: "… does not desire to utilize the services of foreign scientists in the United States, either directly with the Project or with any affiliated organization. This has consistently been my views [sic]. I should like to make it clear, however, that I see no objection to bringing to the United States such carefully screened physicists as would contribute materially to the welfare of the United States and would remain permanently in the United States as naturalized citizens. I strongly recommend against foreign physicists coming in contact with our atomic energy program in any way. If they are allowed to see or discuss the work of the Project the security of our information would get out of control."

The Advisory Committee Staff also revealed:

A number of military research sites recruited Paperclip scientists with backgrounds in aeromedicine, radiobiology and ophthalmology. These institutions included the SAM, where radiation experiments were conducted, and other military sites, particularly the Edgewood Arsenal of the Army's Chemical Corps.

The portfolio of experiments at the SAM was one that would particularly benefit from the Paperclip recruits. Experiments there included total-body irradiation, space medicine and biology studies, and flash blindness stud-

General Leslie Groves oversaw the Manhattan Project, which used former Nazi scientists to construct nuclear weapons for the United States.

ies. Herbert Gerstner, [The committee has no documents at this time indicating that Dr. Gerstner engaged in human experimentation in Germany] a principal investigator in TBI experiments at the SAM, was acting director of the Institute of Physiology at the University of Leipzig: he became a radiobiologist at the SAM.

The Air Force Surgeon General and SAM officials welcomed the Paperclip scientists. In March 1951, the school's Commandant, O. O. Benson Jr., wrote to the Surgeon General to seek more … "first-class scientists and highly qualified technologists from Germany. The first group of Paperclip personnel contained a number of scientists that have proved to be of real value to the Air Force. The weaker and less gifted ones have been culled to a considerable extent. The second group reporting here in 1949 were, in general, less competent than the original Paperclip personnel, and culling process will again be in order."

General Benson's adjutant solicited resumes from a Paperclip list, including a number of radiation biology and physics specialists. The qualifications of a few scientists were said to be known, so curricula vitae were waived. The adjutant wrote, also in March 1951: "In order to systematically benefit from this program this headquarters believes that the employment of competent personnel who fit into our research program is a most important consideration."

ACHRE then addressed the issues of (a) the way in which a race began between the United States and the Soviet Union to acquire the services of the German scientific and medical communities, post-1945; and (b) the extent to which some of the Paperclip scientists had been supporters of the Nazi regime:

Official U.S. government policy was to avoid recruitment of "ardent Nazis," it was stated. However, this was qualified by the following: "Many of the Paperclip scientists were members of Nazi organizations of one sort of another. The documentary record indicates, however, that many claimed inactive status or membership that was a formality, according to files in the National Archives."

Research undertaken by the ACS uncovered the fact that much pressure was exerted in an attempt to ensure that Paperclip succeeded. For example, an April 27, 1948, memorandum from the director of the Joint Intelligence Objectives Agency, Navy captain Bosquet N. Wev, to the Pentagon's director of intelligence stated:

> Security investigations conducted by the military have disclosed the fact that the majority of German scientists were members of either the Nazi Party or one or more of its affiliates. These investigations disclose further that with a very few exceptions, such membership was due to exigencies which influenced the lives of every citizen of Germany at that time.

Wev was critical of over-scrupulous investigations by the Department of Justice and other agencies as reflecting security concerns no longer relevant with the defeat of Germany, and "biased considerations" about the nature of his recruits' fascist allegiances. The possibility of scientists being won to the Soviet side in the Cold War was, according to Captain Wev, the highest consideration.

In a March 1948 letter to the State Department, Wev assessed the prevailing view in the government:

> Responsible officials … have expressed opinions to the effect that, insofar as German scientists are concerned, Nazism no longer should be a serious consideration from a viewpoint of national security when the far greater threat of Communism is now jeopardizing the entire world. I strongly concur in this opinion and consider it a most sound and practical view, which must certainly be taken if we are to face the situation confronting us with even an iota of realism. To continue to treat Nazi affiliations as significant considerations has been phrased as "beating a dead Nazi horse."

The committee then turned its attention to two controversial figures in this particularly notorious saga. The first was Hubertus Strughold. Born in Germany in 1898, Strughold obtained a Ph.D. in biochemistry in 1922, an M.D. in sensory physiology in 1923, and between 1929 and 1935 served as director of the Aeromedical Research Institute in Berlin. In 1947, as a result of Project Paperclip's actions, Strughold joined the staff of the Air Force's School of Aviation Medicine at Randolph Field, Texas; and in 1949 he was named head of the then-newly formed Department of Space Medicine at the school—where, according to documentation uncovered by the ACHRE, he conducted research into "effects of high speed"; "lack of oxygen"; "decompression"; "effects of ultra-violet rays"; "space cabin simulator for testing humans"; "weightlessness"; and "visual disturbances."

//Many of the Paperclip scientists were members of Nazi organizations of one sort of another."

Strughold was naturalized as an American citizen in 1956 and, four years later, became chair of the Advanced Studies Group, Aerospace Medical Center at Brooks Air Force Base. Strughold—whose awards and honors included the USAF Exceptional Civilian Service Award and the Theodore C. Lyster Award of the Aerospace Medical Association—retired in 1968. And, as the Advisory Committee Staff stated:

> Perhaps the most prominent of the Paperclip physicians was Hubertus Strughold, called "the father of space medicine" and for whom the

Aeromedical Library at the USAF School of Aerospace Medicine was named in 1977. During the War, he was director of the Luftwaffe's aeromedical institute; a Strughold staff member was acquitted at Nuremberg on the grounds that the physician's Dachau laboratory was not the site of nefarious experiments.

Strughold had a long career at the SAM, including the recruitment of other Paperclip scientists in Germany. His background was the subject of public controversy in the United States. He denied involvement with Nazi experiments and told reporters in this country that his life had been in danger from the Nazis. A citizen for 30 years before his death in 1986, his many honors included an American Award from the Daughters of the American Revolution.

An April 1947 intelligence report on Strughold stated: "[H]is successful career under Hitler would seem to indicate that he must be in full accord with Nazism." However, Strughold's colleagues in Germany and those with whom he had worked briefly in the United States on fellowships described him as politically indifferent or anti-Nazi.

In his application to reside in this country, he declared: "Further, the United States is the only country of liberty which is able to maintain this liberty and the thousand-year-old culture and western civilization, and it is my intention to support the United States in this task, which is in danger now, with all my scientific abilities and experience."

In a 1952 civil service form, Strughold was asked if he had ever been a member of a fascist organization. His answer: "Not in my opinion." His references therein included the Surgeon General of the Air Force, the director of research at the Lovelace Foundation in New Mexico, and a colleague from the Mayo Clinic. In September 1948, Strughold was granted a security clearance from the Joint Intelligence Objectives Agency director, Captain Wev, who in the previous March had written to the Department of State protesting the difficulty of completing immigration procedures for Paperclip recruits.

The second character of controversy was one who, incredibly, rose to a position of major significance within NASA. Wernher von Braun was born in Wirsitz, Germany, on March 23, 1912, and earned his bachelor's degree at the age of twenty from the University of Berlin, where he also received his doctorate in physics in 1934. Between 1932 and 1937, von Braun was employed by the German Ordnance Department and became technical director of the Peenemünde Rocket Center in 1937, where the V-2 rocket was developed.

Von Braun came to the United States in September 1945 under contract with the Army Ordnance Corps as part of Paperclip and worked on high altitude firings of captured V-2 rockets at the White Sands Proving Ground, until he became project director of the Ordnance Research and Development Division Sub-Office at Fort Bliss, Texas. On October 28, 1949, the secretary of the Army approved the transfer of the Fort Bliss group to Redstone Arsenal; and after his ar-

Wernher von Braun (in civilian clothing) is shown in this 1941 photograph posing with several German officers. Before working for the American space program, von Braun was responsible for the V-2 rocket the Germans used during the London blitz.

rival in Huntsville in April 1950, von Braun was appointed director of development operations.

Major development projects under von Braun's technical direction included the Redstone rocket, the Jupiter Intermediate Range Ballistic Missile, and the Pershing missile. He and his team of German scientists and engineers were also responsible for developing the Jupiter C Reentry Test Missile and launching the free world's first scientific earth satellite, Explorer 1.

On July 1, 1960, von Braun and his team were transferred to the National Aeronautics and Space Administration and became the nucleus of the George C. Marshall Space Flight Center at Redstone Arsenal. He served as director of the Marshall Center until February 1970 when he moved to NASA Headquarters to serve as deputy associate administrator. On 1 July 1972, von Braun left NASA to become vice president of engineering and development for Fairchild Industries in Germantown, Maryland, and was inducted into the Ordnance Corps Hall of Fame in 1973. Von Braun retired in January 1977 because of ill health and died on June 16, 1977. It was not a bad life for the "former" Nazi. And it was a life that never would have existed had it not been for the creation of Paperclip, the ultimate Faustian pact.

The final word on this matter goes to the ACS, who noted in its final report on Paperclip and its investigations of it activities:

The staff believes that this trail should be followed with more research before conclusions can be drawn about the Paperclip scientists and human radiation experiments. That the standard for immigration was "not an ardent Nazi" is troubling; in Strughold's case, investigators had specifically questioned his credentials for "denazification." It is possible that still-classified intelligence documents could shed further light on these connections.

In light of that final sentence from the committee, it seems the story is not yet over.

THE ROSWELL UFO CRASH: MULTIPLE SCENARIOS

No one, not even the U.S. government, disputes that *something* came crashing to earth in the wilds of New Mexico in early July 1947. We are talking about the infamous "Roswell UFO crash." Indeed, history has shown that shortly after rancher Mack Brazel stumbled upon a large amount of mystifying material on the Foster Ranch (and possibly upon a number of unusual corpses, too—it has been suggested), staff at the Roswell Army Air Field issued a press release stating that they had recovered an honest-to-goodness "flying disc."

This was barely two weeks after the famous UFO sighting of pilot Kenneth Arnold at the Cascade Mountains, Washington State—an event that almost single-handedly gave birth to the "flying saucer." Today, we have almost seventy years of "modern era" UFO reports to scrutinize—something that has allowed the extraterrestrial theory to develop and be widely embraced.

But it's difficult to say for sure the extent to which the concept of "flying disc = alien spaceship" was widely accepted, just barely two weeks after the Arnold affair. In other words, when the military said: "Yes, we *have* recovered a flying saucer," it *may* have meant they had an extraterrestrial vehicle on their hands. On the other hand, it could also be interpreted as: "We have recovered a bunch of odd-looking wreckage that we think might be connected to those weird things in the sky people have been seeing for the last week or two—whatever they may be."

Regardless of which scenario is correct, it is an undeniable fact that the recovery of a flying disc *was* confirmed—which is just one of the many things that makes Roswell such an intriguing and enduring case. It's also a fact that, in barely any time at all, the flying disc story was retracted and in its place a weather-balloon explanation surfaced. That's two explanations in two days. In the years that followed, a *dozen* or so additional theories surfaced—some more plausible than others.

The late Jim Keith was the author of a number of conspiracy/UFO-themed books, including *Casebook on the Men in Black*; *The Octopus* (co-written with Kenn Thomas); and *Black Helicopters over America*. In a small article titled "Roswell UFO Bombshell," Keith described his clandestine meeting with "a longtime researcher / instructor of engineering at a school in New Mexico" who claimed to know the truth of Roswell. As for what Keith was told, it goes like this:

The International UFO Museum and Research Center in Roswell, New Mexico, was founded by army information officer Walter Haut and Glenn Dennis in 1992.

According to my source, the true story behind the alleged UFO crash was that there was an accident involving a B-29 flying from the Army Air Force Base in Sandia (Albuquerque) to Roswell … my source states that either an atomic bomb or what is termed a "bomb shape," or "test shape," the shell of a nuke lacking explosives and atomic capability, and sometimes filled with concrete to add weight, was accidentally or purposefully jettisoned above Corona, New Mexico, directly on the flight path between Sandia and Roswell. Along with the bomb, metal foil used for radar jamming, termed "chaff," may have also been dropped.

In 2010, Anomalist Books published the final title from the late Mac Tonnies: *The Cryptoterrestrials*. Highly thought-provoking and deeply controversial in equal measures, the book focused on the idea that UFOs are *not* the products of alien races, but of very ancient, terrestrial people that dwell deep underground and who *masquerade* as extraterrestrials to camouflage their true identity.

Tonnies speculated that the Cryptoterrestrials are likely very impoverished, but utilize subterfuge, hologram-style technology, and staged events to suggest otherwise to us. He even theorized they may have made use of large, balloon-style craft, too. And on this very matter—of the Cryptoterrestrials using balloons in covert missions—Tonnies said in his book: "Maybe the Roswell device wasn't high tech. It could indeed have been a balloon-borne surveillance device brought down in a storm, but it doesn't logically follow that it was one of our own."

Annie Jacobsen's book, *Area 51: An Uncensored History of America's Top Secret Military Base*, created a huge wave of controversy when it was published in 2011, and chiefly for one, specific reason. The book includes a story suggesting that the Roswell craft and bodies were, in reality, the diabolical creations of a near-Faustian pact between the notorious Nazi (and "Angel of Death)", Dr. Josef Mengele and Soviet premier Joseph Stalin.

The purpose of this early Cold War plan: to plunge the United States into a kind of *War of the Worlds*-style panic by trying to convince the U.S. government aliens were invading. And how would the plan work? By placing grossly deformed children (courtesy of the crazed Mengele) inside a futuristic-looking aircraft designed by the brilliant aviation experts, the Horten brothers, and then trying to convince the United States of the alien origins of both. Unfortunately for Stalin—we are told—the plot failed when a storm brought down the craft and its "crew" in the wilds of New Mexico, an event that did not lead to widespread panic, but that instead was hastily covered up by U.S. military authorities.

The Collins Elite is a quasi-official group within the U.S. government that believes the UFO mystery is one of demonic origins. Yes, fork-tails, horns, fiery pits, and maybe even spinning heads—that kind of thing. It must be stressed that the conclusions of the group were chiefly belief-driven, rather than prompted by hard evidence.

One of the conclusions of the group was that Roswell was nothing less than a brilliant Trojan Horse. For the members of the Collins Elite, deceptive demons had, essentially, used a kind of "cosmic alchemy" to create both (A) the so-called "memory-metal" found by Mack Brazel on the Foster Ranch; and (B) the curious bodies—or body-parts—also located on the ranch. In other words, Roswell—perceived by the Collins Elite, at least—was an ingenious ruse, a staged crash, designed to have us believe vulnerable ETs are in our midst, when it's really the all-powerful minions of Satan.

Although no longer active in the UFO community, Timothy Cooper provoked a wealth of controversy in the 1990s, thanks to an enormous body of allegedly leaked, and, supposedly highly secret, documentation in his possession on everything from crashed UFOs to alien autopsies and from sinister deaths in the UFO field to alien viruses. One such document titled *UFO Reports and Classified Projects*, offers a non-UFO-themed explanation for what occurred at Roswell. The relevant extract reads as follows:

> One of the projects underway at that time incorporated re-entry vehicles containing radium and other radioactive materials combined with biological warfare agents developed by I. G. Farben for use against allied assault forces in Normandy in 1944. When a V-2 warhead impacted near the town of Corona, New Mexico, on July 4, 1947, the warhead did not explode and it and the deadly cargo lay exposed to the elements which forced the Armed Forces Special Weapons Project to close off the crash site and a cover story was immediately put out that what was discovered was the remains of a radar tracking target suspended by balloons.

The July 9, 1947, issue of the *Roswell Daily Record* headlined the story about a flying saucer being captured by the military.

When personnel at the Roswell Army Air Field announced in July 1947 that they had recovered a crashed flying disc, one thing was one hundred percent absent: any mention of bodies. And, needless to say, the body angle was also absent from the hasty follow-up explanation of a weather-balloon recovery. The body angle was also denied in the Air Force's July 1994 report on Roswell (titled *Report of Air Force Research Regarding the Roswell Incident*), as the following extract shows: "It should also be noted here that there was little mentioned in this report about the recovery of the so-called 'alien bodies.' The wreckage was from a Project Mogul balloon. There were no 'alien' passengers therein."

Three years later, however, things had changed. In a new document—*The Roswell Report: Case Closed*—it was stated by the Air Force:

"Aliens" observed in the New Mexico desert were probably anthropomorphic test dummies that were carried aloft by U.S. Air Force high altitude balloons for scientific research.... The reports of military units that always seemed to arrive shortly after the crash of a flying saucer to retrieve the saucer and "crew" were actually accurate descriptions of Air Force personnel engaged in anthropomorphic dummy recovery operations.

One of the most controversial theories for the Roswell affair suggests the stories of crashed UFOs and dead aliens were born out of high-altitude experimentation/flights using human test-subjects—*some*, at least, being Japanese individuals, both scientists and prisoners of war. In 1997, *Popular Mechanics* published a story along these very lines. Plus, the well-respected Australian UFO researcher Keith Basterfield was given a near-identical story (in the mid-2000s) by a man whose father worked for British Intelligence. But that's not all.

Another person who was hot on the trail of the "high-altitude/Japanese" angle was the now-deceased UFO investigator Kathy Kasten. Much of Kasten's research on this particular topic took her in the direction of Fort Stanton—which just happens to be situated in Lincoln County, where the still-mystifying events of July 1947 went down. After Kasten's death in 2012, I inherited all of her files, notes, correspondence, documents, and much more—hundreds of pages of which (and maybe even more) were focused on her Roswell/Fort Stanton research. And then there is Kasten's unpublished book on her Roswell research, too, which makes for fascinating reading. I suspect we have not yet heard the last of this particular theory.

Then there is the matter of time travel. One of those who revealed his thoughts on this particular scenario was Lieutenant Colonel Philip Corso, coauthor with William Birnes of the much-debated, championed, and denounced UFO-themed book: *The Day after Roswell*. The unusual bodies found within the wreckage of the craft, Corso claimed, were genetically created beings designed to withstand the rigors of space flight, but they were not the actual creators of the UFO itself.

Right up until the time of his death in 1998, Corso speculated on the distinct possibility that the U.S. government might *still* have no real idea of who constructed the craft, or who genetically engineered the bodies found aboard. Notably, Corso gave much consideration to the idea that the Roswell UFO was a form of time machine, possibly even one designed and built by the denizens of the Earth of a distant future, rather than by the people of a far away solar system.

Following the defeat of Nazi Germany in 1945, numerous German scientists were brought to the United States via a program called Operation Paperclip. And many of those same scientists went to work at the New Mexico-based White Sands Missile Range (or the White Sands Proving Ground, as it was known back then). This has led to a scenario involving a highly secret program to test-fly radical Nazi aircraft captured after Hitler and his cronies were defeated.

One of the most controversial theories for the Roswell affair suggests the stories of crashed UFOs and dead aliens were born out of high-altitude experimentation/flights using human test-subjects....

Someone who has deeply addressed the Nazi/Roswell links is Joseph P. Farrell, the author of *Roswell and the Reich: The Nazi Connection*. Farrell, however, took things in a decidedly different direction. He concludes the Roswell event was *not* caused by the flight and crash of a German craft flown from White Sands. Rather, Farrell believed that "what crashed may have been representative of an independent postwar Nazi power—an extraterritorial Reich monitoring its old enemy, America...."

The Flying Saucer was a science-fiction novel published in 1948 and written by Bernard Newman, a man who penned more than a hundred books on subjects including real-life espionage, global politics, and current affairs. It was his foray into the weird world of crashed UFOs that was perhaps most notable of all, however.

The book was published just eleven months after the alleged recovery by the U.S. military of a flying saucer on the Foster Ranch, Lincoln County, New Mexico, in July 1947. *The Flying Saucer* tells the story of a secret cabal that stages a series of hoaxed UFO crashes, with the express purpose of attempting to unite the world against a deadly alien foe that, in reality, does not exist.

That Newman had numerous, high-level connections to officialdom has given rise to the theory that (a) Roswell was, itself, a staged event—one designed to scare the Soviets into thinking the United States had acquired alien technology; and (b) Newman based his "novel" on data secured by sources with top secret knowledge of the Roswell ruse.

In an article titled *Roswell Explained—Again* (which was published in *Fate* magazine in September 2005, Kevin Randle (a leading figure in the quest to resolve Roswell) stated that during the early part of the 1990s, he "interviewed a man who worked with NASA at the White Sands Missile Range." The man in question was Gerald Brown.

Randle continued that Brown speculated "some kind of flying wing had crashed while carrying five chimps dressed in silver flying suits." So far, no evidence has surfaced to suggest that the alien body stories can be explained away via the chimpanzee scenario. On the other hand, there is no hard, undeniable evidence for *any* theory when it comes to Roswell.

On July 28, 1995, a report surfaced from the National Security and International Affairs Division of the General Accounting Office (today called the Government Accountability Office) that disclosed the results of its investigation of the Roswell affair. Commenting on an Air Force report on Roswell published in July 1994, the GAO noted the following:

> DOD informed us that the U.S. Air Force report of July 1994, entitled *Report of Air Force Research Regarding the Roswell Incident*, represents the extent of DOD records or information concerning the Roswell crash. The Air Force report concluded that there was no dispute that something happened near Roswell in July 1947 and that all available official materials indicated the most likely source of the wreckage recovered was one of the project MOGUL balloon trains. At the time of the Roswell crash, project MOGUL was a highly classified U.S. effort to determine the state of Soviet nuclear weapons research using balloons that carried radar reflectors and acoustic sensors.

And that's where things stand to this very day: *fourteen* theories for just one, near-seventy-year-old event. They are theories that range from the plausible to the unlikely, and with others hazily hovering somewhere in between. Some of those scenarios may be the work of hoaxers; others could be born out of the clandestine worlds of disinformation and psychological warfare. The Air Force's reports on the Mogul Balloon angle and the crash-test-dummy theory are—in *my* opinion, at least—honest attempts to try and resolve a mystery for which today, no files can be found—*anywhere*.

Somewhere, in this confusing mass (and mess) of theories, the truth of Roswell exists ... probably....

MKULTRA: MANIPULATING THE MIND

Within the annals of research into conspiracy theories, there is perhaps no more emotive term than that of "mind-control." Indeed, mention those two words to anyone who is even remotely aware of the term and it will invariably and inevitably (and wholly justifiably, too) provoke imagery and comments pertaining to political assassinations, dark and disturbing CIA chicanery, sexual slavery, secret government projects—and even alien abductions and subliminal advertising on the part of the world's media and advertising agencies.

Yes: the specter of mind-control is one that has firmly worked its ominous way into numerous facets of modern-day society. And it has been doing so for years. Consider, for example, the following (from "Hypnosis Comes of Age," *Science Digest*, April 1971).

"I can hypnotize a man, without his knowledge or consent, into committing treason against the United States," asserted Dr. George Estabrooks, Ph.D., and chair of the Department of Psychology at Colgate University, way back in 1942, and before a select group of personnel attached to the U.S. War Department. Estabrooks added: "Two hundred trained foreign operators, working in the United States, could develop a uniquely dangerous army of hypnotically controlled Sixth Columnists."

Estabrooks's piece-de-resistance, however, was to capitalize on an ingenious plan that had been postulated as far back as the First World War.

As he explained in "Hypnosis Comes of Age":

During World War One, a leading psychologist made a startling proposal to the navy. He offered to take a submarine steered by a captured U-boat captain, placed under his hypnotic control, through enemy mine fields to attack the German fleet. Washington nixed the stratagem as too risky. First, because there was no disguised method by which the captain's mind could be outflanked. Second, because today's technique of day-by-day breaking down of ethical conflicts brainwashing was still unknown.

The indirect approach to hypnotism would, I believe, change the navy's answer today. Personally, I am convinced that hypnosis is a bristling, dangerous armament which makes it doubly imperative to avoid the war of tomorrow.

A perfect example of the way in which the will of a person could be completely controlled and manipulated was amply and graphically spelled out in Estabrooks's 1971 article:

> Communication in war is always a headache. Codes can be broken. A professional spy may or may not stay bought. Your own man may have unquestionable loyalty, but his judgment is always open to question.

> The "hypnotic courier," on the other hand, provides a unique solution. I was involved in preparing many subjects for this work during World War II. One successful case involved an Army Service Corps Captain whom we'll call George Smith.

> Captain Smith had undergone months of training. He was an excellent subject but did not realize it. I had removed from him, by post-hypnotic suggestion, all recollection of ever having been hypnotized.

> First I had the Service Corps call the captain to Washington and tell him they needed a report of the mechanical equipment of Division X headquartered in Tokyo. Smith was ordered to leave by jet next morning, pick up the report and return at once. Consciously, that was all he knew, and it was the story he gave to his wife and friends.

> Then I put him under deep hypnosis, and gave him—orally—a vital message to be delivered directly on his arrival in Japan to a certain colonel—let's say his name was Brown—of military intelligence.

> Outside of myself, Colonel Brown was the only person who could hypnotize Captain Smith. This is "locking."

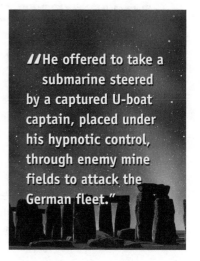

//He offered to take a submarine steered by a captured U-boat captain, placed under his hypnotic control, through enemy mine fields to attack the German fleet."

> I performed it by saying to the hypnotized Captain: "Until further orders from me, only Colonel Brown and I can hypnotize you. We will use a signal phrase *the moon is clear*. Whenever you hear this phrase from Brown or myself you will pass instantly into deep hypnosis."

> When Captain Smith re-awakened, he had no conscious memory or what happened in trance. All that he was aware of was that he must head for Tokyo to pick up a division report.

> On arrival there, Smith reported to Brown, who hypnotized him with the signal phrase. Under hypnosis, Smith delivered my message and received one to bring back. Awakened, he was given the division report and returned home by jet. There I hypnotized him once more with the signal phrase, and he spieled off Brown's answer that had been dutifully tucked away in his unconscious mind.

And with the early, ground-breaking work of George Estabrooks now concisely spelled out for one and all to read, digest and muse upon, let me acquaint you with a concise history of the world of mind-control, mind-manipulation, and what could accurately be termed mind-slavery.

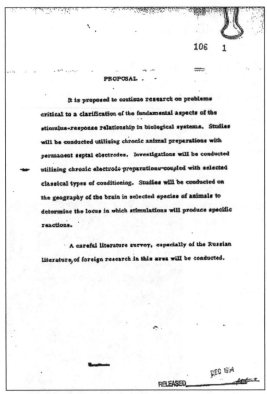

106   1

PROPOSAL .

It is proposed to continue research on problems critical to a clarification of the fundamental aspects of the stimulus-response relationship in biological systems. Studies will be conducted utilising chronic animal preparations with permanent septal electrodes. Investigations will be conducted utilising chronic electrode preparations coupled with selected classical types of conditioning. Studies will be conducted on the geography of the brain in selected species of animals to determine the locus in which stimulations will produce specific reactions.

A careful literature survey, especially of the Russian literature, of foreign research in this area will be conducted.

RELEASED

A sample of declassified documents shows the proposal for MKUltra: the CIA's plan to try and control people's minds.

The picture is not a pretty one—not at all.

Although the U.S. intelligence community, military, and government have undertaken countless official (and off-the-record, too) projects pertaining to both mind-control and mind-manipulation, without any doubt whatsoever, the most notorious of all was Project MKUltra: a clandestine operation that operated out of the CIA's Office of Scientific Intelligence and had its beginnings in the Cold War era of the early 1950s.

The date of the project's actual termination is a somewhat hazy one; however, it is known that it was definitely in operation as late as the latter part of the 1960s—and, not surprisingly and regretfully, has since been replaced by far more controversial and deeply hidden projects.

To demonstrate the level of secrecy that surrounded Project MKUltra, even though it had kicked off at the dawn of the fifties, its existence was largely unknown outside of the intelligence world until 1975—when the Church Committee and the Rockefeller Commission began making their own investigations of the CIA's mind-control-related activities—in part to determine if (a) the CIA had engaged in illegal activity, (b) the personal rights of citizens had been violated, and (c) if the projects at issue had resulted in fatalities—which they most assuredly and unfortunately did.

Rather conveniently, and highly suspiciously, too, it was asserted at the height of the inquires in 1975 that two years earlier, in 1973, CIA director Richard Helms had ordered the destruction of the agency's MKUltra files. Fortunately, this did not stop the Church Committee or the Rockefeller Commission, both of which had the courage and tenacity to forge ahead with their investigations, relying on sworn testimony from players in MKUltra, where documentation was no longer available for scrutiny, study, and evaluation.

The story that unfolded was both dark and disturbing—in equal degrees. Indeed, the scope of the project—and allied operations, too—was spelled out in an August 1977 document titled *The Senate MKUltra Hearings* that was prepared by the Senate Select Committee on Intelligence and the Committee on Human Resources, as a result of its probing into the secret world of the CIA.

The Senate MKULtra Hearings document, available via the Freedom of Information Act, is a lengthy and detailed one. It states:

Research and development programs to find materials which could be used to alter human behavior were initiated in the late 1940s and early 1950s. These experimental programs originally included testing of drugs involving witting human subjects, and culminated in tests using unwitting, non-volunteer human subjects. These tests were designed to determine the potential effects of chemical or biological agents when used operationally against individuals unaware that they had received a drug.

The Select Committee then turned its attention to the overwhelming secrecy that surrounded these early 1940s/1950s projects:

The testing programs were considered highly sensitive by the intelligence agencies administering them. Few people, even within the agencies, knew of the programs and there is no evidence that either the Executive Branch or Congress were ever informed of them.

The highly compartmented nature of these programs may be explained in part by an observation made by the CIA Inspector General that, "the knowledge that the Agency is engaging in unethical and illicit activities would have serious repercussions in political and diplomatic circles and would be detrimental to the accomplishment of its missions."

The research and development programs, and particularly the covert testing programs, resulted in massive abridgments of the rights of American citizens, and sometimes with tragic consequences, too. As prime evidence of this, the Select Committee uncovered details on the deaths of two Americans that were firmly attributed to the programs at issue; while other participants in the testing programs were said to still be suffering from the residual effects of the tests as late as the mid-1970s.

And as the Select Committee starkly noted:

While some controlled testing of these substances might be defended, the nature of the tests, their scale, and the fact that they were continued for years after the danger of surreptitious administration of LSD to unwitting individuals was known, demonstrate a fundamental disregard for the value of human life.

There was far more to come: The Select Committee's investigation of the testing and use of chemical and biological agents also raised serious questions about the adequacy of command and control procedures within the Central Intelligence Agency and military intelligence, and also about the nature of the relationships among the intelligence agencies, other governmental agencies, and private institutions and individuals that were also allied to the early mind-control studies.

For example, the Select Committee was highly disturbed to learn that with respect to the mind-control and mind-manipulation projects, the CIA's normal administrative controls were controversially—and completely—waived for programs in-

> //The research and development programs, and particularly the covert testing programs, resulted in massive abridgments of the rights of American citizens, and sometimes with tragic consequences, too."

volving chemical and biological agents—supposedly to protect their security, but more likely to protect those CIA personnel who knew they were verging upon (if not outright surpassing) breaking the law.

But it is perhaps the following statement from the Select Committee that demonstrates the level of controversy that surrounded—and that still surrounds—the issue of mind-control-based projects:

> The decision to institute one of the Army's LSD field testing projects had been based, at least in part, on the finding that no long-term residual effects had ever resulted from the drug's administration. The CIA's failure to inform the Army of a death which resulted from the surreptitious administration of LSD to unwitting Americans, may well have resulted in the institution of an unnecessary and potentially lethal program.

The Select Committee added:

> The development, testing, and use of chemical and biological agents by intelligence agencies raises serious questions about the relationship between the intelligence community and foreign governments, other agencies of the federal government, and other institutions and individuals.

> The questions raised range from the legitimacy of American complicity in actions abroad which violate American and foreign laws to the possible compromise of the integrity of public and private institutions used as cover by intelligence agencies.

While MKUltra was certainly the most infamous of all the CIA-initiated mind-control programs, it was very far from being an isolated one. Indeed, numerous sub-projects, post-projects, and operations initiated by other agencies were brought to the Select Committee's attention. One was Project Chatter, which the Select Committee described thus:

> Project Chatter was a Navy program that began in the fall of 1947. Responding to reports of "amazing results" achieved by the Soviets in using "truth drugs," the program focused on the identification and the testing of such drugs for use in interrogations and in the recruitment of agents. The research included laboratory experiments on animals and human subjects involving *Anabasis aphylla*, scopolamine, and mescaline in order to determine their speech-inducing qualities. Overseas experiments were conducted as part of the project. The project expanded substantially during the Korean War, and ended shortly after the war, in 1953.

Then there was Projects Bluebird and Artichoke. Again, the Select Committee dug deep and uncovered some controversial and eye-opening data and testimony:

> The earliest of the CIA's major programs involving the use of chemical and biological agents, Project Bluebird, was approved by the Director in 1950. Its objectives were: (a) discovering means of conditioning personnel to prevent unauthorized extraction of information from them by known means, (b) investigating the possibility of control of an individual

Also used for anesthesia and even lethal injection, sodium pentothal is a type of barbituate that has been used in interrogations. It decreases higher cortical brain function, making people less able to lie under pressure.

by application of special interrogation techniques, (c) memory enhancement, and (d) establishing defensive means for preventing hostile control of Agency personnel.

The Select Committee added with respect to Bluebird:

As a result of interrogations conducted overseas during the project, another goal was added—the evaluation of offensive uses of unconventional interrogation techniques, including hypnosis and drugs. In August 1951, the project was renamed Artichoke. Project Artichoke included in-house experiments on interrogation techniques, conducted "under medical and security controls which would ensure that no damage was done to individuals who volunteer for the experiments. Overseas interrogations utilizing a combination of sodium pentothal and hypnosis after physical and psychiatric examinations of the subjects were also part of Artichoke."

Interestingly, the Select Committee noted:

Information about Project Artichoke after the fall of 1953 is scarce. The CIA maintains that the project ended in 1956, but evidence suggests that Office of Security and Office of Medical Services use of "special interrogation" techniques continued for several years thereafter.

MKNaomi was another major CIA program in this area. In 1967, the CIA summarized the purposes of MKNaomi thus:

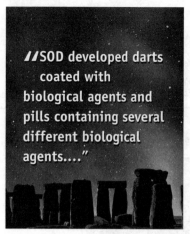

"SOD developed darts coated with biological agents and pills containing several different biological agents...."

(a) To provide for a covert support base to meet clandestine operational requirements. (b) To stockpile severely incapacitating and lethal materials for the specific use of TSD [Technical Services Division]. (c) To maintain in operational readiness special and unique items for the dissemination of biological and chemical materials. (d) To provide for the required surveillance, testing, upgrading, and evaluation of materials and items in order to assure absence of defects and complete predictability of results to be expected under operational conditions.

Under an agreement reached with the Army in 1952, the Special Operations Division (SOD) at Fort Detrick was to assist CIA in developing, testing, and maintaining biological agents and delivery systems—some of which were directly related to mind-control experimentation. By this agreement, the CIA finally acquired the knowledge, skill, and facilities of the Army to develop biological weapons specifically suited for CIA use.

The Select Committee also noted:

SOD developed darts coated with biological agents and pills containing several different biological agents which could remain potent for weeks or months. SOD developed a special gun for firing darts coated with a chemical which could allow CIA agents to incapacitate a guard dog, enter an installation secretly, and return the dog to consciousness when leaving. SOD scientists were unable to develop a similar incapacitant [sic] for humans. SOD also physically transferred to CIA personnel biological agents in "bulk" form, and delivery devices, including some containing biological agents.

In addition to the CIA's interest in using biological weapons and mind-control against humans, it also asked SOD to study use of biological agents against crops and animals. In its 1967 memorandum, the CIA stated:

Three methods and systems for carrying out a covert attack against crops and causing severe crop loss have been developed and evaluated under field conditions. This was accomplished in anticipation of a requirement which was later developed but was subsequently scrubbed just prior to putting into action.

The Select Committee concluded with respect to MKNaomi that the project was

... terminated in 1970. On November 25, 1969, President Nixon renounced the use of any form of biological weapons that kill or incapacitate and ordered the disposal of existing stocks of bacteriological weapons. On February 14, 1970, the President clarified the extent of his earlier order and indicated that toxins—chemicals that are not living organisms but are produced by living organisms—were considered biological weapons subject to his previous directive and were to be destroyed. Although instructed to relinquish control of material held for the CIA by

SOD, a CIA scientist acquired approximately 11 grams of shellfish toxin from SOD personnel at Fort Detrick which were stored in a little-used CIA laboratory where it went undetected for five years.

Recognizing, however, that when it came to mind-control and manipulation, MKUltra was the one project that more than any other was worth pursuing as part of its efforts to determine the extent to which the CIA had bent and broken the law and flouted the rights of citizens, the Select Committee had far more to say on the operation:

Public disclosure of some aspects of MKUltra activity could induce serious adverse reaction in U.S. public opinion....

Time and again the Select Committee returned to Project MKUltra. Not surprising, as it was, after all, the principal CIA program involving the research and development of chemical and biological agents, and was, in the words of the Select Committee: "... concerned with the research and development of chemical, biological, and radiological materials capable of employment in clandestine operations to control human behavior."

The Inspector General's survey of MKUltra, in 1963, noted the following reasons for the profound level of sensitivity that surrounded the program:

A. Research in the manipulation of human behavior is considered by many authorities in medicine and related fields to be professionally unethical, therefore the reputation of professional participants in the MKUltra program are on occasion in jeopardy.

B. Some MKUltra activities raise questions of legality implicit in the original charter.

C. A final phase of the testing of MKUltra products places the rights and interests of U.S. citizens in jeopardy.

D. Public disclosure of some aspects of MKUltra activity could induce serious adverse reaction in U.S. public opinion, as well as stimulate offensive and defensive action in this field on the part of foreign intelligence services.

Over the ten-year life of the program, many "additional avenues to the control of human behavior" were designated as being wholly appropriate for investigation under the MKUltra charter. These included "radiation, electroshock, various fields of psychology, psychiatry, sociology, and anthropology, graphology, harassment substances, and paramilitary devices and materials."

Needless to say, this was a grim list.

A 1955 MKUltra document provides a good example of the scope of the effort to understand the effects of mind-altering substances on human beings, and lists those same substances as follows. In the CIA's own words:

1. Substances which will promote illogical thinking and impulsiveness to the point where the recipient would be discredited in public;

2. Substances which increase the efficiency of mentation and perception.

3. Materials which will prevent or counteract the intoxicating effect of alcohol.

4. Materials which will promote the intoxicating effect of alcohol.

5. Materials which will produce the signs and symptoms of recognized diseases in a reversible way so that they may be used for malingering, etc.

6. Materials which will render the induction of hypnosis easier or otherwise enhance its usefulness.

7. Substances which will enhance the ability of individuals to withstand privation, torture and coercion during interrogation and so-called "brain-washing."

8. Materials and physical methods which will produce amnesia for events preceding and during their use.

9. Physical methods of producing shock and confusion over extended periods of time and capable of surreptitious use.

10. Substances which produce physical disablement such as paralysis of the legs, acute anemia, etc.

11. Substances which will produce "pure" euphoria with no subsequent let-down.

12. Substances which alter personality structure in such a way that the tendency of the recipient to become dependent upon another person is enhanced.

13. A material which will cause mental confusion of such a type that the individual under its influence will find it difficult to maintain a fabrication under questioning.

14. Substances which will lower the ambition and general working efficiency of men when administered in undetectable amounts.

15. Substances which promote weakness or distortion of the eyesight or hearing faculties, preferably without permanent effects.

16. A knockout pill which can surreptitiously be administered in drinks, food, cigarettes, as an aerosol, etc., which will be safe to use, provide a maximum of amnesia, and be suitable for use by agent types on an ad hoc basis.

17. A material which can be surreptitiously administered by the above routes and which in very small amounts will make it impossible for a man to perform any physical activity whatsoever.

In other words, when it came to mind-manipulation, more than half a century ago, the CIA already had all bases covered.

A special procedure, designated MKDelta, was established to govern the use of MKUltra materials when specifically utilized in overseas operations. Such materials were used on a number of occasions. According to the Select Committee: "Because MKUltra records were destroyed, it is impossible to reconstruct the operational use of MKUltra materials by the CIA overseas; it has been determined that the use of these materials abroad began in 1953, and possibly as early as 1950."

The Select Committee further explained:

Drugs were used primarily as an aid to interrogations, but MKUltra/MK-Delta materials were also used for harassment, discrediting, or disabling purposes. According to an Inspector General Survey of the Technical

Services Division of the CIA in 1957—an inspection which did not discover the MKUltra project involving the surreptitious administration of LSD to unwitting, nonvolunteer subjects—the CIA had developed six drugs for operational use and they had been used in six different operations on a total of thirty-three subjects. By 1963 the number of operations and subjects had increased substantially.

// Drugs were used primarily as an aid to interrogations, but MKUltra/MKDelta materials were also used for harassment, discrediting, or disabling purposes."

Aside from the CIA, the Select Committee learned that the Army was up to its neck in mind-control-related projects too. In its 1977 report, the Select Committee wrote:

> There were three major phases in the Army's testing of LSD. In the first, LSD was administered to more than 1,000 American soldiers who volunteered to be subjects in chemical warfare experiments. In the second phase, Material Testing Program EA 1729, 95 volunteers received LSD in clinical experiments designed to evaluate potential intelligence uses of the drug. In the third phase, Projects Third Chance and Derby Hat, 16 unwitting nonvolunteer subjects were interrogated after receiving LSD as part of operational field tests.

But what of the post-MKUltra era: Did the official world really cease its operations and destroy its files en-masse, in 1973, as had been alleged? Probably not: In a 1977 interview, fourteen-year CIA veteran Victor Marchetti stated that the CIA's claim that MKUltra was abandoned was nothing more than a "cover story."

WALT DISNEY AND THE CIA: A SECRET CONNECTION

Ward Kimball, a major player in the Walt Disney Corporation, was famous for his on-screen animations of the Cheshire Cat, Jiminy Cricket, the March Hare, and the Mad Hatter. Not only that: Kimball was the man responsible for Mickey Mouse; at least, in the incarnation he appears today. Kimball joined the Disney Studios in 1934 and rose up the ranks to become a directing animator in such classics as *Snow White and the Seven Dwarfs*, *Pinocchio*, *Fantasia*, and *Peter Pan*. He also directed Disney's Oscar-winning shorts *Toot, Whistle, Plunk* and *Boom* in 1953 and *It's Tough to be a Bird* in 1969.

As strange and as near-unbelievable as it may seem, in the early 1950s Walt Disney, Kimball, and senior elements of the CIA were all tied together in a secret and strange program to influence public opinion on the nature of the UFO controversy. So, how did this odd relationship between Disney and the CIA begin? Let's take a look. The first thing to note is the time frame.

On both July 19 and 20, 1952, there were repeated sightings of unknown aerial objects in the Washington, D.C., airspace, something that, on July 24, led USAF Major General John A. Samford to state in a Secret memorandum for the attention of the Deputy Chief of Staff, Operations:

> We are interested in these reports in that we must always be on the alert for any threat or indication of a threat to the United States. We cannot ignore these reports but the mild hysteria subsequent to publicity given this subject causes an influx of reports which since the nineteenth of July has almost saturated our "Emergency" procedures.

The situation really escalated after the weekend of July 26–27. A two-page U.S. Air Force document, prepared only days later, and made available thanks to Freedom of Information legislation, related the facts:

> This incident involved unidentified targets observed on the radar scopes at the Air Route Traffic Control Center and the tower, both at Washington National Airport, and the Approach Control Radar at Andrews Air Force Base. In addition, visual observations were reported to Andrews and Bolling AFB and to ARTC Center, the latter by pilots of commercial aircraft and one CAA aircraft.

> Varying numbers (up to 12 simultaneously) of u/i targets on ARTC radar scope. Termed by CAA personnel as "generally solid returns," similar to

a/c except slower. Mr. Bill Schreve, flying a/c NC-12 reported at 2246 EDT that he had visually spotted 5 objects giving off a light glow ranging from orange to white; his altitude at time was 2,200. Some commercial pilots reported visuals ranging from "cigarette glow" to a "light."

ARTC crew commented that, as compared with u/i returns picked up in early hours of 20 July 52, these returns appeared to be more haphazard in their actions, i.e. they did not follow a/c around nor did they cross scope consistently on same general heading. Some commented that the returns appeared to be from objects "capable of dropping out of the pattern at will." Also that returns had "creeping appearance." One member of crew commented that one object to which F-94 was vectored just "disappeared from Scope" shortly after F-94 started pursuing. All crew members emphatic that most u/i returns have been picked up from time to time over the past few months but never before had they appeared in such quantities over such a prolonged period and with such definition as was experienced on the nights of 19/20 and 26/27 July 1952.

Although the portions extracted from this report speak for themselves, let us now examine an official transcript of a conversation, dated July 26, between staff at Washington National Airport and personnel from Andrews Air Force Base at the time of the sightings:

Wash: Andrews Tower, do you read? Did you have an airplane in sight west-northwest or east of your airport eastbound?

Andr: No, but we just got a call from the Center. We're looking for it.

Wash: We've got a big target showing up on our scope. He's just coming in on the west edge of your airport—the northwest edge of it eastbound. He'll be passing right through the northern portion of your field on an east heading. He's about a quarter of a mile from the northwest runway—right over the edge of your runway now.

Andr: This is Andrews. Our radar tracking said he's got a big fat target out here northwest of Andrews. He said he's got two more south of the field.

Wash: Yes, well the Center has about four or five around the Andrews Range Station. The Center is working a National Airlines—the Center is working him and vectoring him around his target. He went around Andrews. He saw one of them—looks like a meteor … went by him … or something. He said he's got one about three miles off his right wing right now. There are so many targets around here it is hard to tell as they are not moving very fast.

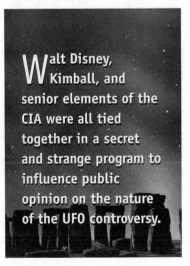

W alt Disney, Kimball, and senior elements of the CIA were all tied together in a secret and strange program to influence public opinion on the nature of the UFO controversy.

Within a matter of hours of hearing of the events of July 26–27, FBI director J. Edgar Hoover instructed N.W. Philcox, the FBI's Air Force liaison representative, to determine what had taken place and to ascertain the Air Force's opinions on the

An illustration depicts what a U.S. Air Force pilot supposedly witnessed near Washington, D.C. in July 1952.

UFO subject as a whole. The FBI's declassified UFO files—from which the following extracts are taken—can be accessed at the FBI's website, The Vault.

On July 29, Philcox made arrangements through the office of the Director of Air Intelligence, Major General John A. Samford, to meet with Commander Randall Boyd of the Current Intelligence Branch, Estimates Division, Air Intelligence, regarding "the present status of Air Intelligence research into the numerous reports regarding flying saucers and flying discs."

Although the Air Force was publicly playing down the possibility that UFOs were anything truly extraordinary, Philcox was advised that "at the present time the Air Force has failed to arrive at any satisfactory conclusion in its research regarding numerous reports of flying saucers and flying discs sighted throughout the United States."

Philcox was further informed that Air Intelligence had set up at Wright-Patterson Air Force Base, Ohio, the Air Technical Intelligence Center, which had been established in part for the purpose of "coordinating, correlating and making research into all reports regarding flying saucers and flying discs."

As Philcox listened very carefully to what Boyd had to say on the matter, he noted that the Air Force had placed its UFO reports into three definable categories. In the first instance there were those sightings

…which are reported by citizens who claim they have seen flying saucers from the ground. These sightings vary in description, color and speeds. Very little credence is given to these sightings inasmuch as in most instances they are believed to be imaginative or some explainable object which actually crossed through the sky.

Philcox then learned that the second category of encounters proved to be of greater significance:

Sightings reported by commercial or military pilots. These sightings are considered more credible by the Air Force inasmuch as commercial or military pilots are experienced in the air and are not expected to see objects which are entirely imaginative. In each of these instances, the individual who reports the sightings is thoroughly interviewed by a representative of Air Intelligence so that a complete description of the object can be obtained.

The third category of encounters, Boyd advised Philcox, were those where, in addition to a visual sighting by a pilot, there was corroboration either from a ground-based source or by radar. Philcox wrote to Hoover:

> Commander Boyd advised that this latter classification constitutes two or three per cent of the total number of sightings, but that they are the most credible reports received and are difficult to explain.

"In these instances … there is no doubt that these individuals reporting the sightings actually did see something in the sky." And to demonstrate that Boyd was well acquainted with the UFO issue on a worldwide scale, he confided in Philcox that "sightings have also recently been reported as far distant as Acapulco, Mexico, Korea and French Morocco … the sightings reported in the last classification have never been satisfactorily explained."

The commander then came out with a true bombshell, as Philcox noted in his report on the meeting: "[Boyd] advised that it is not entirely impossible that the objects may possibly be ships from another planet such as Mars."

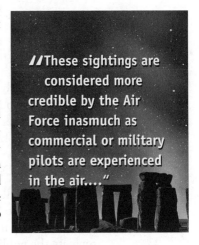

//These sightings are considered more credible by the Air Force inasmuch as commercial or military pilots are experienced in the air…."

The curious and fantastic events of July 1952 deeply troubled the FBI and the Air Force. They greatly worried the CIA, too—and for very intriguing and alternative reasons that had very little to do with literal alien invasion or visitation. On December 2, 1952, the CIA's assistant director H. Marshall Chadwell, noted in a classified report on UFO activity in American airspace: "Sightings of unexplained objects at great altitudes and traveling at high speeds in the vicinity of major U.S. defense installations are of such nature that they are not attributable to natural phenomena or known types of aerial vehicles."

Believing that something really might be afoot in the skies of America, Chadwell prepared a list of saucer-themed recommendations for the National Security Council, which can be found at the CIA's website, CIA.gov:

1. The Director of Central Intelligence shall formulate and carry out a program of intelligence and research activities as required to solve the problem of instant positive identification of unidentified flying objects.

2. Upon call of the Director of Central Intelligence, government departments and agencies shall provide assistance in this program of intelligence and research to the extent of their capacity provided, however, that the DCI shall avoid duplication of activities presently directed toward the solution of this problem.

3. This effort shall be coordinated with the military services and the Research and Development Board of the Department of Defense, with the Psychological Board and other governmental agencies as appropriate.

4. The Director of Central Intelligence shall disseminate information concerning the program of intelligence and research activities in this field to the various departments and agencies which have authorized interest therein.

The curious and fantastic events of July 1952 deeply troubled the FBI and the Air Force.

Forty-eight hours later, the Intelligence Advisory Committee concurred with Chadwell and recommended that "the services of selected scientists to review and appraise the available evidence in the light of pertinent scientific theories" should be the order of the day. Thus was born the Robertson Panel, so named after the man chosen to head the inquiry: Howard Percy Robertson, a consultant to the Agency, a renowned physicist, and the director of the Defense Department Weapons Evaluation Group.

Chadwell was tasked with putting together a crack team of experts in various science, technical, intelligence, and military disciplines and have them carefully study the data on flying saucers currently held by not just the CIA, but the Air Force too—who obligingly agree to hand over all their UFO files for the CIA's scrutiny. Or, at least, the Air Force *said* it was all they had.

Whatever the truth of the matter regarding the extent to which the USAF shared its files with Chadwell's team, the fact that there was a significant body of data to work with was the main thing. And so the team—which included Luis Alvarez, physicist, radar expert (and later, a Nobel Prize recipient); Frederick C. Durant, CIA officer, secretary to the panel, and missile expert; Samuel Abraham Goudsmit, Brookhaven National Laboratories nuclear physicist; and Thornton Page, astrophysicist, radar expert, and deputy director of Johns Hopkins Operations Research Office—quickly got to work.

The overall conclusion of the Robertson Panel was that while UFOs, *per se*, did not appear to have a bearing on national security or the defense of the United States, the way in which the subject could be used by unfriendly forces to manipulate the public mindset and disrupt the U.S. military infrastructure *did* have a bearing—and a major one, too—on matters of a security nature. According to the panel's members:

> Although evidence of any direct threat from these sightings was wholly lacking, related dangers might well exist resulting from: A. Misidentification of actual enemy artifacts by defense personnel. B. Overloading of emergency reporting channels with "false" information. C. Subjectivity of public to mass hysteria and greater vulnerability to possible enemy psychological warfare.

There was also a recommendation that a number of the public UFO investigative groups that existed in the United States at the time, such as the Civilian Flying Saucer Investigators (CFSI) and the Aerial Phenomena Research Organization (APRO), should be "watched" carefully because of "the apparent irresponsibility and the possible use of such groups for subversive purposes."

The panel also concluded that "a public education campaign should be undertaken" on matters relative to UFOs. Specifically, agreed the members, such a program would

... result in reduction in public interest in 'flying saucers' which today evokes a strong psychological reaction. This education could be accomplished by mass media such as television, motion pictures, and popular articles. The basics of such education would be actual case histories that had been puzzling at first but later explained. As in the case of conjuring tricks, there is much less stimulation if the "secret" is known. Such a program should tend to reduce the current gullibility of the public and consequently their susceptibility to clever hostile propaganda.

In this connection, Dr. Hadley Cantril (Princeton University) was suggested. Cantril authored *Invasion from Mars* (a study in the psychology of panic, written about the famous Orson Welles radio broadcast in 1938) and has since performed advanced laboratory studies in the field of perception. The names of Don Marquis (University of Michigan) and Leo Roston were mentioned as possibly suitable as consultant psychologists.

Also, someone familiar with mass communications techniques, perhaps an advertising expert, would be helpful. Arthur Godfrey was mentioned as possibly a valuable channel of communication reaching a mass audience of certain levels. Dr. Berkner suggested the U.S. Navy (ONR) Special Devices Center, Sands Point, L. I., as a potentially valuable organization to assist in such an educational program. The teaching techniques used by this agency for aircraft identification during the past war [were] cited as an example of a similar educational task. The Jam Handy Co. which made World War II training films (motion picture and slide strips) was also suggested, as well as Walt Disney, Inc. animated cartoons.

Robbie Graham, a UFO researcher who has studied the many and varied intricacies of the Robertson Panel and its links to Disney and Ward Kimball, said in his 2011 article, "UFOs and Disney":

The panel's singling-out of Disney made sense given the animation giant's then firmly established working relationship with the US government: during World War II Disney made numerous propaganda shorts for the US military, and in the 1950s corporate and government sponsors helped the company produce films promoting President Eisenhower's "Atoms for Peace" policy, as well as the retrospectively hilarious Duck and Cover documentary, which depicted schoolchildren surviving an atomic attack by sheltering under their desks.

Graham continued in his article:

That the Robertson Panel highlighted Disney is significant in that the Panel's general recommendation to debunk UFOs through media channels is known to have been acted upon in at least one instance: this being the CBS TV broadcast of *UFOs: Friend, Foe, or Fantasy?* (1966), an anti-UFO documentary narrated by Walter Cronkite. In a letter addressed to former Robertson Panel Secretary Frederick C. Durant, Dr

The panel also concluded that "a public education campaign should be undertaken" on matters relative to UFOs.

Animation studio giant Walt Disney (left) stands with rocket engineer Wernher von Braun in this 1954 photo. Von Braun was a technical advisor on three Disney films about space exploration.

Thornton Page confided that he "helped organize the CBS TV show around the Robertson Panel conclusions," even though this was thirteen years after the Panel had first convened. In light of this case alone, it seems reasonable to assume that the government may at least have attempted to follow through on the Robertson Panel's Disney recommendation.

As for Ward Kimball, in 1979, he went public on certain aspects of Disney's links to the UFO conundrum and officialdom and stated that it wasn't just the CIA that Disney was working with when it came to UFOs. At some point during 1955 or 1956 Disney was contacted by representatives of the U.S. Air Force and was asked to secretly cooperate on a documentary about the UFO controversy. As part of the deal, the Air Force offered to supply actual UFO footage, which Disney was told it could include in its film.

According to Kimball, at that time it wasn't at all unusual for either Walt Disney or his studio to go along with the government's wishes—or, perhaps, demands might be a far more accurate term to use. Kimball revealed how, during the Second World War, the military practically took over Disney's Burbank facilities, where dozens of hours of military-training productions and war-effort films featuring Disney characters, like Donald Duck, were made.

The studio began work on the requested UFO documentary; animators were asked to imagine what an alien would look like; while Walt Disney himself eagerly waited for the Air Force to deliver the promised film of actual UFOs. At the last moment, however, the Air Force mysteriously withdrew the offer of the footage, and the planned documentary was canceled.

But, what all this does demonstrate is that Disney had a link to UFOs, the CIA, and secret projects—and specifically, and collectively, in a fashion that revolved around manipulating and controlling public opinion on, and perception of, all things of the flying saucer variety.

FROM NUCLEAR AIRCRAFT TO STOLEN BODIES: COLD WAR SECRETS

"On May 26, 1946, the U.S. Air Force awarded to the Fairchild Engine and Airplane Corporation a contract which established Fairchild as the responsible agency of the Nuclear Energy for Propulsion of Aircraft (NEPA) project. The purpose of the project was twofold: (1) to perform feasibility investigations and research leading toward the adaptation of nuclear energy to the propulsion of aircraft, and (2) to educate the aircraft engine industry in the field of nuclear science and its adaptation to aeronautical propulsion," wrote staff based at the Oak Ridge National Laboratory in Tennessee.

The content above is extracted from a lengthier, secret document that dealt with the feasibility of constructing a nuclear-powered aircraft, one that could be used in a showdown with the Soviets at the height of the Cold War. The content of the document is made particularly controversial for one specific reason. It makes it clear that the military was thinking of using human test-subjects—such as prisoners and even cadavers—in its nuclear experimentation.

In the late summer of 1946 there was a radical shake-up in the Nuclear Energy for Propulsion of Aircraft program. The contract that Fairchild had with the military did not live up to its expectations and was placed into the hands of General Electric, who insisted that the operations be carried out not at Oak Ridge, but at GE's plant in Ohio. More than a few Fairchild staff jumped ship and joined the new version of NEPA. Others, however, stayed at Oak Ridge, which—despite the severing of ties with Fairchild—had already made plans for a new project: the Aircraft Nuclear Program (ANP).

The biggest challenges that faced both NEPA and the ANP were the scientific and technological issues surrounding the development, construction, and deployment of nuclear-powered aircraft into the skies of our world. Could the crew be affected by very close proximity to a nuclear power-source? There were other challenges, too, and chiefly economic ones: Congress balked and frowned upon the ever-escalating costs, and particularly in light of the fact that missiles and supersonic planes were *already* demonstrating their significant worth. So, thought Congress, why are we even giving consideration to extremely costly, and potentially hazardous, nuclear aircraft? Congress's question was a fair and understandable one—to the extent that, not even one year into his presidency, President John F. Kennedy finally had the research programs into nuclear-powered aircraft shut down.

Test Area North (TAN), located in Butte County, Idaho, was used in the late 1950s to test the feasibility of creating a nuclear-powered aircraft. The project was discontinued in 1961.

Although official, and extensive, research into nuke planes went ahead, for around fifteen years before JFK closed it down, it is an acknowledged fact that dark and disturbing research was done on human beings, in an effort to understand and combat the potentially troublesome issues of exposing a crew to such a futuristic vehicle and power-plant. This is amply demonstrated in the papers of NEPA's Medical Advisory Committee, the MAC. A now-declassified June 1948 document (which can be inspected at the National Archives, Maryland) makes it very clear what was going through the minds of the scientists on the program:

> The NEPA Medical Advisory Committee is attempting to determine what will happen to humans exposed at infrequent times to amounts of radiations which are higher than those accepted as permissible for peace time operations. The Committee, with the exception of one member, feels that such information cannot be obtained by animal experiments nor by clinical observations.

MAC made another suggestion, or, as some might call it, an example of crossing the line that should never be crossed. MAC said: "The information sought is sufficiently important to justify the use of humans as experimental subjects."

It was then time for the entire scenario to tumble out. And what a hotbed of controversy it was, and as the official, previously top secret papers show: "The

Committee, therefore recommends, that the Armed Services arrange for and conduct unclassified experiments on man which will make possible the accurate prediction of biological changes resulting from known levels of radiation exposure."

Those very same "experiments on man" were aimed at using nothing less than prisoners then held in American jails:

> The Committee is not in a position to make recommendations as to where these tests can be conducted other than that they should be carried out at some federal, state, or Armed Services prison, where life prisoners are incarcerated and where arrangements can be made with the prison authorities to cooperate in the experiment. The selection of the prison is a matter for top military consideration. Continued cooperation of the prison staff and prisoners for a matter of many years will be required.

Actually, it didn't take years, at all. In fact, it wasn't even *one* year.

By early 1948, MAC's Subcommittee on Human Experimentation recommended that "the Armed Services arrange for and conduct unclassified experiments making possible accurate prediction of biological damage in man from known levels of radiation exposure."

Matters began to progress with speed. In June 1949, the Joint Panel on Medical Aspects of Atomic Warfare gave its support to the program. Four months later, every scientific agency, and arm of the military, that had a vested interest in seeing the nuclear aircraft program come to life was unanimous. An October 4, 1949, memo makes that starkly clear. Experiments on people, the author noted, were the "number one recommendation."

Everything was running smoothly until February 1950. That was when a significant percentage of staff at the Atomic Energy Commission Medical Group (CMG) grew worried about where things were potentially heading. In their eyes and minds, it was one thing to undertake research into the effects of nuclear aircraft on their crews. They saw it as quite another thing entirely, however, to consider, and give the go-ahead for, experiments to be undertaken on American citizens—even those incarcerated in American jails. Unfortunately for the rest of the people allied to the program, the CMG was a large and powerful body, one that, when it flexed its muscles and expressed its concern, was able to put everything into a definitive state of limbo.

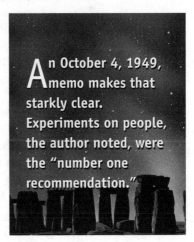

An October 4, 1949, memo makes that starkly clear. Experiments on people, the author noted, were the "number one recommendation."

The arguing went on until September, with many suggesting it was dangerous to go down the path of using human guinea-pigs—and without their consent and even knowledge, too—and just as many others offering that it was no big deal. Unless, that is, one happened to be just such a prisoner. It was in September that NEPA's staff began working on a recommendation-style document that would forcibly argue the need for the program to proceed, and also the need for human test-subjects to be found—and quickly, too.

Matters came to a head in December when NEPA noted that the only thing needed to end the stalemate would be for a major, powerful body to make a final decision, once and for all: "At the meeting of the NEPA Research Guidance Committee, it was recognized that unless AEC or some other highly influential agency recommends human experimentation, the NEPA proposal would never be carried out by the Armed Services."

In essence, this amounted to nothing less than a stern warning, combined with a final ultimatum. NEPA's Medical Advisory Committee also had its say, as a January 5, 1950, report—*Radiation Biology Relative to Nuclear Energy Powered Aircraft Recommendations to NEPA*—shows:

> For many reasons it is desirable that the aircraft carry a crew. This implies that the reactor will be surrounded with shielding adequate to protect the crew against radiations escaping from the reactor. It is necessary to determine the amount of radiation a human can reasonably tolerate in a given number of doses, at given repetition frequencies, and at given intensities, so that shield weights can be minimized. This knowledge is only partially available.

Despite the ultimatum, those against the human experimentation proceeding were unmoved. It was this stance that, on February 12, 1951, provoked M. C. Leverett, who was the technical director of the nuclear aircraft program, to send a memo to Dr. Shields Warren, the director of medicine and biology at the Atomic Energy Commission. It said:

> Dr. Warren,
>
> In connection with our work on Nuclear Powered Flight, we have as you know called together a group of highly qualified experts in the general field of radiology and the effects of radiation upon human beings, in order to assist us in defining the limiting exposure to which we should plan to subject the crew of a nuclear powered airplane.
>
> One of the actions taken by this group of experts was the formulation of a program of recommended research necessary, in their opinion, for adequate coverage of the radiobiological aspects of nuclear flight. Among the recommended research projects was the highly controversial one of human experimentation which this group strongly recommended and gave a position of highest priority.
>
> For almost two years the various members of this Committee have been making efforts to gain governmental approval of their recommendation regarding human experiments. These efforts have been largely unsuccessful and we and they have come finally to the conclusion that further efforts in this direction would be a waste of energy. We are therefore discontinuing our efforts to obtain governmental approval for experiments on humans along the lines recommended by our Advisory Committee.

While the NEPA experimentation did not proceed in the fashion that some dearly hoped it would, the same most certainly cannot be said for other agencies and programs. We know this, thanks to the work of the Advisory Committee on

Human Radiation Experiments (ACHRE), which was created in 1994, and whose staff uncovered the documents cited above and which are contained in its *Final Report: Advisory Committee on Human Radiation Experiments*:

> On 15 January 1994, President Clinton appointed the Advisory Committee on Human Radiation Experiments. The president created the Committee to investigate reports of possibly unethical experiments funded by the government decades ago.

> The members of the Advisory Committee were fourteen private citizens from around the country: a representative of the general public and thirteen experts in bioethics, radiation oncology and biology, nuclear medicine, epidemiology and biostatistics, public health, the history of science and medicine, and law.

> President Clinton asked us to deliver our recommendations to a Cabinet-level group, the Human Radiation Interagency Working Group, whose members are the Secretaries of Defense, Energy, Health and Human Services, and Veterans Affairs; the Attorney General; the Administrator of the National Aeronautics and Space Administration; the Director of Central Intelligence; and the Director of the Office of Management and Budget.

ACHRE continued:

> The controversy surrounding the plutonium experiments and others like them brought basic and crucial questions to the fore: How many experi-

This shop was located at Test Area North in Scoville, Idaho, and was used to produce machinery for the Aircraft Nuclear Propulsion program.

ments were conducted or sponsored by the government, and why? How many were secret? Was anyone harmed? What was disclosed to those subjected to risk, and what opportunity did they have for consent? By what rules should the past be judged? What remedies were due those who were wronged or harmed by the government in the past? How well do federal rules that today govern human experimentation work? What lessons can be learned from the experiments?

The President directed the Advisory Committee to uncover the history of human radiation experiments during the period 1944 through 1974. It was in 1944 that the first known human radiation experiment of interest was planned, and in 1974 that the Department of Health, Education and Welfare adopted regulations governing the conduct of human research; a watershed event in the history of federal protection for human subjects.

With the assistance of hundreds of federal officials and agency staff, the Committee retrieved and reviewed hundreds of thousands of government documents. Some of the most important documents were secret and were declassified at our request. Even after this extraordinary effort, the historical record remains incomplete. Some potentially important collections could not be located and were evidently lost or destroyed years ago.

Nevertheless, the documents that were recovered enabled us to identify nearly 4,000 human radiation experiments sponsored by the federal government between 1944 and 1974. In the great majority of cases, only fragmentary data was locatable and the identity of subjects and the specific radiation exposures involved were typically unavailable.

These case studies, said ACHRE, included:

1. Experiments with plutonium and other atomic bomb materials;
2. The Atomic Energy Commission's program of radioisotope distribution;
3. Non-therapeutic research on children;
4. Total body irradiation;
5. Research on prisoners;
6. Human experimentation in connection with nuclear weapons testing;
7. Intentional environmental releases of radiation;
8. Observational research involving uranium miners and residents of the Marshall Islands.

The testing, revealed ACHRE, was carried out largely to help advance research in "biomedical" fields, and to "advance national interests in defense or space exploration."

They continued:

The Atomic Energy Commission, the Defense Department and the National Institutes of Health recognized at an early date that research should proceed only with the consent of the human subject. The Committee found little evidence of rules or practices of consent except in research with completely healthy subjects. It was commonplace during the 1940s and 1950s for physicians to use patients as subjects of research without their awareness or consent.

Those who sponsored and undertook the experiments, said ACHRE, "are blameworthy for not having had policies and practices in place to protect the rights and interests of human subjects who were used in research from which the subjects could not possibly derive direct medical benefit."

ACHRE then made what was, quite possibly, its starkest comment of all:

Information about human experiments was kept secret out of concern for embarrassment to the government, potential legal liability, and worry that public misunderstanding would jeopardize government programs. There is no evidence that issues of fairness or concerns about exploitation in the selection of subjects figured in policies or rules of the period.

On the matter of the notorious Nuremberg trials that followed the end of the Second World War, the committee recorded the following:

It would be historically irresponsible, however, to rely solely on records related directly to the Nuremberg Medical Trial in evaluating the postwar scene in American medical research. The panorama of American thought and practice in human experimentation was considerably more complex than Ivy acknowledged on the witness stand in Nuremberg.

In general, it does seem that most American medical scientists probably sought to approximate the practices suggested in the Nuremberg Code and the AMA principles when working with "healthy volunteers."

Indeed, a subtle, yet pervasive, indication of the recognition during this period that consent should be obtained from healthy subjects was the widespread use of the term *volunteer* to describe such research participants.

Yet, as Advisory Committee member Susan Lederer has recently pointed out, the use of the word *volunteer* cannot always be taken as an indication that researchers intended to use subjects who had knowingly and freely agreed to participate in an experiment; it seems that researchers sometimes used *volunteer* as a synonym for *research subject*, with no special meaning intended regarding the decision of the participants to join in an experiment.

In the late 1940s American medical researchers seldom recognized that research with patient-subjects ought to follow the same principles as those applied to healthy subjects. Yet, some of those few who asked themselves hard questions about their research work with patients concluded that people who are ill are entitled to the same consideration as those who are not.

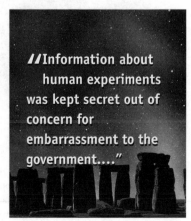

*//*Information about human experiments was kept secret out of concern for embarrassment to the government...."

That some did in fact reach this conclusion is evidence that it was not beyond the horizon of moral insight at that time. Nevertheless, they were a minority of the community of physician researchers, and the organized medical profession did not exhibit a willingness to reconsider its responsibilities to patients in the burgeoning world of postwar clinical research.

Of all the many and varied programs that ACHRE successfully uncovered, none were more controversial than one with the entirely innocent-sounding code name of Project Sunshine. On June 9, 1995, ACHRE completed a report for President Clinton titled *Documentary Update on Project Sunshine "Body Snatching."* Its contents are as shocking as they are revealing:

As part of Project Sunshine, which sought to measure strontium-90, the AEC [Atomic Energy Commission] engaged in an effort to collect the bones of human infants from domestic and foreign sources. As discussed in the prior memorandum, the project involved the use of a cover story (those without clearance being told that the skeleton collection would be used to study naturally occurring radiation, and not that from fallout). Key participants in Project Sunshine at its onset included the AEC's Division of Biology and Medicine (DBM), its Director John Bugher, Columbia University's Dr. J. Laurence Kulp, and the University of Chicago's Dr. Willard Libby (who became an AEC Commissioner).

Libby was the brains that led to Project Sunshine coming to full fruition. In the 1930s, he secured B.Sc. and Ph.D. degrees from the University of California and, at the height of the Second World War, worked on the Manhattan Project that led to the successful development of the atomic bomb. On October 1, 1954, Libby was made a member of the Atomic Energy Commission—at the specific request of President Dwight D. Eisenhower, no less. It's Libby's work on Project Sunshine that is of relevance to us, however.

ACHRE recorded:

A 1955 transcript classified as "secret" (located in the classified materials at the National Archives and recently declassified at the Committee's request), sheds more light on the role of tissue sampling in Project Sunshine. The transcript shows that considerable thought had been devoted to best ways to establish channels to procure "human samples," and the impact of secrecy on the effort. AEC Commissioner Willard Libby, who was a primary proponent of Project Sunshine, explained the great value of "body snatching," and noted that the AEC had even employed an "expensive law firm" to "look up the law of body snatching."

Dr. Willard Libby was a key participant in Project Sunshine. He was one of the developers of radiocarbon dating techniques and was also a member of the Atomic Energy Commission.

The meeting was then turned over to Dr. Libby, who was now an AEC commissioner. Dr. Libby began by stating that there was no effort more important to the AEC than Sunshine. "However, there are great gaps in the data." He explained: "By far the most important [gap] is human samples. We have been reduced to essentially zero level on the human samples. I don't know how to get them but I do say that it is a matter of prime importance to get them and particularly in the young age group.

"The supply of stillborns had evidently been shut off: We were fortunate, as you know to obtain a large number of still-borns as material. This supply, however, has now been cut off also, and shows no signs, I think, of being rejuvenated."

Therefore, Libby told the audience, expertise in "body snatching" would be highly valued: "So human samples are of prime importance and if anybody knows how to do a good job of body snatching, they will really be serving their country."

> **//[H]uman samples are of prime importance and if anybody knows how to do a good job of body snatching, they will really be serving their country."**

Libby recalled that when Project Sunshine was created in 1953, a law firm was hired to study this problem: "I don't know how to snatch bodies. In the original study on the Sunshine at Rand in the summer of 1953, we hired an expensive law firm to look up the law of body snatching. This compendium is available to you. It is not very encouraging. It shows you how very difficult it is going to be to do it legally."

The conferees discussed the need for a wide enough variety of samples to cover age ranges and potential variations among body parts. Dr. Kulp, from Columbia, explained that there were "channels." "We have the channels in these places where we are getting everything. We have three or four other leads where we could get complete age range samples from different other geographic localities. These three are Vancouver, Houston, and New York. We could easily get them from Puerto Rico and other places. We can get virtually everyone that dies in this range...."

Finally, there was discussion of the need for resources from other countries. Colonel Maxwell of the Armed Forces Special Weapons Project suggested the Armed Services could provide some help for specimens of the local population. The possibilities included Germany, a native hospital in Formosa, and the Navy unit in Cairo.

The document goes on and on, in similar, controversial fashion. ACHRE's findings on Project Sunshine—extracted from previously highly classified files—reference (a) "body snatching," (b) radiation experiments on what are described as "specimens" (people, of course), (c) the means by which "human samples" could be secretly obtained, and (d) particularly how those "in the young age group might be secured."

Those findings demonstrate the existence of one of the darkest and most disturbing programs ever established.

FAKING ALIENS: SCIENTOLOGY, SAUCERS, AND SYRINGES

A number of conspiracy theorists have suggested that one spin-off of the MKUltra mind-control experimentation began in the early 1950s: the development of a program to fabricate UFO incidents. In other words, the plan was to subject unwitting individuals to brain-warping and mind-altering technologies to see how effective they might be. One person who might have been subjected to this very technology was none other than L. Ron Hubbard, the brains behind the controversial cult of Scientology—whose beliefs are heavily influenced by matters of an extraterrestrial nature.

Under the terms of the Freedom of Information Act, the FBI has declassified hundreds of pages of formerly classified files on Hubbard and the Church of Scientology. One of those documents cited a letter that Hubbard penned to the FBI. It dealt with something very weird and downright disturbing.

According to the FBI, Hubbard told them that on February 23, 1951, "about two or three o'clock in the morning his apartment was entered. He was knocked out. A needle was thrust into his heart to produce a coronary thrombosis and he was given an electric shock. He said his recollection of this incident was now very blurred, that he had no witnesses and that the only other person who had a key to the apartment was his wife."

It was not long after this that Hubbard's belief in alien life grew to new, stratospheric proportions.

Interestingly, in the following year a man named Karl Hunrath—who hailed from Wisconsin—had a very similar experience to that of Hubbard. In July 1952, Hunrath complained to his local police department about something very weird indeed.

In the early hours of a Sunday morning in July, someone broke into Hunrath's home, injected his arm full of chemicals—which rendered him into a distinctly altered state of mind, and eerily paralleled the claims of L. Ron Hubbard one year earlier—and proceeded to tell him that he, Hunrath, had been chosen to play a significant role in the alien mission on Earth. A very groggy Hunrath could only look on amazed from his bed as the somewhat foreign-sounding—but perfectly human-appearing—alien told him: "I am Bosco. You have been chosen to enter our brotherhood of galaxies."

The files continue that the suit-and-tie-wearing Bosco advised Hunrath the brothers from beyond were deeply worried about our war-like ways, and so, as a result, action had to be taken against those dastardly elements of the human race who wanted to spoil everyone else's fun. There was not to be any *The Day the Earth Stood Still*-style ultimatum for one and all, however. No—The aliens wished to recruit sympathetic humans to aid their righteous cause.

Hunrath, like Hubbard, developed an interest in UFOs that became an obsession. Rather notably, on November 10, 1953, Hunrath, with a colleague named Wilbur Wilkinson, vanished. The pair took to the skies in a small, two-seater plane, from a small airport on the outskirts of Los Angeles. Neither man was ever seen again.

A science fiction novelist and founder of Scientology, L. Ron Hubbard once claimed he had been knocked out and drugged in 1951. It was after this incident that his obsession with aliens came about.

In late July 1953, just four months before he vanished, Hunrath booked a flight from Los Angeles back to his home state of Wisconsin. And after a brief stop in his home town of Racine, Hunrath drove the approximately fifty-mile journey to the city of Delavan, where he met with one Kenneth Goff, a man who was born there in 1914, and who spent his formative years growing up there, too.

Goff is described in now-declassified FBI files of May 6, 1955, as "a self-styled freelance Evangelist who for the past number of years has been speaking around the U.S. regarding the threat of communism to the U.S." Lectures that Goff routinely delivered to interested parties included: *Treason in our State Department*; *Should we use the Atom Bomb?*; *Red Secret Plot for Seizure of Denver*; and *Do the Reds Plan to Come by Alaska?*

As the FBI additionally noted: "Also, some of the titles of Goff's books, which he publishes voluminously, are: *Will Russia Invade America?*, *One World, A Red World*, and *Confessions of Stalin's Agent*." But, the FBI had other concerns about Goff. He had once been a rabid commie himself, and there were certain figures in the bureau who believed Goff was not quite the now-anti-communist that he professed to be. Rather, there was a suspicion that Goff had gone deep-cover and his red-hating ravings were merely a collective, ingenious ruse to camouflage his real intent: establishing networks of communist sympathizers across the United States.

The FBI certainly had a fine stash of material on Goff, who, it was recorded:

"… is a self-admitted former member of the Communist Party," and who "… was found guilty by jury trial on February 25, 1948, in United States District Court, District of Columbia, and was fined $100 as a result of the subject's placing anti-communist signs before the Soviet Embassy in Washington, D.C.

FBI files on Goff also noted:

The *Rocky Mountain News* on October 25, 1951, contained an article stating that three Englewood persons were ordered to appear in Denver Municipal Court as an aftermath of the ripping of the Soviet flag yesterday at Civic Center. Mr. and Mrs. Kenneth Goff were two of these three individuals.

Patriotic Americans might say that protesting outside the Soviet Embassy and tearing up the Soviet flag were very laudable actions for a U.S. citizen to undertake on home-turf at the height of the fraught and dicey Cold War. The FBI wasn't quite so sure, however: "It has been our concern that Goff always ensures he is seen while displaying anti-Soviet tendencies. [Deleted] has remarked that if Goff is still privately 'of a party mind' this might explain his public displays."

> There were certain figures in the Bureau who believed Goff was not quite the now-anti-communist that he professed to be.

Goff was certainly an interesting character and had made comments in the 1950s about communist-based plans to covertly introduce fluoride into the US water-supply, to create a "spirit of lethargy" in the nation. And: guess what? Goff had a deep interest in Flying Saucers. Indeed, one of Goff's regular lectures was titled: *Traitors in the Pulpit, or What's Behind the Flying Saucers—Are They from Russia, Another Planet, or God?* But it was not so much from the perspective of UFOs being alien or even Russian, however, that interested Goff. His concern was how the UFO subject could be utilized as a tool of manipulation and control by government.

In his 1959 publication *Red Shadows*, Goff offered the following to his readers—which, of course, secretly included the FBI:

During the past few years, the flying saucer scare has rapidly become one of the main issues, used by organizations working for a one-world government, to frighten people into the belief that we will need a super world government to cope with an invasion from another planet. Many means are being used to create a vast amount of imagination in the minds of the general public, concerning the possibilities of an invasion by strange creatures from Mars or Venus.

He continued:

This drive began early in the 40's, with a radio drama, put on by Orson Welles, which caused panic in many of the larger cities of the East, and resulted in the death of several people. The Orson Welles program of invasion from Mars was used by the Communist Party as a test to find out how the people would react on instructions given out over the radio. It was an important part of the Communist rehearsal for the Revolution.

The now-infamous Welles broadcast was, of course, based upon H.G. Wells's acclaimed novel *War of the Worlds*. And while, today, it is fashionable and almost *de rigueur* within ufological circles to suggest the conspiratorial and nefarious aspects the Orson Welles's broadcast and deep conspiracy go together hand-in-glove, it was far less so in the 1950s. Goff, then, was quite the prophet—and particularly so when one takes into consideration the fact that he had been mouthing off about *War of the Worlds*, a "one-world government," and a secret program to manipulate the public with staged UFO encounters as far back as 1951. Why 1951? Well, here's where things get even stranger.

In that very year of 1951, Goff—just like L. Ron Hubbard in 1951 and Karl Hunrath in 1952—got a visit in the middle of the night from a shadowy character who pumped his arm full of mind-expanding chemicals. In practically the same scenario that befell Hunrath, lo, a very smartly dressed human-looking alien did appear before an astonished Goff. It was one who wished Goff to spread the word that (a) communism was a very bad thing; and (b) ET hated Reds.

Goff might have been an odd character, but he was most certainly no fool. After the strange figure vanished and Goff finally regained all his senses, he recognized it simply could not have been a coincidence that he—with a fairly significant background in matters of a red nature—should have been warned about the perils of communism.

Coupled with his well-publicized fears about chemicals being introduced into the water supply to affect the mindset of the American populace, Goff—perhaps *very* astutely—came to believe that he had been targeted by some governmental agency that had, at its heart, a program involving (a) the creation of fabricated UFO-themed events; (b) the use of drugs to instill altered states in the targeted individual; and (c) a bigger picture of widespread manipulation and control of the populace via hoaxed UFO events—hence his absolute obsession with the whole *War of the Worlds*/ one world government issue.

The Goff-Hubbard links don't begin and end with late night shenanigans in the bedroom and needles in the arm. In 1955 the Church of Scientology published a booklet titled *Brain-Washing: A Synthesis of the Russian Textbook on Psychopolitics*. Supposedly, it was a summary of the work of one Lavrentiy Beria, a Soviet politician, marshal of the Soviet Union, and chief of the Soviet security and secret police apparatus (NKVD) under Joseph Stalin during the Second World War and Deputy Premier from 1946 to

One of Orson Welles's most famous productions was the 1938 broadcast of *War of the Worlds*, which illustrated how the public could be panicked by the idea of alien invaders.

1953. According to the Church of Scientology, rather intriguingly, *Brain-Washing* was distilled from a lengthy speech that Beria delivered in 1950 on the subject of none other than how psychiatry could be utilized as a tool of social control. Not everyone, however, is quite so sure that Beria had anything to do with it.

L. Ron Hubbard Jr. came straight to the point: "Dad wrote every word of it."

Even more interesting, the introduction to a version of *Brain-Washing* in the hands of Morris Kominsky—the author of *The Hoaxers: Plain Liars, Fancy Liars and Damned Liars*—was written by none other than Kenneth Goff.

Another version attributes the *entire* work to Goff, despite the fact that the document is filled with what is clearly evidence of Hubbard's very own writing style and references to Dianetics. Clearly, then, Goff and Hubbard were somehow inter-connected. Kenneth Goff died in 1972 while still only in his late fifties.

Given that Hubbard, Goff, and Hunrath were all subjected to nighttime visitations from individuals who injected chemicals of who knows what kind into their arms—and that all three men subsequently became well-known players within the arena of UFO research—this begs an important question: are shadowy forces, whose agenda is to roll in a New World Order, intent on using a non-existing alien threat to control each and every one of us, just as Kenneth Goff believed was going to, one day, happen?

THE BROOKINGS REPORT: CLOSE ENCOUNTER IMPLICATIONS

In the December 1960 / January 1961 issue of the *NICAP UFO Investigator* journal, a small article was published under the heading of "Space-Life Report Could be Shock." It read as follows:

> The discovery of intelligent space beings could have a severe effect on the public, according to a research report released by the National Aeronautics and Space Administration. The report warned that America should prepare to meet the psychological impact of such a revelation.

> The 190-page report was the result of a $96,000 one-year study conducted by the Brookings Institution for NASA's long-range study committee.

> Public realization that intelligent beings live on other planets could bring about profound changes, or even the collapse of our civilization, the research report stated. "Societies sure of their own place have disintegrated when confronted by a superior society," said the NASA report. "Others have survived even though changed. Clearly, the better we can come to understand the factors involved in responding to such crises the better prepared we may be."

> Although the research group did not expect any immediate contact with other planet beings, it said that the discovery of intelligent space races "could nevertheless happen at any time."

NICAP—the National Investigations Committee on Aerial Phenomena, which was a public UFO research study group—continued:

> Even though the UFO problem was not indicated as a reason for the study, it undoubtedly was an important factor. Fear of public reaction to an admission of UFO reality was cited as the main reason for secrecy in the early years of the AF [Air Force] investigation.

> Radio communication probably would be the first proof of other intelligent life, said the NASA report. It added: "Evidences of its existence might also be found in artifacts left on the moon or other planets."

> NICAP further noted that the document gave weight to "... previous thinking by scholars who have suggested that the earth already may be under close scrutiny by advanced space races." In 1958, Prof. Harold D.

Lasswell of the Yale Law School stated: "The implications of the UFOs may be that we are already viewed with suspicion by more advanced civilizations and that our attempts to gain a foothold elsewhere may be rebuffed as a threat to other systems of public order."

NICAP concluded:

The NASA warning of a possible shock to the public, from the revelation of more advanced civilizations, supports NICAP's previous arguments against AF [Air Force] secrecy about UFOs. All available information about UFOs should be given to the public now, so that we will be prepared for any eventuality.

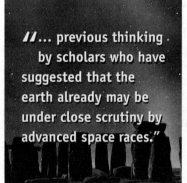

// ... previous thinking by scholars who have suggested that the earth already may be under close scrutiny by advanced space races."

The document to which NICAP was referring was titled *Proposed Studies on the Implications of Peaceful Space Activities for Human Affairs*. It was a document written by an employee of the Brookings Institution named Donald N. Michael. The report was contracted by the Committee on Long Range Studies, which was an arm of NASA. The document was completed and provided to the House of Representatives in the 87th U.S. Congress on April 18, 1961.

More than half a century after it was completed, the document is still noted for its intriguing and controversial content, much of which has potential impact on the UFO phenomenon. One of the most notable entries reads:

While face-to-face meetings with it will not occur within the next twenty years (unless its technology is more advanced than ours, qualifying it to visit earth), artifacts left at some point in time by these life forms might possibly be discovered through our space activities on the Moon, Mars, or Venus.

It has been suggested by UFO theorists that this "artifacts" statement might imply Brookings and NASA had already uncovered data on—and secured photographs of—the controversial "Face on Mars," which is discussed in an earlier chapter. The report then makes what can only be interpreted as a thinly veiled threat, regarding what the future might bring, if the presence of intelligent, extraterrestrial life in our midst was confirmed:

Anthropological files contain many examples of societies, sure of their place in the universe, which have disintegrated when they have had to associate with previously unfamiliar societies espousing different ideas and different life ways; others that survived such an experience usually did so by paying the price of changes in values and attitudes and behavior.

On this very issue, in 2004 Mac Tonnies told me, in a personal interview:

If our own history is any example, technologically robust civilizations inevitably subsume less sophisticated cultures, not merely by violently dismantling them, but by introducing a virulent strain of apathy. The infamous Brookings report to NASA, recommending that the discovery of extraterrestrial artifacts be covered up for fear of paralyzing research and development enterprises, stands as perhaps the most explicit elucidation of this idea.

The Michaels paper continued:

Since intelligent life might be discovered at any time via the radio telescope research presently under way, and since the consequences of such a discovery are presently unpredictable because of our limited knowledge of behavior under even an approximation of such dramatic circumstances, two research areas can be recommended:

Continuing studies to determine emotional and intellectual understanding and attitudes—and successive alterations of them if any—regarding the possibility and consequences of discovering intelligent extraterrestrial life.

> //Anthropological files contain many examples of societies, sure of their place in the universe, which have disintegrated when they have had to associate with previously unfamiliar societies...."

Historical and empirical studies of the behavior of peoples and their leaders when confronted with dramatic and unfamiliar events or social pressures. Such studies might help to provide programs for meeting and adjusting to the implications of such a discovery. Questions one might wish to answer by such studies would include: How might such information, under what circumstances, be presented to or withheld from the public for what ends? What might be the role of the discovering scientists and other decision makers regarding release of the fact of discovery?

The questions were many. Granted they were theoretical, but they provoked raised eyebrows and concerned thoughts within NASA and the U.S. government.

An individual's reactions to such a radio contact, said Brookings, "would in part depend on his cultural, religious, and social background, as well as on the actions of those he considered authorities and leaders, and their behavior, in turn, would in part depend on their cultural, social, and religious environment."

And, as the Brookings team also noted:

The discovery would certainly be front-page news everywhere; the degree of political or social repercussion would probably depend on leadership's interpretation of (1) its own role, (2) threats to that role, and (3) national and personal opportunities to take advantage of the disruption or reinforcement of the attitudes and values of others. Since leadership itself might have great need to gauge the direction and intensity of public attitudes, to strengthen its own morale and for decision making purposes, it would be most advantageous to have more to go on than personal opinions about the opinions of the public and other leadership groups.

Brookings noted an important issue that the conformation of alien life might have on the human race, as a whole:

The Brookings Institution is a private, nonprofit organization located in Washington, D.C., that researches and writes studies that influence public policy.

The knowledge that life existed in other parts of the universe might lead to a greater unity of men on earth, based on the "oneness" of man or on the age-old assumption that any stranger is threatening. Much would depend on what, if anything, was communicated between man and the other beings.

One of the most controversial issues that occupied Brookings was that relative to the impact that the existence of alien life would have on the world of religion:

The positions of the major American religious denominations, the Christian sects, and the Eastern religions on the matter of extraterrestrial life need elucidation. Consider the following: "The Fundamentalist (and anti-science) sects are growing apace around the world. For them, the discovery of other life—rather than any other space product—would be electrifying. Some scattered studies need to be made both in their home centers and churches and their missions, in relation to attitudes about space activities and extraterrestrial life."

If plant life or some subhuman intelligence were found on Mars or Venus, for example, there is on the face of it no good reason to suppose these discoveries, after the original novelty had been exploited to the fullest and worn off, would result in substantial changes in perspectives or philosophy in large parts of the American public, at least any more than, let us say, did the discovery of the coelacanth or the panda.

The matter of extraterrestrial existence, and specifically its impact on religion, was still impacting on NASA in the 2000s. As evidence of this, in November 2009, NASA announced:

This past week in Rome as part of the International Year of Astronomy, the Pontifical Academy of Sciences hosted a Study Week on Astrobiology. Their discussion ranges from what it would mean to the Church if alien life were found, to whether or not science needs religion.

This final sentence, from NASA's November 2009 press release, is highly significant, since it extremely closely echoes the words and recommendations of the Brookings report of 1960.

The human race stood a very good chance of having its collective ego bruised by a close encounter with aliens, Brookings advised NASA:

If super intelligence is discovered, the results become quite unpredictable. It is possible that if the intelligence of these creatures were sufficiently superior to ours, they would choose to have little if any contact with us. On the face of it, there is no reason to believe that we might learn a great deal from them, especially if their physiology and psychology were substantially different from ours.

Ironically, Brookings noted, those most likely to be "devastated" by the discovery of extraterrestrial life might not be the general public but the scientific community—the very people looking for the aliens. Brookings explained its stance on this matter:

> It has been speculated that, of all groups, scientists and engineers might be the most devastated by the discovery of relatively superior creatures, since these professions are most clearly associated with the mastery of nature, rather than with the understanding and expression of man. Advanced understanding of nature might vitiate all our theories at the very least, if not also require a culture and perhaps a brain inaccessible to earth scientists.
>
> It is perhaps interesting to note that when asked what the consequences of the discovery of superior life would be, an audience of *Saturday Review* readership chose, for the most part, not to answer the question at all, in spite of their detailed answers to many other speculative questions.
>
> A possible but not completely satisfactory means for making the possibility "real" for many people would be to confront them with present speculations about the I.Q. of the porpoise and to encourage them to expand on the implications of this situation.
>
> Such studies would include historical reactions to hoaxes, psychic manifestations, unidentified flying objects, etc. Hadley Cantril's study, *Invasion from Mars* (Princeton University Press, 1940), would provide a useful if limited guide in this area. Fruitful understanding might be gained from a comparative study of factors affecting the responses of primitive societies to exposure to technologically advanced societies. Some thrived, some endured, and some died.

It is, perhaps, this final sentence that humankind had—and still has—the most to worry about. If extraterrestrials—friendly or hostile—one day show themselves to us, en masse, there is a very good chance that, as the Brookings report noted all those decades ago, from a psychological perspective we might not survive the encounter, at least not intact. This is one of the reasons why Brookings made what turned out to be its most controversial statement of all. It was a statement that said NASA should think very carefully about not *when* it should reveal, to the public, the truth about confirmed alien visitation, but *if* it should do so.

//It has been speculated that, of all groups, scientists and engineers might be the most devastated by the discovery of relatively superior creatures...."

Given that events such as the infamous Roswell UFO crash of July 1947 remain enveloped by a wide and thick cloak of secrecy, one can make a valid argument that the decision to deny the public the truth of Roswell may have been, in part or in whole, influenced by the words, comments, and conclusions of Brookings.

MARILYN MONROE: DRIVEN TO DEATH

There can be no doubt that when it comes to Hollywood legends, they don't get more legendary than Marilyn Monroe, the ultimate blond bombshell. Born in 1925, she became one of the biggest stars of Hollywood's Golden Age, starring in such hit movies as *Bus Stop*, *Some Like It Hot*, and *Gentlemen Prefer Blondes*. With worldwide fame, millions of adoring fans, and a lifestyle that saw her mixing with the rich, the famous, and the leading lights of both Hollywood and the world of politics, Monroe's life should have been a dream. It was, however, more like a nightmare: failed marriages, depression, anxiety, a fragile state of mind, and a cast of characters who used and abused Monroe, were all parts of the short life of the famous star—one whose life tragically came to an end at just thirty-six. It was a death that, more than half a century after it occurred, still provokes a mass of debate.

That Monroe is acknowledged to have had affairs with both President John F. Kennedy and his brother Robert Kennedy (the attorney general under JFK), has led to suspicions that she was murdered as a result of certain, top secret data shared with her by the Kennedy brothers—as a means to impress her into the bedroom, before being callously dumped. There's no doubt that Monroe was a prestigious keeper of journals—one of which, dubbed "The Red Book," reportedly contained the facts surrounding a wealth of data on everything from the U.S. government's plans to invade Cuba, a CIA-Mafia connection, attempts to have Cuba's Fidel Castro assassinated, and even crashed UFOs and dead aliens—all provided by the recklessly talkative Kennedy boys.

If Marilyn Monroe was considered a potential security threat for what she knew, surely we should see some evidence of it, correct? Yes, correct. And we do see that evidence—thanks to the Freedom of Information Act. Now available, but previously classified, documents reveal that as far back as 1955 both the FBI and the CIA were watching Monroe closely. It was all as a result of the fact that, in the very same year, she applied for a visa to visit the former Soviet Union.

The FBI's files also show that J. Edgar Hoover was keeping watch on all the many and varied rumors of links between Monroe and both JFK and RFK. Her links to mob buddy Frank Sinatra were also secretly noted by officialdom—and were frowned upon, too. Doubtless, the official, secret surveillance of Marilyn would have continued, had something not intervened. That "something" was her death, on August 5, 1962.

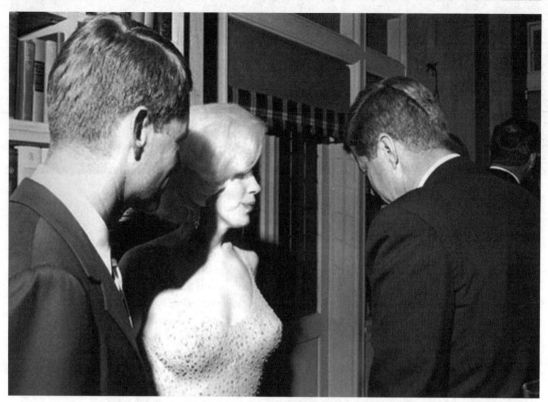

Actress Marilyn Monroe (center) is seen in this May 19, 1962, photo with U.S. attorney general Robert Kennedy (left) and President John F. Kennedy (right). It was believed that Monroe knew a great many government secrets that the Kennedys divulged to her, and that that might be why she was killed.

Despite extensive investigations, the passing of Marilyn Monroe remains the enigma it was back in 1962. The story begins on August 4, one day before the actress's death. The afternoon was taken up by a visit to Monroe's Brentwood, Los Angeles home by her psychiatrist, Dr. Ralph Greenson. He was attempting to get Monroe out of her depressive state of mind. A few hours later, at around 7.00 P.M., Monroe chatted on the phone with Joe DiMaggio Jr. (the son of her former husband, and baseball legend, Joe DiMaggio) and was, said DiMaggio Jr. in a good frame of mind. Not long after that, the actor Peter Lawford invited Marilyn over to his house for dinner. She chose not to go. Lawford was reportedly concerned by Monroe's stoned, slurry tones and decided to call her again later. This is where things become confusing—and potentially conspiratorial.

So the story goes—Lawford tried to reach Monroe several times again that night—all to no avail. He was, however, able to speak with her housekeeper, Eunice Murray, who assured Lawford that all was well. He was not so sure. Murray would later state that at roughly 10.00 P.M. she saw a light coming from Monroe's bedroom but heard nothing, and assumed the actress had fallen asleep and left the light on.

Around half an hour later, rumors were circulating that Marilyn had overdosed, something confirmed by Monroe's lawyer, Mickey Rudin, and her publicist, Arthur P. Jacobs. The nail in the coffin came at approximately 1.00 A.M. when Peter Lawford got a call from Rudin, stating the star was dead. That is somewhat curious, however, as at 3.00 A.M.—two hours later—Eunice Murray reportedly tried to wake Monroe by knocking on the bedroom door and the French windows.

Dr. Greenson was soon on the scene again, having been phoned by Murray; he quickly smashed the windows to gain entry. Sure enough, the world's most famous blond was no more. The police soon arrived to a scene filled with confusion and suspicious activity. Murray was hastily washing the bed sheets when the investigating officers descended on Marilyn's home. Both Greenson and Murray made changes to their stories, specifically in regard to who called who and when, and in relation to the particular time at which they believed she died—around 4.00 A.M. This was completely at odds with the conclusion of the undertaker, Guy Hockett, who put the time of death at around 9.30 P.M., a significant number of hours earlier. On top of that, pathologist Dr. Thomas Noguchi was suspicious of the fact that even if Monroe had taken an overdose—of what was deemed to be Nembutal—she had not swallowed it, via a glass of water, for example. A study of her intestines demonstrated that. How the drugs got into the system of the actress remained a puzzle. Actually, everything remained a puzzle—and it pretty much still does.

Marilyn Monroe was laid to rest on August 8, 1962, at the Los Angeles, California-based Westwood Village Memorial Park Cemetery. Was her death due to a combination of her fragile state of mind, anger, and turmoil at the way the Kennedy brothers treated her, and overwhelming depression? Such a scenario isn't impossible. It's worth noting, however, that not long after Marilyn's death, the FBI received something startling, something that was not declassified until decades later, and that shed shocking new light on the strange saga.

One of the most fascinating—and deeply controversial—pieces of documentation that has surfaced concerning the death of Marilyn Monroe originated with an unknown individual who the FBI identified, in its now declassified dossier on the Hollywood legend, as a "former Special Agent, who is currently Field Representative, Appointment Section, Governor's Office, State of California."

Written and sent to the FBI in 1963, its contents are eye-opening in the extreme, since they suggest that the attorney general, himself, Bobby Kennedy, was involved in a plot to "induce" Monroe's suicide. The lengthy document to the FBI begins as follows:

A fan left these flowers at the crypt of Marilyn Monroe at Westwood Village Memorial Park Cemetery in Los Angeles, California.

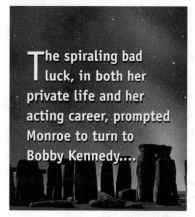

The spiraling bad luck, in both her private life and her acting career, prompted Monroe to turn to Bobby Kennedy....

Robert Kennedy had been having a romance and sex affair over a period of time with Marilyn Monroe. He had met her, the first date being arranged by his sister and brother-in-law, Mr. and Mrs. Peter Lawford. Robert Kennedy had been spending much time in Hollywood during the last part of 1961 and early 1962, in connection with his trying to have a film made of his book dealing with the crime investigations. He used to meet with producer Jerry Wald. He was reported to be intensely jealous of the fact that they had been making a film of John F. Kennedy's book of the PT boat story.

The unidentified special agent of the FBI continued that RFK was "deeply involved emotionally" with Marilyn Monroe, and had repeatedly promised to divorce his wife to marry Marilyn. Eventually, however, she realized that Bobby had no intention of marrying her, at all—and almost certainly never had any such plans. Adding to that woe was the fact that, as the Bureau was also informed,

> ... about this time, 20th Century Fox studio had decided to cancel [Monroe's] contract. She had become very unreliable, being late for set, etc. In addition, the studio was in financial difficulty due to the large expenditures caused in the filming of "Cleopatra." The studio notified Marilyn that they were canceling her contract. This was right in the middle of a picture she was making. They decided to replace her with actress Lee Remick.

The spiraling bad luck, in both her private life and her acting career, prompted Monroe to turn to Bobby Kennedy yet again, even though it was clear to her that the relationship was doomed to go nowhere. It was a decision that may well have cost Marilyn her life, as the words of the FBI's confidante demonstrate:

> Marilyn telephoned Robert Kennedy from her home at Brentwood, California, person-to-person, at the Department of Justice, Washington, D.C. to tell him the bad news. Robert Kennedy told her not to worry about the contract—he would take care of everything. When nothing was done, she again called him from her home to the Department of Justice, person-to-person, and on this occasion they had unpleasant words.

> She was reported to have threatened to make their affair public. On the day that Marilyn died, Robert Kennedy was in town, and registered at the Beverly Hills Hotel. By coincidence, this is across the street from the house in which a number of years earlier his father, Joseph Kennedy, had lived for a time, common-law, with Gloria Swanson.

It was at this point in the informant's story that things turned decidedly dark. Hardly surprising, since he outlined something controversial in the extreme: a cold-hearted plot to manipulate Marilyn Monroe into taking her own life. It began like this, FBI documents state:

> Peter Lawford knew from Marilyn's friends that she often made suicide threats and that she was inclined to fake a suicide attempt in order to

arouse sympathy. Lawford is reported as having made a "special arrangement" with Marilyn's psychiatrist, Dr. Ralph Greenson, of Beverly Hills. The psychiatrist was treating Marilyn for emotional problems and getting her off the use of barbiturates. On her last visit to him, he prescribed [illegible] tablets, and gave her a prescription for 60 of them, which was unusual in quantity, especially since she saw him frequently.

That "special arrangement" had one goal: the death of the Hollywood goddess. The statement to the FBI continued:

[Monroe's] housekeeper put the bottle of pills on the night table. It is reported the housekeeper and Marilyn's personal secretary and press agent, Pat Newcombe, were cooperating in the plan to induce suicide. Pat Newcombe was rewarded for her cooperation by being put on the head of the Federal payroll as top assistant to George Stevens, Jr., head of the Motion Pictures Activities Division of the U.S. Information Service. His father, George Stevens, Sr., is a left-wing Hollywood director, who is well known for specializing in the making of slanted and left-wing pictures. One of these was the "Diary of Anne Frank."

On the day of Marilyn's death, said the "former Special Agent," Robert Kennedy checked out of the Beverly Hills Hotel and flew from Los Angeles International Airport via Western Airlines to San Francisco, where he checked into the St. Francis Hotel, the owner of the hotel being a Mr. London, a friend of Robert Kennedy. From there, Kennedy phoned Peter Lawford "to find out if Marilyn was dead yet."

FBI records reveal what reportedly happened next:

Peter Lawford had called Marilyn's number and spoke with her, and then checked again later to make sure she did not answer. Marilyn expected to have her stomach pumped out and to get sympathy through her suicide attempt. The psychiatrist left word for Marilyn to take a drive in the fresh air, but did not come to see her until after she was known to be dead.

Marilyn received a call from Joe DiMaggio, Jr., who was in the U.S. Marines, stationed at Camp Pendleton, California. They were very friendly. Marilyn told him she was getting very sleepy. The last call she attempted to make was to Peter Lawford to return a call he had made to her. Joe DiMaggio, Sr., knows the whole story and is reported to have stated when Robert Kennedy gets out of office, he intends to kill him. [Deleted] knew of the affair between Robert Kennedy and Marilyn.

Marilyn Monroe's body was found in her home in Brentwood, California. She had no clothes on, which added to the gossip that she and Robert Kennedy were having an affair.

The story was not over—however, in fact far from it. The FBI's source had far more to add:

> While Robert Kennedy was carrying on his sex affair with Marilyn Monroe, on a few occasions, John F. Kennedy came out and had sex parties with [deleted], an actress. Chief of Police Parker, of the Los Angeles Police Department, has the toll call tickets obtained from the telephone company on the calls made from Marilyn's residence telephone. They are in his safe at Los Angeles Headquarters.

From there, things got even more controversial:

> Florabel Muir, the columnist, has considerable information and knowledge of the Robert F. Kennedy and Marilyn Monroe affair. She personally saw the telephone call records. Marilyn Monroe's psychiatrist, although he knew she had taken the pills, did not come to her home until after she was dead. He made contact with the coroner and an arrangement was made for a psychiatric board of inquiry to be appointed by the coroner, an unheard of procedure in the area. This was so the findings could be recorded that she was emotionally unbalanced. It was reported this arrangement was to discredit any statements she may have made before she died.

> During the period of time that Robert F. Kennedy was having his sex affair with Marilyn Monroe, on one occasion a sex party was conducted at which several other persons were present. Tape recording was secretly made and is in the possession of a Los Angeles private detective agency. The detective wants $5,000 for a certified copy of the recording, in which all the voices are identifiable.

We may never know for sure to what extent the data provided to the FBI was acted upon—even if at all. We can say one thing for certain, however—just as with the deaths of JFK, Robert Kennedy, and Martin Luther King, nagging suspicions remain that the official explanation may not be the correct explanation.

THE JFK ASSASSINATION: WHODUNNIT?

In the slightly more than half a century that has now passed since President John F. Kennedy was shot and killed in Dealey Plaza, Dallas, Texas, on November 22, 1963, a wealth of theories has been put forward to explain the death of the only man to whom Marilyn Monroe sang, or rather purred, "Happy Birthday." Those theories range from plausible to paranoid and bizarre to out of this world.

On November 29, 1963, an investigation began that still provokes huge debate in conspiracy-themed circles, decades after JFK bought the bullet(s). The ten-month-long study was undertaken by the President's Commission on the Assassination of President Kennedy. Or, as it is far better, and unofficially, known: the Warren Commission—which took its name from its chairman, Chief Justice Earl Warren.

The commission's job was to get to the bottom of the big question that everyone was itching to see answered: who *really* shot JFK? According to the Warren Commission, it was Lee Harvey Oswald. And it was *only* Oswald. Not everyone agreed with that controversial conclusion, however.

In 1978, fourteen years after the Warren Commission laid all the blame firmly on the shoulders of Oswald, the U.S. House Select Committee on Assassinations came to a different conclusion. The lone gunman, said the committee, was not such a lone gunman, after all. President Kennedy's death was the result of nothing less than a full-on conspiracy.

The HSCA agreed with the Warren Commission that Kennedy was killed by Oswald and no one else. The committee went one step further, however, by concluding that Oswald was not the only gunman prowling around Dallas on that deadly day.

Forensic analysis suggested to the HSCA's investigators that *four* shots rang out, not the three that the Warren Commission attributed to Oswald. That's to say there was another gunman. In the minds of the HSCA's staff, this mysterious second character completely missed his target. Nevertheless, a pair of shooters meant a conspiracy was at the heart of the JFK assassination. In other words: take that, Warren Commission.

Was JFK the victim of both an assassin and friendly fire? Two men, totally unconnected to each other, but who, in a strange set of circumstances, ultimately

This photo was taken of President Kennedy and the First Lady just before the assassination in Dallas, Texas, on November 22, 1963.

sealed the fate of the president? This was the theory postulated in a 1992 book, *Mortal Error: The Shot That Killed JFK*, by Bonar Menninger.

The scenario presented by Menninger had Oswald as the chief culprit, but not the only one. George Hickey was a Secret Service agent travelling in the vehicle immediately following the presidential car. After the bullets fired by Oswald slammed into JFK, Menninger suggested, Hickey accidentally discharged his weapon, delivering the fatal head-shot that killed Kennedy.

In 1992, when *Mortal Error* was published, Hickey was still alive. He was not pleased to see himself portrayed as the second gunman in the Kennedy assassination. Unfortunately for Hickey, he let three years pass before trying to take legal action against the publisher, St. Martin's Press.

U.S. District Court judge Alexander Harvey II dismissed the defamation case on the grounds that Hickey had waited too long to file suit. In 1998, however, Hickey received an undisclosed sum of money from St. Martin's Press that led Hickey's attorney, Mark S. Zaid, to state: "We're very satisfied with the settlement."

Prior to his death in 1976, Johnny Roselli was a notorious and much feared figure in the Chicago, Illinois, Mafia. His influence and power extended to the heart of tinsel-town and the slots and tables of Vegas. In 1960, Roselli was quietly contacted by a man named Robert Maheu, a former employee of the CIA and the FBI.

A startling proposal was put to Roselli. The CIA, Maheu explained, wanted Roselli's help in taking care of Fidel Castro. In mob-speak, "taking care of" meant "whacking." Thus was born a controversial program that saw the CIA and the mob work together, hand in glove.

As history has shown, Roselli and his goons never did take out Castro. But, say conspiracy theorists, they may have ended the life of JFK, with help from the CIA. The mob was no fan of the Kennedy administration. Robert Kennedy, as U.S. attorney general, went after the Mafia in definitive witch-hunt style. Did the mob decide to return the favor? Maybe it did.

Following Kennedy's killing, Roselli and a number of other mobsters, including Santo Trafficante Jr. and Carlos Marcello, were suspected of having been implicated. Even the House Select Committee on Assassinations admitted there were "credible associations relating both Lee Harvey Oswald and Jack Ruby to figures having a relationship, albeit tenuous, with Marcello's crime family or organization."

Just perhaps, it's not such a whacked-out theory, after all.

JFK taken out of circulation to prevent him from revealing the truth about what really crashed at Roswell, New Mexico, in 1947? So say UFO researchers, who said that on getting elected in 1960, JFK got the lowdown on all-things E.T.-based in a secret briefing from the CIA: "Bad news, Mr. President: E.T. is real. Worse news: he really doesn't like us." Kennedy was determined to warn the public of the alien menace. A secret and ruthless cabal in the heart of officialdom, however, was having none of it. The president had to go before he spilled the bug-eyed beans. It sounds crazy. But even crazier, the JFK assassination really *is* littered with characters who were tied to the strange world of flying saucers.

Back in 1947, a man named Fred Crisman claimed to have recovered debris from an exploded UFO in Tacoma, Washington. Crisman also alluded to having worked for decades as a deep-cover agent with U.S. Intelligence. Jim Garrison was New Orleans's district attorney from 1961 to 1973 and the man portrayed by Kevin Costner in Oliver Stone's *JFK*. In 1968, Garrison subpoenaed Crisman while investigating JFK's death. The reason: Crisman had connections to a CIA asset believed by many researchers to have been linked to the killing of Kennedy. His name was Clay Shaw. The case against Shaw collapsed and Crisman breathed a big sigh of relief.

Guy Bannister, a retired FBI agent at the time of the JFK assassination, was also linked to Clay Shaw by Garrison. As the Freedom of Information Act has shown, Bannister undertook numerous UFO investigations for the FBI in 1947. There's even a Lee Harvey Oswald connection. In October 1962, Oswald went to work for a Texas-based company called Jaggars-Chiles-Stovall. It undertook classified photo analysis connected to the CIA's U-2 spy plane program. Where was

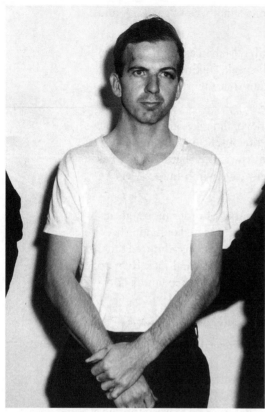

Lee Harvey Oswald took the fall for killing President Kennedy. He was shot dead by Jack Ruby two days after the Kennedy assassination.

the U-2 developed? Area 51, that's where. And we all know what goes on out there, right?

One of the oddest theories concerning the Kennedy assassination tumbled out in the pages of a 1975 book, *Appointment in Dallas*. It was written by Hugh McDonald, formerly of the LAPD. According to McDonald, Oswald was indeed a patsy, but in a very strange fashion.

Oswald was supposedly told, by shadowy sources, that his expertise was needed in Dallas on November 22, 1963. But Oswald wasn't required to kill the president. Quite the contrary, Oswald was told to ensure all his bullets *missed* JFK.

The operation, Oswald was assured, was designed to demonstrate how inadequate the Secret Service was by staging a mock-assassination attempt of the president. Unbeknownst to Oswald, however, a team of *real* assassins was in Dealey Plaza. Their bullets, however, did not miss.

The gunmen made quick exits, leaving Oswald as the man guaranteed to take the fall—simply because he really *did* fire bullets across Dealey Plaza. A panicked Oswald, realizing he had been set up, fled the scene, thus setting in motion the wheels that led to his arrest and death.

Forget Oswald. JFK was killed by the man behind the wheel, in full view of the people of Dallas and thousands of cameras. That was the outrageous claim of one of the most vocal conspiracy theorists of the 1980s and 1990s. His name was Milton William "Bill" Cooper.

The man who Cooper fingered as the guilty party was William Greer, a Secret Service agent who drove the presidential limousine on the day that JFK was destined not to leave Dallas alive. When shots echoed around Dealey Plaza, Greer slowed the car down and turned back to look at the president. For Cooper, Greer's actions were not due to confusion caused by the chaos breaking out all around him. No. Cooper claimed that analysis of the famous footage taken by Abraham Zapruder, on the Grassy Knoll on November 22, showed Greer pointing some form of device at JFK.

That device, Cooper maintained to anyone who would listen, was nothing less than a sci-fi-style weapon developed by government personnel that had acquired the technology from extraterrestrials.

By the time Cooper got on his rant, which began in the late 1980s, Greer wasn't around to defend himself. He passed away in 1985 from cancer, having retired from the Secret Service in 1966 as a result of problems caused by a stomach ulcer.

In a strange piece of irony, Cooper himself died by the bullet. In the summer of 1998, he was formerly charged with tax evasion. Cooper told the government where to go and what to do. What the government did, on November 5, 2001, was to dispatch deputies to Cooper's Arizona home. A shoot-out soon erupted. Cooper, like JFK, was soon full of lead.

In October 1959, Lee Harvey Oswald—a self-admitted Marxist—made his way to the Soviet Union. Oswald reached Moscow on October 16 and announced that he wished to remain in Russia. Although the Soviets were, initially, reluctant

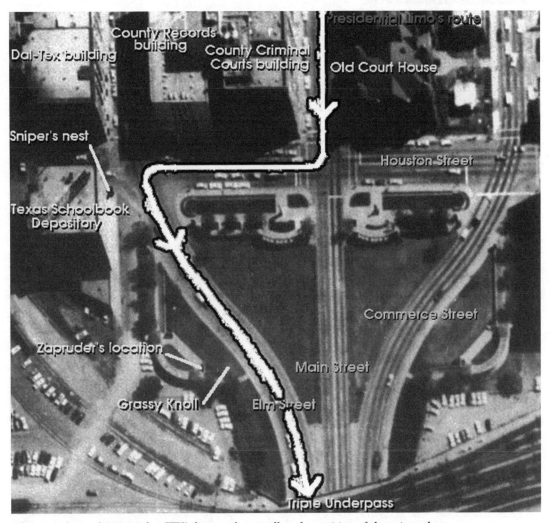

This map shows the route that JFK's limo took, as well as the position of the sniper, the Grassy Knoll, and where Abraham Zapruder was standing when he shot the film.

Khrushchev was determined to exact his revenge. Oswald was chosen to ensure that revenge was achieved.

to allow Oswald residency, that soon changed. It wasn't long before Oswald had a job and a home. In 1961, he had a wife: Marina. Fatherhood soon followed. Claiming to have become disillusioned with a dull life in the Soviet Union, however, Oswald moved his family to the United States in 1962.

Was Oswald recruited by the KGB during his time in Russia? Was his return to the States actually nothing to do with disillusionment? Had the elite of the Kremlin convinced Oswald to kill Kennedy? One person who has commented on such matters is Ion Mihai Pacepa.

In 1978, Pacepa, a general with Romania's Department of State Security, defected to the United States. One of Pacepa's revelations was that JFK was killed on the orders of Soviet premier Nikita Khrushchev. Still seething from backing down in the Cuban missile crisis of 1962, Khrushchev was determined to exact his revenge. Oswald was chosen to ensure that revenge was achieved.

Notably, Pacepa asserted that Khrushchev made a last-minute decision not to go ahead with the plan to kill JFK. Unfortunately, the Russians failed to make timely contact with Oswald and inform him of the change in plans. The countdown to assassination could not be stopped.

As far back as the late 1950s, the CIA planned to have Cuba's president, Fidel Castro, assassinated. The Kennedy administration sought to destabilize the Cuban government on many occasions. Castro was enraged. Not as enraged as he became in the wake of the Bay of Pigs invasion of 1961 and the missile crisis of 1962, however.

So angered was Castro that he decided to teach the United States a terrible lesson by having the most powerful man on the planet, JFK, murdered. Or, so this particular conspiracy theory goes. None other than Kennedy's successor, Lyndon B. Johnson, suspected the Cubans were behind the president's killing. Stating that he could "accept that [Oswald] pulled the trigger," Johnson felt that Castro had a significant hand in matters somewhere.

Not surprisingly, Castro has consistently denounced such claims. Castro also asserts, perhaps with justification, that had the United States proved Cuba was involved, his country would have been wiped off the map. Castro was certainly not a fan of JFK. But would he have risked the very existence of Cuba to see Kennedy killed? The question lives on.

In January 1961, outgoing president Dwight D. Eisenhower made a speech, part of which has become inextricably tied to the murder of JFK. Eisenhower said: "In the councils of government, we must guard against the acquisition of unwarranted influence, whether sought or unsought, by the military-industrial complex."

In the minds of many JFK assassination researchers, it is this military-industrial complex that we should look to for the answers on the fifty-year-old killing of the president. JFK had a vision of creating a state of lasting peace between the

United States and the Soviet Union. In short, Kennedy wanted to end the Cold War. We're talking permanently.

Powerful figures in the military, the Intelligence community, and companies that raked in millions of dollars in lucrative defense contracts secretly agreed to do the unthinkable. Profits from war were more important than the life and goals of the president.

Today, more than half a century after President John F. Kennedy was assassinated, we're still none the wiser as to what really went down. Or didn't. Those who see conspiracies around every corner will continue to see them. As for those who don't, well, they won't. And, in all likelihood, the full and unexpurgated facts, whether pointing in the direction of deep conspiracy or Lee Harvey Oswald, will never surface.

One thing does seem likely, however. In another 50 years, when the hundredth anniversary of the JFK assassination looms large, theorizing, finger pointing, and *Deep Throat*-style testimony will still be the order of the day. But definitive answers? Don't bet on it.

MARTIN LUTHER KING: SLAIN BY A HYPNOTIZED KILLER

Very few people would dispute that Martin Luther King Jr. was the foremost, leading, and most influential figure in the arena of civil rights in the twentieth century. King, who was born on January 15, 1929, in Atlanta, Georgia, was a man upon whose words millions of African Americans hung—and still do. He changed the face of American society and culture. He was awarded the Nobel Peace Prize in 1964. And, he died—before he was even forty—under circumstances that many theorists and researchers believe were dominated by conspiracy and cover-up.

The official story of the shooting of Martin Luther King Jr. goes like this: in early February 1968, a major dispute broke out in Memphis, Tennessee. Local African Americans, employed in the city's sanitation industry, were becoming more and more angered by the fact that their wages were significantly lower than those of their white colleagues. The result was that they went on strike, protesting against what they saw as an outrageous, racist practice on the part of Memphis' mayor, Henry Loeb. King agreed with them, to such an extent that he decided to fly out to Memphis to offer his support for the striking workers and to condemn the practices of Loeb. King could not have known it at the time, but his actions had just firmly sealed his fate.

The countdown to King's final moments really began on April 3. That was when King spoke before an audience at Memphis's Church of God in Christ— which, today, has no less than five million, predominantly African-American, followers. Looking back on the day in question, one can practically see the air of menace and death growing before King's very eyes. When he was due to fly to Memphis, King's flight was almost canceled—the result of a claim that there was an explosive device aboard. Fortunately, that proved not to be the case. The ominous atmosphere was not about to go away anytime soon, however. While he passionately delivered a speech to the large throng at the Church of God in Christ, a huge storm wailed and thundered outside. The rain poured, the heavens flashed, and the sky boomed.

Somewhat eerily, what turned out to be King's final, public speech—ever— was cloaked with references to finality, to death, and to God. King told the audience:

> I don't know what will happen now. We've got some difficult days ahead. But it doesn't matter with me now, because I've been to the mountaintop.

And I don't mind. Like anybody, I would like to live a long life. Longevity has its place. But I'm not concerned about that now. I just want to do God's will. And He's allowed me to go up to the mountain. And I've looked over and I've seen the Promised Land. I may not get there with you. But I want you to know tonight, that we, as a people, will get to the Promised Land. And so I'm happy, tonight. I'm not worried about anything; I'm not fearing any man. My eyes have seen the glory of the coming of the Lord.

Followers of Christianity might say that the Lord, hearing King's words, came calling on him—and very soon, too.

While he was visiting Memphis, King stayed at the Lorraine Motel, specifically in room 306, which he shared with Reverend Ralph David Abernathy—who, after King's death, ran the "Poor People's Campaign," which saw thousands of angry African Americans descending upon Washington, D.C., to protest about their living conditions.

It was just one-minute after 6.00 P.M. on the evening of April 4 that King's life was violently and viciously ended. At the time in question, King was positioned on a second-floor balcony of the Lorraine Motel. Suddenly, a single, solitary shot rang out. It wrought immediate and irreversible devastation on King: it slammed into his cheek, utterly shattering his right jawbone, breaking into shards

The Lorraine Motel in Memphis, Tennessee, where Martin Luther King Jr. was assassinated (the spot is marked by the wreath on the second floor). It is now part of the National Civil Rights Museum.

a number of vertebrae, and creating a gaping hole in his jugular vein. One of these injuries, alone, could have proved fatal. With all of them, however, King really didn't stand a chance. He was unconscious even before he hit the balcony floor.

Despite the fact that King was driven, at breakneck speed, to Memphis's St. Joseph Hospital, and despite the very best efforts of the hospital's medical staff, King could not be saved from the reaper. A little more than an hour after he was shot, King was dead. He was just thirty-nine years of age. Adding to that odd and unsettling sense of finality that surrounded King's last days, when his body was autopsied it was determined that his heart was in very bad shape—something that may well have taken him to an early grave anyway, even if he had avoided that deadly bullet. As for who shot and killed King, this is where things become decidedly murky.

The official version of events that concerns the shooting of Martin Luther King Jr. is actually quite straightforward. Not long after that fatal shot rang out, a man named James Earl Ray was seen leaving—with possibly incriminating speed—a lodging house that was situated on the other side of the road from the Lorraine Motel. That Ray was renting a room at the house at the time is not a matter of any doubt, nor is the fact that less than a week before the shooting Ray purchased a rifle, using a bogus name. That same rifle—along with a pair of binoculars—was found in a bundle covered in Ray's fingerprints. It must be noted, too, that Ray had a long and checkered history as a career criminal.

He was found guilty of burglary in 1949, served two years in prison for armed robbery in 1952, and was convicted of mail fraud three years later. In 1959, and after yet another armed robbery, Ray was hit with a two-decade sentence. It was a sentence destined not to last, however. In 1967, Ray escaped from the Jefferson City-based Missouri State Penitentiary, after which he spent time in, variously, Mexico, Los Angeles, and Birmingham, Alabama—the latter being where, on March 30, 1968, he purchased a Remington Gamemaster 760 .30-06 caliber rifle and twenty bullets.

In the aftermath of the shooting, Ray made his careful, stealthy way to the Canadian city of Toronto, the reason being that he had previously secured bogus ID there. Exactly one month after he returned to the city, Ray used that same, faked, documentation to fly to the United Kingdom. It was at London's Heathrow Airport that Ray was finally arrested—while trying to leave the U.K. for pastures new. He was quickly returned to the United States and, ultimately, charged with the murder of Martin Luther King Jr. Not only that, Ray offered up that yes, he did shoot and kill King. The date of the confession was March 10, 1969—Ray's forty-first birthday. For his actions, Ray got ninety-nine years. He died, still incarcerated, on April 23, 1998, from the effects of Hepatitis C. He was seventy years old.

Just like Lee Harvey Oswald, James Earl Ray was portrayed as a definitive lone gunman, even by himself. At least, for a short period: only seventy-two hours after admitting to having shot and killed King, Ray, by now in custody, had a sudden and radical change of mind. Not only that, he made some curious statements concerning the assassination of the civil-rights legend. According to Ray's odd words, while he was not the man who shot and killed King, he just might have been, "partially responsible without knowing it." Then there was the matter of a mysterious character known as "Raoul."

According to Ray, he met the enigmatic Raoul in Canada, sometime after escaping from the Missouri State Penitentiary. Writer Pan Shannan (in "Former CIA Participant Says He Was Part of It—Raoul Identified as FBI Agent") said of the Ray-Raoul connection that Raoul "quickly began to give James money in exchange for his help with importing some kind of contraband."

Shannan continued:

In Memphis on April 4th, the afternoon of the murder, Raoul had suggested that James go to a movie, but James declined. After several tries at getting rid of James for awhile, Raoul finally sent him on an errand only minutes before King was shot. James said that he was going to get the worn tires changed on the Mustang but that the man at the tire store was too busy and could not get to it that day. When James returned to the flophouse/ Lorraine Motel location, it was surrounded by police cars with flashing lights, and he decided it would be prudent to leave the area, as it certainly was not a place for an escaped con to be hanging around.

James Earl Ray's mugshot, taken after he was captured and charged with killing Martin Luther King Jr. Many believe that the petty criminal could not have acted alone, however.

It was, said Ray, Raoul who told him to purchase the rifle, who instructed Ray to meet with him in Memphis, and who even told Ray in which boarding house he should rent a room. The story continues that, although he did not realize it at the time, Ray was being set up as the fall guy—the patsy—in the assassination. A case for this *can* be made: the bundle containing the rifle and binoculars was dumped in the doorway of a building adjacent to the rooming house.

The website *What Really Happened* noted in "The Death of Martin Luther King. Raoul Proven!":

Less than two minutes after the fatal shot was fired, a bundle containing the 30.06 Remington rifle allegedly used in the assassination and some of Ray's belongings was conveniently found in the doorway of the Canipe Amusement Company next door to the boarding house. Ray would have had to fire the shot that killed King from his contorted position in the bathroom, exit the sniper's nest, go to his room to collect his belongings and wrap and tie it all in a bundle, leave his room, run down the stairs and out of the boarding house, stash the bundle next door, and then get away from the scene unnoticed—all within two minutes!

Ray may have been a long-term criminal, but he was certainly no fool. Why leave the incriminating evidence, with his fingerprints just about here, there, and everywhere, right below the room in which he allegedly carried out the assassination—and for one and all to see?

In June 2000, the U.S. Department of Justice released a document titled *Investigation of Recent Allegations Regarding the Assassination of Dr. Martin Luther King, Jr.* It contains a section titled "Findings Regarding Raoul," which makes for fascinating reading.

On August 26, 1998, the attorney general directed the Civil Rights Division of the U.S. Department of Justice, assisted by the Criminal Division, to investigate two separate, then-recent allegations related to the April 4, 1968, assassination of King. The allegations emanate from two people: Loyd Jowers, a former Memphis tavern owner, and Donald Wilson, a former agent with the FBI.

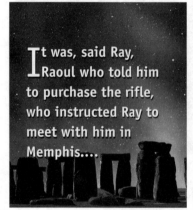

It was, said Ray, Raoul who told him to purchase the rifle, who instructed Ray to meet with him in Memphis....

In 1993, twenty-five years after the murder, Jowers claimed that he had participated in a conspiracy to kill King, along with an alleged Mafia figure, Memphis police officers, and a man named Raoul. According to Jowers, one of the conspirators shot Dr. King from behind his tavern.

Wilson alleged in 1998 that shortly after the assassination, while working as an FBI agent, he took papers from the abandoned car of James Earl Ray. Wilson claims he concealed them for thirty years. Some of the papers contained references to a Raoul and figures associated with the November 1963 assassination of President John F. Kennedy. According to Wilson, someone who later worked in the White House subsequently stole the other papers he took from Ray's car, including one with the telephone number of an FBI office.

The Department of Justice had much to say on all this. Its staff began:

Both the Jowers and the Wilson allegations suggest that persons other than or in addition to James Earl Ray participated in the assassination. Ray, within days of entering his guilty plea in 1969, attempted to withdraw it. Until his death in April 1998, he maintained that he did not shoot Dr. King and was framed by a man he knew only as Raoul. For 30 years, others have similarly alleged that Ray was Raoul's unwitting pawn and that a conspiracy orchestrated Dr. King's murder.

These varied theories have generated several comprehensive government investigations regarding the assassination, none of which confirmed the existence of any conspiracy. However, in *King v. Jowers*, a recent civil suit in a Tennessee state court, a jury returned a verdict finding that Jowers and unnamed others, including unspecified government agencies, participated in a conspiracy to assassinate Dr. King.

The DoJ was not persuaded by the words of Jowers and Wilson:

> Our mission was to consider whether the Jowers or the Wilson allegations are true and, if so, to detect whether anyone implicated engaged in criminal conduct by participating in the assassination. We have concluded that neither allegation is credible. Jowers and Wilson have both contradicted their own accounts. Moreover, we did not find sufficient, reliable evidence to corroborate either of their claims. Instead, we found significant evidence to refute them.

> Nothing new was presented during *King v. Jowers* to alter our findings or to warrant federal investigation of the trial's conflicting, far-ranging hearsay allegations of a government-directed plot involving the Mafia and African American ministers closely associated with Dr. King. Ultimately, we found nothing to disturb the 1969 judicial determination that James Earl Ray murdered Dr. King or to confirm that Raoul or anyone else implicated by Jowers or suggested by the Wilson papers participated in the assassination.

Dr. Martin Luther King Jr. is seen here with President Lyndon Johnson at a 1966 White House meeting. Some people, such as Loyd Jowers, believed King was killed as a result of a joint Mafia-government plot.

The DoJ also noted:

> More than 30 years after the crime, there still is no reliable information suggesting Raoul's last name, address, telephone number, nationality, appearance, friends, family, location, or any other identifying characteristics. The total lack of evidence as to Raoul's existence is telling in light of the fact that Ray's defenders, official investigations, and others have vigorously searched for him for more than 30 years. The dearth of evidence is also significant since Ray often claimed that he was repeatedly with Raoul in various places, cities, and countries, and many of Ray's associations unrelated to the assassination have been verified.

> Because the uncorroborated allegations regarding Raoul originated with James Earl Ray, we ultimately considered Ray's statements about him. Ray's accounts detailing his activities with Raoul related to the assassination are not only self-serving, but confused and contradictory, especially when compared to his accounts of activities unrelated to the assassination. Thus, Ray's statements suggest that Raoul is simply Ray's creation. For these reasons, we have concluded there is no reliable evidence that a Raoul participated in the assassination.

As persuasive as many might find the words of the Department of Justice to be, the story does not end there. It's now time for us to take a look at the controversial world of mind-control. It is a fact that after he escaped from prison, in 1967, Ray underwent plastic surgery—reportedly, notes Brad Steiger—on the orders of Raoul. Steiger continued:

> A link to MK-ULTRA, the CIA's mind-control project, may have occurred when Ray was recuperating from the plastic surgery. Dr. William Joseph Bryan, Jr. had programmed individuals when he was with the air force as chief of Medical Survival Training, the air force's covert mind-control section. Bryan, whom some called pompous and arrogant, liked nothing better than to talk about himself and his accomplishments. He was known as an expert on brainwashing, and he served as a consultant on *The Manchurian Candidate*, a motion picture that portrayed a programmed political assassin. In informal discussions, Bryan "leaked" that he had programmed Sirhan Sirhan and James Earl Ray to commit assassinations and to forget their participation in the act.

The *It Was Johnson* website (that is dedicated to the study of the theory that President John F. Kennedy's death was orchestrated by his successor, President Lyndon B. Johnson) noted:

> Dr. Bryan, like many other figures directly involved in the murders of the Kennedy brothers and King, would die under mysterious circumstances in the spring of 1977; this at a time when the JFK case was reopened and key witnesses and conspirators everywhere conveniently died (e.g., John Rosselli, Sam Giancana). In Bryan's case, the coroner determined he died of natural causes before any autopsy was performed.

The Ray family was determined to have its say, too. In April 2008, Ray's brother, John Larry Ray, wrote and published a book on the death of his sibling. Its title was *Truth at Last*. The Alabama-based *Birmingham News* noted, in an article penned by Rahkia Nance, that:

> For years, John Larry Ray has tried to reveal what he said is an uncovered page in history about his older brother's role in the assassination of Martin Luther King, Jr. He always has contended James Earl Ray was a government "patsy," the fall guy for a sophisticated government plot.

//A link to MK-ULTRA, the CIA's mind-control project, may have occurred when Ray was recuperating from the plastic surgery."

Nance noted that John Larry Ray stated that his brother had been "caught in a web of hypnosis, brainwashing and government-backed mind-control programs that all began with the shooting of a black soldier named Washington in 1948. As a military police officer in Germany, James Earl Ray was directed to shoot the soldier, only identified as Washington, who had been arrested for beating up Jews. Army records showed that prior to the incident, Ray had received two spinal taps, which John Larry suggests may have been part of a drug experiment," one which may have involved the administering of LSD and other hallucinogens.

The shooting, Ray said in his book,

… identified James Earl Ray as a programmable personality and would eventually thrust him into the center of the King assassination. Upon his general discharge from the Army in 1948, James Earl Ray would spend the next 20 years falling deeper into the government network, first used as an undercover operative investigating Communists and eventually landing in and out of prisons, supposedly under the guidance of federal agents.

Was Martin Luther King Jr. the victim of nothing stranger than a violent career criminal, one who had killed *another* black man, some twenty years earlier? Or, were King and James Earl Ray *both* victims in this strange and (so far) unending saga? The final word, for now, goes to Ray's brother, John Larry Ray, who, said: "James got caught up in something he didn't understand. He didn't know what was going down."

THE DEATH OF ROBERT KENNEDY: THE MANCHURIAN CANDIDATE

Almost two months to the day after Martin Luther King Jr. was shot and killed in Memphis, Tennessee, the life of yet another formidable figure in American history was brought to a violent, bloody, and controversial end. That figure was Robert Francis Kennedy. He was better known as Bobby, the younger brother of President John F. Kennedy—himself shot and killed under suspicious circumstances in Dallas, Texas, in November 1963—and as the man who served as the attorney general of the United States while JFK was in power. Just like with the deaths of Martin Luther King Jr. and that of President Kennedy, the circumstances surrounding the shooting of RFK are steeped in mystery. And, also as with the deaths of King and JFK, there is more than one version of events.

The version that is accepted by the U.S. government is that Kennedy was shot and killed in the early hours of June 5, 1968, in Los Angeles, California, by a man named Sirhan Sirhan—and *only* by Sirhan Sirhan. At the time, Kennedy was aggressively campaigning to be the Democratic nominee for president. Sirhan's actions ensured Bobby never, ever, held presidential office. Sirhan received a life-sentence for murdering Robert Kennedy—which he continues to serve to this day, at the San Diego, California-based Richard J. Donovan Correctional Facility.

On the other side of the coin are the claims of deep conspiracy, of mind-controlled assassins, of Manchurian candidates, and of shadowy gunmen—all of whom were determined to ensure that another Kennedy never reached the White House. Let's now try and sort fact from rumor and what we can deduce versus what we have been told.

At the time of his killing on June 5, RFK was in a distinctly good mood. Had he not been shot, Kennedy might very well have been elected president. The timeframe of the election was important, as was the run-up to the tragic events. Kennedy announced his decision to run on March 16, 1968. Significant portions of the United States were soon thereafter in states of flux, as a direct result of the killing of Martin Luther King Jr. There was vehement, and violent, opposition to the Vietnam War, race riots were breaking out, and tens of thousands were demanding new legislation to help lessen the overwhelming amount of poverty that was blighting certain cities.

Lyndon Johnson, who was campaigning to be re-elected, realized that his time was running out and he dropped out of the race. Vice President Hubert

Humphrey jumped in and quickly became a major contender. Indeed, at the time of RFK's death, Humphrey was ahead of Kennedy: the latter had 561 delegates to Kennedy's figure of less than four hundred. It was clear, however, that things were turning in favor of RFK, something that was particularly defined by the results of the California poll.

An enthused RFK knew that he had to continue the tidal wave of campaigning, speaking to the voters, and getting the nation behind him if he was to secure the White House for the next four years—at least. This involved Kennedy thanking his campaign team, and followers, in the Embassy Room of the Ambassador Hotel. Had RFK already been elected president, there's a good chance he would have survived the assassination—at the time the Secret Service, specifically in the wake of the assassination of JFK in November 1963, had majorly beefed-up the security for the U.S. president. Unfortunately, the Secret Service provided *zero* protection for presidential candidates. As for Kennedy, he had just three people protecting him—a couple of bodyguards and William Barry, previously of the FBI. Little did he know it, but time was running out for Robert Kennedy—drastically so.

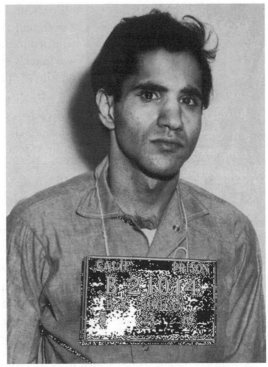

Mugshot of Sirhan Sirhan, a Jordanian citizen living in the United States who was convicted of killing Robert F. Kennedy.

With Kennedy now riding a distinct wave, the original plan—for him to meet with his team and supporters—was put on hold, the reason being that the media demanded a statement from RFK, something that, if done quickly, would still allow the story to make the next day's, early-morning newspapers. Since this would continue the campaign momentum, Kennedy—following the suggestion of his aide Fred Dutton—agreed that the best approach was to speak with the media first. To reach that rapidly growing band of media, Dutton directed RFK through the hotel's kitchen, which was the most optimum route.

Kennedy gave the press what they wanted, after which there was a sudden change of plans, in terms of his exit. The number of people present, by now, was a definitive throng. Kennedy couldn't even get back to the kitchen via the original route, and he was forced to take another to finally make it. Kennedy and Karl Uecker, who was the maitre d', increased their step, as they walked along a passageway, one in which Kennedy stopped to shake hands with a busboy named Juan Romero. At that moment, Sirhan Sirhan raced forward, letting loose with a salvo of bullets. Complete and utter chaos broke out, as Sirhan's .22 caliber Iver-Johnson Cadet revolver took down Kennedy and injured a number of other peo-

Unfortunately, the Secret Service provided *zero* protection for presidential candidates. As for Kennedy, he had just three people protecting him....

ple present, including one of RFK's campaign volunteers, Irwin Stroll, and ABC News's William Weisel. Sirhan was quickly wrestled to the ground, but it was all to no avail. Kennedy's life was quickly ebbing away—as the media looked on and captured on film the final, grim moments of his life.

RFK's wife, Ethel, was, unsurprisingly, hysterical. She knelt by her dying husband, whose final words were, "Don't lift me," as paramedics attempted to do just that, onto a stretcher. For a while it seemed that things might be okay, despite the severe physical damage that Kennedy had suffered. His heartbeat was still strong—something confirmed by Ethel, who had the opportunity to listen to it via a stethoscope—despite the fact that he soon passed out. For roughly half an hour, attempts were made to save the life of RFK, after which he was quickly driven to the nearby Hospital of the Good Samaritan. Unfortunately, the good Samaritans on hand just weren't good enough.

This was hardly surprising: as the medical team assigned to Kennedy carefully examined their patient, they were devastated by the damage that Sirhan's bullets had wrought: one bullet was embedded in RFK's neck. Another impacted through his right armpit and then tore out of his chest. And a third slammed into his skull, at the rear of his right ear. One such injury would have been bad enough, but three practically sealed RFK's fate. He took his last breaths at 1.44 A.M., a little more than one full day after he was shot. Robert Kennedy's funeral took place on June 8. He was, just like his brother, JFK, buried at Arlington National Cemetery. Although Hubert Humphrey won the Democratic nomination, it was a Republican, Richard M. Nixon, who ultimately won the race for the White House.

But what of RFK's assassin, Sirhan Sirhan: Was he really the solitary shooter that he was portrayed as?

Sirhan Sirhan's background is a significant part of the story. He was born in Jerusalem, was a citizen of Jordan, and was vehemently anti-Zionist. That RFK was a noted supporter of the state of Israel deeply grated on Sirhan's mind, to the point where loathing of Kennedy eventually turned into outright hatred. This can be illustrated in no greater and graphic fashion than in Sirhan's very own journal. Under the May 19, 1968, date, he wrote: "My determination to eliminate RFK is becoming more and more of an unshakable obsession. RFK must die. RFK must be killed. Robert F. Kennedy must be assassinated. Robert F. Kennedy must be assassinated before 5 June 68."

Almost certainly, these words had specific significance to Sirhan. June 5 marked the date on which—one year earlier, in 1967—the so-called Six Day War, between Israel and its opponents in the Middle East (Syria, Jordan, and Egypt), began.

Since the evidence against Sirhan was seen as being cast-iron, on April 17, 1969, he was found guilty of the murder of Robert Kennedy, which resulted in him

Robert F. Kennedy was buried at Arlington National Cemetery. After his death, Hubert Humphrey won the Democratic Party nomination but lost the presidential election to Richard Nixon.

being given a sentence of death—which was later changed to life imprisonment. But was the evidence really that cast-iron solid? To some, it wasn't.

It transpires that doubts about Sirhan's guilt surfaced very soon after he was found guilty of killing RFK. While Sirhan was interviewed in San Quentin prison in 1969, he was interviewed by a man named Dr. Eduard Simson-Kallas, who was an expert in the field of hypnosis and believed Sirhan had been subjected to some form of subliminal programming of the mind-control kind. On top of that, the coroner in the RFK case, Thomas Noguchi, offered his conclusion that the bullet that entered the senator's skull, behind his right ear, had been fired at a distance of barely one-inch. That suggests even if Sirhan was a hypnotically controlled assassin, he must have had an accomplice, since he was most definitely further away than one inch when he shot Kennedy.

What was without a doubt the biggest development in the saga of who really shot RFK surfaced in 2011, when papers were filed, in federal court, maintaining that Sirhan Sirhan was "manipulated by a seductive girl in a mind-control plot to shoot Sen. Robert F. Kennedy."

The papers, noted the media, "point to a mysterious girl in a polka-dot dress as the controller who led Sirhan to fire a gun in the pantry of the Ambassador Hotel. But the documents suggest a second person shot and killed Kennedy while using Sirhan as a diversion."

The story of the mysterious girl is not a new one, as the late Jim Keith—a leading figure in conspiracy research, until his own controversial death in 1999—said in his 1998 book *Mind Control, World Control*:

Immediately after the Kennedy shooting a woman named Sandra Serrano saw a Caucasian woman in a white dress with black polka dots, and a young man, tentatively identified as Mexican-American, and wearing a white shirt and gold sweater, running down the stairs that provided exit from the hotel. The woman in the polka dots said, "We've shot him! We've shot him!" Serano asked, "Who did you shoot?" and the woman responded, "We shot Senator Kennedy."

The 2011 revelations take the story much further, as the media noted. For the first time, Sirhan said, and while under hypnosis, on a specific cue from the polka-dotted girl he went into "range mode," believing he was at a firing range and seeing circles with targets in front of his very eyes.

"I thought that I was at the range more than I was actually shooting at any person, let alone Bobby Kennedy," Sirhan was quoted as saying during interviews with Daniel Brown, a Harvard University professor and an expert in trauma memory and hypnosis.

The U.K's *Daily Mail* newspaper noted of this issue in a 2011 article titled "Bobby Kennedy assassin still claims he was 'victim of mind control and his gun didn't fire fatal shot' in new appeal after parole is denied":

> Sirhan's lawyers, William Pepper and Laurie Dusek, are using a defense that is eerily familiar to another Kennedy murder—that there was more than one shooter. They say the sixty-seven-year-old Christian Palestinian born in Jerusalem was hypnoprogrammed to divert attention from a shooter who actually killed Mr. Kennedy in 1968. They also allege he was an easy scapegoat because he is Arab.

> "The public has been shielded from the darker side of the practice. The average person is unaware that hypnosis can and is used to induct antisocial conduct in humans," the court papers stated. Those same papers also noted that Sirhan was "an involuntary participant in the crimes being committed because he was subjected to sophisticated, hypnoprogramming and memory implantation techniques which rendered him unable to consciously control his thoughts and actions at the time the crimes were being committed."

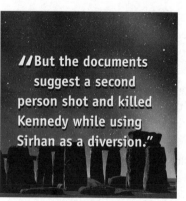

//But the documents suggest a second person shot and killed Kennedy while using Sirhan as a diversion."

Then, in 2012, a writer for the *Huffington Post* noted (in "RFK Assassination Witness Nina Rhodes-Hughes Says Sirhan Sirhan Didn't Act Alone"): "Nina Rhodes-Hughes, a key witness to the Robert F. Kennedy assassination at the Ambassador Hotel in 1968, is making bombshell claims in a CNN interview, suggesting that convicted murderer Sirhan Sirhan didn't act alone."

In Rhodes-Hughes's very own words: "What has to come out is that there was another shooter to my right. The truth has got to be told. No more cover-ups."

The *Post* added: "Rhodes-Hughes, now 78, claims the FBI 'twisted' her statements to investigators after the incident in order to come up with the conclusion that she had only heard 8 shots, an account that was used as evidence that Sirhan carried out the act without an accomplice."

The late Jim Keith referred to an odd—and, perhaps, highly revealing—discussion between Sirhan Sirhan and a psychiatrist based at UCLA: Dr. Bernard Diamond. Keith stated that when Diamond was speaking with Sirhan about certain entries in his notebooks, he, Diamond, asked, "Is this crazy writing?"

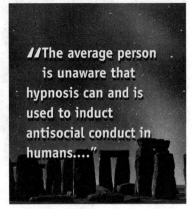

//The average person is unaware that hypnosis can and is used to induct antisocial conduct in humans...."

Sirhan chose to reply in writing, rather than verbally:

"YES. YES. YES."

"Are you crazy?" the doctor pressed.

"NO. NO."

"Well, why are you writing crazy?"

"PRACTICE PRACTICE PRACTICE."

"Practice for what?"

"MIND CONTROL MIND CONTROL MIND CONTROL."

The final word goes to Charles R. McQuiston, one of the originators of Psychological Stress Evaluator (PSE) technology, and a member of U.S. Army Intelligence. Jim Keith quoted McQuiston in his book *Mind Control, World Control*:

I'm convinced that Sirhan wasn't aware of what he was doing. He was in a hypnotic trance when he pulled the trigger and killed Senator Kennedy. Everything in the PSE charts tells me that someone else was involved in the assassination—and that Sirhan was programmed through hypnosis to kill RFK. What we have here is a real live "Manchurian Candidate."

WATERGATE: WILL THE REAL DEEP THROAT PLEASE STAND UP?

On August 8, 1974, U.S. President Richard Milhous Nixon did something that no other American president has ever done, before or since: he resigned from office in disgrace. It was the inevitable fallout in one of the nation's biggest-ever scandals: Watergate. The events that led to Nixon's decision to walk away from his presidency can be traced back to the early hours of June 17, 1972. That was when a break-in occurred at the headquarters of the Democratic National Committee (DNC), which was housed in the Washington, D.C.-based Watergate Complex. This was not a case of burglary, however.

The intruders were there to install covert listening devices and make copies of important papers of the DNC. Five men were given the task of getting the job done. They were: Eugenio Martinez, James McCord, Virgilio Gonzalez, Bernard Barker, and Frank Sturgis. They failed miserably. Good work on the part of Watergate's security staff, and in particular a guard named Frank Wills, combined with the actions of the D.C. police, soon meant that the five conspirators were in custody. It was not long before the sensational truth of the affair started to surface, bit by bit.

Money found in the possession of the five was traced back to the Committee for the Reelection of the President. This was not good news for Nixon. Worse news was to follow. Also in on the conspiracy were three powerful figures: John Mitchell, the attorney general; Jeb Magruder, the acting-chair of the Committee for the Reelection of the President; and John Dean, the White House counsel. Panicky attempts by Nixon's staff to distance the president from the guilty parties fell apart when the press learned that Nixon had attempted to bury the story. It was only a matter of time before the death-knell for Nixon was signaled.

On the night of his resignation, Nixon made a speech to the American people that, in part, went as follows:

> In all the decisions I have made in my public life, I have always tried to do what was best for the Nation. Throughout the long and difficult period of Watergate, I have felt it was my duty to persevere, to make every possible effort to complete the term of office to which you elected me.

> In the past few days, however, it has become evident to me that I no longer have a strong enough political base in the Congress to justify continuing that effort. As long as there was such a base, I felt strongly that it was nec-

essary to see the constitutional process through to its conclusion, that to do otherwise would be unfaithful to the spirit of that deliberately difficult process and a dangerously destabilizing precedent for the future.

But with the disappearance of that base, I now believe that the constitutional purpose has been served, and there is no longer a need for the process to be prolonged.

I would have preferred to carry through to the finish whatever the personal agony it would have involved, and my family unanimously urged me to do so. But the interest of the Nation must always come before any personal considerations.

From the discussions I have had with Congressional and other leaders, I have concluded that because of the Watergate matter I might not have the support of the Congress that I would consider necessary to back the very difficult decisions and carry out the duties of this office in the way the interests of the Nation would require.

Richard M. Nixon became the first president in U.S. history to resign from that office.

I have never been a quitter. To leave office before my term is completed is abhorrent to every instinct in my body. But as President, I must put the interest of America first.

America needs a full-time President and a full-time Congress, particularly at this time with problems we face at home and abroad.

To continue to fight through the months ahead for my personal vindication would almost totally absorb the time and attention of both the President and the Congress in a period when our entire focus should be on the great issues of peace abroad and prosperity without inflation at home.

Therefore, I shall resign the Presidency effective at noon tomorrow. Vice President Ford will be sworn in as President at that hour in this office.

In terms of the American media's investigations, it was without a doubt the team of Bob Woodward and Carl Bernstein—of the *Washington Post* and who went on to pen the best-selling book on the affair, *All the President's Men*, which was published in 1974—that made Watergate the nation-changing event it became. What set the Woodward-Bernstein investigation apart from those of other news outlets was the fact that the duo had an ace up their sleeves: a high-level, government whistleblower, infamously dubbed "Deep Throat."

Although senior staff of the *Washington Post* knew of the existence of Deep Throat, the rest of the nation's media and the general public were kept in the dark until *All the President's Men* was published—which told the whole secrecy-filled,

Journalist Bob Woodward (shown here) teamed up with Carl Bernstein at the *Washington Post* to break the story about Watergate.

shadowy saga. Such was the success of the book, the movie-rights were quickly sold and, in 1976, a Hollywood version of the events that led to Nixon's resignation surfaced, with Robert Redford and Dustin Hoffman playing Woodward and Bernstein. For more than thirty years after Nixon's resignation, the real identity of Deep Throat was never formerly acknowledged. In 2005, however, that all changed—the world finally learned the true identity of the man who helped Woodward and Bernstein uncover the story that destroyed the presidency of Richard Nixon.

Deep Throat was Mark Felt, at the time of Watergate the associate director of the FBI. When the world learned of the identity of Deep Throat, it quite naturally thrust Watergate back into the public domain and became a major talking point for not just the nation's media, but for the world's, too. But, was Felt really Deep Throat? Was he just one of *many* Deep Throat-style sources? Was Felt acting as a witting stooge, carefully protecting the *real* source of Woodward and Bernstein's information? To answer those questions, it's necessary for us to return to the events of the early 1970s.

As for the name "Deep Throat," it was the idea of the *Washington Post's* managing-editor, Howard Simons, who was inspired by the famous 1972 porno-flick *Deep Throat* that starred Linda Lovelace. From the outset, Woodward and Bernstein stated they would not identify their source. The only circumstances under which they would do so, the pair said, would be (a) if Deep Throat died; or (b) if Deep Throat, himself, wanted to go public—in which case, the pair would offer support to him and confirm his claim to be the United States' most infamous whistleblower of the decade. What do we know about Mark Felt?

Born in Idaho, in 1913, Felt joined the FBI in 1942 and had a prestigious career. During the Second World War, he worked in the bureau's Espionage Section—the work of which revolved around tracking down Nazi spies, sympathizers, and saboteurs in the United States. By the mid-1950s, Felt was running the Salt Lake City, Utah, office of the FBI. He returned to the Washington, D.C-based FBI headquarters in 1962. Two years later, he was assistant director. And, in 1971, Felt was offered the position of deputy associate director. It was a position he enthusiastically accepted. It wasn't long before Felt was associate director, the most powerful figure in the FBI next to J. Edgar Hoover himself. Little wonder, then, that Felt was in a prime position to know the lowdown on Watergate.

In terms of how Felt became known to Woodward and Bernstein, most of the revelations on this issue came from Woodward. He first met Felt around the turn of the 1970s—the date remains unclear—at the White House and kept in periodic touch with him from thereon. There was a good reason for this. Woodward noted that Felt was an "incurable gossip." This was good news for an investigative journalist like Woodward. Felt's inability to keep his mouth shut meant that, from time to time, Woodward got more than a few tasty morsels of information on important stories, such as the attempted assassination of presidential candidate George Wallace Jr. in May 1972.

Woodward was no fool—he quickly recognized the significance of the Watergate affair and contacted Felt to see if he could offer any insight, information, and guidance. It turned out that, yes, Felt could do that—provided that Woodward was willing to keep his mouth shut about from whom the information was coming. That was good enough for Woodward, particularly

Mark Felt, who was second associate director of the FBI at the time of the Watergate break-ins, admitted in 2005 that he was Deep Throat.

when Felt was able to provide verifiable information that linked the Watergate break-ins to senior figures in the Nixon administration.

Such was the concern about how far, and how deep, the story ran. Woodward and Felt arranged their meetings in a paranoia-soaked fashion that would have been worthy of an episode of *The X-Files*. When Woodward wanted to meet with Felt, he signaled him by prominently placing a flower pot containing a red flag on the balcony of his apartment. After the identity of Deep Throat became known, Woodward said of this curious situation, in a June 2005 article for the *Washington Post*, titled "How Mark Felt Became Deep Throat":

> How he [Deep Throat] could have made a daily observation of my balcony is still a mystery to me. At the time, the back of my building was not enclosed so anyone could have driven in the back alley to observe my balcony. In addition, my balcony and the back of the apartment complex faced onto a courtyard or back area that was shared with a number of other apartment or office buildings in the area. My balcony could have been seen from dozens of apartments or offices. There were several embassies in the area. The Iraqi embassy was down the street, and I thought it possible that the FBI had surveillance or listening posts nearby. Could Felt have had the counterintelligence agents regularly report on the status of my flag and flowerpot? That seems unlikely, but not impossible.

As for Felt, when he had something he wanted to share with Woodward, he would make a note on the copy of the *New York Times* that Woodward had delivered to his door on a daily basis. It was as a result of this strange set of affairs that Woodward and Bernstein became famous and President Richard Nixon became downright infamous. But, is that all there is to it? No, possibly not.

It was on May 31, 2005, that Mark Felt finally stood up and said that he was, indeed, the mysterious and enigmatic Deep Throat. His story appeared in an issue of *Vanity Fair*, something that ensured the floodgates were open and could not be closed again. Now that the world knew the truth, there was no need for Woodward and Bernstein to stay silent: they had pledged never to reveal Felt as their source until he did so, himself, or he passed away. The two writers were backed up—in their assertion that Felt was Deep Throat—by the *Washington Post's* Ben Bradlee, who held the position of executive editor of the newspaper when Watergate occurred.

A number of individuals were neither impressed nor convinced by Felt's words, or by the back-up testimony of Woodward, Bernstein, and Bradlee. One was L. Patrick Gray, who spent just under a year as acting director of the FBI after J. Edgar Hoover's death in 1972. Gray—the coauthor with his son Ed of the book, *In Nixon's Web: A Year in the Crosshairs of Watergate*—didn't dispute that Felt provided *some* of the data that allowed Woodward and Bernstein to get to the heart of the conspiracy. Gray was, however, of the opinion that Felt was just one of a number of sources that the Woodward-Bernstein team was using. In that sense, Deep Throat was a convenient composite behind which not just Mark Felt could be hidden.

Then there was Leonard Garment, the White House counsel after John Dean, who had his suspicions that Felt might have been Deep Throat, but was also troubled by the theory:

Watergate, where the 1972 scandal started, is a complex of five buildings that include offices, apartments, and a hotel. It is still in use today and is on the U.S. Register of Historic Places.

The Felt theory was a strong one. Felt had a personal motive for acting. After the death of J. Edgar Hoover, Felt thought he was a leading candidate to succeed Hoover. The characteristics were a good fit. The trouble with Felt's candidacy was that Deep Throat in *All the President's Men* simply did not sound to me like a career FBI man.

There were other issues that some found suspicious. For example, there was the matter of that red-flagged flowerpot on Woodward's balcony—the one he used to signal Deep Throat when a meeting was needed. Adrian Havill is the author of the 1993 book *Deep Truth: The Lives of Bob Woodward and Carl Bernstein.* Havill had significant issues with the idea that the layout of the apartment complex that Woodward lived in would have allowed Felt to see the flowerpot, never mind the flag. The reason being: Wooodward's balcony overlooked an interior courtyard, not the street. Havill also had issues with whether or not copies of the *New York Times* were really delivered to the front doors of the residents of the block. Woodward said yes, they were.

In view of all this, it's hardly surprising that other candidates have been suggested, aside from Mark Felt. First on our list are members of President Nixon's Secret Service. The allegation goes that since they were specifically responsible for installing and maintaining the many and varied listening- and recording-devices that Nixon secretly had placed throughout the White House, the Secret Service would have been the ideal candidates to overhear incriminating conversations and then provide summaries of those same conversations to Woodward and Bernstein.

Nixon's successor, President Gerald R. Ford, also had the finger pointed in his direction, the theory being that Ford saw Watergate as a convenient way to get rid of Nixon and take control of the White House and the presidency for himself—which, is actually what happened, whether due to any duplicity on Ford's part or not. Pat Buchanan—Nixon's special assistant—was accused on more than a few occasions of being Deep Throat. His response was amusing and fiery, to say the least: the last time he cooperated with *The Washington Post*, said Buchanan, was in 1952, when he was a paper boy delivering copies of the newspaper in northwest Washington. Interestingly, Buchanan was of the opinion that Deep Throat was not just one person, but many.

And the list goes on. It includes John Daniel Ehrlichman, counsel and assistant to the president for domestic affairs, William Colby, who was the director of the CIA from September 1973 to January 1976; Colby's immediate successor at the CIA (and future president), George Herbert Walker Bush; Nixon's Press Secretary, Ron Ziegler; Raymond Price, Nixon's speechwriter (which included his resignation speech); and even ABC News's Diane Sawyer, who was brought into the Nixon administration by the aforementioned Ron Ziegler.

The likelihood is that the controversy will never truly go away. Woodward and Bernstein stand by their position of Felt, and *only* Felt, being Deep Throat, as did Ben Bradlee before his death. As for Mark Felt, whatever the true nature of his involvement in secretly spilling the beans on the Watergate fiasco, he took the secrets with him to the grave, when he died, at the age of ninety-five, on December 18, 2008.

CATTLE MUTILATIONS: SECRET FILES AND SCARED FARMERS

Since at least 1967, reports have surfaced throughout the United States of animals—but, chiefly, cattle—slaughtered in bizarre fashion. Organs are taken and significant amounts of blood are found to be missing. In some cases, the limbs of the cattle are broken, suggesting they have been dropped to the ground from a significant height. Evidence of extreme heat, to slice into the skin of the animals, has been found at mutilation sites. Eyes are removed, tongues are sliced off, and, typically, the sexual organs are gone.

While the answers to the puzzle remain frustratingly outside of the public arena, theories abound. They include extraterrestrials, engaged in nightmarish experimentation of the genetic kind; military programs involving the testing of new bio-warfare weapons; occult-based groups that sacrifice the cattle in ritualistic fashion; and government agencies secretly monitoring the food-chain, fearful that something worse than "Mad Cow Disease" may have infected the U.S. cattle herd—and, possibly, as a result, the human population, too.

Cattle mutilations are a favorite topic of UFO researchers and conspiracy theorists. From the mid-1970s to the dawning of the 1980s, however, the phenomenon was of deep interest to another body: the FBI. We know this, as the FBI has now declassified all of its files on the subject, thanks to Freedom of Information provisions. Not only that, the FBI has posted its file collection online at its website—The Vault—from where the lengthy dossier can be downloaded in PDF format.

From January to March 1973, the state of Iowa was hit hard by cattle mutilations. Many of the ranchers who lost animals also reported seeing strange lights and black-colored helicopters in the direct vicinities of the attacks. That the FBI took keen notice of all this is demonstrated by the fact that, as the Freedom of Information Act has shown, it collected and filed numerous media reports on the cattle-mutes in Iowa. The next piece of data dates from early September 1974. That's when the FBI's director, Clarence M. Kelley, was contacted by Senator Carl T. Curtis, who wished to inform the bureau of a wave of baffling attacks on livestock in Nebraska—the state in which Curtis resided and represented.

At the time, the FBI declined to get involved, as Director Kelley informed the senator: "It appears that no Federal Law within the investigative jurisdiction of the FBI has been violated, inasmuch as there is no indication of interstate transportation of the maimed animals."

One year later, in August 1975, Senator Floyd K. Haskell, of Colorado, made his voice known to the FBI, on the growing cattle mutilation controversy:

> For several months my office has been receiving reports of cattle mutilations throughout Colorado and other western states. At least 130 cases in Colorado alone have been reported to local officials and the Colorado Bureau of Investigation (CBI); the CBI has verified that the incidents have occurred for the last two years in nine states. The ranchers and rural residents of Colorado are concerned and frightened by these incidents. The bizarre mutilations are frightening in themselves: in virtually all the cases, the left ear, rectum and sex organ of each animal has [sic] been cut away and the blood drained from the carcass, but with no traces of blood left on the ground and no footprints.

The senator had much more to say, too:

> In Colorado's Morgan County area there has [sic] also been reports that a helicopter was used by those who mutilated the carcasses of the cattle, and several persons have reported being chased by a similar helicopter. Because I am gravely concerned by this situation, I am asking that the Federal Bureau of Investigation enter the case.

> Although the CBI has been investigating the incidents, and local officials also have been involved, the lack of a central unified direction has frustrated the investigation. It seems to have progressed little, except for the recognition at long last that the incidents must be taken seriously. Now it appears that ranchers are arming themselves to protect their livestock, as well as their families and themselves, because they are frustrated by the unsuccessful investigation. Clearly something must be done before someone gets hurt.

Again, the FBI—some ranchers and media people thought, rather suspiciously—declined to get involved in the investigation of the phenomenon. It was a stance the FBI rigidly stuck to (despite collecting numerous, nationwide newspaper and magazine articles on the subject) until 1978. That was when the FBI learned of an astonishing number of horse and cattle mutilations in Rio Arriba County, New Mexico—mutilations that actually dated back to 1976. They had all been scrupulously investigated and documented by Police Officer Gabe Valdez of Espanola.

FBI director Clarence M. Kelley (pictured) dismissed the problem of cattle mutilations by saying no federal laws had been violated because the livestock had not been transported across state lines.

It was when the FBI was contacted by New Mexico senator Harrison Schmitt (also the twelfth person to set foot on the Moon—in December 1972), who implored the FBI to get involved, that action was finally taken. In March 1979, Deputy Attorney General Philip Heymann prepared a summary on the New Mexico cases for the FBI, and—for good measure—photocopied all of Officer Valdez's files to the bureau's director. Things were about to be taken to a new level.

As Valdez's voluminous records showed, from the summer of 1975 to the early fall of 1978, no fewer than twenty-eight cattle mutilation incidents occurred in Rio Arriba County. One of the most bizarre events occurred in June 1976, as Valdez's files demonstrate:

> Investigations revealed that a suspected aircraft of some type had landed twice, leaving three pod marks positioned in a triangular shape. The diameter of each pod was 14 inches. Emanating from the two landings were smaller triangular shaped tripods 28 inches and 4 inches in diameter. Investigation at the scene showed that these small tripods had followed the cow for approximately 600 feet. Tracks of the cow showed where she had struggled and fallen. The small tripod tracks were all around the cow. Other evidence showed that grass around the tripods, as they followed the cow, had been scorched. Also a yellow oily substance was located in two places under the small tripods. This substance was submitted to the State Police Lab. The Lab was unable to detect the content of the substance.

> A sample of the substance was submitted to a private lab and they were unable to analyze the substance due to the fact that it disappeared or disintegrated. Skin samples were analyzed by the State Police Lab and the Medical Examiner's Office. It was reported that the skin had been cut with a sharp instrument.

Seventy-two hours later, Valdez liaised with Dr. Howard Burgess of the New Mexico-based Sandia Laboratories, with a view to having the area checked for radiation. It was a wise move. The radiation level was double that which could normally be expected. Valdez's conclusions on this issue: "It is the opinion of this writer that radiation findings are deliberately being left at the scene to confuse investigators."

The case was not over, however. Whatever, or whoever, was responsible for the mutilation made a return visit. Once again, we need to take a look at the official files on the affair. In Valdez's own, official words, extracted from New Mexico State Police files:

> There was also evidence that the tripod marks had returned and removed the left ear. Tripod marks were found over Mr. Gomez's tire tracks of his original visit. The left ear was intact when Mr. Gomez first found the cow. The cow had a 3-month-old calf which has not been located since the incident. This appears strange since a small calf normally stays around the mother even though the cow is dead.

On the matter of whether or not the mutilations were the work of cults or natural predators, Valdez said:

Both have been ruled out due to expertise and preciseness and the cost involved to conduct such a sophisticated and secretive operation. It should also be noted that during the spring of 1974 when a tremendous amount of cattle were lost due to heavy snowfalls, the carcasses had been eaten by predators. These carcasses did not resemble the carcasses of the mutilated cows. Investigation has narrowed down to these theories which involve (1) Experimental use of Vitamin B12 and (2) The testing of the lymph node system. During this investigation an intensive study has been made of (3) What is involved in germ warfare testing, and the possible correlation of these 3 factors (germ warfare testing, use of Vitamin B12, testing of the lymph node system).

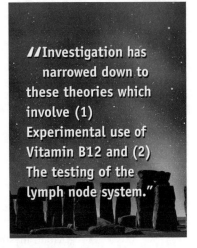

//Investigation has narrowed down to these theories which involve (1) Experimental use of Vitamin B12 and (2) The testing of the lymph node system."

A further, very strange, report can be found in Valdez's files, from 1978:

> This four year old cross Hereford and Black Angus native cow was found lying on left side with rectum, sex organs, tongue, and ears removed. Pinkish blood from [illegible] was visible, and after two days the blood still had not coagulated. Left front and left rear leg were pulled out of their sockets apparently from the weight of the cow which indicates that it was lifted and dropped back to the ground. The ground around and under the cow was soft and showed indentations where the cow had been dropped. 600 yards away from the cow were the 4-inch circular indentations similar to the ones found at the Manuel Gomez ranch on 4-24-78.

> This cow had been dead approximately [illegible] hours and was too decomposed to extract samples. This is the first in a series of mutilations in which the cows' legs are broken. Previously the animals had been lifted from the brisket with a strap. These mutilated animals all dehydrate rapidly (in one or two days).

As the summer of 1978 progressed, so did the number of reports where elevated radiation readings were found, as Valdez noted in his records:

> It is believed that this type of radiation is not harmful to humans, although approximately 7 people who visited the mutilation site complained of nausea and headaches. However, this writer has had no such symptoms after checking approximately 11 mutilations in the past 4 months. Identical mutilations have been taking place all over the Southwest. It is strange that no eye witnesses have come forward or that no accidents [have] occurred. One has to admit that whoever is responsible for the mutilations is very well organized with boundless financing and secrecy. Writer is presently getting equipment through the efforts of Mr. Howard Burgess, Albuquerque, N.M. to detect substances on the cattle which might mark them and be picked up by infra-red rays but not visible to the naked eye.

A lengthy document, prepared by Forrest S. Putman, the FBI's special-agent-in-charge at Albuquerque, New Mexico, was soon thereafter sent to the FBI's headquarters in Washington, D.C. It read:

//Officer Valdez theorizes that clamps are being placed on the cow's legs and they are being lifted by helicopter...."

Information furnished to this office by Officer Valdez indicates that the animals are being shot with some type of paralyzing drug and the blood is being drawn from the animal after an injection of an anti-coagulant. It appears that in some instances the cattle's legs have been broken and helicopters without any identifying numbers have reportedly been seen in the vicinity of these mutilations.

Officer Valdez theorizes that clamps are being placed on the cow's legs and they are being lifted by helicopter to some remote area where the mutilations are taking place and then the animal is returned to its original pasture. The mutilations primarily consist of removal of the tongue, the lymph gland, lower lip and the sexual organs of the animal.

Much mystery has surrounded these mutilations, but according to witnesses they give the appearance of being very professionally done with a surgical instrument, and according to Valdez, as the years progress, each surgical procedure appears to be more professional. Officer Valdez has advised that in no instance, to his knowledge, are these carcasses ever attacked by predator or scavenger animals, although there are tracks which would indicate that coyotes have been circling the carcass from a distance. Special Agent Putman then informed the Director of the outcome of Valdez's run-ins with officials.

He also advised that he has requested Los Alamos Scientific Laboratory to conduct investigation for him but until just recently has always been advised that the mutilations were done by predatory animals. Officer Valdez stated that just recently he has been told by two assistants at Los Alamos Scientific Laboratory that they were able to determine the type of tranquilizer and blood anti-coagulant that have been utilized.

Putnam then demonstrated to headquarters the astonishing scale of the mutilation puzzle:

Officer Valdez stated that Colorado probably has the most mutilations occurring within their State and that over the past four years approximately 30 have occurred in New Mexico. He stated that of these 330, 15 have occurred on Indian Reservations but he did know that many mutilations have gone unreported which have occurred on the Indian reservations because the Indians, particularly in the Pueblos, are extremely superstitious and will not even allow officers in to investigate in some instances. Officer Valdez stated since the outset of these mutilations there have been an estimated 8,000 animals mutilated which would place the loss at approximately $1,000,000.

Putman additionally advised the director that:

It is obvious if mutilations are to be solved there is a need for a coordinated effort so that all material available can be gathered and analyzed and further efforts synchronized. Whether the FBI should assume this role is a matter to be decided. If we are merely to investigate and direct our efforts toward the 15 mutilated cattle on the Indian reservation we, I believe, will be in the same position as the other law enforcement agencies at this time and would be seeking to achieve an almost impossible task.

It is my belief that if we are to participate in any manner that we should do so fully, although this office and the USA's office are at a loss to determine what statute our investigative jurisdiction would be in this matter. If we are to act solely as a coordinator or in any other official capacity the sooner we can place this information in the computer bank, the better off we would be and in this regard it would be my recommendation that an expert in the computer field at the Bureau travel to Albuquerque in the very near future so that we can determine what type of information will be needed so that when the invitation for the April conference is submitted from Senator Schmitt's Office that the surrounding States will be aware of the information that is needed to place in the computer.

It should be noted that Senator Schmitt's Office is coordinating the April conference and will submit the appropriate invitations and with the cooperation of the USA, Mr. Thompson will chair this conference. The FBI will act only as a participant.

Putnam went on to describe the theories that had been advanced to try and explain the phenomenon:

Since this has not been investigated by the FBI in any manner we have no theories whatsoever as to why or what is responsible for these cattle mutilations. Officer Gabe Valdez is very adamant in his opinion that these mutilations are the work of the U.S. government and that it is some clandestine operation either by the CIA or the Department of Energy and in all probability is connected with some type of research into biological warfare. His main reason for these beliefs is that he feels that he was given the "run around" by Los Alamos Scientific Laboratory and they are attempting to cover up this situation. There are also theories that these are cults (religious) of some type of Indian rituals resulting in these mutilations and the wildest theory advanced is that they have some connection with unidentified flying objects.

In the closing section of his report, Putman said:

If we are to assume an investigative posture into this area, the matter of manpower, of course, becomes a consideration and I am unable to determine at this time the amount of manpower that would be needed to give this our full attention so that a rapid conclusion

An April 20, 1979, issue of *UFO & Outer Space* reported on a cattle mutilation case outside of St. Louis, Missouri. Strange lights had been seen before the dead livestock were discovered.

could be reached. The Bureau is requested to furnish its comments and guidance on this whole situation including, if desired, the Legal Counsel's assessment of jurisdictional question. An early response would be needed, however, so that we might properly, if requested to do so, obtain the data bank information. If it appears that we are going to become involved in this matter, it is obvious that there would be a large amount of correspondence necessary and Albuquerque would suggest a code name be established of BOVMUT.

As a result of the growing concern surrounding the cattle mutilations, a conference on the subject was held, on April 20, 1979, at the Albuquerque Public Library. There was a heavy concentration of FBI agents at the conference, something that resulted in the following official document being prepared by the FBI, which summarized the various theories, cases, and ideas advanced at the conference:

> Forrest S. Putman, Special Agent in Charge (SAC), Albuquerque Office of the FBI, explained to the conference that the Justice Department had given the FBI authority to investigate those cattle mutilations which have occurred or might occur on Indian lands. He further explained that the Albuquerque FBI would look at such mutilations in connection with mutilations occurring off Indian lands for the purpose of comparison and control, especially where the same methods of operation are noted. SAC Putman said that in order for this matter to be resolved, the facts surrounding such mutilations should be gathered and computerized.

> District Attorney Eloy Martinez, Santa Fe, New Mexico, told the conference that his judicial district had made application for a $50,000 Law Enforcement Assistance Administration (LEAA) Grant for the purpose of investigating the cattle mutilations. He explained that there is hope that with the funds from this grant, an investigative unit can be established for the sole purpose of resolving the mutilation problem. He said it is his view that such an investigative unit could serve as a headquarters for all law enforcement officials investigating the mutilations and, in particular, would serve as a repository for information developed in order that this information could be coordinated properly. He said such a unit would not only coordinate this information, but also handle submissions to a qualified lab for both evidence and photographs. Mr. Martinez said a hearing will be held on April 24, 1979, for the purpose of determining whether this grant will be approved.

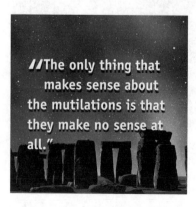

//The only thing that makes sense about the mutilations is that they make no sense at all."

> Gabe Valdez, New Mexico State Police, Dulce, New Mexico, reported he has investigated the death of 90 cattle during the past three years, as well as six horses. Officer Valdez said he is convinced that the mutilations of the animals have not been the work of predators because of the precise manner of the cuts. Officer Valdez said he had investigated mutilations of several animals which had occurred on the ranch of Manuel Gomez of Dulce, New Mexico.

Manuel Gomez addressed the conference and explained he had lost six animals to unexplained deaths which were found in a mutilated condition within the last two years. Further, Gomez said that he and his family are experiencing fear and mental anguish because of the mutilations.

David Perkins, Director of the Department of Research at Libre School in Farasita, Colorado, exhibited a map of the United States which contained hundreds of colored pins identifying mutilation sites. He commented that he had been making a systematic collection of data since 1975, and has never met a greater challenge. He said, "The only thing that makes sense about the mutilations is that they make no sense at all."

Tom Adams of Paris, Texas, who has been independently examining mutilations for six years, said his investigation has shown that helicopters are almost always observed in the area of the mutilations. He said that the helicopters do not have identifying markings and they fly at abnormal, unsafe, or illegal altitudes.

Dr. Peter Van Arsdale, Ph.D., Assistant Professor, Department of Anthropology, University of Denver, suggested that those investigating the cattle mutilations take a systematic approach and look at all types of evidence is discounting any of the theories such as responsibility by extraterrestrial visitors or satanic cults.

Richard Sigismund, Social Scientist, Boulder, Colorado, presented an argument which advanced the theory that the cattle mutilations are possibly related to activity of UFOs. Numerous other persons made similar type presentations expounding on their theories regarding the possibility that the mutilations are the responsibility of extraterrestrial visitors, members of Satanic cults, or some unknown government agency.

Dr. Richard Prine, Forensic Veterinarian, Los Alamos Scientific Laboratory (LASL), Los Alamos, New Mexico, discounted the possibility that the mutilations had been done by anything but predators. He said he had examined six carcasses and in his opinion predators were responsible for the mutilation of all six.

Dr. Claire Hibbs, a representative of the State Veterinary Diagnostic Laboratory, New Mexico State University, Las Cruces, New Mexico, said he recently came to New Mexico, but that prior to that he examined some mutilation findings in Kansas and Nebraska. Dr. Hibbs said the mutilations fell into three categories: animals killed and mutilated by predators and scavengers, animals mutilated after death by "sharp instruments" and animals mutilated by pranksters.

Tommy Blann, Lewisville, Texas, told the conference he has been studying UFO activities for twenty-two years and mutilations for twelve years. He explained that animal mutilations date back to the early 1800's in England and Scotland. He also pointed out that animal mutilations are not confined to cattle, but cited incidents of mutilation of horses, dogs, sheep, and rabbits. He also said the mutilations are not only nationwide, but international in scope.

Chief Raleigh Tafoya, Jicarilla Apache Tribe, and Walter Dasheno, Governor, Santa Clara Pueblo, each spoke briefly to the conference. Both spoke of the cattle which had been found mutilated on their respective Indian lands. Chief Tafoya said some of his people who have lost livestock have been threatened.

Carl W. Whiteside, Investigator, Colorado Bureau of Investigation, told the conference that between April and December 1975, his Bureau investigated 203 reports of cattle mutilations.

One month later, the district attorney's office for Santa Fe, New Mexico, secured $50,000 in funding, to allow a detailed study of the evidence to commence—specifically in New Mexico. Very suspiciously, when it was announced that the program was going ahead, the FBI noted that the mutilations came to a sudden halt. This gave rise to deep suspicions that the mutilators were done by humans who, having heard of the planned investigation, hastily backed away until matters calmed down—which they did, when the number of new reports trailed off to nothingness.

> **V**ery suspiciously, when it was announced that the program was going ahead, the FBI noted that the mutilations came to a sudden halt.

With a distinct lack of new data to go on, the ambitious program was left to study a mere handful of cases—all of which it relegated to the work of predators and absolutely nothing else. Hardly surprisingly, this gave rise to the suspicions, among conspiracy theorists, that this was the goal all along: launch an investigation and assert that the mutes were the work of predators and nothing else, whatsoever, and then close the investigation down. If that was the case, then it worked all too well: the world of officialdom walked away from the mutilation problem, asserting that it had resolved the entire matter in down-to-earth terms, and assuring the public and the ranching community that there was nothing to worry about.

Evidently, however, there *was* something to worry about: no sooner had the project closed down, when the mutilations began again. And they still continue to this day. Whether the work of the government, the military, satanic cults, or deadly extraterrestrials, all that can be said of the cattle mutilations is that, officially, at least, they are no longer of any interest to the FBI or to any other arm of officialdom.

HAZARDS IN SPACE: RADIATION SECRETS

On Christmas day 2000, the Russian government announced it had lost contact with its *Mir* space station for a terrifying twenty hours. As the 140-ton station hurtled around the Earth, speculation was rife that *Mir* would spiral out of control and a disaster was imminent like that depicted in the film *Deep Impact*, in which a meteor hits our planet and causes devastation.

A calamity was averted when, as mission-control chief Vladimir Sololyov revealed on December 26, contact with, and control of, *Mir* had been re-established. "*Mir* will not fall on your heads on New Year's Eve," he said. "We have a plan to bid farewell to *Mir* in a civilized and organised way." He said *Mir* would be brought down in a controlled descent in the Pacific between February 27 and 28, 2001. It transpired that the actual date was March 23.

Throughout one of the tensest moments in the history of Russia's space program, officialdom was quick to state that the possibility of *Mir* crashing to Earth and wreaking untold havoc was remote. Or, maybe it wasn't: In the wake of the affair, a source inside the British Ministry of Defense leaked a classified document that revealed the truth about the hazards posed by the likes of secret spy-satellites in Earth orbit, and particularly those that might pose dangers of the atomic kind. The documents—and the attendant story—were big news.

The document, titled *Satellite Accidents with Radiation Hazards*, was prepared in 1979 by the British government's Home Office and was circulated to every chief officer of police, every chief fire officer, and every county council in England and Wales. "Similar circulars are being issued by the Scottish Office and the Northern Ireland Office," said the author of the paper.

An examination of the 1979 file makes it clear that the Home Office's decision to circulate the document on such a large scale was, ostensibly at least, because of an event that had occurred twelve months previously—as the following extract from the file reveals: "Following the descent of a nuclear-powered satellite in Canada on 24 January 1978, consideration has been given to contingency arrangements for dealing with the possibility of a similar incident in the United Kingdom."

The Home Office added that the possibility of a nuclear-powered satellite crashing within the British Isles was "remote." It was, however, careful to add that "the special considerations that affect the use of nuclear materials and the safety standards applied to them make it prudent to devise plans to deal with such an incident."

According to the file, one of the hardest predictions to make was when and where a stricken, nuclear-powered space vehicle, possibly spiraling wildly out of control and at hundreds, or even thousands, of miles-per-hour would impact. On this issue, the author of the document stated:

> Although it is likely that knowledge of changes in the orbital pattern which might lead to premature return to Earth would be available many hours or even days before re-entry occurred, it would not be such that a reasonably accurate prediction of the final orbit over the Earth could be made until 12 to 24 hours before impact. Even then forecasts of the precise point of re-entry along this track might still be in error by thousands of kilometers. It is possible accurate warning would not be available till a few minutes before impact and it is possible there might be no warning.

The document also makes it very clear that the Home Office was well acquainted with the more technical aspects of satellite technology: "Some satellites are designed in such a way that they will disintegrate on re-entry; others are so designed that fairly large components will remain intact on entering Earth's atmosphere."

And, if a space vehicle were to impact on the British Isles, what would be the outcome? The author of the document had a few ideas:

> Although the parameters of the orbit of a crashing satellite can be fairly closely defined, debris might fall over an area 2,000 kilometers wide. It would not be possible to alert police forces on a selective basis. In the event of a warning that a satellite might crash in or near the UK, all police forces would be alerted.

The *Mir* space station reentered Earth's atmosphere on March 23, 2001, breaking up harmlessly over the South Pacific, but only after the Russians were able to regain control of the craft.

In other words, official authorities all across the nation would potentially be put on stand-by to deal with the crash and recovery of exotic, space-based technologies. And that would only be the beginning, as the file demonstrates.

The crash of a nuclear-powered satellite would present problems such as: "There would be a possible radiation hazard; debris from the crashed satellite might be scattered over a very large area, perhaps the greater part of the country; and the individual pieces of debris might be very small, yet each might present a small radiation hazard."

Most significant of all, however, is a section of the document that refers not to *when*, but *if* the public should be informed of such a disaster:

A government decision would then be sought on whether the police should be alerted and whether a public statement should be made. If such actions were to be decided upon, overall responsibility for the measures to deal with an incident would be exercised from a central point in Whitehall, in a manner similar to procedures already established to handle a terrorist incident.

And who, precisely, would play a role in such recoveries? The list is intriguing, to say the least, and focused primarily upon the Atomic Weapons Research Establishment (AWRE) at Aldermaston; the National Radiological Protection Board (NRPB); the Ministry of Defense; and representatives from NAIR: the National Arrangements for Incidents involving Radioactivity. The Home Office then turned its attention to what would happen in the event that a crash was fully confirmed:

> When reports of suspected or actual locations have been received, the police should take such steps as may be needed locally to prevent people entering areas which may be dangerous because of radioactive material. All persons should be told to keep well away from possible radioactive debris. Although highly unlikely, some large pieces of debris might have radiation fields of significance over distances the order of 100 meters and some limited evacuation might be necessary; widespread continuous contamination is, however, unlikely.

In the wake of such a crash, the Home Office realized, the identification and collection of highly hazardous debris would be a painstaking process:

> Since much of the debris would be very small, many of the fragments would not be sighted and unnoticed irradiated debris might well be scattered over thousands of square kilometers. A major search operation might have to be mounted to locate radioactive fragments. Whether to mount a search, and if so what area should be covered, would be decided by the central control point. Arrangements would be made to deploy the resources of every available technical support service, including teams from the Ministry of Defense, National Radiological Protection Board, United Kingdom Atomic Energy Authority, British Nuclear Fuels and Electricity Generating Boards, using specialist aircraft and vehicle search techniques. In rural areas, the most effective initial search to locate major sources of radioactivity might be from the air.

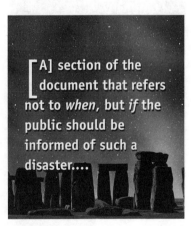

[A] section of the document that refers not to *when*, but *if* the public should be informed of such a disaster....

Two further sections of the document stand out as being worthy of comment. The first, titled *Public Warning About Radioactivity*, provides further insight into the British government's position on informing the populace at large of a disaster involving the crash of a contaminated spacecraft on British soil:

> It is for the government to decide whether, and by what means, a public warning of danger from radioactivity should be given. In reaching that decision, the need to prevent unnecessary alarm would be carefully con-

sidered. Chief Officers should therefore ensure that nothing is done locally to anticipate a government statement.

So much for the public: but what of the media? Under the heading *Press and Publicity*, we learn the following:

It is essential that those dealing with a satellite accident and the government team in Whitehall should not issue inconsistent statements. Chief Officers should ensure that all local press enquiries are directed to a senior officer at force headquarters, who is briefed to deal with them, working in close liaison with government information officers who would make appropriate arrangements to coordinate the national dissemination of information from Whitehall.

In essence, that is the document. And although the leaked paper is now more than three decades old, there are several points worthy of comment. First, the Home Office was—and, logic dictates, still is—very concerned by the possible scenario of a radioactive space vehicle crashing on British soil. Second, the fact that the public might be kept in the dark, if circumstances dictated, is highly worrying. One might ask: what gives the government the right to decide whether members of the public are informed of the possibility that radioactive space debris might rain down on their heads? Should not such information be made public at the earliest opportunity?

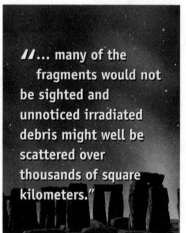

//... many of the fragments would not be sighted and unnoticed irradiated debris might well be scattered over thousands of square kilometers."

A call to the Home Office's press room—when the document surfaced—enticed a somewhat cagey response that affirmed the involvement of the Home Office in such matters today—along with the tracking station at RAF Fylingdales, in Yorkshire, England. Official concern that one day a cosmic calamity will occur, of the sort that almost befell the *Mir* space station over Christmas 2000, apparently, continues.

And, finally, the document briefly references an early 1979 meeting between representatives of the British Ministry of Defense and the United States Department of Defense, to discuss the matter of hazards posed by decaying, nuclear-powered spy satellites. To date, the files on that meeting remain classified. Clearly, the potential for disaster is as much a matter of secret concern for the Pentagon as it is for the Brits.

THE MURDER OF JOHN LENNON: A ROCK STAR CONSPIRACY

The countdown to the murder of rock music legend, and former Beatle, John Lennon, arguably began hours before it actually occurred, which was at 10:50 P.M. on December 8, 1980. During the afternoon of Lennon's last day alive, he and Yoko Ono were photographed at their apartment—in New York's Dakota Hotel—by Annie Leibowitz, who was there to secure pictures for a *Rolling Stone* magazine story. When the shoot was over, Lennon did a radio interview with San Francisco host Dave Sholin.

Somewhat eerily, Lennon said during the course of the interview: "I still believe in love, peace. I still believe in positive thinking. And I consider that my work won't be finished until I'm dead and buried, and I hope that's a long, long time." Lennon did not know it, but the end was getting closer by the minute.

With the interview complete, John and Yoko left the hotel and headed to a waiting limousine, which was to take them to the New York-based Plant Studio. As they strolled towards the vehicle, Lennon was approached by a young, bespectacled man who said absolutely nothing whatsoever. It was Mark David Chapman, whose only action was to push a copy of Lennon's *Double Fantasy* album into the hands of the former Beatle. Lennon, always willing to meet with fans, signed the album, which seemingly satisfied Chapman, who went on his way—as did John and Yoko.

It was shortly before 11.00 P.M. that the pair returned to the Dakota Hotel. Chapman was still there, hanging around since Lennon gave him an autograph just a few hours earlier. Yoko exited the limousine first and John followed. Tragedy was only mere moments away. As Lennon passed Chapman—and apparently recognized him from earlier—the words "Mr. Lennon!" rang out. Lennon turned in time to see Chapman assuming a combat-style position and gripping a pistol with both hands. It was all too late, however.

Chapman—who later said that, at that very moment, he heard a voice in his head say "Do it, do it, do it!"—fired on Lennon. Two bullets slammed into his back and two more into his left shoulder. Chapman had chosen his method of killing Lennon carefully. Chapman's pistol was loaded with hollow-tipped bullets, which are designed to cause maximum, pulverizing damage. They did exactly that. Lennon, covered in blood, and fatally injured, managed to stagger up the

The entrance to the Dakota Hotel in New York, where John Lennon was shot by Mark Chapman on December 8, 1980.

steps of the hotel, collapsing as he uttered the words, "I'm shot." For his part, Chapman simply removed his hat and coat and sat down on the sidewalk.

It became clear to all those present—which included the Dakota's concierge, Jay Hastings, and the doorman, José Sanjenis Perdomo, formerly an agent of both Cuba's secret police and the CIA—that Lennon needed emergency attention, immediately. There wasn't even a second to lose. Police officers James Moran and Bill Gamble were quickly on the scene and raced Lennon to the St. Luke's Roosevelt Hospital Center. Although Lennon was, initially, vaguely conscious in the back of the pair's car, he soon slipped into complete unconsciousness.

Despite the very best efforts of the responding doctors and nurses, Lennon could not be saved. The sheer level of destruction to his internal organs, arteries, and blood vessels sealed his fate back at the Dakota. As for Mark Chapman, although a battery of psychologists deemed him psychotic (five of whom stated he was suffering from full-blown schizophrenia), he was perceived as able to stand trial. He pleaded guilty to the murder of John Lennon and received a sentence of twenty-five years to life. Chapman remains incarcerated, to this day, despite having had seven parole hearings—all of which ended in denials. And now we come to the most controversial aspect of the shooting of John Lennon.

The *Atomic Poet* website noted:

After Mark David Chapman shot and killed John Lennon, he calmly opened up *Catcher in the Rye* and proceeded to read it—before being apprehended. John Hinckley, the man who attempted to kill Ronald Reagan, also was in possession of the book. It is also alleged Lee Harvey Oswald was quite fond of the book, though this is disputed. *Catcher in the Rye* has sold 65 million copies. Of the millions who have enjoyed the book, perhaps three have become well-known assassins. Still, we should ask: is there any merit to the book being an assassination trigger?

Writer Aidan Doyle said:

There are enough rumors about murders linked to J. D. Salinger's classic that the unwitting assassins in the Mel Gibson film *Conspiracy Theory* are portrayed as being brainwashed with the urge to buy the novel. John Lennon's murderer, Mark David Chapman, was famously obsessed with *The Catcher in the Rye*. Chapman wanted to change his name to Holden

Caulfield and once wrote in a copy of the book "This is my statement," and signed the protagonist's name. He had a copy of the book in his possession when the police arrested him.

But why, exactly, should the book have any bearing—whatsoever—on Mark Chapman's crazed killing of John Lennon? So conspiracy theorists maintain, trained, mind-controlled assassins—born out of the CIA's controversial MKUltra program—are "switched on" by certain key, "trigger words" that appear in the text of *The Catcher in the Rye*.

Lawrence Wilson, MD, notes that a hypnotist can implant the suggestion that when the phone rings twice, or when the doorbell rings, a post-hypnotic suggestion such as to kill whomever is in the room, even if it is your wife, will go into effect. This is used by some foreign police agencies to train hypnotized assassins.

In other words, and so the theory goes, Mark Chapman may have been a victim of deep hypnosis on the part of MKUltra operatives. But, rather than relying on a phone or doorbell ringing, they used *The Catcher in the Rye*—or segments of the text—as the trigger that turned Chapman into a ruthless killer, one who had no control over his deadly actions on December 8, 1980.

The blog, *CIA Killed Lennon*, records that:

While a teenager in Decatur, Georgia, Chapman did a lot of LSD, then found Jesus, and devoted his life to working with the YMCA, which, according to Philip Agee (*CIA Diary*, 1975), was prime recruiting grounds for CIA stations in Latin America. Chapman's YMCA employment records are missing. In June 1975, Chapman volunteered to work in the YMCA office in Beirut, Lebanon, as the civil war erupted. Returning to the U.S., Chapman was sent to work with newly resettled Vietnamese refugees (and CIA assets) in Fort Chaffee, Arkansas, run by World Vision, an evangelical organization accused of CIA collaboration in Honduras and El Salvador.

Let's not forget, too, that the doorman at the Dakota Hotel, José Sanjenis Perdomo, had worked with both Cuba's secret police and the CIA. On the matter of Perdomo, *Rumor Mill News* stated in 2004:

Newly discovered information about doorman José Perdomo suggests he may have been John Lennon's true assassin and Mark David Chapman was merely a patsy who confessed to the crime while under the spell of relentless mind control techniques such as hypnosis, drug abuse, shock treatment, sleep

John Lennon is seen in this photo rehearsing his song "Give Peace a Chance." It is felt by some conspiracy theorists that he was killed by a pro-war government that saw Lennon as a troublemaker.

deprivation, and so on. Perdomo was tasked to provide security for Lennon at the rock star's upscale apartment complex, the Dakota, the night of the murder. Records reveal a "José Joaquin Sanjenis Perdomo" (aliases: "Joaquin Sanjenis" and "Sam Jenis") was an anti-Castro Cuban exile and member of Brigade 2506 during the Bay of Pigs Invasion in 1961, a failed CIA operation to overthrow Fidel Castro.

To understand why someone may have wished to see John Lennon terminated, we have to turn to the writings of British conspiracy theorist Jon King:

> In his book *Who Killed John Lennon?* author Fenton Bresler presents evidence that the former Beatle's death was not the work of a "lone nut," but that Mark David Chapman was a CIA asset and that the CIA itself—or a faction within it—was behind the assassination. Bresler cited Lennon's political activism as a primary motive.
>
> In support of his claim, Bresler quotes late radio host, Mae Brussell, who broke the Watergate scandal, along with *Washington Post* reporters Bob Woodward and Carl Bernstein.
>
> "It was a conspiracy," Brussell affirmed. "Reagan had just won the election. They knew what kind of president he was going to be. There was only one man who could bring out a million people on demonstration in protest at his policies—and that was Lennon."
>
> Indeed, a year after Lennon's death, CIA-backed forces famously massacred more than a thousand civilians in El Salvador, where America was busy fighting a particularly dirty war.
>
> Lennon was opposed to that war, and word is the White House feared he may have spoilt the party had he remained alive and resumed his role as a political activist—which, according to those closest to him, he was planning to do.

Now-declassified FBI surveillance files on John Lennon (available online at the FBI's website, The Vault) make it very clear that the man was not at all approved of in official quarters. Both the bureau and President Richard M. Nixon viewed Lennon as a troublesome agitator. As a result, and as the papers that have surfaced through the Freedom of Information Act show, a number of attempts

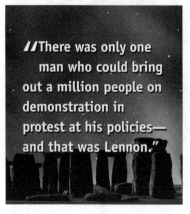

*//*There was only one man who could bring out a million people on demonstration in protest at his policies— and that was Lennon."

were made to try and find substantial dirt on Lennon that would allow the government to send him packing and back to his native England. One area of investigation that was followed revolved around various financial donations that Lennon had made to left-wing groups in the United States. It was something that angered the FBI but which was not seen as something strong enough to have Lennon deported. Drug-based charges certainly would have worked, but the bureau was never in a position to firmly pin anything on Lennon.

One issue that was of particular concern to the FBI was the fact that, in 1972, Lennon had donated money to a group called EYSIC, the Election Year Strategy Information Center. The FBI noted in its files:

The Election Year Strategy Information Center has been formed to direct movement activities during coming election year to culminate with demonstrations at Republican National Convention, August next. Sources advise John Lennon, former member of The Beatles singing group, has contributed seventy-five thousand dollars to assist in formation of EYSIC.

The FBI shared this data with none other than the Immigration and Naturalization Service, as the following 1972 memo demonstrates:

EYSIC, apparently dedicated to creating disruptions during Republican National Convention, obviously being heavily influenced by John Lennon, British citizen who is currently in U.S. attempting to obtain U.S. citizenship. Inasmuch as he is attempting to stay permanently in U.S., it is anticipated pertinent information concerning him will be disseminated to State and INS.

The battle to have Lennon deported continued. On March 16, 1972, the following was prepared by the FBI's Communications Section:

On March 16th Mr. Vincent Schiano, Chief Trial Attorney, Immigration and Naturalization Service, New York City advised that John Lennon and his wife Yoko Ono appeared at INS, NYC, this date for deportation proceedings. Both individuals thru their attorney won delays on hearings. Lennon requested delay while he attempted to fight a narcotics conviction in England. Yoko Ono requested delay on basis of child custody case in which she is involved. Mr. Schiano advised that new hearings would be held on April 18 next. If Lennon wins overthrow of British narcotic conviction, INS will reconsider their attempts to deport Lennon and wife.

Three days later, the FBI reported:

Lennon and his wife might be preparing for lengthy delaying tactics to avert their deportation in the near future.... Careful attention should be given to reports that he is a heavy narcotics user and any information developed in this regard should be furnished to narcotics authorities and immediately furnished to Bureau.

It was all to no avail, however. In 1974, the FBI finally relented—in the face of no direct, incriminating evidence of outright criminal activity on the part of Lennon—and the legendary Beatle was allowed to stay in the States. Sadly, as we have seen, Lennon's stay was not for long. It

John Lennon's wife, Yoko Ono, was also taken to the immigration hearings in which the U.S. government was trying to send the couple to England.

all came to a crashing halt in December 1980, when Mark David Chapman intervened.

For those who cannot bring themselves to accept that Chapman's actions were due to subliminal programming, it's worth noting the 1942 words of Dr. George Estabrooks, Ph.D., and chair of the Department of Psychology at Colgate University ("Hypnosis Comes of Age," *Science Digest*, April 1971): "I can hypnotize a man, without his knowledge or consent, into committing treason against the United States."

If a person could be hypnotized into committing treason against the U.S. at the dawning of the 1940s, then hypnotizing someone into a similar state four decades later—and having them kill a famous rock star known for his political activism, and his ability to influence the mindset of millions—seems not so unlikely, after all.

THE CHALLENGER DISASTER: NASA ATTACKED?

Not long before midday on January 28, 1986, NASA suffered what was, without doubt, its worst catastrophe ever: the destruction of the *Challenger* space shuttle. Worse still, all of the crew lost their lives in the fiery explosion that took out the shuttle. They were: pilot Michael J. Smith, payload specialists Gregory Jarvis and Christa McAuliffe, mission specialists Ellison Onizuka, Judith Resnik, Ronald McNair, and flight commander Dick Scobee. And, although the official verdict was that the *Challenger* disaster occurred as a result of wholly down-to-earth reasons, a wealth of conspiracy theories surfaced in the wake of the affair, all of which were carefully investigated by none other than the FBI. Before we get to the conspiracy theories, however, let's first take a look at what we know for sure, based upon NASA's careful study of all the evidence available.

The flight of *Challenger*—dubbed Mission 51-L—commenced at 11:38 A.M. EST. In no time whatsoever, it was all over. Just seventy-three seconds into the flight, a deadly explosion of oxygen and hydrogen propellants blew up the shuttle's external tank. The result, as NASA noted, was that this "exposed the Orbiter to severe aerodynamic loads that caused complete structural breakup. All seven crew members perished. The two Solid Rocket Boosters flew out of the fireball and were destroyed by the Air Force range safety officer 110 seconds after launch."

But, how did such a thing happen? Inquiring minds—including the government, the media, and the general public—wanted answers. NASA responded with a detailed study of the evidence. Thus was born the *Report of the Presidential Commission on the Space Shuttle* Challenger *Accident*, which was published by the U.S. Government Printing Office in 1986.

NASA's investigative team noted in its report on the disaster:

At 6.6 seconds before launch, the *Challenger*'s liquid fueled main engines were ignited in sequence and run up to full thrust while the entire Shuttle structure was bolted to the launch pad. Thrust of the main engines bends the Shuttle assembly forward from the bolts anchoring it to the pad. When the Shuttle assembly springs back to the vertical, the "Solid Rocket Boosters" restraining bolts are explosively released. During this prerelease "twang" motion, structural loads are stored in the assembled structure. These loads are released during the first few seconds of flight in a structural vibration mode at a frequency of about 3 cycles per second.

The maximum structural loads on the aft field joints of the Solid Rocket Boosters occur during the "twang," exceeding even those of the maximum dynamic pressure period experienced later in flight.

Just after liftoff, at .678 seconds into the flight, said NASA, "photographic data show a strong puff of gray smoke was spurting from the vicinity of the aft field joint on the right Solid Rocket Booster."

NASA continued that the two pad 39B cameras that would have recorded the precise location of the puff were inoperative. Computer graphic analysis of film from other cameras indicated the initial smoke came from the aft field joint of the right solid rocket booster. This area of the solid booster faces the External Tank. Eight more distinctive puffs of increasingly blacker smoke were recorded between .836 and 2.500 seconds, said NASA:

> The smoke appeared to puff upwards from the joint. While each smoke puff was being left behind by the upward flight of the Shuttle, the next fresh puff could be seen near the level of the joint. The multiple smoke puffs in this sequence occurred at about four times per second, approximating the frequency of the structural load dynamics and resultant joint flexing. Computer graphics applied to NASA photos from a variety of cameras in this sequence again placed the smoke "puffs" origin in the 270- to 310-degree sector of the original smoke spurt.

As the shuttle increased its upward velocity, it flew past the emerging and expanding smoke puffs. The last smoke was seen above the field joint at 2.733 seconds. At 3.375 seconds the last smoke was visible below the solid rocket boosters and became indiscernible as it mixed with rocket plumes and surrounding atmosphere.

The black color and dense composition of the smoke puffs suggested to NASA that the grease, joint insulation, and rubber O-rings in the joint seal were being burned and eroded by the hot propellant gases. Launch sequence films from previous missions were examined in detail to determine if there were any prior indications of smoke of the color and composition that appeared during the first few seconds of the 51-L mission, NASA noted in its official report on the disaster. None were found, however. Other vapors in this area were determined to be melting frost from the bottom of the external tank or steam from the rocket exhaust in the pad's sound suppression water trays.

The Space Shuttle *Challenger* is shown here being towed to the launch pad at the Kennedy Space Center.

The space shuttle's main engines were throttled up to 104 percent of their rated thrust level, the *Challenger* executed a programmed roll maneuver, and the engines were throttled back to 94 percent. At approximately thirty-seven seconds, NASA explained, *Challenger* encountered

Not long after takeoff on January 26, 1986, the Space Shuttle *Challenger* exploded, killing all seven crew members. A faulty O-ring on the Solid Rocket Booster was later blamed as the official cause.

the first of several high-altitude wind shear conditions, which lasted until about the sixty-four-second mark. The wind shear created forces on the vehicle with relatively large fluctuations. These were immediately sensed and countered by the guidance, navigation, and control system. It was all to no avail, however.

At forty-five seconds into the flight, NASA noted, three bright flashes appeared downstream of the *Challenger's* right wing. Each flash lasted less than one-thirtieth of a second. Similar flashes had been seen on other flights. Another appearance of a separate bright spot was diagnosed by film analysis to be a reflection of main engine exhaust on the Orbital Maneuvering System pods located at the upper rear section of the orbiter. The conclusion was that the flashes were unrelated to the later appearance of the flame plume from the right solid rocket booster.

Both the shuttle main engines and the solid rockets operated at reduced thrust, approaching and passing through the area of maximum dynamic pressure of 720 pounds per square foot, NASA determined, adding:

Main engines had been throttled up to 104 percent thrust and the Solid Rocket Boosters were increasing their thrust when the first flickering flame appeared on the right Solid Rocket Booster in the area of the aft field joint. This first very small flame was detected on image enhanced film at 58.788 seconds into the flight. It appeared to originate at about 305 degrees around the booster circumference at or near the aft field joint.

It was at the seventy-two-second mark, NASA demonstrated, that what the space agency described as a "series of events occurred extremely rapidly that terminated the flight." The agency continued:

At about 72.20 seconds the lower strut linking the Solid Rocket Booster and the External Tank was severed or pulled away from the weakened hydrogen tank permitting the right Solid Rocket Booster to rotate around the upper attachment strut. This rotation is indicated by divergent yaw and pitch rates between the left and right Solid Rocket Boosters.

Things had now reached the point of no return: overwhelming death and disaster were all but inevitable:

At 73.124 seconds, a circumferential white vapor pattern was observed blooming from the side of the External Tank bottom dome. This was the beginning of the structural failure of the hydrogen tank that culminated in the entire aft dome dropping away. This released massive amounts of liquid hydrogen from the tank and created a sudden forward thrust of about 2.8 million pounds, pushing the hydrogen tank upward into the intertank structure. At about the same time, the rotating right Solid Rocket Booster impacted the intertank structure and the lower part of the liquid oxygen tank. These structures failed at 73.137 seconds as evidenced by the white vapors appearing in the intertank region.

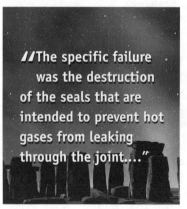

//The specific failure was the destruction of the seals that are intended to prevent hot gases from leaking through the joint...."

Within milliseconds, NASA's records show, there was massive, almost explosive, burning of the hydrogen streaming from the failed tank bottom and the liquid oxygen breach in the area of the intertank. At this point in its trajectory, while traveling at a Mach number of 1.92 at an altitude of 46,000 feet, the *Challenger* was totally enveloped in the explosive burn. The *Challenger*'s reaction control system ruptured and a hypergolic burn of its propellants occurred as it exited the oxygen-hydrogen flames. The reddish brown colors of the hypergolic fuel burn are visible on the edge of the main fireball. The orbiter, under severe aerodynamic loads, broke into several large sections that emerged from the fireball. Separate sections that can be identified on film include the main engine/tail section with the engines still burning, one wing of the orbiter, and the forward fuselage trailing a mass of umbilical lines pulled loose from the payload bay.

NASA's conclusion on the affair reads as follows:

The consensus of the Commission and participating investigative agencies is that the loss of the Space Shuttle *Challenger* was caused by a failure in the joint between the two lower segments of the right Solid Rocket Motor. The specific failure was the destruction of the seals that are intended to prevent hot gases from leaking through the joint during the propellant burn of the rocket motor. The evidence assembled by the Commission indicates that no other element of the Space Shuttle system contributed to this failure. In arriving at this conclusion, the Commission reviewed in detail all available data, reports, and records; directed and supervised numerous tests, analyses, and experiments by NASA, civilian contractors and various government agencies; and then developed specific failure scenarios and the range of most probable causative factors.

With regard to the crew, the NASA said:

The findings are inconclusive. The impact of the crew compartment with the ocean surface was so violent that evidence of damage occurring in the seconds which followed the disintegration was masked. Our final conclusions are: the cause of death of the *Challenger* astronauts cannot be positively determined; the forces to which the crew were exposed during Orbiter breakup were probably not sufficient to cause death or serious injury; and the crew possibly, but not certainly, lost consciousness in the seconds following Orbiter breakup due to in-flight loss of crew module pressure.

Although NASA's official conclusion was that the destruction of *Challenger* and the deaths of the crew were the collective result of a terrible accident, in no

The ill-fated crew of the *Challenger* included (front row, left to right) Michael J. Smith, Dick Scobee, Ron McNair, and (back row, left to right) Ellison S. Onizuka, Sharon Christa McAuliffe, Greg Jarvis, and Judy Resnik.

Some of the FBI agents on the case expressed their suspicions that there might have been more to the matter than met the eye.

time at all conspiracy theories surfaced, all of which suggested the event was not the accident that many concluded it to be. They were conspiracy theories that reached the very heart of the FBI. Interestingly, the FBI did not ignore or write off the claims. Instead, they launched concerted investigations to get to the truth. We know this, as the FBI's lengthy file on the *Challenger* conspiracy has now been declassified, thanks to the provisions of the Freedom of Information Act. The file is titled "Space Shuttle Challenger" and can be viewed online at the FBI's website The Vault, from which all of the following extracts are taken:

Less than twenty-four hours after the *Challenger* explosion took place, the office of William H. Webster, then the director of the FBI, received a memorandum from the agency's office in Boston, Massachusetts. It was a memo that described something disturbing and controversial. Barely forty-eight hours before the shuttle was destroyed, a reporter at the city's Channel 7 news took a phone call from an anonymous man who claimed that, according to the FBI's files, "he was part of a group of three people who were going to sabotage the Shuttle, causing it to blow up and kill all aboard."

Boston-based FBI agents wasted no time at all in hitting the offices of Channel 7. The staff was extensively interviewed as the bureau sought to gather all the available facts. Unfortunately, they were scant, but revolved around the caller's claims that "horrible things" were about to befall NASA and the *Challenger* crew, and that no less than "five people are going to be killed." By whom was the big mystery facing the FBI.

It turned out, however, that the bureau *assumed* it would be a big mystery, given that the caller was anonymous and seemingly long gone. That was not quite the case. For one of the agents, this was all too familiar, as a particularly notable, and now-declassified, FBI report shows. In part, the document reports that:

During briefing of SAC [Special Agent in Charge], ASAC [Assistant Special Agent in Charge], and appropriate supervisory personnel relative to aforementioned and employment of agent personnel, it was recalled that in September of 1985, a walk in complainant, of questionable mentality, had intimated that he had been responsible for the delay of previous Shuttles, plane crashes and other catastrophic events.

Agents who worked on the case well remembered the odd man, who clearly displayed far more than a few psychological issues. As a result, it didn't take them long to find and arrest the man. He was quickly subjected to what was described as a "five-day mental evaluation." It was clear to the FBI that the man was not faking his deranged mindset. As a result, he was released without charge, providing he underwent therapy and took whatever drugs the responding doctors determined he needed to take to try and ensure at least a degree of stability.

It must be said, though, that even some of the FBI agents on the case expressed their suspicions that there might have been more to the matter than met the eye. Yes, admittedly, the man had made a number of prior predictions about a terrible disaster concerning the *Challenger* space shuttle. But, this one was unlike any of the previous ones: not only did the man correctly predict the destruction of the shuttle; he also predicted it just two days before the disaster actually happened.

The FBI was far from done with space shuttle-based conspiracy theories, however.

At the same time that agents of the Boston office of the FBI were pursuing leads on the destruction of *Challenger*, something of a very similar nature was going down in California. The story is told in a summary document, one that was prepared by FBI agents in April 1986, after the investigation was finally closed. The document in question is titled *Space Shuttle* Challenger, *Information Concerning Launch Explosion, Kennedy Space Center, Florida, January 28, 1986*, dated April 18, and reads as follows:

> On January 31, 1986, the FBI Resident Agency in Santa Ana, California, was advised by [identity deleted] that he believes the *Challenger* exploded due to its being struck by laser beams fired from either Cuba or an aircraft. [Source] stated that a review of film footage of the explosion revealed brown puffs of smoke coming from the Space Shuttle just prior to the explosion. He stated leaks from the fuel tanks would produce white smoke, not brown smoke. [Source] said that the brown smoke would be produced each time the craft took a "hit" by the laser beam, and the explosion occurred when the laser beam penetrated the skin of the craft.

The FBI took careful steps to speak with leading figures in the field of laser-based weaponry—both in the U.S. military and the private sector. Interestingly, just about everyone told the FBI that the scenario was theoretically possible—and disturbingly so—but was considered unlikely. Precisely why the scenario was dismissed—when there was a near unanimous consensus that just such a thing could really be achieved—is curious. Unfortunately, certain portions of the documents that have been declassified on this matter are significantly redacted, thus making it practically impossible to secure the full story.

Moving on from Massachusetts and California, the story then takes us to Dallas, Texas. It was early March when the bureau's office in Dallas began investigating the claims of a man who worked in the movie industry. He believed that footage he recorded and carefully analyzed showed "something" flying through the sky and hitting one of the two boosters responsible for getting the shuttle into the skies, and "subsequently causing the explosion." FBI agents were sufficiently concerned to secure the footage—which they did, after a lengthy interview with the man, whose name is deleted from the available files.

The matter was ultimately dismissed; although it should be noted that the files reflect the man was perceived as nothing less than a good, concerned citizen, and not someone displaying mental issues, or working to a suspicious agenda. The most bizarre story of all was still to come, however.

He believed that footage he recorded and carefully analyzed showed "something" flying through the sky and hitting one of the two boosters....

Demonstrating that the FBI's study of the *Challenger* explosion was very much a nationwide one, the story now takes us to Washington, D.C. It's a strange saga, made even stranger by the fact that, even today, nearly thirty pages of material on the affair remain classified—specifically for reasons having a bearing on the safety of the nation. It revolved around the claims of a woman who maintained two things: (a) that the destruction of the space shuttle was the work of Japanese terrorists, and (b) that her information on the matter was channeled into her mind by highly advanced extraterrestrials.

From practically the very beginning, the FBI's files detail the controversy surrounding the woman in question. The bureau recorded in its documents on the case that the woman

> ... claims to be in contact with certain psychic forces that provide her with higher information on selected subjects. She refers to these forces as "Source" and when providing information from Source she often speaks in the collective "we." [She] claimed that she had come to Washington, D.C. to provide information concerning the *Challenger* Space Shuttle explosion on 1/28/86.

She did precisely that and provided the information on February 24, 1986.

Her claims were controversial: she maintained that the terrorist group in question was partly comprised of two workers at the Kennedy Space Center and one of the astronauts that died in the disaster: mission specialist Ellison Onizuka. As the FBI agents working on the case listened carefully—and, perhaps, a bit dubiously too—they were told that the group in question had a deep hatred of the United States and, by destroying the shuttle, wished to destabilize the U.S. space program and American morale. Whether the woman's story was true or not, it is a fact that the U.S. public was indeed shocked to the core, and the space shuttle program was put on hold for no less than thirty-two months.

When the agents asked the woman how the sabotage was achieved, they got a detailed answer:

> The explosion was effected by a device placed inside the external fuel tank of the Shuttle. An individual whose description seems to match that of an engineer or technician placed this charge. The charge was triggered by a second saboteur using a hand-held transmitter while standing in the crowds watching the Shuttle lift-off. The individual matches the description of a guard or security person. The astronaut saboteur chose to die in the explosion as a sort of ritual death or "cleansing."

As with all of the previous cases that the FBI had looked into, this one led nowhere—at least, that is the assumption, since no arrests were made. The odd affair came to a complete halt just weeks after it commenced.

The destruction of the *Challenger* space shuttle, on January 28, 1986, remains to this day one of the worst moments in NASA's history. Whether it was a moment provoked by nothing stranger than a terrible accident, or something filled to the brim with conspiracy theories and sinister, ruthless characters, very much depends on who you ask.

DEATHS IN THE DEFENSE INDUSTRY: NOT WHAT THEY SEEM

To many, it might sound like the ultimate plotline of the equally ultimate conspiracy-thriller: dozens of scientists and technicians—all working on highly classified programs, and all linked to one, particular company—dead under highly controversial and unusual circumstances. It's a controversy that ran from the early 1970s to 1991 and remains unresolved to this very day. And it all revolves around the top secret work of a company called Marconi Electronic Systems, but which, today, exists as a part of BAE Systems Electronics Limited. Its work includes the development of futuristic weaponry and spy-satellite technology.

As far as can be ascertained, the first to die was a man named Robert Wilson, who by 1971 had carved for himself a successful career with Marconi, specifically at its facility in Chelmsford, England. By that time, however, Wilson was ready to move on and take his work to a new level and to a new company. It was a decision that may have spelled his doom. One Sunday afternoon in the following year, Wilson decided to finally get around to tidying up the attic of his home. As he did so, and to his concern, he stumbled upon a stash of files from his old employer. He could not imagine how they got there and, deeply worried, contacted Marconi. A major investigation was quickly launched.

Although Marconi's security staff were seemingly satisfied that this was simply a case of Wilson having misplaced the files and forgotten about them, the story was about to turn both tragic and sinister—and quickly too. Less than twenty-four hours later, Wilson put a bullet into his chest. He had been cleaning a gun—a *loaded* gun, no less, and one that had the barrel pointing directly at him as he cleaned it—when it accidentally discharged. Luckily for Wilson, the bullet missed his heart, as well as his vital arteries. He survived. Not for long, however. In 1973, Wilson's lifeless body was found in his garage, the result of carbon-monoxide poisoning.

Wilson's death was quickly followed by the passing of yet another employee of the very same Chelmsford facility: Jack Darlow. Whereas Wilson had shot himself in the chest, Darlow had stabbed himself with a long, sharp blade. Death came quickly. There was then a lull in the deaths, one that recommenced in 1982—and with a vengeance.

It was in March 1982 that Professor Keith Bowden, whose computer expertise made him a valuable employee of Marconi, lost his life in a car accident. His vehicle left a three-lane highway at high speed and slammed into a railway line. Death was instantaneous. In March 1985, Roger Hill, a draughtsman with Marconi, died of a shotgun blast. His death was deemed a suicide. Just months later, the body of Jonathan Wash, an employee of a department within British Telecom that had extensive links to Marconi, was found on the sidewalk of an Ivory Coast hotel. Wash suffered a fatal fall, or was perhaps pushed, from the balcony of his room. That Wash had told friends and family he believed someone was watching and following him, and that he suspected his life was in danger, added to the suspicions that his death was not due to accident or suicide.

As 1985 became 1986, the death toll increased dramatically. On August 4, 1986, a highly regarded young man named Vimal Bhagvangi Dajibhai jumped from England's Clifton Suspension Bridge into the deep waters below. He did not survive the fall. Dajibhai held a secret clearance with Marconi Underwater Systems, a subsidiary of the main company. Only around eight weeks later, one of the most grisly of all the Marconi scientist deaths occurred. The victim was a computer programmer named Arshad Sharif. Such was the terrible and bizarre nature of Sharif's death, it even made the news thousands of miles away, in the United States. The *Los Angeles Times* reported that Sharif had "died in macabre circumstances ... when he apparently tied one end of a rope around a tree and the other around his neck, then got into his car and stepped on the accelerator. An inquest ruled suicide."

The coroner in the Sharif case, Donald Hawkins, commented wryly on the fact that Marconi was experiencing an extraordinary number of odd deaths: "As James Bond would say—this is beyond coincidence."

As the months progressed, so did the deaths. The case of Dr. John Brittan was particularly disturbing, since he had *two* run-ins with death, the second of which he did not survive. During Christmas 1986, Brittan ended up in a ditch after his car violently, and inexplicably, lurched across the road. He was lucky to survive. The Grim Reaper was not happy that Brittan had escaped his icy clutches, however. Less than two weeks into January 1987 (and immediately after Brittan returned to the U.K. from the States, where he had been on official, secret business) Brittan's body was found in his garage. He was an unfortunate victim of the effects of deadly carbon monoxide.

Also dead in January 1987 was Richard Pugh, a computer expert who had done work for Marconi and whose death the Ministry of Defense dismissed with the following words: "We have heard about him but he had nothing to do with us."

Then there is the extremely weird saga of Avtar Singh-Gida. An employee of the British Ministry of Defense, who worked on a number of Marconi programs, he vanished from his home in Loughborough, England, right around the same time that Dr. John Brittan died. His family feared the worst. Fortunately, Singh-Gida did not turn up dead. Quite the opposite, in fact: he was found, bafflingly, in Paris, fifteen weeks later. He had no memory of where he had been or what he had done during that period.

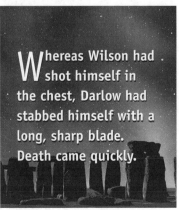

Whereas Wilson had shot himself in the chest, Darlow had stabbed himself with a long, sharp blade. Death came quickly.

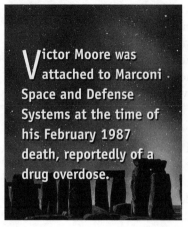

Victor Moore was attached to Marconi Space and Defense Systems at the time of his February 1987 death, reportedly of a drug overdose.

The deaths of Brittan, Dajibhai, and Sharif—coupled with the odd case of Singh-Gida—prompted a Member of Parliament, John Cartwright, to state authoritatively that the deaths "stretch the possibility of mere coincidence too far."

Cartwright's words proved to be eerily prophetic.

On February 22, 1987, Peter Peapell, a lecturer at the Royal College of Military Science, who had been consulted by Marconi on various projects, was yet another figure whose death was due to carbon-monoxide poisoning in his own garage—in the English county of Oxfordshire. In the same month, David Skeels, a Marconi engineer, was found dead under *identical* circumstances. Victor Moore was attached to Marconi Space and Defense Systems at the time of his February 1987 death, reportedly of a drug overdose. At the time, he was said to be under investigation by MI5, the British equivalent of the FBI.

One month later, in March 1987, one David Sands killed himself under truly horrific circumstances. He was in the employ of what was called Elliott Automation Space and Advanced Military Systems Ltd., which just happened to have a working relationship with Marconi at the time. Sands, whose family and colleagues said he was exhibiting no signs of stress or strain, loaded his car with containers of gasoline and drove—at "high voltage," as the police worded it—into an empty restaurant. A fiery death was inevitable.

In April 1987, there was yet another death of an employee of the Royal College of Military Science: Stuart Gooding, whose car slammed head-on into a truck on the island of Cyprus. Colleagues of Gooding expressed doubt at the accidental death verdict. On the very same day as Gooding died, David Greenhalgh died after falling (or being pushed) off a railway bridge at Maidenhead, Berkshire. Greenhalgh just happened to be working on the same program as David Sands.

Just seven days after Greenhalgh and Gooding died, and only a short distance away, a woman named Shani Warren took her last breaths. Warren worked for Micro Scope, a company taken over by Marconi just weeks later. Despite being found in just a foot and a half of water, and with a gag in her mouth, her feet bound, and her hands tied behind her back, the official verdict was—wholly outrageously—suicide.

May 3, 1987, was the date on which Michael Baker was killed—in a car "accident" in Dorset, England. He worked on classified programs for Plessey. Twelve years later, Plessy became a part of British Aerospace when the latter combined with Marconi. Ten months after, Trevor Knight, who worked for Marconi Space and Defense Systems in Stanmore, Middlesex, England, died—as had so many others—from carbon-monoxide poisoning in his garage. There were other unexplained deaths in 1988: midway through the year, Brigadier Peter Ferry (a business-development manager with Marconi) and Plessey's Alistair Beckham both killed themselves via electrocution. And, finally, there was the mysterious

1991 death of Malcolm Puddy. He had told his bosses at Marconi he had stumbled on something amazing. What that was, no one knows. Within twenty-four hours Puddy was dead. His body was hauled out of a canal near his home.

So, what was the cause of such a huge catalog of mysterious and sinister deaths? Here is where we reach decidedly controversial territory.

It's an undeniable fact that many of those who met untimely ends were working directly and indirectly with the U.S.-based Strategic Defense Initiative (SDI) program championed by President Ronald Reagan. It was a program that famously became known as "Star Wars." Even those who weren't directly allied to SDI were employed on issues that were tangential to the project, such as advanced laser-based technologies and outer space-based operations for the British Ministry of Defense.

The Department of Defense's Missile Defense Agency (MDA) notes of "Star Wars" that:

> By the early eighties, a number of strategic analysts had begun to worry that the Soviets had achieved a first strike capability that would allow them to cripple U.S. strategic forces and still retain enough nuclear weapons to destroy America's cities. In February 1983, this situation led the Joint Chiefs

Part of the Strategic Defense Initiative "Star Wars" program, this Delta II rocket was launched in 1989 from Cape Canaveral, Florida. The murder victims were all tied, in some way, to the SDI project.

of Staff to recommend to President Ronald Reagan that the U.S. begin to place greater emphasis in its strategic plans on developing missile defenses.

President Reagan was highly receptive to this recommendation. In a nationally televised speech on March 23, 1983, the president announced his decision to initiate an expanded research and development program to see if strategic defenses were feasible.

In April 1984, following a year of technical and strategic studies to determine how best to pursue the president's goal, the Defense Department established the Strategic Defense Initiative Organization (SDIO) under the leadership of its first director, Lieutenant General James A. Abrahamson of the U.S. Air Force. This organization was to carry out the SDI program of research and development (R&D) to resolve the feasibility issue.

After two and a half years of R&D, at the end of 1986 the President and Secretary of Defense decided to enter a missile defense system into the defense acquisition process. SDIO began to develop defenses against widespread missile attacks.

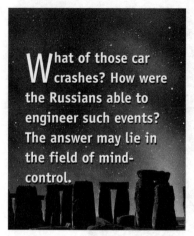

What of those car crashes? How were the Russians able to engineer such events? The answer may lie in the field of mind-control.

Thus was born the Strategic Defense Initiative. Things did not work out quite as well as President Reagan had hoped, however. Overly ambitious and lacking in adequate technologies to bring it to fruition, it was placed on the back burner, ultimately mutating into the Clinton-era Ballistic Missile Defense Organization, which has since been reorganized as the aforementioned Missile Defense Agency.

Conspiracy theorists suggest that at the height of SDI research, the former Soviet Union became deeply concerned by the distinct possibility that its entire nuclear arsenal might very well be rendered useless by an orbiting armada of laser-based weapons. In this scenario, the Soviets took a deadly and controversial decision: they decided to assassinate just about as many people as conceivably possible who were linked to the SDI program—from those directly involved to those only tangentially attached. But how could such a thing have been achieved? How could so many seemingly tragic suicides actually be murder? What of those car crashes? How were the Russians able to engineer such events? The answer may lie in the field of mind-control.

Whistleblowers have suggested the answers to the deaths of the Marconi personnel can be found in the pages of a formerly classified U.S. Defense Intelligence Agency document, dated March 1976: *Biological Effects of Electromagnetic Radiation (Radiowaves and Microwaves)—Eurasian Communist Countries*. Written by Ronald L. Adams and Dr. R. A. Williams, of the U.S. Army (and specifically of the Medical Intelligence and Information Agency), it notes in part:

> The Eurasian Communist countries are actively involved in evaluation of the biological significance of radiowaves and microwaves. Most of the research being conducted involves animals or in vitro evaluations, but active programs of a retrospective nature designed to elucidate the effects on humans are also being conducted.

Of deep concern to the United States was the incredible revelation that the Soviets had developed technology that allowed them to beam "messages" into the minds of targeted individuals. Rather notably, the DIA and the Army concluded that such messages might direct a person to commit nothing less than suicide. Even if the person was not depressed, said Adams and Williams, the technology could be utilized to plunge them into sudden states of "… irritability, agitation, tension, drowsiness, sleeplessness, depression, anxiety, forgetfulness, and lack of concentration."

The authors added: "Sounds and possibly even words which appear to be originating intracranially can be induced by signal modulation at very low average-power densities."

They concluded:

> The Soviets will continue to investigate the nature of internal sound perception. Their research will include studies on perceptual distortion and

other psycho-physiological effects. The results of these investigations could have military applications if the Soviets develop methods for disrupting or disturbing human behavior.

Were the Marconi personnel wiped out by a Soviet hit-squad, one that was determined to do its absolute utmost to ensure the SDI program failed? As incredible and as sci-fi-like as it seems, that just might have been *exactly* what happened.

AREA 51: COSMIC CONSPIRACIES

There can be very few people who have not heard of its infamous name. Many will be familiar with the extraordinary claims of what, allegedly, goes on there. It's a place that is saturated in secrecy, cloaked in conspiracy theories, and, according to many, is home to Uncle Sam's very own, highly classified collection of dead aliens, crashed UFOs, and extraterrestrial technology. Highly fortified, and guarded by personnel who have the right to use "deadly force" to protect its secrets, it is Area 51.

Although Area 51—as a classified installation, as a piece of popular culture, and as a magnet for UFO sleuths—has been known of since the late 1980s (when a maverick scientist, about whom much more later, spilled the beans), its origins can be found in the very earliest years of the Cold War.

It may surprise many to learn that, contrary to what the worlds of Hollywood and UFO research suggest, Area 51 is not buried deeply in the heart of nowhere and miles away from civilization. In fact, the surprising reality (to many) is that it is situated barely eighty miles outside of the city of Las Vegas. And, while Area 51 is the title that it is most associated with, the official name of the installation is far less infamous and far more bureaucratic: The Nevada Test and Training Range. It's located on a dry lake bed called Groom Lake, which has been converted into a highly classified—and decidedly off-limits—facility, one that is supplemented with huge airstrips, runways, hangars, and, so the rumor-mill goes—deep, underground installations that stretch for miles.

Accessing the base is near-impossible, unless, that is, of course, one has the relevant, top secret clearance to do so. The airspace above Area 51 is officially designated a no-fly zone, to anyone and everyone except those attached to the base. Trying to drive to the installation is a pointless task, too: motion-sensor equipment and armed guards dominate the desert terrain, ensuring that no one can get even within miles of the base. Try and do so and you run the very real risk of being detained, arrested, jailed, or, worse still, shot dead.

As far as the origins of Area 51 are concerned, they date back to the height of the Second World War. Just one year after the Japanese attack on Pearl Harbor, what was then known as the Indian Springs Air Force Auxiliary Field was created at the 4,409-foot-elevation lake. Its remote location provided the perfect

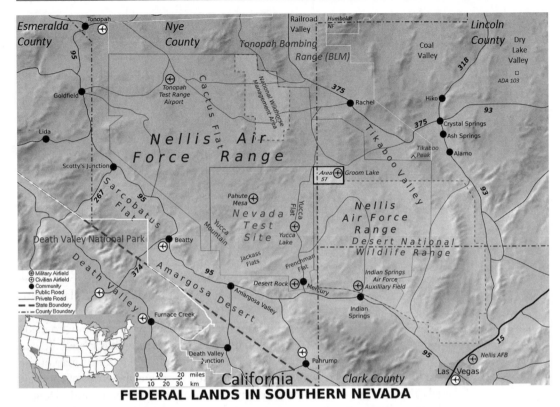

FEDERAL LANDS IN SOUTHERN NEVADA

A map of Area 51 now shows the once-secret area to be just to the northeast of the Nevada Test Site.

cover for the military to undertake practice bombing missions and the testing of new weaponry. Even though the facility was scarcely of the proportions that it is today, the seeds of deep secrecy and conspiracy were already being quietly sown.

It may not be exactly jaw-dropping to learn that the definitive origins of Area 51 began with none other than the Central Intelligence Agency, the CIA. Although the CIA was established in 1947, it was not until around the turn of the 1950s that serious consideration was given to constructing a secret, out-of-the-way, well-protected installation from which highly classified research could be undertaken. Given the timeframe, the Cold War era of the 1950s, the U.S. government knew that it had to take steps to ensure that, at the very least, a balance of power existed between the United States and the former Soviet Union.

Richard M. Bissell Jr. was a CIA officer who from 1961 to 1962 held down the job of first co-director of the super-secret National Reconnaissance Office (NRO), which operates much of the United States' satellite-based surveillance technology. Back in the early 1950s, and before his NRO career began, Bissell astutely realized that there was a pressing need to keep careful watch on what the Soviets were doing, specifically in terms of constructing new military bases, atomic

Rober M. Bissell Jr. was the man in charge of secret reconnaissance programs at the CIA. His main concern was keeping an eye on the Soviets.

facilities, and aircraft that might pose distinct, serious threats to the security of the United States. So, a plan was initiated to develop a fleet of aircraft—reconnaissance planes designed to fly very fast and very high—that could secretly spy on the Soviets, by penetrating their airspace and securing high-resolution photography of what the Reds were up to. The aircraft was the Lockheed U-2 and the operation was code named Project Aquatone.

Obviously, secrecy was paramount and the definite name of the game. Since intelligence data had shown the Soviets had spies in place all across the United States, and even within seemingly secure military facilities and aircraft research centers, a decision was made to have the project developed not at an existing plant or installation, but at an entirely new one, specifically built for the task. Bissell was the man who made it all happen. The first thing that Bissell did was to make a careful study of a detailed map of the entire United States. He was specifically looking for somewhere out of the way, largely inaccessible, easily protected, and that would offer a panoramic view of the surrounding landscape—in the event that communist spies attempted to engage in a bit of localized espionage.

One of those that Bissell approached was a man Clarence "Kelly" Johnson, a brilliant aircraft engineer and designer, and the brains behind both the U-2 and the SR-71 *Blackbird*. He scouted out various places in the United States, eventually settling on one that he felt most fit the bill that Bissell and the CIA were looking for. In the words of Air Force colonel Osmond J. Ritland (a major player in the development of Area 51), regarding the now famous scouting operation that he and Johnson were involved in:

> We flew over it and within thirty seconds you knew that was the place. It was right by a dry lake. Man alive, we looked at that lake, and we all looked at each other. It was another Edwards, so we wheeled around, landed on that lake, taxied up to one end of it. It was a perfect natural landing field … as smooth as a billiard table without anything being done to it.

Ritland was, of course, talking about Groom Lake. Area 51 was about to be born.

Given that the location was blisteringly hot, inhospitable in the extreme, and filled with nothing but deserts, dry beds, and mountains, something had to be done to entice people to come out and work there. Johnson had a brainwave: he decided to christen it Paradise Ranch. It paid off. It was during the first week of

1955 that things really got moving: that was when a group of surveyors arrived on-site, primarily to figure out the logistics involved in constructing a huge, 5,000-foot-long runway. It wasn't just the construction of the primary runway that began in earnest; the building of workplaces, a couple of rudimentary hangars, and even more rudimentary places to house the workers commenced. In other words, back then, Area 51 was little more than a desert equivalent of a North Pole outpost. As the months progressed, however, the workers were blessed with a couple of sports halls and a small cinema.

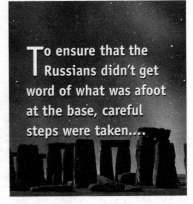

To ensure that the Russians didn't get word of what was afoot at the base, careful steps were taken to ensure that, at any and every given moment, the numbers of people on-site were kept to the bare minimum. That meant, essentially, hardly anyone would stay for lengthy periods of time (all of the workers would be flown in from, and back to, the Lockheed plant), and discussion of what was going on less than 100 miles from Las Vegas was strictly off-limits. The secrecy level was amped up even further when, in July 1955, two things happened: (a) a small, permanent CIA presence was established; and (b) the very first U-2 made its arrival at the base, having been secretly flown in aboard a large, cargo aircraft that was leased out to the CIA. Only days afterwards, the first of a near-unending series of flights began between Lockheed's Burbank facility and Area 51.

In the years that followed, such groundbreaking aircraft as the U-2, the *Blackbird*, and the A-12 were tested, refined, and flown at Area 51—all to try and find ways to keep the Soviet threat to a minimum.

As the demand increased for yet further advanced aircraft to be produced, taken to the skies, and modified, so did the need for Area 51 to be expanded in both scope and size. As a new decade dawned, a company called the Reynolds Electrical and Engineering Company—which, in the 1980s, did contract work for President Ronald Reagan's Strategic Defense Initiative (SDI) program—got involved. A huge new runway—in excess of 10,000 feet—was designed and built by REEC. Numerous hangars, in which the many and varied prototype aircraft could be hidden from any and all aircraft that might intrude too close to the base, were soon constructed. The Department of the Navy provided more than 120 prefabricated, small homes for those who had long-term contracts.

To cope with the concerns that the Soviets might try and figure out what was going on, by making high-level flights over Area 51, just two weeks into 1962, highly classified legislation was prepared by the Federal Aviation Administration to ensure that even more airspace was denied to anyone and everyone without official clearance. There was a good reason for this: February 1962 marked the date on which the first A-12 was flown into Area 51 for testing.

As the 1960s progressed, so did the work of staff at Area 51. One part of that work—a very significant part—revolved around the capture and exploitation of foreign technology. Over the years, the U.S. military acquired a number

Soviet fighter jets like the MIG-17 (this now-mothballed one at a Ukraine facility) were sometimes captured by the Americans and studied at Area 51.

of Soviet military aircraft, specifically MIGs. Some were the result of defections by Soviet pilots; others were secured after aerial accidents. Numerous, studious examinations of the Soviet technology were undertaken at Area 51, under such projects as Have Ferry and Have Drill.

By the time the 1970s were up and running, Area 51's finest were focusing a great deal on what has since become termed as Stealth technology—in essence, the ability to render an aircraft invisible to radar. Much of the highly classified research that led to the construction and deployment of the Lockheed F-117 *Nighthawk* (more popularly referred to as the Stealth Fighter) and the Northrop B-2 *Spirit* (better known as the Stealth Bomber) was undertaken out at Area 51— by which time the word "vast" barely begins to describe the base. A countless number of aircraft hangars underground labs, facilities built into the sides of the surrounding mountains, and new runways were part and parcel of Area 51.

For the most part, no one—aside from those elite figures in the military, the intelligence community, and the government—knew anything of Area 51 from its creation in the 1950s and right up until the latter part of the 1980s. The late eighties, however, was when everything changed and Area 51 became not just a big name, but somewhere that was forever thereafter inextricably tied to the UFO phenomenon.

On a now near-legendary night in March 1989 a man named Robert Scott Lazar made distinct waves amongst the Las Vegas media—and, ultimately, amongst the staff and highest echelons of Area 51, too. According to Lazar—who would only speak under the pseudonym of "Dennis"—for a few months in the latter part of 1988, he worked at what one might term a subsidiary of Area 51. Its name: S-4. George Knapp, a TV host at KLAS in Las Vegas, listened intently as Lazar told his story. It was one of fantastic and out-of-this-world proportions—quite possibly, literally.

Lazar claimed that at least nine alien spacecraft were stored at Area 51, all of which were being studied by a small group of scientific personnel who were having varying degrees of success in understanding and duplicating the technology. As an alleged, full-blown whistleblower, Lazar was a man both scared and sporting a target on his back.

Before we get into the intricacies of the Area 51–Bob Lazar story, let's see what we know about this still-mysterious character. Lazar was born in Florida in 1958; that is a verifiable fact. That, with his education complete, he was employed by Fairchild—which was created at the end of the 1960s by William Shockley, the man behind the development of the transistor—is not in doubt, either. What is in doubt is Lazar's claim to have obtained an M.S. from Caltech and another from MIT—in electronics and physics, respectively. So far, and despite his assertion, nothing has ever surfaced to support Lazar's claims about Caltech and MIT.

Moving on, and demonstrating that Lazar was plugged into intriguing and notable circles as far back as the early 1980s, he appears on the front-page of the *Los Alamos Monitor*, a New Mexico-based newspaper. It profiled Lazar's interest in cars, particularly super-charged cars—more to the point: cars powered by nothing less than jet engines. The *Monitor* also noted that, at the time, Lazar was employed at the Los Alamos Meson Physics Facility where he was working on projects concerning the field of particle physics. He also claimed a friendship, of sorts, with the legendary theoretical physicist Edward Teller—who, Lazar said, helped get him the job at Area 51. It was a claim that Teller would not outright deny; he squirmed in just about every way possible when asked about it. It wasn't long after speaking with Teller that Lazar was contacted by an employee of Edgerton, Germeshausen, and Grier, Inc. (EG&G), a U.S. defense contractor. One meeting became a second meeting, and finally turned into

Robert Lazar claimed to have worked on extraterrestrial technology while at S-4, a subsidiary of Area 51, and that there were at least nine UFOs at the secret military facility.

a job offer, although Lazar was not told what the job would be, only that he would find it amazing. No prizes for guessing where the project was based.

Flown out of Las Vegas's McCarran Airport—after which, he was required to travel a short distance in a vehicle with blacked-out windows—Lazar arrived at Area 51's S-4, still not entirely sure what he would be doing there. He soon found out, however. On arrival, Lazar found himself confronted by the sort of futuristic installation one might expect to see on the surface of the Moon, in a high-tech sci-fi production—but certainly not in the heart of the Nevada desert. The security was extreme: machine-guns were shoved in his face, he was warned that his life would be in danger if he ever disclosed what he was about to see, and there were threats of the use of mind-altering drugs to make him forget what he might encounter.

What he did see, Lazar claimed—to George Knapp, in 1989—was a veritable squadron of UFOs, sitting in hangars, some in pristine condition, one or two somewhat damaged, but still sitting there, all the same. Lazar was beginning to perceive the enormity of the situation; something that became even clearer when he was given a mass of highly classified files to read on the extraterrestrial presence on Earth. The aliens' link to religion, their technology, reports of alien autopsies, attempts to duplicate the fantastic non-human technology: it was all in there.

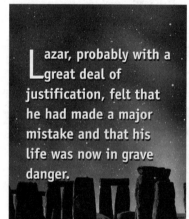

Lazar, probably with a great deal of justification, felt that he had made a major mistake and that his life was now in grave danger.

As for his specific job, Lazar was told it would be based around trying to understand and duplicate the power source of the UFOs: a super-heavy element called Element 115, which does not naturally exist on Earth, something that convinced Lazar of the non-human origin of the technology before him.

According to Lazar, his time at the base was brief—something that was prompted by his highly unwise decision to confide in family and friends what he had seen and read at Area 51. Lazar, probably with a great deal of justification, felt that he had made a major mistake and that his life was now in grave danger. It may well have been: someone shot out one of the tires on his vehicle, there were veiled threats of what was going to happen to him, and he feared being taken back to the base and vanishing—*forever*. As a result, Lazar did the only thing he felt he could do, under the circumstances. That was to go public with the help of George Knapp and the KLAS-TV team. Area 51 soon was featured in the likes of *The X-Files* and *Independence Day* and quickly became a part of popular culture.

And it still is. Area 51: the world's most highly classified, and most widely known, secret installation on the planet. The extraterrestrial angle of Area 51 is not solely reliant on the words of Bob Lazar, however.

In the early 1970s, a man named Arthur Stansel—who held a master's degree in engineering, and who, during the Second World War, took part in the D-Day Landings at Normandy, France—went public with a story relative to what he knew of classified UFO activity that, as would later become apparent, had a connection to Area 51. It was late one night in 1953, and while he was working at the ultra-secret Nevada Proving Ground, that Stansel and a colleague viewed nothing less than a flying saucer-shaped UFO soar across the skies near the site of a then very recent atomic-bomb test that was part of a larger series of tests known as *Operation Upshot-Knothole*. This was just the latest in a whole series of atmospheric nuclear weapons-based tests that fell under the jurisdiction of the Atomic Energy Commission (AEC) and that were conducted at the Nevada Proving Ground from March 17 to June 4, 1953.

Ultimately, however, Stansel had far more to impart than the details of a hard-to-define aerial encounter. There was another UFO event in which he was involved; one that was even more controversial. Stansel said that the incident had occurred during his brief tenure with the U.S. Air Force's UFO investigation program known as Project Blue Book. He had received a telephone call from the base-commander at Wright-

Arthur Stansel asserted that while he was working at the Nevada Proving Ground he saw a UFO fly by the site of a recent nuclear test.

Patterson AFB in Dayton, Ohio, on one particular day in 1953, with orders for him to fly to Phoenix, Arizona. From there, Stansel was driven to the crash site of what he was told was a then-secret aircraft of the Air Force.

On arrival at the site—which he was sure was situated on the fringes of Kingman—Stansel could not fail to see some form of unusual object. This was no classic flying saucer, however. Rather, the object was shaped like a cross between a teardrop and a cigar. Not only that: it was barely twelve feet in length. But that was not all. Also at the site was a body, and at only four feet in height it was no human body. Yes, it had arms, legs, a torso, and head, but its skin was dark in color and its facial features were manifestly different from what one would normally see. Stansel claimed not to know what happened to the craft—or to the curious creature—or where it was taken. But someone did.

One of the most intriguing figures to surface with regard to the Kingman affair was Bill Uhouse, a retired mechanical engineer from Las Vegas who claimed to have worked on classified projects at certain governmental locations in Nevada that focused upon the reverse engineering of crashed-and-recovered UFO technology, including Area 51. With specific regard to the Kingman crash, the UFO researcher, Bill Hamilton, dug deep into the claims of Uhouse, who asserted that no fewer than four alien entities were found alongside the Kingman UFO—and that all of them had survived the crash, albeit with varying degrees of injury.

Somewhat ominously, Uhouse additionally said that a number of the team that was involved in the retrieval of the Kingman UFO had been afflicted by what was suspected of being an unknown biological agent. This latter point was expanded upon in early 2006 when new and provocative data surfaced on the Kingman crash via an unnamed source who claimed a background within the United States' Intelligence community, and whose story can be found at the website www.serpo.org.

According to data posted to the *Serpo* website, the Kingman event did indeed occur, and that, just like Bill Uhouse claimed, four alien beings were found at the site—two severely injured and two in reasonably good condition. And, again just like Uhouse: the unnamed source whose words are now preserved at

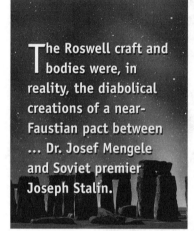

The Roswell craft and bodies were, in reality, the diabolical creations of a near-Faustian pact between ... Dr. Josef Mengele and Soviet premier Joseph Stalin.

the *Serpo* website maintained that a number of the military retrieval team were adversely, physically affected by their exposure to the craft and bodies—which were taken to Area 51 for secret study.

Also on the issue of UFOs at Area 51, one of the strangest of all developments surfaced in 2011. It was a story that appeared in the pages of a book written by author and journalist Annie Jacobsen. Its title was *Area 51: An Uncensored History of America's Top Secret Military Base*. The book included a thought-provoking story suggesting that the legendary "UFO crash" at Roswell, New Mexico, in the summer of 1947, was actually nothing of the sort at all. The Roswell craft and bodies were, in reality, the diabolical creations of a near-Faustian pact between the notorious Nazi (and "Angel of Death") Dr. Josef Mengele and Soviet premier Joseph Stalin. The purpose of this early Cold War plan: to plunge the United States into a kind of *War of the Worlds*–style panic, all by trying to convince the U.S. government that alien beings were invading.

And how would the plan work? By placing grossly deformed children (courtesy of the crazed Mengele, who was noted for his obscene, nightmarish experimentation on people) inside a futuristic-looking aircraft designed by a pair of brilliant aviation experts, the Horten brothers—Walter and Reimar—and then try and convince the United States of the alien origins of both. Unfortunately for Stalin, the plot failed when a storm brought down the craft and its "crew" in the wilds of New Mexico, an event that did not lead to widespread panic, but that, instead, was hastily covered up by U.S. military authorities.

Was the story true? Was Jacobsen duped? Is it a blend of fact and fiction specifically weaved by government insiders to even further confuse the true nature of what did, or did not, happen outside of Roswell back in the summer of 1947?

When Jacobsen's book was published, it garnered a great deal of publicity—much of it focusing on the Roswell story that she had been given. The story was reportedly provided to Jacobsen by an elderly man who, before his retirement, worked for a company with deep ties to Area 51: Edgerton, Germeshausen, and

Grier, Inc. (EG&G), a U.S. defense-contractor-based body created in 1931 by Harold Edgerton, who was a professor at MIT, and one of Edgerton's students, Kenneth Germeshausen. Three years later, Herbert Grier—also of MIT—became the third member. The initials of their surnames prompted the name of the company. They were soon, thereafter, joined by Bernard O'Keefe. EG&G was involved in (a) the Manhattan Project that created the atomic bomb, (b) the development of night-vision goggles, and (c) the testing of new technologies at a certain place in the Nevada desert—Area 51.

As controversial and eye-catching as the story of Annie Jacobsen's source was, it was not without its problems. First, there was the matter of Josef Mengele. Mengele was a member of Adolf Hitler's dreaded SS, and someone whose notorious and horrific experiments were carried out at Auschwitz (many of which *were* carried out on deformed children). Mengele fled Auschwitz in January 1945, specifically before the Soviet military arrived on the scene. He was, months later, taken into custody by Allied forces, before being let go because of catastrophic, bureaucratic mistakes on the part of his captors. He laid low for years, secretly fleeing to South America in 1949—first to Argentina, then to Paraguay, and finally, to Brazil, where he died in 1979. In short, Mengele was *never* in the employ of Soviet premier Joseph Stalin.

[T]he chances of the U.S. government being duped by a Horten-created craft ... are unlikely in the extreme.

There is also a problem with the theory that the Roswell craft was designed and built by the Horten brothers. Yes, they were aviation geniuses, ones who designed some of the most advanced and weird-looking aircraft of the Second World War. Documentation of 1946, however—which was declassified under the terms of the U.S. Freedom of Information Act—demonstrates that just one year after the war was over, the U.S. military had in its hands *all* of the many and varied designs of the Horten brothers. Therefore, the chances of the U.S. government being duped by a Horten-created craft one year later, in 1947, are unlikely in the extreme. That's not to say that Annie Jacobsen's source lacked credibility, however; quite opposite, in fact, as UFO researcher Tony Bragalia noted in a 2011 article, "Book Exposed: Jacobsen's Secret Source Revealed with Interview":

> Ms. Jacobsen's source about this Roswell story is unnamed by her in the blockbuster book. He wanted to remain anonymous. Annie Jacobsen kept her promise. I did not learn her source from her or from anyone associated with her publishing company. His identity and his background is revealed here and now: Alfred O'Donnell is nearly 89 years old and he is one of Annie Jacobsen's key sources about this Roswell crash story "interpretation." O'Donnell is indeed exactly who he claims to have been. In the early 1950's he was at the "Nevada Test Site" where atomic bombs were tested regularly. O'Donnell was indeed part of the nucleus of top management and engineers for EG&G—one of our nation's top defense contractors.

Bragalia's conclusion is that O'Donnell was, indeed, told the story that he later told to Jacobsen. Bragalia, however, is of the opinion that the Stalin–Mengele story was deliberately, secretly, and officially, spread to confuse the truth surrounding what Bragalia believes to have been the *real* story of Roswell—the crash of a vehicle constructed from another world.

The reference to EG&G brings us right back to Bob Lazar, who claimed it was none other than EG&G who set him up with the brief job he held at Area 51's S-4. In the more than a quarter of a century that has now passed since Lazar came out of the shadows with his story of UFOs at Area 51, controversy continues to reign: Was Lazar telling the truth? Was he the whistleblower he claimed to be? Might he—unknowingly—have been set up, as part of a strange psychological warfare-themed operation, one that was designed to try and scare the Soviets into believing that the U.S. government had in its hands fantastically advanced alien technology? Or was the whole thing nothing but a big joke on Lazar's part?

It must be said that while certain parts of Lazar's background don't check out, others certainly do, including his time spent working on classified programs at Los Alamos. That Edward Teller refused to deny that he knew or had met Lazar is puzzling, if the whole thing was just a big con on the part of Lazar. That there has never been an official denial of Lazar's claims is intriguing, too. Also intriguing is the fact that Lazar has stood by his story since 1989; he has never wavered from the story he told back in 1989. There is no evidence he has made significant monetary gains from telling his story.

In that sense, nothing makes much sense, unless one accepts Lazar's story as valid. Or, one takes the view that Lazar is a man who enjoys stirring the pot, so to speak, and his goal was not money but notoriety. He certainly got the latter.

Of only one thing can we be sure of when it comes to Bob Lazar: whatever the truth of the man's story and his claims, it was Lazar—and largely, Lazar alone—who put Area 51 on the map, and on the radar of the world's media, of Hollywood, and of the general public.

CROP CIRCLE SECRETS: MESSAGES IN THE FIELDS

In 1989 George Wingfield, who worked at the Royal Greenwich Observatory, and who had a fascination for the crop circle enigma, revealed his awareness of a secret British government meeting held in September 1990 to discuss the nature and implications of the ever-increasing mystery of the circles. It was a fear of the government having to admit its ignorance of the phenomenon that provoked the meeting, Wingfield's sources told him.

Crop circle conspiracies? It might sound outlandish and extreme. It's not. It's all too real.

Secret government interest in crop circles dates back to the height of the Second World War, when Britain's MI5—the equivalent of the United States' FBI—took note of the curious phenomenon, and which was decades before the term "crop circle" was even created. The story is told in a formerly top secret MI5 file that is available for viewing at the National Archives, England. In part, it reveals:

> This account is not concerned with the activities of fifth columnists such as sabotage, capturing airfields and key points, and harassing the defending army, but in the methods used in communicating to each other and to the enemy. Reports from Poland, Holland, France, and Belgium showed that they used ground markings for the guidance of bombers and paratroops (and of lights by night).

The MI5 agent who prepared the report (whose name is blacked out on the available records) added that:

> Such ground markings might be the cutting of cornfields into guiding marks for aircraft, painting of roofs and the inside of chimneys white, setting haystacks on fire, and laying out strips of white linen in pre-arranged patterns. For guiding and giving information to advancing troops they would conceal messages behind advertisement hoardings and leave markings on walls and telegraph poles.

Now, we get to the most significant part of the file. It notes that intelligence data coming out of Poland, the United States, and the U.K. had revealed that German agents were believed to have been contacting Nazi pilots by "beating out signs," twenty meters in diameter, "on harrowed fields or mowing such signs on

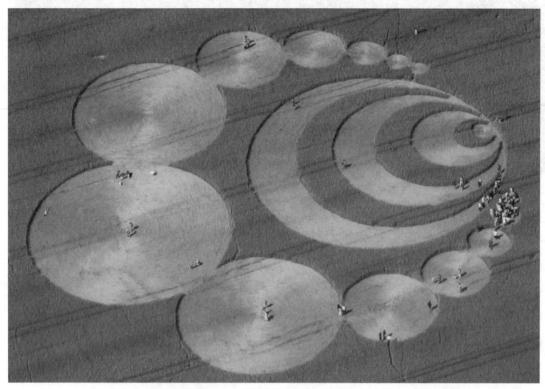

Back during World War II, England's MI5 thought crop circles like this one recently seen in Switzerland were secret signals for the benefit of German pilots.

meadows or cornfields." It doesn't take a genius to realize that what MI5 was describing sounds very much like crop circles.

There is something even more significant, too, about all this: the idea that the huge formations Allied pilots had seen in European fields were the work of the Nazis was simply a theory and nothing more. Moreover, it was a theory that was never, ever proved—even after the hostilities came to their close in 1945. Captured German spies and Luftwaffe pilots claimed no knowledge of the formations, even though they admitted having seen them too, and presumed they were the work of the Allies.

As a result of these curious formations popping up in Europe, MI5 kept a very careful watch on what was going on at home.

An MI5 document, with the title of *Examples of Ground Markings Investigated*, reveals the following on British-based formations found in fields:

Field, north of Newquay, Cornwall—Aircraft noticed, in May 1940, strange marking in this field and it was photographed. Enquiries were made and it was found that the lines were formed by heaps of lime used for agricultural purposes. The farmer concerned was above reproach and removed the lime heaps.

A further report noted: "Field at Little Mill, Monmouthshire: In May 1941, a report was made that an unusual mark was visible amongst the growing corn. Near one of the gates was a mark in the form of the letter G, some 33 yards long. This mark had been made by sowing barley transversely through the grain."

And then there is this:

Air photographs were taken and it was seen that the tail of the marking pointed towards the Ordnance factory at Glascoed. The farmer, a man of good character, was interviewed, and admitted that he had sown the field himself. He explained that he had sold the field in April.

Shortly after, having a drilling machine nearby which had a small quantity of barley seed in it, and wishing to empty it as he had to return it to the farmer from whom he had borrowed it that night, he turned his team of horses into the grain field and drilled it into the ground thickly to get rid of it. He did this because it is extremely difficult to remove the grain in the machine by hand, and to sow it was the quickest way of getting rid of it.

He agreed to plough up this part of the field. As a satisfactory explanation had been reached, the case was carried no further.

And the reports kept on coming:

Field, near Staplehurst, Kent: In October, 1943, aircraft saw a faint white circle on the ground. Enquiries were made, and it was discovered that before the war the field was used as an emergency landing ground by Imperial Airways; the mark was made by them, and they paid a small yearly rent to the farmer. At the beginning of the war the mark was obliterated in some way, but this had worn thin. Steps were taken to obliterate it again.

Obviously, all of these particular formations had wholly down-to-earth explanations. It's important to stress, however, that the investigations were prompted by the truly unknown ones found across various parts of Europe, such as the fields of Holland, Poland, and France.

During the early part of 1995, the British Ministry of Defense declassified hundreds of pages of formerly withheld files on UFOs, all of which dated from 1964. Contained within the file was the following letter, submitted to the MoD, via the National Physical Laboratory at Teddington, England, in March 1964. The subject matter was a curious, circular area of flattened ground found on land in the town of Penrith, Cumbria, England.

As the file demonstrates, on March 23, 1964, T. E. T. Burbury, the rector at Clifton Rectory, Penrith, Cumberland, England, wrote to the National Physical Laboratory at Teddington describing an encounter that had occurred some days previously. I quote from the rector's letter:

Dear Sirs:

Does an apparent column of blue light about 8-feet in diameter and about 15-feet high which disappears and leaves a

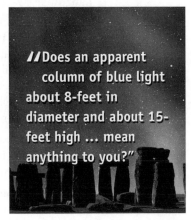

//Does an apparent column of blue light about 8-feet in diameter and about 15-feet high ... mean anything to you?"

mark of very slightly disturbed earth, the same diameter, mean anything to you? This occurred about 9.30 P.M. last Saturday night about 2 miles from here. It was seen by a person who is very short sighted who would have been unable to see anything, except the light, even if it had been present.

I examined the ground which is about 100 Yards from the nearest building and there are no pylons near. There was no sign of burning, either by sight or smell, the grass growing between the exposed ground appeared quite normal. There were no signs of bird tracks or droppings: the ground simply appeared to have been lightly raked over in an almost perfect circle.

For your information only, I told the farmer to have a sample of the earth collected and analyzed for bacteria content, but don't know whether he has done so. Yours faithfully: T. E. T. Burbury.

Note the words of the rector: "The ground simply appeared to have been lightly raked over in an almost perfect circle."

Does this not sound somewhat familiar?

Furthermore, Burbury's reference to "the farmer" strongly suggests that the circle was found on farmland. And: what of the column of blue light? Realizing that this was out of their jurisdiction, staff at the National Physical Laboratory forwarded a copy of the rector's letter to the Meteorological Office at London Road, Bracknell. In turn, Mr. H. M. Race of the Meteorological Office advised Burbury: "This does not appear to be a meteorological matter and we are therefore passing your letter to a London office who may be able to deal with it."

The "London office" to which Race was referring was an element of the old Air Ministry called S4. For its part, S4 seemed largely unconcerned, even amused, by the rector's report, as the following opening words of a memorandum of 16 April 1964 from R. A. Langton of S4 to a colleague, Flight Lieutenant A. Bardsley showed: "I should be grateful for your advice on the report in the attached correspondence. Could it be Will o' the Wisp?"

The attached correspondence was, of course, Burbury's letter. Two months later, Flight Lieutenant Bardsley stated the following in a good-humored reply to Langton:

This is quite a corker! The explanation could be one of several things, depending really, on the state of the investigator's liver. One explanation could be aurora borealis. This phenomenon, however, is so unpredictable that it would be rather hopeless to expect someone to have seen the aurora at the same date/time as our short-sighted observer. Professor Paton at Edinburgh is an aurora expert, but I cannot really justify pestering him with this one.

Bardsley continued: "Again your 'will o' the wisp' theory may be correct. However whilst following this line, the Royal Geographic Society confirmed that Penrith did not exist—at least in Bradshaw's Gazetteer."

Further, information on the geological structure around Penrith again confirmed that there probably would not, but possibly could be, local ignitions of methane gas—absolutely no use these experts! Our myopic observer may possibly have seen car headlights shining up into a low cloud base. There is no mention of any sound in this report—could the observer be also deaf!

He concluded:

One comment by the rector intrigues me: Could it be the rector thinks the object could be a phoenix? Finally: There once was a rector of Penrith, who reported that one of his Kith, saw blue light in the night, got a terrible fright, and the rector thinks it's a "myth."

Although Flight Lieutenant Bardsley signed off his reply in fine poetic style, he did not see fit to comment on the "almost perfect circle" reported by the rector, nor did he express an interest in following up on the rector's suggestion to the farmer that a sample of earth should be collected for study.

Moreover, an examination of the Air Ministry file in question reveals no further reference to this particular case, and the entire matter appears to have been summarily dismissed—which is in stark contrast to the situation during the Second World War.

Moving on to the 1990s, Pentagon personnel attended the first European meeting of the Society for Scientific Exploration, which was held from August 7 to 8, 1992, in Munich, Germany, and that had the crop circle subject on its agenda. A secret document on the meeting, now available via the Freedom of Information Act, describes its flavor:

The expressed aim of the SSE meeting was to promote the exchange of ideas, results and goals among researchers in various fields of anomalies, and inform the public of the discussion among active scientists concerning current controversial issues. Papers and communications were in English, and German language abstracts of the various parapsychology (PS) papers presented were distributed at the beginning of the meeting.

The conference sessions examined PSI and other extraordinary mental phenomena, crop circles (were they messages or hoaxes), geophysical variables and their influences on human behavior, astro-psychology, the Earth and unidentified flying objects (UFO), and additional highlights, to include near death experiences (NDE).

And Nick Pope, who investigated UFO sightings for the Ministry of Defense between 1991 and 1994, said to me in a January 1997 interview:

I draw a parallel between the way in which incredibly complex patterns appear in a field, with the way in which we broadcast through radio astronomy. Perhaps it is an attempt at communication. Where that communication comes from, whether it's extraterrestrial or something to do with the earth, I don't know.

Whether *someone else* in the Ministry of Defense—or within MI5 or the Pentagon—may secretly know, however, is quite a different matter.

SECRET PSYCHIC SPYING: MIND-BASED ESPIONAGE

For decades, numerous nations, all around the world, have done their utmost to try and harness the mysterious powers of the mind and utilize them as tools of nothing less than espionage. Extrasensory perception (ESP), clairvoyance, precognition, and astral projection have all been utilized by the CIA, the KGB, and British Intelligence on more than a few occasions. As astonishing as it may sound, the world of psychic 007s is all too real. It's a subject that has been researched, with varying degrees of success, for decades.

The earliest indication of serious interest on the part of the U.S. government in the field of psychic phenomena can be found in a formerly classified CIA document written in 1977 by Dr. Kenneth A. Kress—then an engineer with the CIA's Office of Technical Services—and titled *Parapsychology in Intelligence*.

According to Kress:

Anecdotal reports of extrasensory perception (ESP) capabilities have reached U.S. national security agencies at least since World War II, when Hitler was said to rely on astrologers and seers. Suggestions for military applications of ESP continued to be received after World War II. In 1952, the Department of Defense was lectured on the possible usefulness of extrasensory perception in psychological warfare.

In 1961, the CIA's Office of Technical Services became interested in the claims of ESP. Technical project officers soon contacted Stephen I. Abrams, the Director of the Parapsychological Laboratory, Oxford University, England. Under the auspices of Project ULTRA, Abrams prepared a review article which claimed ESP was demonstrated but not understood or controllable.

Kress added: "The report was read with interest but produced no further action for another decade."

Indeed, it was in the early 1970s that the research began in earnest. In April 1972, Dr. Russell Targ, a laser physicist with a personal interest in parapsychology and the power of the human mind, met with CIA personnel from the Office of Strategic Intelligence, specifically to discuss paranormal phenomena.

Of paramount concern to the CIA was the fact that Targ informed them that the Soviet Union was deeply involved in researching psychic phenomena, mental telepathy, and ESP. It did not take the CIA long to realize that the purpose of the Soviet research was to determine if ESP could be used as a tool of espionage. As one CIA agent said:

> Can you imagine if a bunch of psychic 007's from Russia could focus their minds to short-circuit our missile systems or our satellite surveillance equipment and get access to classified information in this way? The possibilities—if it worked—would be disastrous.

It was this realization that galvanized the CIA into action. As the Kress report stated, in 1973: "The Office of Technical Services funded a $50,000 expanded effort in parapsychology."

The initial studies utilized a variety of people who were carefully and secretly brought into the project, and who demonstrated a whole range of seemingly paranormal skills. Those same skills could not be reliably replicated on every occasion, however.

As evidence of this, Kenneth Kress informed his superiors:

> One subject, by mental effort, apparently caused an increase in temperature; the action could not be duplicated by the second subject. The second subject was able to reproduce, with impressive accuracy, information inside sealed envelopes. Under identical conditions, the first subject could reproduce nothing.

Similarly, some government-sponsored psychics in the period from 1973 to 1974 located secret missile installations in the Soviet Union, found terrorist groups in the Middle East, and successfully remotely viewed the interior of the Chinese embassy in Washington, D.C. Others, meanwhile, provided data that was sketchy and, at times, simply wrong.

And it was the continuing rate of success versus the frequency of failure that led to heated debate within the CIA about the overall relevancy and validity of the project.

In *Parapsychology in Intelligence*, Kenneth Kress confirmed this. After the CIA's remote viewing team attempted to broaden the range of its operation and secure extra funding in mid-1973, said Kress: "I was told not to increase the scope of the project and not to anticipate any follow-on in this area. The project was too sensitive and potentially embarrassing."

Despite this, the CIA's research continued, with many of its advances due to a skilled psychic named Pat Price, who had achieved a num-

Physicist Russell Targ met with representatives of the Office of Strategic Intelligence to discuss paranormal phenomena in the 1970s.

ber of extraordinary successes in the field of ESP, including successfully remotely viewing a sensitive installation that fell under the auspices of the National Security Agency and psychically penetrating missile sites in Libya.

Price's sudden and untimely death from a heart attack in 1975 indirectly led the CIA—according to the official story, at least—to minimize its research into psychic espionage.

Tim Rifat, the author of a 2001 book, *Remote Viewing*, has deeply studied the world of top secret, governmental research into psychic spying. He said of Pat Price's death:

> It was alleged at the time that the Soviets poisoned Price. It would have been a top priority for the KGB to eliminate Price as his phenomenal remote-viewing abilities would have posed a significant danger to the USSR's paranormal warfare buildup. He may also have been the victim of an elite group of Russian psi-warriors trained to remotely kill enemies of the Soviet Union.

The scenario of research being minimized in the aftermath of Price's potentially suspicious passing was reinforced when, in 1995, a CIA-sponsored report, titled *An Evaluation of the Remote-Viewing Program—Research and Operational Applications*, was produced by the American Institutes for Research (AIR). In essence the report stated that from an espionage and intelligence-gathering perspective, remote viewing and related phenomena were largely useless.

Price's sudden and untimely death from a heart attack in 1975 indirectly led the CIA ... to minimize its research into psychic espionage.

Not everyone agreed with that conclusion, however, including W. Adam Mandelbaum, author of *The Psychic Battlefield* and a former U.S. intelligence officer, who said: "The AIR report was US-intelligence-purchased disinformation intentionally formatted to misrepresent the true states of remote-viewing research, and the true operational utility of the phenomenon."

Regardless of whether or not the CIA's role in remote viewing operations was downsized, terminated, or simply hidden from prying eyes, it is a matter of fact that additional agencies within the U.S. government, military, and Intelligence community took—and still continue to take—a deep interest in psychic espionage.

The Defense Intelligence Agency (DIA), for example, has had longstanding involvement and interest in understanding and using paranormal powers both on the battlefield and in the cloak and dagger world of espionage.

As an illustration of this, a DIA report from 1972 titled *Controlled Offensive Behavior—USSR*, made an astonishing claim:

> Before the end of the 1970s, Soviet diplomats will be able to sit in their foreign embassies and use ESP to steal the secrets of their enemies. A spy would be hypnotized, then his invisible "spirit" would be ordered to leave his body, travel across barriers of space and time to a foreign government's

security facility, and there read top-secret documents and relay back their information.

The Soviets are at least 25 years ahead of the U.S. in psychic research and have realized the immense military advantage of the psychic ability known as astral projection (out of the body travel).

Similarly, in 1973 and 1975, the DIA commissioned two lengthy reports that delved deep into the heart of Soviet research of psychic phenomena and included details of one extraordinary experiment undertaken by the Russian military in the 1950s.

A somewhat disturbing extract from the DIA's files on this particular experiment stated: "Dr. Pavel Naumov conducted animal bio-communication studies between a submerged Soviet Navy submarine and a shore research station. These tests involved a mother rabbit and her newborn litter and occurred around 1956."

The author of the report continued:

According to Naumov, Soviet scientists placed the baby rabbits aboard the submarine. They kept the mother rabbit in a laboratory on shore where they implanted electrodes in her brain. When the submarine was submerged, assistants killed the rabbits one by one. At each precise moment of death, the mother rabbit's brain produced detectable and recordable reactions.

It was also noted by the DIA that "as late as 1970 the precise protocol and results of this test described were believed to be classified."

Nevertheless, the DIA was able to determine that the Soviets' reasoning behind such experimentation was to try and understand the nature of ESP, astral projection, and the power of the mind—and even the existence of a soul—in animals such as dogs, rabbits and primates. And if eventually understood in the animal kingdom, said the DIA, the Soviets' next step would be to focus on human beings and the way in which those same phenomena might be used as a weapon of war and espionage.

In Britain, the situation was broadly similar: at the height of the Second World War, formerly classified files at the National Archives in Kew that reveal elements of the British Police Force occasionally and stealthily employed the use of dowsers—normally associated with underground searches for water—to locate victims buried under the rubble of inner city destruction wrought by Nazi bomber pilots.

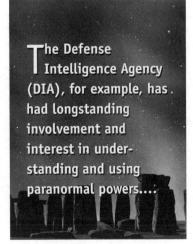

The Defense Intelligence Agency (DIA), for example, has had longstanding involvement and interest in understanding and using paranormal powers....

Such was the controversy surrounding this unique brand of psychic police work that even the government's wartime Ministry of Home Security became embroiled in the affair, urging caution in endorsing "support for the mysterious" at such a "particularly dangerous time"—this despite the apparent success of its "dowsing detectives."

Still on the matter of Britain's secret spies, there is the matter of a "novel" titled *The Psychic Spy*. Written by Irene Allen-Block in 2013, it contains the following endorsement from me:

> In late 1970s London, a young woman is secretly recruited to work for British Intelligence. Her world soon becomes dominated by psychic-spying, enemy agents, assassinations, and suspicious deaths. Add to the mix, the Lockerbie tragedy, the Falklands War, and the classified world of MI6, and you have a great story filled with adventure, intrigue and shadowy characters. As Irene Allen-Block skillfully shows, the mind is a mysterious and dangerous tool.

The publisher of the book, Glannant Ty, noted:

> *The Psychic Spy* tells the story of Eileen Evans, a beautiful young woman and talented psychic who is unwittingly recruited by MI6 to join their new top secret Remote Viewing program "Blue Star" during the heart of the Cold War in the 1970's and 80's. Eileen quickly finds herself embroiled in excitement and danger as she quickly becomes a "psychic spy" for British Intelligence. Finding forbidden love with another agent, Eileen descends into a dark world filled with political intrigue, danger and death. Not only must she cope with the possibility of losing her life, she must also struggle with the very real threat of losing her soul.

> Smart, sexy and filled with humor and peril, *The Psychic Spy* is a thrilling adventure that explores a little-known but very real world where governments use actual psychics to spy on their enemies, and in some cases, even their allies! Using her own real-life experiences as a remote viewer, Irene Allen-Block has created a powerful tale that should entertain and educate readers on a piece of history that has been hidden in the shadows.

The Psychic Spy is made all the more intriguing by the fact that the book is actually a thinly veiled version of the *real-life* exploits of the author while, from the late 1970s onwards, she was in the secret employ of British Intelligence, in the field of psychic spying.

The Psychic Spy is made all the more intriguing by the fact that the book is actually a thinly veiled version of the *real-life* exploits of the author....

What of today's world: Are psychic spies engaged in helping to end the War on Terror? In November 2001, it was revealed in the media that the FBI had quietly approached private remote viewing companies with a view to predicting likely targets of future terrorist attacks.

As Lyn Buchanan, the author of *The Seventh Sense*—a book that examines Buchanan's personal role in the U.S. government's remote viewing story—said on this specific subject: "We want the message to get to terrorists everywhere that no one attacks our country and kills our people and gets away with it. We can, and we will, find you."

Decades after official research began into remote viewing and ESP it seems that the worlds of the psychic and the spy continue to cross paths.

SECRET AIRCRAFT VS. STEALTHY ALIENS

Since the 1980s, sightings of large, triangular-shaped UFOs, usually described as being black in color, making a low humming noise, and very often with rounded rather than angled corners, have been reported throughout the world. The sheer proliferation of such reports has led some ufological commentators to strongly suspect that the Flying Triangles (as they have come to be known) are prime examples of still-classified aircraft, the development of which was secretly begun in the 1980s by elements of the U.S. Department of Defense.

In March 1993 a series of earth-shattering Flying Triangle encounters occurred in British airspace that went on to have a profound effect on high-ranking sources within both the Royal Air Force and the Ministry of Defense. More importantly, it was that single wave of encounters that ultimately led senior military and defense personnel to liaise with their American counterparts to try and determine, once and for all, if the FTs are of terrestrial or extraterrestrial origins. The story comes from one of those at the forefront of the study into the aforementioned sightings: Nick Pope, who for three years (1991–1994) investigated—at an official level—UFO incidents on behalf of the Ministry of Defense.

Long-since retired from the MoD, Pope, in a January 1997 interview with me, revealed his role in—and his knowledge of—the March 1993 UFO encounters over the United Kingdom:

> I arrived at the office at about 8.30 A.M. or 9.00 A.M. on the morning of March 31, 1993, and my telephone was ringing. I picked it up and there was a police officer on the other end making a UFO report. Now, he was based in Devon and told me an account of an incident that had taken place in the early hours of that particular day when he and a colleague who had been on night patrol saw a triangular-shaped UFO at fairly high altitude. He said that the motion was fairly steady and that there were lights at the edges with a fainter light in the middle.

> To me, this was already a description that was becoming quite familiar both from one or two reports that I'd received at the Ministry of Defense over the years and from my own study and research into the UFO literature. In other words, I was aware that this was a commonly reported shape for a UFO.

Pope continued:

I was also quite pleased to get a report from a police officer. I won't say that it was rare, but it was slightly unusual to have reports from trained observers like police and military. I would say that, of the reports I received in my time at the UFO desk, less than five per cent came from, collectively, pilots, military officers, and the police. I had spoken, socially, to numerous Royal Air Force pilots who'd had personal sightings, but who had never reported them for fear of ridicule.

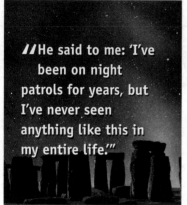

//He said to me: 'I've been on night patrols for years, but I've never seen anything like this in my entire life.'"

But that police report was very much the first of many that came in that day and over the next week or so. When taken together, the sightings described took place in a range of times—the earliest was about 11–11.30 P.M. on the evening of the thirtieth and the latest was about 1.45 A.M. in the early hours of the thirty-first.

What was it precisely that made the police officer's report stand out?

He said to me: "I've been on night patrols for years, but I've never seen anything like this in my entire life." Well, reports such as this came through thick and fast over the course of the next week or so; more and more reports came in from police stations, the public and local RAF stations. In fact, I would say that the total number of reports easily exceeded one hundred.

It is clear from what Pope had to say that there were three reports in particular that stood out more than any other—the first of which concerned a family based in Rugeley, Staffordshire, England, who had viewed a remarkable aerial vehicle near the sprawling forest that is Cannock Chase. Pope revealed the facts:

This report was brought to my attention by the Community Relations Office at RAF Cosford [Shropshire]. The report had come direct from the family and sounded particularly interesting because, unlike some of the other sightings, this one was of an object flying at very low level. There had been a family gathering and several members of the family were out on the drive—really just saying goodbye to their relatives who were about to drive off. Suddenly, this large, triangular-shaped craft flew over them very, very slowly. This was a flat triangle, with a light in each corner and a larger light in the direct centre of the underside of the craft.

In fact, not unlike the report filed by the police reports from Devon?

Exactly. But there was something else that I'd come across in my investigations that was also present in the Rugeley case. This was a low-frequency humming sound coming from the UFO; a humming that they actually described as being quite unpleasant. Imagine standing in front of the speakers at a pop concert and almost feeling the sound as well as hearing it—that was the effect that they reported. Well, they were so excited and overwhelmed that two of them leapt into the car to give chase!

As they did so, they came to a point where they thought the UFO was so low that it must have come down in a nearby field. Well, they parked the car, jumped out and looked around. But there was absolutely nothing there; the UFO had gone.

The night's activities had barely begun:

The two most significant reports began at RAF Cosford shortly after the encounter at Rugeley. This was definitely the highlight and was one of the best sighting reports I received in my entire posting. The report itself came from a guard patrol at Cosford. They were on duty manning entrance points, checking the perimeter fence and such like. All the members of the patrol saw the UFO and, again, the description was pretty much the same as most of the others. In this case, though, the UFO was at medium-to-high altitude.

Pope makes an important observation:

Remember that these witnesses were people who see in a normal course of business all sorts of aircraft activity, meteorites, fireballs and so on, and they considered it absolutely out of the ordinary.

He was looking at this massive, triangular-shaped craft flying at what was a height of no more than two hundred feet....

They didn't make a standard report: what they did was to submit an actual 2–3 page report which went up their chain of command and then the report was forwarded on to me. In that report, they stated that the UFO passed directly over the base and that this was of particular concern to them. They made immediate checks with various Air Traffic Control radar centres but nothing appeared on the screens. It was this factor that made them particularly keen to make an official report. This was at around 1.00 A.M.

Whatever the origin of the unknown vehicle, it appeared that its activities were far from over.

They noticed that this *Flying Triangle* was heading on a direct line for RAF Shawbury, which is some twelve to fifteen miles on. Now, the main concern of the Cosford patrol was to alert Shawbury that the UFO was coming their way; but they also wanted confirmation that they weren't having a mass hallucination.

They took a decision to call Shawbury and this was answered by the Meteorological Officer. You have to realize that at that time there was literally just a skeleton staff operating, so the Met. Officer was, essentially, on his own. So, he took a decision to go outside, look in the direction of RAF Cosford and see what he could see.

Sure enough, he could see this light coming towards him and it got closer and closer and lower and lower. Next thing, he was looking at this massive, triangular-shaped craft flying at what was a height of no more than two hundred feet, just to the side of the base and only about two hundred feet from the perimeter fence.

Bearing in mind the fact that the Meteorological Officer at RAF Shawbury could be considered a reliable witness, and someone well-trained in recognizing numerous types of aerial phenomena, was he able to gauge the size of the object? Pope said:

> Very much so: military officers are very good at gauging sizes of aircraft and they're very precise. His quote to me was that the UFO's size was midway between that of a C-130 Hercules and a Boeing 747 *Jumbo Jet.* Now, he had eight years worth of experience with the Royal Air Force, and a Met. Officer is generally much better qualified than most for looking at things in the night sky. And there were other factors too: like the family in Rugeley, he heard this most unpleasant low-frequency hum; but unlike their experience, he saw the craft fire a beam of light down to the ground. He felt that it was something like a laser beam or a searchlight. The light was tracking very rapidly back and forth and sweeping one of the fields adjacent to the base.

> He also said—and he admitted this was speculation—that it was as if the UFO was looking for something. Now, the speed of the UFO was extremely slow—no more than twenty or thirty miles per hour, which in itself is quite extraordinary. As far as the description is concerned, he said that it was fairly featureless—a sort of flat, triangular-shaped craft, or possibly a bit more diamond-shaped. But if all the descriptions had been identical I would have been surprised.

Perhaps the most eye-opening and revealing aspect of the RAF Shawbury encounter was the way in which the object made its exit, as Nick Pope reveals:

> He said that the beam of light retracted into the craft, which then seemed to gain a little bit of height. But then, in an absolute instant, the UFO moved from a speed of about twenty or thirty miles per hour to a speed of several hundreds of miles per hour—if not thousands! It just suddenly moved off to the horizon and then out of sight in no more than a second or so—and there was no sonic boom. Well, of course, when I received this report and the one from Cosford, I launched as full an investigation as I possibly could.

The entrance to the RAF Shawbury base. In 1993, there was a wave of sightings of a "Flying Triangle," both over the base and in the surrounding counties. No commercial or military aircraft were in the area at the time.

As Nick Pope now makes abundantly clear, that investigation proved to be extraordinary, to say the least: "Even though it was fairly obvious to me that there were a number of things that this object was not, I still made the checks anyway to try and eliminate absolutely every possibility." Pope also noted: "I had a feeling that this one was going to go right up the chain of command." He was not wrong.

Checks were also made with various Air Traffic Control Centers, with Air Defense experts and Air Defense radar systems; and although at one point we thought we had caught the UFO on radar, it eventually turned out that there was nothing. After these checks were made and we were able to establish that the UFO hadn't been caught on radar, the Royal Air Force was quite interested. There isn't really a corporate view on UFOs; it really does go down to the belief of the individual. But, enough people realized that there was something exciting and out of the ordinary going on and they, too, got caught up in all that excitement.

Initially, suggestions were put forward that all of the sightings were simply the result of a satellite re-entering the Earth's atmosphere: "I spoke to the Space Information Officer at RAF Fylingdales; this is the Ballistic Missile Early Warning Centre. They've got very powerful space-tracking radar that can pick up and track all sorts of objects at orbital heights. Now, they raised the possibility that we were looking at the re-entry of one of the Russian *Cosmos* satellites.

> Contrary to what some people have said, however, Fylingdales were very unsure as to whether or not the satellite would even have been visible from the U.K. at all during that time. But even if there was a re-entering satellite in the skies, it certainly couldn't explain the very close encounter at RAF Shawbury. Don't forget, too, that a satellite burn-up is very much like a meteor shower with a few tracks of light flashing across the sky. In this sighting, however, it was a case of one military base actually reporting to another and saying: "It's coming your way...." So this rules out a satellite burn-out.

Pope then took his investigation to another level.

> My next step was to get a map and plot out the various locations where the UFO—or UFOs—had been seen. Well, that didn't work out. I was confronted with a map of haphazard sightings all around the country. There was certainly a concentration of sightings in Devon, Cornwall, South Wales, and the Midlands. But there were also sightings from Southampton and Yorkshire; and I knew that there were reports from Ireland, Belgium, and elsewhere in Europe. And these were just the tip of the iceberg.

One interesting point that then occurred to me was that we were dealing with activity on exactly the same night—but three years later—to a very famous wave of sightings of very similar craft seen over Belgium. And my favorite theory about this—or at least an idea I floated about—was that this was a deliberate move on the part of whoever was operating the craft.

//... three years later ... a very famous wave of sightings of very similar craft [was] seen over Belgium."

Pope explains his line of thinking:

> For example, if the media had got a hold of this, it would have been too late to get it in the newspapers on March 31; so, the earliest date that the story could have run would have been April 1—April Fools' Day! Again, a little indicator, perhaps, of an intelligence and possibly even some form of humor.

The Lockheed SR-71 Blackbird was a Mach-3 reconaissance aircraft used by the U.S. Air Force. One theory about the Flying Triangles was that the air force was experimenting with a craft to replace the SR-71.

Of course, it could be argued that this would serve as excellent cover if the Flying Triangle that was seen near RAF Shawbury was a terrestrial aircraft (albeit a distinctly secret one) as opposed to something extraterrestrial. Pope acknowledges this.

We decided that we couldn't ignore the various rumors that were doing the rounds about a supposed Top Secret aircraft developed by the U.S. government and called *Aurora*—or, indeed, *any* hypersonic and/or prototype aircraft operated by the Americans.

There had been persistent rumors in the aviation world and amongst the UFO lobby that the SR-71 *Blackbird* had been replaced by a hypersonic aircraft code-named *Aurora* and that that was what the Flying Triangles really were. I was well aware that there had been some interesting stories about visual and radar sightings around certain air bases; however, I hadn't put much store in these rumors—not least because there had been some very definitive denials from the Americans.

I know there's a lot of cynicism about government and the military. And although officialdom may refuse to answer a question and may sometimes give a misleading answer, outright lying is incredibly rare. And when it does occur, if it's uncovered it almost certainly leads to resignation.

But with the March 1993 sightings—and in spite of the denials from the Americans that they were responsible for the Flying Triangles—we did contact them to make inquiries. This was because they have the responsibility pertaining to the U.S. presence in Britain. Those inquiries bore absolutely no fruit at all. The Americans said: "No. We can shed no light at all on the UFO sightings that have led to your inquiry."

Pope is able to disclose, however, that the liaison with the Americans was not without its moment of intrigue. "If anything," he now related:

[T]here was an interesting little hint that the Americans, too, were seeing these Flying Triangles over their territory. As we were making our inquiries, they turned the question around and wanted to know if our Royal Air Force had a triangular-shaped, hypersonic prototype aircraft of some sort. So, presumably, the Americans were having Flying Triangle sightings, too.

But this was interesting, in light of the fact that the Americans supposedly got out of UFO investigations back in 1969 when the Air Force's Project Blue Book closed down. Of course, you may not officially be in the UFO game, but you are certainly going to be aware of—and take an interest in—reports of structured craft in your airspace. So, essentially, we drew blanks with the Americans.

At the time, Nick Pope and the secretariat of the Air Staff were not the only ones who were addressing the issue of whether or not the Americans were flying an *Aurora*-type craft in British airspace. In early 1995, for example, this very issue was brought up in none other than the Houses of Parliament. It was January 26, and the following exchange took place between Llew Smith MP and Nicholas Soames, the then minister for the Armed Forces:

> *Mr. Llew Smith:* To ask the Secretary of State for Defense how many *Aurora* Prototype aircraft of the United States Air Force are based at the Machrihanish Air Force Base in Argyll; and for what period permission has been given for basing these aircraft in the United Kingdom.

> *Mr. Soames:* There are no United States Air Force prototype aircraft based at RAF Machrihanish and no authorization has been given by Her Majesty's government to the United States Air Force, or any other U.S. body, to operate such aircraft within or from the United Kingdom.

As this exchange made abundantly clear, even during a Parliamentary debate, nothing had surfaced to suggest—officially, at least—the American government was in any way implicated in the mystery of the Flying Triangles. Back to Nick Pope:

> Bearing in mind that the Americans had inquired—at an official level, no less—if the British Royal Air Force had in its employ something broadly fitting the description of a Flying Triangle, and we had said "No," I still felt obliged to address the issue of whether or not the rumors about secret aircraft being flown by us were true.

> First, from my own knowledge of prototype aircraft, un-manned aerial vehicles and so on, the Triangles don't fit into the typical pattern, and I'll explain why. Where we do have such pieces of kit, they're not tested over the heads of "Joe Public;" they're tested in a small number of clearly defined ranges and danger areas—mostly out at sea such as the Abberporth Range in Cradigan Bay.

Pope also states on this highly controversial matter:

> You simply do not fly a prototype craft over a military base or over the centre of Rugeley or wherever, and run the risk that someone will either (a) scramble a [Tornado] F-3 [aircraft] to try and intercept it; or (b) take a photograph of it which will end up on the front page of *The Sun* or *Jane's Defense Weekly*. It's simply not the way that things are done.

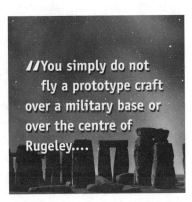

//You simply do not fly a prototype craft over a military base or over the centre of Rugeley....

> We checked domestically anything that might have been flying. But if we'd have been poking our noses into something that didn't concern us, the investigation would have been quietly switched off. In fact, the opposite happened. We were making big waves throughout the Royal Air Force, the Min-

Triangle-shaped objects were spotted by the Belgian airforce near Brussels in 1990.

istry of Defense and at an international level. So the domestic secret aircraft theory is interesting but it doesn't hold water.

Three years prior to the extraordinary events at RAF Cosford and RAF Shawbury, similar objects were seen on repeated occasions in Belgian airspace in 1989 and 1990. In view of this, was any form of approach made to the Belgian military to ascertain their views? "Yes," said Pope:

I approached the Belgians to get a comparison after their sightings. I phoned the Air Attaché at the British Embassy in Brussels and he spoke to one of the F-16 pilots who had been scrambled to intercept a Flying Triangle over Belgium back in 1990. Well, the Air Attaché reported back to me that the corporate view of the Belgian Defense Staff was that they did believe that they were dealing with a solid, structured craft.

Apparently, the word from the Belgians was: "Thank God it was friendly." If it hadn't been, it was made clear to me that there was very little that the Belgian Air Force could have done anyway—despite the fact that the F-16 is no slouch.

With the secret weapon angle disposed of as far as Nick Pope was concerned, what was his next step in the investigation?

There was only one place to go and that was up the chain of command and I briefed my head of division. He was notoriously skeptical about UFOs and generally made no secret of the fact that he thought that it was all a waste of time and resources. But he had been quite impressed by the Shawbury and Cosford events—even to the point of making some attempts to plot the course of the UFO.

In fact, I recall him bounding into the office in a state of some considerable excitement when he thought that he had found indications of a straight-line track. I had copied some of the reports; but what he didn't have was a batch of reports that had just come in and that painted a totally different picture.

Well, I just thought that this needed to go up the chain of command. The main addressee was the Assistant Chief of the Air Staff; so what I did was to summarize the events on a couple of sides of paper and attach the original reports—the typed report submitted by the patrol sighting at Cosford and my own write-up of the RAF Shawbury sighting.

He took a few days to have a look at all the paperwork and then passed it back down the chain of command with a message that said: "This is extremely interesting. It is a genuine mystery but clearly you've made all the checks that we could reasonably make and it's difficult to see how we can take this any further." And that was essentially where the matter rested.

Today, does Nick Pope feel that the assessment of the Assistant Chief of the Air Staff was a fair one?

Well, yes and no. I felt extremely uncomfortable that we had a clear breach of the U.K. air defense region; and we had two Royal Air Force bases pretty much being over-flown by a structured craft and yet we had nothing on radar and absolutely no explanation. I applied our own standard line on UFOs and asked myself the questions: Is this of no defense significance? What if the craft had been hostile? What if a bomb-bay had suddenly opened up and it had attacked these bases? If that had been the case, and with the UFO not appearing on radar, the first we would have known would have been when the bombs were falling. So, I came to the conclusion that this was of extreme defense significance.

I'm naturally suspicious of anyone that doesn't declare their hand. And although there may be some very good reasons for them remaining covert, I think that from a military and defense point of view, you have to say that there is a potential UFO threat.

Personally, I felt that saying *"Object Unexplained; Case Closed"* was not satisfactory. On the other hand, I had every sympathy with the Assistant Chief of the Air Staff; there was no faulting his logic. What else could he have done? Really, it was an impossible situation. I can tell you, however, that after this, there were a lot more believers in the extraterrestrial hypothesis amongst the RAF and the MoD than there had been previously.

Given that the 1993 UFO encounters had a profound effect on a number of Pope's colleagues, would it be fair to say that he, too, found his views on the subject altering?

Yes, they did, definitely. I don't know if it was the single turning point that switched me from being an open-minded skeptic to a believer; but it was certainly one of the key events. In fact, if you were to ask me to take my best shot, I would say that this was the real article; *this was extra-terrestrial.*

STORMS ON THE BATTLEFIELD: A NEW CONCEPT IN WARFARE

April 28, 1997, was the date on which a startling statement was made by William S. Cohen—at the time, the U.S. secretary of defense in the Clinton administration. The location was the University of Georgia, which was playing host to The Conference on Terrorism, Weapons of Mass Destruction, and U.S. Strategy. As a captivated audience listened intently, Cohen revealed something that was as remarkable as it was controversial.

Hostile groups—that Cohen, whether by design or not, did not name—were actively

> … engaging in an eco-type of terrorism whereby they can alter the climate, set off earthquakes, volcanoes remotely through the use of Electro-Magnetic waves. So there are plenty of ingenious minds out there that are at work finding ways in which they can wreak terror upon other nations. It's real.

Cohen was not wrong: in 1996 the U.S. Air Force unveiled to the public and the media an astonishing document. It read like science fiction. It was, however, nothing less than amazing, controversial, science-fact. The title of the document was *USAF 2025*. It was, basically, a study of where the Air Force hoped to be—technologically and militarily speaking—in 2025.

Researched and written by the 2025 Support Office at the Air University, Air Education and Training Command, and developed by the Air University Press, Educational Services Directorate, College of Aerospace Doctrine, Research, and Education, Maxwell Air Force Base, Alabama, the document was "designed to comply with a directive from the chief of staff of the Air Force to examine the concepts, capabilities, and technologies the United States will require to remain the dominant air and space force in the future."

Beyond any shadow of a doubt, the most controversial section of the entire *USAF 2025* report was that titled "Weather as a Force Multiplier: Owning the Weather in 2025." Forget missiles, bombs, bullets, troops, and aircraft. The future, very possibly, lies in defeating the enemy via global weather manipulation. The report stated:

> In 2025, US aerospace forces can "own the weather" by capitalizing on emerging technologies and focusing development of those technologies to

war-fighting applications. While some segments of society will always be reluctant to examine controversial issues such as weather-modification, the tremendous military capabilities that could result from this field are ignored at our own peril. Weather-modification offers the war fighter a wide-range of possible options to defeat or coerce an adversary.

The authors also noted:

The desirability to modify storms to support military objectives is the most aggressive and controversial type of weather-modification. While offensive weather-modification efforts would certainly be undertaken by U.S. forces with great caution and trepidation, it is clear that we cannot afford to allow an adversary to obtain an exclusive weather-modification capability.

It's very clear that a great deal of thought had gone into the production of this particular section of the report. It begins by providing the reader with a theoretical scenario, one filled with conflict, but which may very well be resolvable by turning the weather into a weapon:

Former secretary of defense William Cohen believed that hostile groups were targeting the United States with ecoterrorism and the manipulation of earthquake and volcanic activity.

Imagine that in 2025 the US is fighting a rich, but now consolidated, politically powerful drug cartel in South America. The cartel has purchased hundreds of Russian- and Chinese-built fighters that have successfully thwarted our attempts to attack their production facilities. With their local numerical superiority and interior lines, the cartel is launching more than 10 aircraft for every one of ours. In addition, the cartel is using the French *system probatoire d'observation de la terre* (SPOT) positioning and tracking imagery systems, which in 2025 are capable of transmitting near-real-time, multispectral imagery with 1 meter resolution. The US wishes to engage the enemy on an uneven playing field in order to exploit the full potential of our aircraft and munitions.

At this point, a decision is taken to focus carefully on making the local weather work for the United States and against the cartel:

Meteorological analysis reveals that equatorial South America typically has afternoon thunderstorms on a daily basis throughout the year. Our intelligence has confirmed that cartel pilots are reluctant to fly in or near thunderstorms. Therefore, our weather force support element (WFSE), which is a part of the commander in chief's (CINC) air operations center (AOC), is tasked to forecast storm paths and trigger or intensify thunderstorm cells over critical target areas that the enemy must defend with their aircraft. Since our aircraft in 2025 have all-weather capability, the thunderstorm threat is minimal to our forces, and we can effectively and decisively control the sky over the target.

The WFSE, the report notes, has the necessary sensor and communication capabilities to observe, detect, and act on weather-modification requirements to support U.S. military objectives. These capabilities, we are told, "are part of an advanced battle area system that supports the war-fighting CINC. In our scenario, the CINC tasks the WFSE to conduct storm intensification and concealment operations. The WFSE models the atmospheric conditions to forecast, with ninety percent confidence, the likelihood of successful modification using airborne cloud generation and seeding."

The countdown to Weather War One is about to begin.

According to *USAF 2025*, by 2025 "uninhabited aerospace vehicles (UAV) are routinely used for weather-modification operations. By cross-referencing desired attack times with wind and thunderstorm forecasts and the SPOT satellite's

A Cessna-210 fitted with cloud-seeding equipment prepares for takeoff. Cloud seeding works by spraying fine particulates (such as from silver iodide) into clouds that serve as seed around which water and ice crystals can form.

projected orbit, the WFSE generates mission profiles for each UAV. The WFSE guides each UAV using near-real-time information from a networked sensor array.

> Prior to the attack, which is coordinated with forecasted weather conditions, the UAVs begin cloud generation and seeding operations. UAVs disperse a cirrus shield to deny enemy visual and infrared (IR) surveillance. Simultaneously, microwave heaters create localized scintillation to disrupt active sensing via synthetic aperture radar (SAR) systems such as the commercially available Canadian search and rescue satellite-aided tracking (SARSAT) that will be widely available in 2025. Other cloud seeding operations cause a developing thunderstorm to intensify over the target, severely limiting the enemy's capability to defend. The WFSE monitors the entire operation in real-time and notes the successful completion of another very important but routine weather-modification mission.

The Air Force admitted that "this scenario may seem far-fetched" but remained fully confident that "technological advances in meteorology and the demand for more precise weather information by global businesses will lead to the successful identification and parameterization of the major variables that affect weather."

It was then time for the *USAF 2025* team to do a bit of hypothetical future-forecasting:

> By 2025, advances in computational capability, modeling techniques, and atmospheric information tracking will produce a highly accurate and reliable weather prediction capability, validated against real-world weather. In the following decade, population densities put pressure on the worldwide availability and cost of food and usable water. Massive life and property losses associated with natural weather disasters become increasingly unacceptable.

> These pressures prompt governments and/or other organizations who are able to capitalize on the technological advances of the previous 20 years to pursue a highly accurate and reasonably precise weather-modification capability. The increasing urgency to realize the benefits of this capability stimulates laws and treaties, and some unilateral actions, making the risks required to validate and refine it acceptable.

By 2025, the world, it seems, will be vastly different to the one we inhabit today. The Air Force noted that entire nations would have the ability to "shape local weather patterns by influencing the factors that affect climate, precipitation, storms and their effects, fog, and near space."

And as the team astutely observed:

> These highly accurate and reasonably precise civil applications of weather-modification technology have obvious military implications. This is particularly true for aerospace forces, for while weather may affect all mediums of operation, it operates in ours.

With the above in mind, the combined brains behind the reported advocated that …

//These highly accurate and reasonably precise civil applications of weather-modification technology have obvious military implications."

the DoD explore the many opportunities (and also the ramifications) resulting from development of a capability to influence precipitation or conducting "selective precipitation modification." Although the capability to influence precipitation over the long term (i.e., for more than several days) is still not fully understood. By 2025, we will certainly be capable of increasing or decreasing precipitation over the short term in a localized area.

Demonstrating the military advantage to such a program was made clear to the DoD:

Before discussing research in this area, it is important to describe the benefits of such a capability. While many military operations may be influenced by precipitation, ground mobility is most affected. Influencing precipitation could prove useful in two ways. First, enhancing precipitation could decrease the enemy's trafficability by muddying terrain, while also affecting their morale. Second, suppressing precipitation could increase friendly trafficability by drying out an otherwise muddied area.

Much attention was given to a phenomenon that no one can deny is on the increase: storms. It's one thing to manipulate precipitation, but to engineer a storm as a means to defeat our foes? Yes, such a possibility is actively being discussed and researched, as the document clearly demonstrates:

The desirability to modify storms to support military objectives is the most aggressive and controversial type of weather-modification. The damage caused by storms is indeed horrendous. For instance, a tropical storm has an energy equal to 10,000 one-megaton hydrogen bombs, and in 1992 Hurricane Andrew totally destroyed Homestead AFB, Florida, caused the evacuation of most military aircraft in the southeastern US, and resulted in $15.5 billion of damage.

The controversial document stated:

At any instant there are approximately 2,000 thunderstorms taking place. In fact 45,000 thunderstorms, which contain heavy rain, hail, microbursts, wind shear, and lightning form daily. Anyone who has flown frequently on commercial aircraft has probably noticed the extremes that pilots will go to avoid thunderstorms. The danger of thunderstorms was clearly shown in August 1985 when a jumbo jet crashed killing 137 people after encountering microburst wind shears during a rain squall. These forces of nature impact all aircraft and even the most advanced fighters of 1996 make every attempt to avoid a thunderstorm.

Once again, speculating on the future, the authors ask an important question: "Will bad weather remain an aviation hazard in 2025?" Their response follows:

The answer, unfortunately, is "yes," but projected advances in technology over the next 30 years will diminish the hazard potential. Computer-controlled flight systems will be able to "autopilot" aircraft through rapidly changing winds. Aircraft will also have highly accurate, onboard sensing systems that can instantaneously "map" and automatically guide the aircraft through the safest portion of a storm cell. Aircraft are envisioned to have hardened electronics that can withstand the effects of lightning strikes and may also have the capability to generate a surrounding electropotential field that will neutralize or repel lightning strikes.

Assuming that the US achieves some or all of the above outlined aircraft technical advances and maintains the technological "weather edge" over its potential adversaries, we can next look at how we could modify the battlespace weather to make the best use of our technical advantage.

If storms do become future weapons of choice, precisely how might this be achieved? The answer might already be available. The *USAF 2025* team carefully addressed the scientific issues surrounding this very question:

> Weather-modification technologies might involve techniques that would increase latent heat release in the atmosphere, provide additional water vapor for cloud cell development, and provide additional surface and lower atmospheric heating to increase atmospheric instability.

Critical to the success of any attempt to trigger a storm cell, noted the authors, "is the pre-existing atmospheric conditions locally and regionally."

A Civil Air Patrol cadet examines airplane wreckage in Punta Gorda, Florida, after Hurricane Charley in 2004. While advancements in technology are predicted to mitigate hazards to air travel in the future, inclement weather will always remain a hazard.

That's to say, the atmosphere must already be conditionally unstable and the large-scale dynamics must be supportive of vertical cloud development. The focus of the weather-modification effort would be to provide additional "conditions" that would make the atmosphere unstable enough to generate cloud and eventually storm cell development. The path of storm cells once developed or enhanced is dependent not only on the mesoscale dynamics of the storm but the regional and synoptic (global) scale atmospheric wind flow patterns in the area which are currently not subject to human control.

The Air Force conceded that "the technical hurdles for storm development in support of military operations are obviously greater than enhancing precipitation or dispersing fog as described earlier." They added, however:

One area of storm research that would significantly benefit military operations is lightning modification. Most research efforts are being conducted to develop techniques to lessen the occurrence or hazards associated with lightning. This is important research for military operations and resource protection, but some offensive military benefit could be obtained by doing research on increasing the potential and intensity of lightning.

Now it's time to take a look at the conclusions of the *USAF 2025* report:

The lessons of history indicate a real weather-modification capability will eventually exist despite the risk. The drive exists. People have always wanted to control the weather and their desire will compel them to collectively and continuously pursue their goal. The motivation exists. The potential benefits and power are extremely lucrative and alluring for those who have the resources to develop it. This combination of drive, motivation, and resources will eventually produce the technology.

History also teaches that we cannot afford to be without a weather-modification capability once the technology is developed and used by others. Even if we have no intention of using it, others will. To call upon the atomic weapon analogy again, we need to be able to deter or counter their capability with our own. Therefore, the weather and intelligence communities must keep abreast of the actions of others.

And, finally:

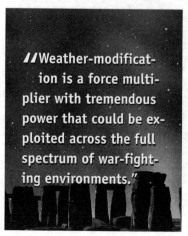

//Weather-modification is a force multiplier with tremendous power that could be exploited across the full spectrum of war-fighting environments."

Weather-modification is a force multiplier with tremendous power that could be exploited across the full spectrum of warfighting environments. From enhancing friendly operations or disrupting those of the enemy via small-scale tailoring of natural weather patterns to complete dominance of global communications and counter-space control, weather-modification offers the war fighter a wide-range of possible options to defeat or coerce an adversary. But, while offensive weather-modification efforts would certainly be undertaken by US forces with great caution and trepidation, it is clear that we cannot afford to allow an adversary to obtain an exclusive weather-modification capability.

One has to wonder, however, if just such a hostile adversary—whether a particular nation, terrorists, or a shadowy cabal—has *already* developed and even deployed technology that allows them to wreak havoc on our environment in a fashion and have the attack blamed on Mother Nature.

If, one day, you find yourself caught up in the heart of a terrible storm, a violent tsunami, a sudden and powerful earthquake, or a catastrophic deluge, you may wish to give consideration to the possibility that this is *not* Mother Nature's doing, after all. It may be a prime example of someone waging war via the weather.

CHEMTRAILS: POLLUTING THE POPULATION

The controversy of chemtrails has attracted the attention of conspiracy theorists, the mainstream media, the U.S. Air Force, and the governments of both the United Kingdom and Canada. On the one hand, there are those who suggest it's all a matter of conspiratorial nonsense and fear-mongering. On the other hand, it's perceived by many as something dark and deadly; something that may even threaten our very existence as a species.

The official line is that chemtrails—in essence, trails in the sky, left by large aircraft—are simply regular contrails of the kind that can be seen in the skies at pretty much anytime and pretty much everywhere. They are created when a high-flying aircraft reaches an altitude cold enough to cause exhaust vapor to transform into crystals of ice, something that allows them to be seen as long trails of cloud-like vapor.

The unofficial view, however, is very different. It suggests that chemtrails are nothing less than prime evidence that someone is pumping massive amounts of potentially deadly chemicals into the atmosphere. The theories as to why such actions might be taking place are just about as many as they are varied: (a) to provoke widespread illness and death, as a means to lower the planet's ever-growing population levels; (b) to reduce the effects of global-warming; (c) to alter the Earth's weather (whether for good or bad is a matter of dispute amongst theorists); and (d) to adversely affect the human brain, and turn us into subservient, morose cattle. Somewhere in this mass of tangled theories and claims lies the answer. But whose answer is the real one? That's the big question.

It was in 1996 that the seeds of the chemtrail mystery were first sewn. And it was all thanks to the U.S. Air Force's *USAF 2025* report, the salient points of which were discussed in the previous chapter of this book. They were points that focused, to a significant degree, on how the Air Force was planning to manipulate and control the weather as a tool of warfare.

The data contained in the *USAF 2025* document was presented in a distinctly theoretical fashion—its authors were, after all, trying to second-guess where technology would be almost thirty years after the report was written and published. Those suspicious of anything and everything that comes out of the mouth of officialdom weren't buying it; not at all. In mere weeks after the document was declassified into the public domain, rumors were afoot that (a) the weather-altering technology was already in use; and (b) evidence of its existence could be seen in the contrails—soon to be termed chemtrails—above our heads. Interestingly, the conspiracy theorists quickly came to believe they had support in high places.

Recall that, in 1997, just one year after the *USAF 2025* report was published, U.S. secretary of defense William Cohen stated that dark forces were

> engaging in an eco-type of terrorism whereby they can alter the climate, set off earthquakes, volcanoes remotely through the use of Electro-Magnetic waves. So there are plenty of ingenious minds out there that are at work finding ways in which they can wreak terror upon other nations. It's real.

Chemtrail proponents offered the opinion that Cohen's words amounted to a less-than-subtle attempt to get the word out about what was secretly going on in the Earth's atmosphere. Maybe they were right. It wasn't long, however, before the weather-control theory was elbowed out in favor of one focused on population control and a sinister New World Order.

Such was the sheer level of finger-pointing in the direction of the Air Force that a forthright statement on the matter was issued by USAF staff. In part, it read:

> The Air Force's policy is to observe and forecast the weather. The Air Force is focused on observing and forecasting the weather so the information can be used to support military operations. The Air Force is not conducting any weather modification experiments or programs and has no

Most people have looked up into the sky and observed one or several contrail streaks, but there are some who suspect they contain chemicals that may deliberately spread illnesses, affect global warming, or somehow turn people into subservient slaves.

plans to do so in the future. The "Chemtrail" hoax has been investigated and refuted by many established and accredited universities, scientific organizations, and major media publications.

In 1999, the New Mexico attorney general's office contacted New Mexicans for Science and Reason (NMSR) member Kim Johnson to help answer questions from constituents regarding the alleged dangers of "chemtrails." After his investigation, Johnson told the attorney general (in a letter that can be found in the online article "Kim Johnson's Chemtrail Analysis—Updated"):

> I have viewed a number of photos purporting to be of aircraft spraying the chemical or biological material into the atmosphere. I have also discussed these letters with another scientist familiar with upper atmospheric phenomena from Sandia National Laboratory and a retired general and fighter pilot who is an Air Force Hall of Fame member. In summary, there is no evidence that these "chemtrails" are other than expected, normal contrails from jet aircraft that vary in their shapes, duration, and general presentation based on prevailing weather conditions.

> That is not to say that there could not be an occasional, purposeful experimental release of, say, high altitude barium for standard wind tracking experiments. There could also be other related experiments that occur from time-to-time which release agents into the atmosphere. However, not one single picture that was presented as evidence indicates other than normal contrail formation.

Mark Pilkington, an observer of, and commentator on, conspiracy theories, was doubtful of the idea that chemtrails were part of some terrible plot to kill whole swathes of the population or to manipulate the weather. Nevertheless, he did note the following:

Author and curator Mark Pilkington—in a 2014 article, "Plane Truth on the Conspiracy Trail"—doubted there was a conspiracy to kill people with contrails, but he did note their effects on the environment.

> The contrail threat isn't entirely imagined, however. NASA has been carrying out genuine research into the possible effects of contrails and increased air activity on the environment. An average contrail can last for hours before evolving into cirrus clouds—the largest measured covered 2,000 square miles (5,180sq km) of west America. Scientists have long been concerned that, with an expected six-fold increase in plane flights, such cirrus spreads might trap heat in the Earth's atmosphere, so contributing to global warning. According to NASA research, cirrus cloud cover over America has increased five per cent since 1971, with the figure higher in the north-east.

At the height of the controversy, chemtrails researcher Ken Adachi said in "Chemtrails":

> Chemtrail spraying seems to be heaviest and most constant over North America and most countries of eastern Europe. Some countries in Asia are being sprayed (Japan and Korea), but the greatest exception to any chemtrail activity whatsoever is China. The Chinese are being spared completely because China is being groomed by the NWO to replace the United States as the leading nation of the world, both economically and militarily.

Adachi also noted something that suggested it wasn't the entire human race that was under assault, but possibly just specific portions of it:

> It is being reported that people with average or below average immunity are experiencing pneumonia-like respiratory symptoms, while people with stronger immunity are only experiencing slight discomfort for a day or two or no symptoms at all. Some people have gotten very ill and the symptoms seem to keep returning after a short period of improvement. It's possible that some of these sprayings might contain special bioengineered pathogens designed to affect only certain racial groups.

Even the world of mainstream media couldn't ignore the chemtrails. *USA Today* writer Traci Watson said in 2001, in in "Conspiracy Theories Find Menace in Contrails":

> Federal bureaucracies have gotten thousands of phone calls, e-mails and letters in recent years from people demanding to know what is being sprayed and why. Some of the missives are threatening.
>
> It's impossible to tell how many supporters these ideas have attracted, but the people who believe them say they're tired of getting the brush-off from officials. And they're tired of health problems they blame on "spraying."
>
> "This is blatant. This is in your face," said Philip Marie Sr., a retired nuclear quality engineer from Bartlett, N.H., who said the sky above his quiet town is often crisscrossed with "spray" trails.
>
> "No one will address it," he said. "Everyone stonewalls this thing."

Some people have gotten very ill and the symptoms seem to keep returning after a short period of improvement.

Writer William Thomas, one of the leading researchers of the chemtrails phenomenon, and who is a firm believer they are the work of classified programs and represent a major hazard, noted in his paper "Stolen Skies: The Chemtrail Mystery":

> On December 8, 2000, Terry Stewart, the Manager for Planning and Environment at the Victoria International Airport, responded to a caller's complaint about the strange patterns of circles and grids being woven over the British Columbia capitol. Stewart left a message on an answering machine tape—a message that later was heard by more than 15 million radio

listeners. Stewart explained: "It's a military exercise, [a] US and Canadian Air Force exercise that's going on. They wouldn't give me any specifics on it."

Thomas expanded further:

> Canadian Forces Base (CFB) Comox on Vancouver Island is Canada's biggest radar installation. CFB Comox is easily capable of tracking the US formations coming up from the south. When asked for a response to Stewart's statement, the base information officer at CFB Comox replied tersely: "No military operation is taking place." Stewart later told the *Vancouver Courier* that his information had come directly from Comox.

//**High altitude aerial spraying of pesticides does not occur in Canada and any spraying that is currently done in Canada does not encompass the use of large military type jet aircraft."**

Not surprisingly, Canadians kept a wary and concerned watch on what was going on above their heads.

In 2003, and in an attempt to put to rest concerns exhibited by Canadian citizens, in relation to the controversy, the Canadian government issued a statement on chemtrails. It included the following words, taken from a longer statement that can be read in an article titled "Chemtrails—Spraying in Our Sky":

> There is no substantiated evidence, scientific or otherwise, to support the allegation that there is high altitude spraying conducted in Canadian airspace. The term "chemtrails" is a popularized expression, and there is no scientific evidence to support their existence. Furthermore, weather modification experiments carried out over Canadian airspace legally require that Environment Canada be notified. We have no information of any such efforts. High altitude aerial spraying of pesticides does not occur in Canada and any spraying that is currently done in Canada does not encompass the use of large military type jet aircraft.

Absolutely no word was made of the December 8, 2000, saga of Stewart.

As the controversy grew, certain elements of the British government got caught up in the chemtrails controversy. On November 8, 2005, questions were asked about the chemtrails in none other than the Houses of Parliament. Specifically, the secretary of state for environment, food, and rural affairs was asked what research had been undertaken into "the polluting effects of chemtrails for aircraft."

The response from Elliott Morley (who held the position of minister of state for the environment and agri-environment) was intriguing, but ultimately dismissive. Published at parliament.uk, in November 2005, it states:

> The Department is not researching into chemtrails from aircraft as they are not scientifically recognized phenomena. However, condensation trails (contrails) are known to exist and have been documented since the 1940s. Contrails are composed of ice crystals forming on the small particles and water vapor emitted by aircraft as the result of the combustion

process they form behind high-flying aircraft depending on the temperature and humidity of the atmosphere.

A major scientific report, *Aviation and the Global Atmosphere*, was published in 1999 by the Intergovernmental Panel on Climate Change. The report assessed the current contribution of aviation to climate change and, based on a range of scenarios and assumptions, forecast its contribution up to 2050. It estimated that contrails covered about 0.1 per cent of the Earth's surface in 1992 and projected this cover would grow to 0.5 per cent by 2050 (on middle range assumptions). More recently this work has been updated from the results of the EU 5th Framework Project, TRADEOFF.

Contrails continue to be the subject of research to help better understand both how they are formed and what effects they have on the atmosphere.

To date, that remains the British government's official verdict on chemtrails.

Moving on to 2008, one of the most well-known and respected investigators of conspiracy theories, Jim Marrs, is quoted in Ben Radford's 2009 article "Curious Contrails: Death from the Sky?" as saying: "Chemtrails often occur at altitudes and in conditions where it would be impossible for a contrail to form." He noted that a 2007 report undertaken by a television station in Louisiana—KSLA—revealed something startling. Investigative reporter Jeff Ferrell, said Marrs, tested water captured under a crosshatch of alleged chemtrails. According

Television station KSLA in Shreveport, Louisiana, conducted an analysis of water from chemtrails, discovering toxic levels of barium.

to Ferrell, and referenced by Marrs: "KSLA News 12 had the sample tested at a lab. The results: high level of barium, 6.8 parts per million (ppm). That's more than three times the toxic level set by the Environmental Protection Agency."

The results were disputed by physicist David E. Thomas, who concluded the errors were simply the result of bad math on the part of Ferrell. That Thomas was a contributing editor to the *Skeptical Inquirer* left many of the chemtrail proponents ... well ... skeptical.

In May 2014, a new angle surfaced, one that suggested chemtrails were, in part at least, aimed at destroying the organic food market. At least one of the guilty parties in this affair, said GeoEngineering Watch, was Monsanto, a major, multinational, bio-technology corporation based out of St. Louis, Missouri. On this matter, taken from "Chemtrails Killing Organic Crops, Monsanto's GMO Seeds Thrive," is the following:

> Organic farmers and our food supply have a huge environmental hazard to contend with compliments of the U.S. government—chemtrails. Chemtrails are chemical or biological agents deliberately sprayed at high altitudes for purposes undisclosed to the general public in programs directed by various government officials. These sprays pollute the soil, water and air while compromising the health of humans, animals and plants. But wait—Monsanto has developed seeds that will weather the effect of the sprays, creating a tidy profit for the corporation while organics suffer.
>
> Monsanto's GMO seeds are specially designed to grow in the high presence of aluminum. Aluminum is the chemical found in chemtrails. If this poisoning continues, true organic farming may become impossible in the not so distant future. When aluminum pollutes soil and water it kills crops. It collects in people and causes diseases!

Today, the debate over chemtrails continues to rage on. As prime evidence of this, visitors to *The Sheep Killers* website are told, in "Chemtrails":

> Our health is under attack as evidenced by the skyrocketing rates of chemtrail induced lung cancer, asthma, and pulmonary/respiratory problems. Our natural environment and planetary weather systems are under attack resulting in freak lightening strikes, bizarre weather, 20% less sunlight reaching the Earth's surface, the alarming, nearly complete collapse in certain areas of the west coast marine ecosystem and the creation of some of the largest tornadoes and hurricanes on record. Our skies are increasingly hazed over with fake barium/aluminum particulate, ethylene dibromide chemtrail clouds. Whether in the atmosphere or in the Ocean this added particulate matter is a hazard to the health of every living thing on this planet.

You have been warned. Keep your eyes on the skies. You know: just in case....

BLACK HELICOPTERS: SPIES IN THE SKIES

Since the mid-1960s, countless people, all around the globe, have had encounters with what have become infamously known in conspiracy circles as "black helicopters." Typically, as the name suggests, these craft are completely black in color and lack any markings that might, otherwise, provide an explanation as to who, exactly, is flying them and why.

Black helicopters are most often seen: (a) in areas where UFO activity is prevalent, (b) where so-called cattle mutilation events have occurred, and (c) in close proximity—sometimes in *perilously* close proximity—to the homes of people who have become known as alien abductees. Oddly, the craft are very often described as flying in almost complete silence. Hardly surprisingly, this collective data has led many conspiracy theorists and UFO investigators to conclude that the black helicopters originate with clandestine, government-run groups that keep a careful and concerned watch on the UFO phenomenon, as well as its interactions with us, the human race.

On October 11, 1966, for example, a notable UFO encounter occurred at the Wanaque Reservoir, New Jersey. It involved a group of police officers who all had a very close encounter with a classic, saucer-shaped UFO that hovered over the reservoir for a brief period, thus allowing the astonished officers to see the craft up close and personal, before it vanished in the vicinity of nearby woods. Within minutes, half a dozen unmarked helicopters—presumed by the officers to have been military in origin—were seen flying in the direction where the UFO disappeared.

In mid January 1974, the British media was tipped off by government insiders that there was deep concern on the part of officialdom that someone— someone unknown and maybe of hostile intent—was flying unmarked helicopters around the skies of the United Kingdom, and in the dead of night, no less. All across the north of England the curious crafts were seen, as is evidenced by the following official statement put out by Cheshire police when the story reached the media (Cheshire Police Force, press release, January 14, 1974):

> We don't know of any reason why the helicopter should make these trips
> at night. Obviously we are anxious to find out. Apart from anything else,
> the helicopter crosses one of the main flight paths to Manchester Air-

port. There is an obvious danger to the aircraft going into the airport. We are very interested to know what is happening. We hope to be able to trace the pilot and put some suggestions to him. It would appear the pilot is in breach of civil aviation laws. A special license is needed to fly a helicopter at night.

Police from Derbyshire, England, acknowledged they had received such reports, too: "All sorts of things spring to mind but we have pretty much ruled out that it is anything to do with illegal immigrants, and nothing appears to have been stolen in the areas where the aircraft have been sighted."

As the encounters with the black and unmarked helicopters continued, an elite arm of the British Police Force known as Special Branch—whose work primarily revolves around combating terrorism within the U.K.—got involved in the investigation. This is made clear via a now-declassified Special Branch file on the affair titled *Alleged Unauthorized Helicopter Flights in Derbyshire and Cheshire.*

The Special Branch files record that:

The machine was observed on a number of occasions over a period of two weeks to be apparently practicing landings in the vicinity of the sites of quarries and explosive stores in the Derbyshire countryside. Special Branch Constable [deleted] has made numerous enquiries to discover the ownership and reasons for the flights from various sources but has yet to establish any positive facts.

He has contacted an experienced Royal Air Force helicopter pilot with night flying experience who explained that night flying in the Derbyshire areas would be extremely dangerous due to the nature of the terrain and to the number of overhead pylons in the area.

Two months after the British press first got wind of what was afoot, the sightings were still going on, something that led the British Ministry of Defense, Special Branch, and a whole variety of regional police forces to pool their thoughts and recommendations at Horseferry House, London, on March 21, 1974. Rather oddly—some might say suspiciously—when a decision was taken to increase the investigation, possibly using Royal Air Force aircraft to pursue the helicopters, the curious wave came to a sudden end.

This photo, taken in 2005, appears to show a UFO (circled) being towed by a helicopter near Humberside Airport in England. What is the connection between some UFO sightings and helicopters?

Six months after the events in England ceased, a black helicopter surfaced in the United States. It was late on the evening September 26, 1974, when the Richley family of Lynchburg, Ohio, saw a strange object high in the sky above their home. That it was stationary and appeared to be circular in shape prompted Walter Richley to hit the UFO with the beam of a large searchlight that was affixed to his truck. The UFO responded by doing likewise: the truck was bathed with an eerie, red glow. Not surprisingly, the Richleys raced for their home and locked the doors. Things were not quite over, however.

A little more than twenty-four hours later, Walter's son, Dan, was reading in bed when he heard the unmistakable sound of rotor-blades—seemingly almost outside the window. He flung open the curtains. Sure enough, a large helicopter was in view. Not only that, it was sitting on the ground, just a short distance from the family home. Dan quickly roused his father, who later told UFO researcher Leonard Stringfield (who published the story in his 1978 book, *Situation Red: The UFO Siege*): "I think I put my light beam on something that was a military secret. That 'copter came here to warn me. I'm not about to press it; I'd rather forget it."

In a previous chapter of this book, a study was made of the FBI's formerly classified files on so-called cattle mutilations. One particular FBI document makes a distinct connection between the mutilations and mysterious, black helicopters. Dated February 2, 1979, and viewable at the FBI's website, The Vault, under the heading of "Animal Mutilation," it noted:

> For the past seven or eight years, mysterious cattle mutilations have been occurring throughout the United State of New Mexico. Officer Gabe Valdez, New Mexico State Police, has been handling investigations of these mutilations within New Mexico. Information furnished to this office by Officer Valdez indicates that the animals are being shot with some type of paralyzing drug and the blood is being drawn from the animal after an injection of an anti-coagulant.

///I think I put my light beam on something that was a military secret. That 'copter came here to warn me."

> It appears that in some instances the cattle's legs have been broken and helicopters without any identifying numbers have reportedly been seen in the vicinity of the mutilations. Officer Valdez theorizes that clamps are being placed on the cow's legs and they are being lifted by helicopter to some remote area where the mutilations are taking place and then the animal is returned to its original pasture.

> Officer Valdez is very adamant in his opinion that these mutilations are the work of the US government and that it is some clandestine operation either by the CIA or the Department of Energy and in all probability is connected with some type of research into biological warfare.

Tom Adams, a researcher who spent many years investigating the mutilation problem, said in his booklet, *The Choppers and the Choppers*:

> The helicopters are of military origin. The government of the United States possesses a very substantial amount of knowledge about the mutilators, their means, motives and rationale. The government may be attempting to persuade mutilation investigators and the populace as a whole that perhaps the military might be behind the mutilations, a diversion away from the real truth.

One of the most famous of all alien abductees is Betty Andreasson, whose encounters with large-eyed, diminutive extraterrestrials have been chronicled in a number of books, most notably *The Andreasson Affair*. For years, Andreasson and her family have been plagued by unwanted visits from black helicopters. Lawrence Fawcett and Barry Greenwood, who, in the early 1980s, spent a great deal of time addressing the many and varied intricacies of the Andreasson case, said, in their 1984 book, *Clear Intent*, of Betty and her husband, Bob Luca:

> They reported that their home was over flown numerous times by black, unmarked helicopters of the Huey UH-1H type and that these helicopters would fly over their homes at altitudes as low as 100 feet. The Lucas described these helicopters as being black in color, with no identifiable marking on them. They noticed that the windows were tinted black also, so that no one could see inside. During many of the over flights, Bob was able to take close to 200 photos of the helicopters.

Angered and frustrated as to what was going on—and, more importantly, *why*—Luca fired off a communication to the U.S. Army's Office of the Adjutant General. Luca demanded answers. All he got was a brief, and hardly satisfying, reply: "It is difficult to determine what particular aircraft is involved or the owning unit."

Debbie Jordan, whose alien encounters are detailed in her book *Abducted!*, said of her very own run-ins with the black helicopters:

> These could be seen almost daily around our houses. They are so obvious about their flights it's almost comical. On occasions too numerous to even remember, they have hovered around my house, above my house, and above me for several minutes at a time, not trying to hide themselves or the fact that they are watching us.

The black, unmarked helicopters resembled Huey UH-1H types used by the military.

> Even when I am outside and obviously watching back, it doesn't seem to bother them. They just sit there in midair, about sixty to ninety feet above the ground, whirling and watching. They are completely without identification and are always low enough so that I could easily see the pilot, if the windshield were clear glass. But the windshield is smoky black, with a finish that makes it impossible to see who's inside.

The late Jim Keith—a conspiracy theorist who died under controversial circumstances in 1999—was an acknowledged expert on black helicopters and someone who penned two books on the subject. He recalled—in his book *Black Helicopters II*—one incident that demonstrated sightings of black helicopters were occurring well into the 1990s:

On May 23, 1994, at the Big Meadows on the Blue Ridge Parkway, Virginia, a citizen came upon a blocked-off road leading into the Shenandoah National Park. He observed a black chopper coming in for a landing a short distance away, and took photos of the craft. When he asked a park ranger what the black choppers were doing there, the ranger said, "They help us with search and rescue."

When the man pointed out to the ranger that the helicopter was equipped with a grenade launcher and added that this hardly seemed to gel with the "search and rescue" comment, the ranger suddenly became noticeably hostile.

As to who, precisely, is overseeing all of these classified operations, perhaps the most likely scenario is that which was offered to a long-time UFO investigator named Tommy Blann. In the early 1980s Blann had the opportunity to speak with a confidential, U.S. military source who was willing to share at least a limited amount of solid data on the black helicopter phenomenon.

Blann (referenced in Leonard Stringfield's 1982 booklet, *UFO Crash/Retrievals: Amassing the Evidence*) said that his informant told him of "underground installations, as well as isolated areas of military reservations [that] have squadrons of unmarked helicopters, which have sophisticated instrumentation on board, that are dispatched to areas of UFO activity to monitor these craft or airlift them out of the area if one has malfunctioned."

NEW WORLD ORDER

THE TWIN TOWERS: FROM CONSPIRACY TO DEMOLITION

September 11, 2001, will go down as one of the worst days in the history of the United States of America, if not *the* worst. In terms of tragedy and outrage, it is equaled only by the terrible events of December 7, 1941, when Japanese forces attacked Pearl Harbor, Hawaii, killing nearly twenty-five hundred Americans in the process.

In shockingly quick progression—and with equally shocking ease—nineteen al-Qaeda terrorists seized control of four, large passenger planes and, essentially, turned them into the equivalents of missiles. On the morning of September 11, United Airlines Flight 175 and American Airlines Flight 11 slammed, respectively, into the South and North towers of New York's World Trade Center. Another American Airlines plane, Flight 77, hit the Pentagon, and United Airlines Flight 93 hurtled to the ground outside of Shanksville, Pennsylvania, when a number of passengers attempted to wrestle control of the plane from the hijackers. There were suspicions that the plan of the hijackers was to target none other than the White House itself. Before the day was over, a nation was stunned to its core and almost three thousand people had lost their lives.

Although the United States had been subjected to terrorist attacks in the past, none equaled the levels of horror that 9/11 provoked. They were attacks that, near-singlehandedly, prompted the invasions of both Iraq and Afghanistan, as the Bush administration sought to bring the guilty parties to justice and prevent any future, similar events from occurring. It wasn't just horror and outrage that resulted from 9/11; the events also ensured the rapid development of a wide and varied body of conspiracy theories, all suggesting that the story told to the public and the media—that the attacks were the work of al-Qaeda—was very wide of the mark.

Rather oddly, given that Osama bin Laden made no bones about his hatred of the West, and the United States in particular, he denied any involvement in the attacks of September 11, 2001, at all—until 2004. Precisely why the one man who, more than any other, wished to do significant harm to the United States would deny his involvement in committing the worst atrocity on U.S. soil since 1941 makes very little sense. In terms of the propaganda value, and of instilling fear in the minds of American citizens, bin Laden should have been all over 9/11 from day one. That he was not is something many have failed to realize and even more do not understand.

New York City's World Trade Center belches flames after being struck by two passenger aircraft on September 11, 2001. The attack was blamed on al-Qaeda terrorists, but their leader, Osama bin Laden, denied involvement.

There is also the matter of how less than two dozen men, armed with nothing more than box-cutters, were able to kill thousands of Americans, destroy both of the Twin Towers, and cause major damage to the Pentagon. It's almost as if the terrorists were *allowed* to carry out their deadly actions, while the authorities looked the other way and turned a blind eye. Maybe, that's precisely what did occur. Let's begin with the events at the World Trade Center.

Steve Alten is a best-selling author, probably most widely known for his controversial novel *The Shell Game*, a 2009 story that tells of the next 9/11-style event on U.S. soil. Alten makes no bones about the fact that he has major suspicions that we have not been told the real story of what happened on September 11, 2001. In a foreword to his novel, Alten correctly noted that on the morning of 9/11, then-Vice President Dick Cheney oversaw a series of war games that, in

Alten's opinion, "purposefully diverted all of our jet fighters away from the North-eastern Air Defense Sector (NEADS) where the four hijackings took place, sending them over Alaska, Greenland, Iceland, and Canada."

Alten also significantly noted:

One of these exercises, *Vigilant Guardian*, was a hijack drill designed to mirror the actual events taking place, inserting twenty-two false radar blips on the FAA's radar screens so that flight controllers had no idea which blips were the hijacked aircraft and which were the war game blips.

The result: mass confusion over what was real and what was not, and a lack of adequate military defense at the time when the Twin Towers were struck.

Then there is the matter of certain, highly suspicious stock trading that went on in the immediate days before the attacks, something that led to vocal assertions from the conspiracy-minded that those engaged in the trading secretly knew of what was about to hit the United States. Most of the activity revolved around the very two airlines whose planes were used in the attacks: American Airlines and United Airlines.

Allen M. Poteshman, of the *Journal of Business* (quoted in "Unusual Option Market Activity and the Terrorist Attacks of September 11, 2001"), said of this curious state of affairs:

A measure of abnormal long put volume was also examined and seen to be at abnormally high levels in the days leading up to the attacks. Consequently, the paper concludes that there is evidence of unusual option market activity in the days leading up to September 11 that is consistent with investors trading on advance knowledge of the attacks.

It wasn't just airlines that were experiencing abnormal stock-based activity right before 9/11. The world of insurance did, too. Both Morgan Stanley and Citigroup Inc. had massive increases in trading from September 8 and right up until the time of the attacks. Indeed, Citigroup Inc.'s trading was in excess of *forty times* its normal level. Citigroup stood to pay out millions in insurance claims from the World Trade Center attacks. Morgan Stanley had its offices *within* the World Trade Center. One of the United States' leading defense companies, Raytheon, saw trading leap more than five times its normal, approximate level on September 10.

One of the United States' leading defense companies, Raytheon, saw trading leap more than five times its normal, approximate level on September 10.

Also on the matter of advance knowledge of 9/11, there is a curious, and downright surreal, story that has a link to none other than *The X-Files*. Although Mulder and Scully were the focus of just about every episode, from time to time they received significant help, in their efforts to uncover the truth of a number of cosmic conspiracies, from a trio of eccentric conspiracy theorists. They were John Byers, Melvin Frohike, and Richard Langly, who published the *Magic Bullet Newsletter*. The three characters became better known as the Lone Gunmen. Such was the enthusiasm that the show's fans had for Langly,

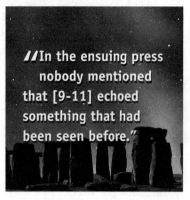

//In the ensuing press nobody mentioned that [9-11] echoed something that had been seen before."

Frohike, and Byers, in early 2001 they were given their very own, short-lived series. The name of the series surprised no one: *The Lone Gunmen.*

The first episode aired on March 4, 2001. Its title was *Pilot.* The plot-line was chillingly similar to the events that went down on 9/11. In the show, a computer hacker takes control of a Boeing 727 passenger plane and flies it towards the World Trade Center, with the specific intention of crashing the plane into one of the Twin Towers. It's only at the very last moment that the Lone Gunmen are able to hack the hacker and avert disaster and death for those aboard the plane and those inside the World Trade Center.

The story gets even more intriguing: the hacker is not just some random, crazy guy. It's all the work of a powerful group buried deep within the U.S. government. The secret plan, had it worked, was to put the blame for the World Trade Center attacks on one or more foreign dictators who are "begging to be smart-bombed" by the U.S. military. It should be stressed that there is no evidence that the creators of *The Lone Gunmen* had any advance knowledge of 9/11. It is worth noting, however, that there seemed to be a deep reluctance on the part of the media to address the storyline of *Pilot* and its parallels to 9/11—not to mention that the episode had its premiere broadcast in Australia just *thirteen days* before the events of September 11 occurred.

One of those who commented on this odd state of affairs was Christopher Bollyn. He said, in "Did Rupert Murdoch Have Prior Knowledge of 9-11?":

> [R]ather than being discussed in the media as a prescient warning of the possibility of such an attack, the pilot episode of *The Lone Gunmen* series seemed to have been quietly forgotten. While an estimated 13.2 million Fox TV viewers are reported to have watched the pilot episode … when life imitated art just six months later on 9-11, no one in the media seemed to recall the program.

Frank Spotnitz was one of the executive producers of *The Lone Gunmen.* He said (and is also quoted in Christopher Bollyn's article):

> I woke up on September 11 and saw it on TV and the first thing I thought of was *The Lone Gunmen.* But then in the weeks and months that followed, almost no one noticed the connection. What's disturbing about it to me is, you think as a fiction writer that if you can imagine this scenario, then the people in power in the government who are there to imagine disaster scenarios can imagine it, too.

Robert McLachlan was the director of photography on *The Lone Gunmen.* He had words to say, too (also cited by Bollyn): "It was odd that nobody referenced it. In the ensuing press nobody mentioned that [9-11] echoed something that had been seen before."

Jeffrey King, who has carefully studied the 9/11 events, asked, in his article, "The Lone Gunmen Episode 1: Pilot:"

Is this just a case of life imitating art, or did [the production company] know something about the upcoming attacks? Was this an attempt to use the highly visible platform of the first episode of a new series (and a spin-off from the very popular *X-Files*) to make enough people aware of the scenario that it would become too risky to implement? Or was it just one of those ideas that was "in the air" at the time, an expression of the zeit-geist?

King had more to impart:

Great and traumatic events always seem to be preceded by certain fore-shadowings [sic], like the upstream standing waves that form behind a rock in the streambed. Perhaps this is just another in the endless string of odd synchronicities surrounding the events of 9-11, peculiar juxtaposi-tions of events that must eventually strain the credulity of even the most devoted coincidence theorist, though no single one rises to the level of a smoking gun.

Then there is the matter of the speed, and ease, with which the Twin Towers fell to the ground. Many people claimed that the ways in which the South and North Towers collapsed were far less consistent with what one could expect from aircraft collisions, and far more consistent with the likes of a carefully con-trolled demolition. And those people were not all conspiracy theorists.

It should be noted that when the towers were constructed they were specif-ically designed to survive a direct strike from an aircraft the size of a Boeing 707.

The World Trade Center Memorial honors the 2,977 people who died during the September 11, 2001, attacks, as well as the six who died in the 1993 WTC terrorist attack.

They were also built to withstand winds of up to 160 miles per hour. Instead, both towers did not continue to stand. Quite the opposite: they crumbled to the ground, causing even more terror and death for the people of New York. The South Tower fell just short of an hour after it was hit, while the North Tower stood for just one hour and forty-two minutes.

One person who carefully studied the data suggesting the towers were brought down in definitive demolition style was Steven Jones, a physics professor at Brigham Young University. In 2005, Jones helped to establish an organization called Scholars for 9/11 Truth. Jones suffered for his cause: after publishing his theories that the collapse of the Twin Towers was caused by explosives, he was placed on leave by the university. He responded by retiring on January 1, 2007. It was Jones' theory that the specific type of substance used was likely to have been nano-thermite, used by the military in explosives (See: Associated Press, "9/11 Conspiracy Theorist to Leave Brigham Young").

"I am electing to retire so that I can spend more time speaking and conducting research of my choosing," said the professor, as he bid the university goodbye.

Global Research (in "9/11 Theologian Says Controlled Demolition of World Trade Center Is Now a Fact, Not a Theory") noted:

> The massive core columns—the most significant structural feature of the buildings, whose very existence is denied in the official 9/11 Commission Report—were severed into uniform 30 foot sections, just right for the 30-foot trucks used to remove them quickly before a real investigation could transpire.

> There was a volcanic-like dust cloud from the concrete being pulverized, and no physical mechanism other than explosives can begin to explain how so much of the buildings' concrete was rendered into extremely fine dust. The debris was ejected horizontally several hundred feet in huge fan shaped plumes stretching in all directions, with telltale "squibs" following the path of the explosives downward.

> These are all facts that have been avoided by mainstream and even most of the alternative media. Again, these are characteristics of the kind of controlled demolitions that news people and firefighters were describing on the morning of 9/11.

It's important to note that it was not just the North and South Towers that fell on 9/11. A third tower, completely untouched by the aircraft that ploughed into the towers, also collapsed. It was Tower 7 of the World Trade Center complex. Dylan Avery, who directed the 9/11-themed film, *Loose Change*, said (and is quoted in "The Evolution of a Conspiracy Theory"): "The truth movement is heavily centered on Building 7 and for very good reason a lot of people are very suspicious about what went down that day." The BBC noted, in "The Evolution of a Conspiracy Theory":

> Avery points out that Tower 7 housed some unusual tenants: the CIA, the Secret Service, the Pentagon and the very agency meant to deal with

disasters or terrorist attacks in New York—the Office of Emergency Management. And some people think Tower 7 was the place where a 9/11 conspiracy was hatched.

The official explanation, the BBC noted, was that "ordinary fires" were to blame for the fall of Tower 7. But, the BBC also said, this "makes this the first and only tall skyscraper in the world to have collapsed because of fire."

Then there is the theory that, as per the claims surrounding the December 7, 1941, attack on Pearl Harbor, 9/11 was allowed to happen to justify an invasion of the Middle East. Michael Meacher was the British government's environment minister from 1997 to 2003. His words (published by Britain's *Guardian* newspaper in 2003, in an article titled "This War on Terror Is Bogus"), as a senior official of the government, did not go by unnoticed. They were picked up widely:

> [I]t is clear the US authorities did little or nothing to preempt the events of 9/11. It is known that at least 11 countries provided advance warning to the US of the 9/11 attacks. Two senior Mossad experts were sent to Washington in August 2001 to alert the CIA and FBI to a cell of 200 terrorists said to be preparing a big operation. The list they provided included the names of four of the 9/11 hijackers, none of whom was arrested.

> It had been known as early as 1996 that there were plans to hit Washington targets with airplanes. Then in 1999 a US national intelligence council report noted that "al-Qaida suicide bombers could crash-land an aircraft packed with high explosives into the Pentagon, the headquarters of the CIA, or the White House."

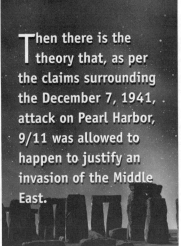

Then there is the theory that, as per the claims surrounding the December 7, 1941, attack on Pearl Harbor, 9/11 was allowed to happen to justify an invasion of the Middle East.

Fifteen of the 9/11 hijackers obtained their visas in Saudi Arabia. Michael Springman, the former head of the American visa bureau in Jeddah, has stated that since 1987 the CIA had been illicitly issuing visas to unqualified applicants from the Middle East and bringing them to the US for training in terrorism for the Afghan war in collaboration with Bin Laden. It seems this operation continued after the Afghan war for other purposes. It is also reported that five of the hijackers received training at secure US military installations in the 1990s.

With that all said, let us now take a look at the events that occurred on September 11, 2001, at the Pentagon and over Shanksville, Pennsylvania.

FROM THE PENTAGON TO FLIGHT 93: MISSILES AND MYSTERIES

Of the four aircraft that were involved in the 9/11 attacks, three succeeded in reaching their intended targets: United Airlines Flight 175 and American Airlines Flight 11 slammed into the Twin Towers of the World Trade Center, and American Airlines Flight 77 hit the Pentagon. The one exception was United Airlines Flight 93, which failed to reach its target—which may have been the White House, although this is, admittedly, speculation. Instead, it crashed in a field near Shanksville, Pennsylvania. Although Flight 93, a Boeing 757, could hold almost two hundred passengers, there were less than forty onboard when, at 8.42 A.M., on the morning of September 11, the plane took to the skies from Newark International Airport, New Jersey, under the control of Captain Jason Dahl. Forty-six minutes later, the plane was under siege.

Terrorists had control of the plane. Each and every one of them had practically breezed their way through security. They were Ziad Jarrah, Saeed al-Ghamdi, Ahmed al-Nami, and Ahmed al-Haznawi. Only the latter was subjected to a high degree of screening, but it was a screening that raised no red flags whatsoever. All four men were sitting in first-class, which made it relatively easy for them to invade the cockpit with speed.

It was just a couple of minutes before 9:30 A.M. that the hijackers launched their attack on the cockpit—which occurred after the Twin Towers had already been hit. Although United Airlines staff sent messages to their crews, Captain Dahl did not receive the message until just mere minutes before the hijack began. A study of the cockpit recordings retrieved after the crash showed that the hijackers successfully breached the cockpit and overpowered the crew, possibly critically injuring, or killing, Captain Dahl in the process.

A few moments later, a voice, coming from the cockpit, echoed around the plane: "Ladies and gentlemen: this is the captain. Please sit down and keep remaining seated. We have a bomb on board. So sit."

Not surprisingly, the frantic passengers and flight attendants quickly phoned friends and family and, in doing so, learned of the attacks on the World Trade Center. They soon learned, too, of the attack on the Pentagon, which occurred just minutes after the hijacking of Flight 93. As a result, the passengers formulated a plan to try and wrestle the plane out of the hands of the terrorists. The recordings reveal a wealth of confusion, shouting, screaming, and moaning, all of which graphically demonstrated the nightmarish, terrifying situation onboard the plane. Friends and family were told the pilots were dead or dying, that men with bombs strapped to their bodies were in the cabin, and that the hijackers were supposedly going to return to the airport to make their demands known to U.S. authorities.

When a group of passengers attempted to storm the cockpit—by ramming the door with the food and drink cart—the hijackers knew their time was short, as the black-box data showed. Instead of continuing onto their destination of San Francisco, California, or heading back to Newark, they first put the plane through a violent series of maneuvers, to specifically try and knock the passengers off their feet. When that failed to work and the passengers continued, the hijackers chose to end things there and then. Shortly after 10:00 A.M., the plane crashed into the ground between Shanksville and Indian Lake, Pennsylvania. No one survived the impact. Although there is no definitive proof, it has been suggested that some of the passengers may have made it into the cockpit and managed to prevent the hijackers from continuing on with their mission to hit whatever their intended target was.

In terms of the conspiracy theories that surround the events of September 11, 2001, the most enduring, when it comes to Flight 93, is that the plane was not deliberately crashed by the hijackers, or as a result of a confrontation between the hijackers and the passengers, but was blasted out of the skies by a U.S. military aircraft.

On September 15, CBS 58 News reported (see "FBI Does Not Rule Out Shootdown of Hijacked 757 Over Pennsylvania"):

> Federal investigators said on Thursday they could not rule out the possibility that the United jet was shot down. "We have not ruled out that," FBI agent Bill Crowley told a news conference when asked about reports that a U.S. fighter jet may have fired on the hijacked Boeing 757. "We haven't ruled out anything yet."

This photo, taken on September 8, 2001, is of the United Airlines plane that was scheduled as Flight 93 on that fateful day of September 11, 2001.

Then, in November, journalist William Bunch spoke with the mayor of Shanksville, Ernie Stuhl, on the issues surrounding the crash of Flight 93. Bunch reported, in "Flight 93: We Know It Crashed but Not Why":

> Ernie Stuhl is the mayor of this tiny farming borough that was so brutally placed on America's psychic map on the morning of September 11, when United Airlines Flight 93 slammed nose-down into the edge of a barren strip-mine moonscape a couple of miles outside of town.

> A 77-year-old World War II veteran and retired Dodge dealer, he's certainly no conspiracy theorist.

> And, when you ask Stuhl for his theory of what caused the jetliner to crash that morning, he will give you the prevailing theory—that a cockpit battle between the hijackers and burly, heroic passengers somehow caused the Boeing 757 to spiral out of control. "There's no doubt in my mind that they did put it down before it got to Washington and caused more damage," he said.

> But press the mayor for details, and he will add something surprising:

> "I know of two people—I will not mention names—that heard a missile," Stuhl said. "They both live very close, within a couple of hundred yards. This one fellow's served in Vietnam and he said he's heard them, and he heard one that day." The mayor adds that based on what he knows about that morning, military F-16 fighter jets were "very, very close."

In April 2009, writer Paul Joseph Watson reported in "Military Whistleblower Claims She Witnessed Flight 93 Shootdown Order":

> A woman who claims she was stationed at Fort Meade on September 11, 2001, has given an explosive interview about how she personally heard military commanders make the decision to shoot down United Airlines Flight 93 on 9/11.

> A person using the pseudonym Elizabeth Nelson [said] that she personally heard officials agree on the order to shoot down Flight 93. The decision was apparently made because the plane was flying in a no-fly zone near to Camp David and heading toward *Site R*, a military facility known as the "backup Pentagon."

> Nelson stresses that at no time was there any talk of "hijackers," and the plane was shot down purely because communication had been lost and standard operating procedure mandated that the plane be intercepted and destroyed.

Christopher Bollyn, of *American Free Press*, penned "Eyewitnesses Saw Military Aircraft at Scene of Flight 93" and said:

> Susan McElwain, a local teacher, also reported seeing a white "military" plane at the scene of the crash before witnessing an explosion. Ms. McElwain told *The Daily Mirror* what she saw:

"It came right over me, I reckon just 40 or 50 feet above my mini-van," she recalled. "It was so low I ducked instinctively. It was traveling real fast, but hardly made any sound.

Then it disappeared behind some trees. A few seconds later I heard this great explosion and saw this fireball rise up over the trees, so I figured the jet had crashed. The ground really shook. So I dialed 911 and told them what happened. I'd heard nothing about the other attacks and it was only when I got home and saw the TV that I realized it wasn't the white jet, but Flight 93."

None of this proves that Flight 93 was shot down, and the fact that some of the data has been offered anonymously weakens the case. Nevertheless, whatever the truth of the matter, the claim that Flight 93 was brought down by the U.S. military continues to endure.

Only minutes after Flight 93 was hijacked, the crew and passengers of American Airlines Flight 77 suffered a near-identical fate. They too found themselves hijacked and on a course with death. Just like Flight 93, the aircraft involved was a Boeing 757. It was piloted by Captain Charles Burlingame and left Washington Dulles International Airport for Los Angeles International Airport, California, at 8:20 A.M. on the morning of 9/11. It was around twenty to twenty-five minutes into the flight that terror broke out across the plane: a group of five men took control of the aircraft. The ringleader was Hani Saleh Hasan Hanjour, a Saudi-

An aerial photo of the site in Somerset County, Pennsylvania, where Flight 93 crashed.

The Pentagon in Washington, D.C., suffered enormous damage when Flight 77 rammed into one side of the building.

Arabian who possessed a commercial pilot's certificate, which gave him significant skills when it came to directing the 757 into the Pentagon.

Much of what happened onboard the plane remains a mystery to this very day—chiefly because the cockpit voice recorder was so badly damaged in the fiery crash that nothing of any use was ever recovered. What is known for certain is that air traffic controllers lost contact with Captain Burlingame and his crew at 8:50 A.M. Given that the first attack on the World Trade Center had already occurred, it was clear to ground control that something serious was going on, and almost certainly a hijacking. A couple of people—including Barbara Olson, the wife of U.S. solicitor general Theodore Olson—managed to contact family and confirmed the plane had been hijacked by men armed with knives. Barbara Olson told her husband that everyone—including the crew—had been ordered to the rear of the plane. The hijackers now had complete control of the cockpit.

Hanjour, a skilled pilot, took his plane towards Washington, D.C., and on a course for the Pentagon. Somewhat incredibly, he managed to not only aim the huge 757 at the Pentagon, but actually managed to fly low and horizontal and right into the building at a speed of more than five hundred miles an hour. So low was the plane, it actually destroyed a number of street-level lampposts as it smashed directly into its target. The result was complete chaos and devastation: everyone on board—six crew members, fifty-three passengers, and all five hijackers—was killed, as were 125 people in the Pentagon. It was almost a miracle that more Pentagon employees didn't lose their lives, since the aircraft penetrated the building by more than three hundred feet and sent a massive fireball into the skies above.

Mike Walter, a *USA Today* writer, witnessed the terrible event and was referenced in Porter Anderson's "Witnesses to the Moments":

> I looked out my window and I saw this plane, this jet, an American Airlines jet, coming. And I thought, "This doesn't add up, it's really low." And I saw it. I mean it was like a cruise missile with wings. It went right there and slammed right into the Pentagon.

Despite all the evidence suggesting that the plane had been hijacked and crashed into the Pentagon—something confirmed by Walter and others—a controversial conspiracy soon took shape: that the Pentagon was not hit by a hijacked aircraft, at all, but by a missile.

Major General Albert N. Stubblebine, the commanding general of the United States Army Intelligence and Security Command from 1981 to 1984, said that he saw a photograph …

… taken by one of the sensors on the outside of the Pentagon. Now, all of the sensors had been turned off, which is kind of interesting—isn't it? That day, why would all of the sensors around the Pentagon be turned off? That's strange. I don't care what the excuse is. That's strange.

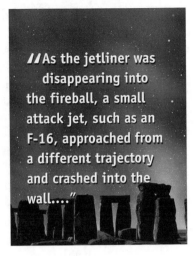

//As the jetliner was disappearing into the fireball, a small attack jet, such as an F-16, approached from a different trajectory and crashed into the wall....

There happened to be one that apparently did not get turned off. And in that picture, coming in, flying into the Pentagon, you see this object, and it obviously hits the Pentagon. When you look at it, it does not look like an airplane. Sometime later, after I'd gone public, that imagery was changed. It got a new suit around it that now looked like an airplane. But, when you take the suit off, it looks more like a missile—not like an airplane.

Stubblebine's words can be found at Ross Pitman's "9/11 Must See."

The website *911review* noted—in an article titled "What Hit the Pentagon?"—that, in 2002, a theory was advanced suggesting:

[A] Boeing 757 did indeed swoop down toward the west block of the Pentagon, but disappeared into a blinding pyrotechnic display, making it appear that it had crashed into the building, while in fact it had cleared the facade, overflown the Pentagon, and then banked sharply to land at Reagan National Airport, whose runways are only about two miles away from the Pentagon. As the jetliner was disappearing into the fireball, a small attack jet, such as an F-16, approached from a different trajectory and crashed into the wall, producing, in combination with a missile, the damage to the facade and interior.

This theory has the advantage over other no-757-crash theories that it is consistent with the many credible eyewitness reports of a jetliner. However, it neither explains the eyewitness statements that the plane collided with the building, nor the lack of a single eyewitness statement supporting the idea that a 757 overflew the Pentagon and then landed at the nearby National airport. Also, the theory raises questions about the fate of the passengers of Flight 77.

On the tenth anniversary of 9/11, Britain's *Guardian* newspaper reported (see Chris McGreal's "September 11 Conspiracy Theories Continue to Abound") in its summary of the conspiracy theories that had risen over the past decade:

A French author, Thierry Meyssan, had a bestseller—*9/11: The Big Lie*—within months of the attacks by claiming the Pentagon was destroyed by a missile and aircraft parts were brought to the scene to fake the crash. It is a theory supported by Dean Hartwell who claims in his books—*Planes without Passengers: The Faked Hijackings of 9/11* and *Osama bin Laden Had Nothing to Do with 9/11*—to have uncovered documentary evidence that two of the hijacked flights never took off and the other two landed safely in secret.

So, asked the *Guardian*, quite reasonably, what happened to those who we are assured died on all four aircraft on the morning of September 11, 2001? According to Hartwell:

The people who got on the planes were simply pawns. They were, whether wittingly or unwittingly, directed to show up at the airport terminal just to show people who were watching that there were passengers. They were simply agents and they were given new identities. The government wanted to fake plane attacks to scare the public. We saw horrible images on television that were designed to provoke us into supporting wars in Afghanistan and Iraq.

It's also important to remember that we saw images of normal, everyday Washington D.C. residents assuring us that they saw a Boeing 757 hit the Pentagon.

As with the killings of the Kennedy brothers, John and Robert, the death of Martin Luther King Jr. and the events at Pearl Harbor in 1941, it's most unlikely that the conspiracy theories surrounding 9/11 will fade away anytime soon. Many have said they shouldn't fade away, since they tell the truth of what really happened.

Michael Lerner, a political activist, rabbi, and the editor of *Tikkun* magazine, gets the last words. Daniel Treiman quotes those words in "A 9/11 Conspiracy? 'I Would Not Be Surprised," Says Tikkun Editor.

I would not be surprised to learn that some branch of our government conspired either actively to promote or passively to allow the attack on 9/11. For those who watched the reactionary political uses made of this tragedy, it's easy to conjure up a variety of possible conspiratorial motives that would have led the president, the vice president, or some branch of the armed forces or CIA or FBI or other "security" forces to have passively or actively participated in a plot to re-credit militarism and war.

THE ANTHRAX ATTACKS: DELIVERIES OF THE DEADLY KIND

Exactly one week after the terrible, nation-changing events that have since become known as 9/11 occurred, the United States was plunged into another, equally fraught and fear-filled, situation. It became known as *Amerithrax*. This was the official title of the subsequent FBI investigation into the affair, one in which anonymously mailed envelopes, containing deadly anthrax spores, were sent to significant individuals and bodies in the world of politics and the media.

It was an affair of deeply conspiratorial proportions and one that, in a most curious fashion, pre-dates 9/11 itself. It is a seldom discussed fact that on the night of September 11, then-Vice President Dick Cheney—along with members of his staff—was given an antibiotic called Ciprofloaxin. It has the ability to treat and defend against a wide and varied body of bacterial infections and conditions, including anthrax. We are assured that it is purely down to coincidence that the V.P. was given protection from anthrax exposure just seven days before *Amerithrax* began.

On September 18, no fewer than five letters—sent by sources then unknown—arrived at the offices of *NBC News*, *ABC News*, the *National Enquirer*, *CBS News*, and the *New York Post*. Or, rather, it's *presumed* that is the case. While the letters sent to *NBC News* and the *New York Post* certainly were found and recovered for forensic analysis by the FBI, the remaining three were not found—ever. That staff at *ABC News*, *CBS News*, and the *National Enquirer* were quickly infected by anthrax has led to the assumption that letters were the delivery method involved, too. That may well be the case. Certainly, it's a logical, solid assumption, but it is still an unproven assumption. Matters, however, had barely begun.

On October 9, things were taken to an entirely new level, when two Democratic senators—Tom Daschle and Patrick Leahy (of South Dakota and Vermont, respectively)—were also the recipients of envelopes containing potentially deadly anthrax spores. Such was the growing concern, the U.S. government briefly shut down its own mail service. Ultimately, around two dozen people were infected and five died, and all as a result of the series of letters mailed between September 18 and October 9, 2001. As for where, exactly, the letters were mailed from, the most likely location was a box situated just a short distance from Princeton University. The hunt was immediately on for the culprit or culprits.

U.S. senators Tom Daschle (D-SD) and Patrick Leahy (D-VT) were both targeted by an unknown person or persons who sent deadly anthrax spores inside envelopes mailed to their offices.

It's notable that, as history and investigative journalism have shown, great steps were taken to try and prove—and convince the mainstream media and the entire populace—that the source of the anthrax was none other than Iraq: the iron-fisted regime of Saddam Hussein, in other words. The media quickly bought the story. As just one example of several, less than three weeks after the targeting of Daschle and Leahy occurred, *ABC News*'s Brian Ross stated: "Sources tell ABC-NEWS the anthrax in the tainted letter sent to Senate Majority Leader Tom Daschle was laced with bentonite. The potent additive is known to have been used by only one country in producing biochemical weapons—Iraq."

It turned out that while Hussein had used bentonite (a form of clay) in his bio-weapons program, the claim that it was found in the anthrax spores was not just in error; it was downright false. How such an incorrect claim became fact in the minds of many remains a matter of deep debate.

Notably, it wasn't just Saddam Hussein who was being blamed for the attacks. Fingers were also pointed in the direction of Al Qaeda and Osama bin Laden. Indeed, senior figures in the White House did their absolute utmost to have FBI director Robert Mueller confirm this as a fact. That he did not, reportedly led him to be chewed out by presidential high-rankers. The FBI was far from happy. FBI personnel, by now heavily involved in the investigation of the attacks, had already concluded that the kind of anthrax used was highly unlikely to have been concocted by, as one agent memorably worded it, "some guy in a cave."

As the months progressed, and with no meaningful data pointing in the direction of Iraq or Afghanistan, the FBI began looking in what many considered to be an even more controversial direction: the very heart of the United States itself. One of those who the FBI had major concerns about was a man named Steven Jay Hatfil, an undeniable expert in the field of germ warfare. From 1997 to 1999, Hatfil was employed at the United States Army Medical Research Institute of Infectious Diseases (USAMRIID), which is, essentially, the Department of Defense's primary research facility in the field of biological weapons and is housed at Fort Detrick, Maryland.

In 1941 President Franklin D. Roosevelt secretly ordered the establishment of what came to be officially known as the U.S. Biological Warfare Program. As a result of Roosevelt's historic move, in 1943 the newly designated Camp Detrick, Maryland, was assigned to the Army Chemical Warfare Service for the specific development of a center dedicated to biological-warfare issues. Twelve months later, Camp Detrick was established as an installation focused on the research and diligent development of both offensive and defensive biological-warfare techniques and agents.

In 1956, the name of the installation was changed from Camp Detrick to Fort Detrick, although its workload remained very much the same. Then, on April 1, 1972, following the official closure of offensive biological-warfare studies in the United States, the control of Fort Detrick was transferred from the U.S. Army Material Command, to the Office of the Surgeon General, Department of the Army. One year later, Fort Detrick was assigned to the newly created U.S. Army Health Services Command. And in 1995, the HSC was itself reorganized—into the U.S. Army Medical Command.

Ironically, the FBI was put on the trail of Hatfil not by its own agents, but by media sources and activists. Falling into the former category was Nicholas Donabet Kristof. Commencing in 2002, Kristof—a Pulitzer-Prize-winning journalist with the *Washington Post* and the *New York Times*—wrote a number of articles that suggested Hatfil was possibly the guilty party in the anthrax attacks. In the latter category was Dr. Barbara Hatch Rosenberg, who also suggested a home-grown terrorist as the probable source, one acting with the "unwitting assistance of a sophisticated government program."

The biological warfare laboratory at Fort Detrick in Maryland was created by President Franklin D. Roosevelt in 1943.

The FBI was soon digging deeply into the world, career, and life of Steven Jay Hatfil, to the extent that his home was extensively searched (twice, as it transpired: in July and August 2002), and an admittance was made by FBI staff that Hatfil was considered someone of interest in its quest for the truth of the anthrax attacks. It turned out that Hatfil was wholly innocent of *any* and *all* involvement, whatsoever. Justifiably outraged, he sued the U.S. government and was awarded almost $6 million in damages. It was time for the FBI to focus on yet another character in this curious saga.

The next person on the FBI's list—and the person it concluded that most likely behind the attacks, and who also happened to be the *final* person on its list—was Dr. Bruce Edwards Ivins. He was a microbiologist, also employed at the Fort Detrick-based USAMRIID, and someone who had held his position for almost two decades. Although Steven Jay Hatfil had been targeted by the FBI as far back as 2002, it wasn't until 2007 that Ivins found himself in the bureau's sights.

For the FBI's investigative team, there was a valid reason why Ivins was now considered its chief suspect: the strain of anthrax used in the attacks was taken, in 1981, from a cow in Sarita, South Texas. It was then sent to none other than USAMRIID for analysis. Despite all the efforts to put the blame on Saddam Hussein and Osama bin Laden, the trail actually led led to the front door of Fort Detrick.

Rather ironically, Ivins played a significant role in analyzing the very anthrax samples that had caused so much chaos and death in late 2001. And they were analyses that Ivins conducted for the FBI, no less. Such was the respect that Ivins had achieved amongst his colleagues in 2003 he received the Decoration for Exceptional Civilian Service award from the Department of Defense. It is presently the highest award that the DoD can give to a civilian employee.

By 2007 the FBI was watching Ivins closely—*very* closely, it is now known. Ivins's home was raided, it was intimated to him by the FBI that he was now its primary suspect, threats of the death penalty for a guilty verdict were discussed, and his normal state of mind became one dominated by depression, stress, and anxiety. He was subsequently hospitalized in March 2008.

The FBI noted in "Amerithrax or Anthrax Investigation":

> At a group therapy session on July 9, 2008, Dr. Ivins was particularly upset. He revealed to the counselor and psychologist leading the group, and other members of the group, that he was a suspect in the anthrax investigation and that he was angry at the investigators, the government, and the system in general. He said he was not going to face the death penalty, but instead had a plan to "take out" co-workers and other individuals who had wronged him. He noted that it was possible, with a plan, to commit murder and not make a mess. He stated that he had a bullet-proof vest, and a list of co-workers who had wronged him, and said that he was going to obtain a Glock firearm from his son within the next day, because federal agents were watching him and he could not obtain a weapon on his own. He added that he was going to "go out in a blaze of glory."

Three months later, the FBI advised Ivins that he was very likely going to be charged with committing one of the worst terrorist attacks in American history. It did not happen, however. On July 27, 2008, Ivins committed suicide. His weapon of choice was a significant and deadly amount of Tylenol, which took its fatal toll on his kidneys and liver. For the FBI, the case was closed. The FBI may not have got its man, so to speak, but the verdict was that Ivins was almost certainly the guilty party. Not everyone agreed with the FBI, however. In fact, a substantial and highly credible body of people didn't.

One of those who stood up in support of Ivins was Dr. Henry S. Heine, who worked with Ivins at USAMRIID. Heine very vocally rejected the idea that Ivins could have perfected such a strain of anthrax and avoided any and all detection in the process. He also maintained that within USAMRIID, no one was of the opinion that Ivins was the culprit.

A senior researcher at the U.S. Army Medical Research Institute of Infectious Diseases in Fort Derick, Maryland, Dr. Bruce Edwards Ivins was a primary suspect in the anthrax attacks of 2001.

There was far more damning data to follow. Having scrupulously studied the FBI's investigation of Ivins, the National Academy of Sciences, in April 2010, came to a controversial conclusion that placed the bureau in a distinctly uncomfortable light. The NAS said that the FBI had "overstated the strength of genetic analysis linking the mailed anthrax to a supply kept by Bruce E. Ivins."

Not only that, the NAS added that it was "impossible to reach any definitive conclusion about the origins of the anthrax in the letters, based solely on the available scientific evidence."

Democratic senator Patrick Leahy—one of the very people targeted by the attacker—had his say on the matter of Ivins's involvement or lack of involvement. His words were not well received by the FBI or the Bush administration (see Lara Jakes Jordan's article, "Senator: Anthrax Not 1 Man's Work," published by the *Denver Post*).

"If [Ivins] is the one who sent the letter, I do not believe in any way, shape, or manner that he is the only person involved in this attack on Congress and the American people. I do not believe that at all."

Then there was Dr. Meryl Nass, a noted expert on anthrax and its effects. While it was indeed quite possible to link a particular strain of anthrax to one particular facility, said Ness, further linking that same strain to one person—such as Ivins—was nigh-on impossible to achieve.

The FBI shut down its investigation on February 19, 2010, still perceiving Ivins as the brains....

The words of Dr. Henry S. Heine, the National Academy of Sciences, Senator Patrick Leahy, and Dr. Meryl Nass mattered very little at the end of the day. The FBI shut down its investigation on February 19, 2010, still perceiving Ivins as the brains—and the *only* brains—behind the attacks. Perhaps the FBI was right and Ivins was the man, after all. But, what if he wasn't? What if the FBI got it catastrophically wrong?

If not Saddam Huessein, Osama bin Laden, Dr. Bruce Edwards Ivins, or Steven Jay Hatfil, then who, exactly, was the guilty party? A highly disturbing theory—one supported by those of a conspiracy-themed mindset—offered a distinctly alaraming scenario: that the events of September 18 to October 9, 2001, were orchestrated by powerful figures within, or attached to, the White House. The purpose behind their deranged plot: to place the blame for the anthrax attacks on Iraq or Al Qaeda, as a means to engineer further support for the War on Terror and the eventual annexing and control of the entire Middle East.

Some conspiracy theorists point to another factor that is highly suggestive of the Bush administration playing at least some form of role in the anthrax affair, whether officially or off the record. It revolves around Democratic senators Tom Daschle and Patrick Leahy. It's important to note the timeframe when the anthrax attacks occurred: late 2001. This was the very time in which President Bush was pushing to have the Patriot Act passed.

Neither Daschle nor Leahy had much love for the controversial act. Daschle, the Senate majority leader, did not believe Congress should rush the bill through without giving it—and all its many and varied implications—deep thought and study. And, as the Senate majority leader, Daschle held significant sway over the amount of time the act would likely take to pass.

Moving on to Senator Leahy, only five days before *Amerithrax* erupted, he openly accused the Bush presidency of reneging on a certain agreement contained in the bill. Just like Daschle, Leahy had the ability to majorly slow down the passing of the Patriot Act. Such a possibility did not occur, however. On October 24—and after significant media outlets and two senators had been targeted by the anthrax attacker—the Patriot Act was passed, and all without the Senate actually reading it.

Republican congressman Ron Paul noted: "It's my understanding the bill wasn't printed before the vote—at least I couldn't get it. They played all kinds of games, kept the House in session all night, and it was a very complicated bill. Maybe a handful of staffers actually read it, but the bill definitely was not available to members before the vote."

Forty-eight hours later, President Bush signed the necessary paperwork that made the Patriot Act law. That the anthrax attacks directly hastened the passing of the act is not in doubt.

And finally, and of potential support for this same "the government did it" theory, is the fact that the type of anthrax used in the 2001 mailings also goes by the name of "Militarized anthrax." It was the brainchild of William C. Patrick III. He was a man with a prestigious career, one that—in 1986—culminated in him becoming the programs analysis officer at Fort Detrick's USAMRIID.

Patrick, who died in 2010—the same year in which the FBI's file on Ivins was closed—near-singlehandedly created a system by which anthrax spores could be concentrated at a level of one trillion spores per gram. And what was the level of concentration in the spores found in all the anthrax letters of 2001? You guessed it: one trillion spores per gram. To date, the United States is the only nation on the planet that has succeeded in achieving such a specific level of concentration.

THE PATRIOT ACT: ORWELLIAN SURVEILLANCE

The events of September 11, 2001—coupled with the anthrax attacks that occurred shortly afterwards—provoked terror, fear, and feelings of deep paranoia and angst within the American population. They also provoked something else: the rapid passing of what became known as the Patriot Act. It was—and still, to this very day, remains—without doubt one of the most controversial pieces of legislation ever put into place by government officials. Very few people doubted that post-9/11, America needed to create new policies and programs to combat terror-driven attacks on the nation and its people. For many, however, the controversial content of the Patriot Act was seen as being way over the top and something that had the excessive ability to take away the rights, freedoms, and everyday existences of American citizens—and to do so with shocking speed, if it was so deemed necessary.

It was on October 24, 2001—only a month and a half after 9/11 forever changed the United States—that Congress passed the act. It was not an act that everyone in government was happy about, however. The vote was 357 to 66 in the House. Twenty-four hours later, in the Senate, things were very different: 98 to a dissenting 1. Like it or not, the Patriot Act was now a reality and one that was here to stay.

Given that the Patriot Act was designed to help lessen the potential for terror attacks on the United States, and on its overseas interests, why did it so quickly become the target of critics? The answer is as simple as it is disturbing—the act allowed for widespread monitoring of U.S. citizens in ways that had never before been used. It allowed for extreme measures to be taken—all in the name of national security—to keep the nation safe, and, said the critics, could be enforced to try and turn America into a nation of Orwellian proportions. One does not have to be a conspiracy theorist to see how such a sorry state of affairs could, one day, come to pass.

Included in the Patriot Act are clauses that allow government agencies and personnel to (a) access someone's home without its permission or even his or her knowledge; (b) hold individuals, in prison-style facilities, indefinitely; and (c) dig through emails, phone calls, and personal bank records—and all without any need for permission from a court or a judge. Particularly chilling: the Patriot Act gives the government carte blanche access to the reading habits of each, and every, U.S. citizen and resident. It does so by allowing government agencies to record the title of every single book taken out of a library, to note who is borrowing the book, and to store their physical address in relevant databanks. It should be noted that while many—even within government and in the court system—have argued loudly and soundly that all of this is outrageously unconstitutional, it has not made a single bit of difference. Although certain changes were made to the legislation in 2005, the Patriot Act continues to stand as an example of the kind of thing that would have given the likes of the aforementioned George Orwell nightmares.

President George W. Bush signed the Patriot Act on October 26, 2001, supposedly to help secure the nation after the terrorist attacks the month before.

But let's not get ahead of ourselves. Let's see how the act came to be, and how and why its very existence has created such a furor.

Only eight days after the attacks on the World Trade Center and the Pentagon, new legislation was presented to Congress by the Department of Justice. It was a bill entitled the Anti-Terrorism Act. It was also a bill that introduced Congress to the Patriot Act. It's an act whose very title has meaning. "Patriot" stands for "Provide Appropriate Tools Required to Intercept and Obstruct Terrorism." In one sense, that was all well and good, since the act would clearly help in the fight against those who wish to do us harm. It was, however, the negative impact that the tools used in the fight could have on American society that concerned so many. Indeed, the Anti-Terrorism Act swept aside pre-existing acts designed to protect the rights of each and every U.S. citizen, including the Bank Secrecy Act, the Electronic Communications Privacy Act, the Money Laundering Control Act, and the Foreign Intelligence Surveillance Act.

One of the most outrageous aspects of the story of the Patriot Act is how it came to be so easily passed, and why there was only one dissenter, Senator Russell Feingold of Wisconsin. Put simply, and astonishingly, the overwhelming majority who voted to enact the new legislation did not read it prior to agreeing to its creation. Worse still, there are solid indications that it was deliberately made difficult for senators to see the bill before passing it.

Alex Jones wrote in *A Brief Analysis of the Domestic Security Enhancement Act 2003*:

> Congressman Ron Paul (R-Tex) told the *Washington Times* that no member of Congress was allowed to read the first Patriot Act that was passed by the House on October 27, 2001. The first Patriot Act was universally decried by civil libertarians and Constitutional scholars from across the political spectrum.

Jones also noted that William Safire, writing for the *New York Times*, detailed the first Patriot Act's powers by saying that "President Bush was seizing dictatorial control." He continued:

U.S. senator Russ Feingold of Wisconsin was the lone dissenter against the passage of the Patriot Act.

The secretive tactics being used by the White House and Speaker Hastert to keep even the existence of this legislation secret would be more at home in Communist China than in the United States. The fact that Dick Cheney publicly managed the steamroller passage of the first Patriot Act, insuring that no one was allowed to read it and publicly threatening members of Congress that if they didn't vote in favor of it that they would be blamed for the next terrorist attack, is by the White House's own definition terrorism. The move to clandestinely craft and then bully passage of any legislation by the Executive Branch is clearly an impeachable offense.

This scenario was further noted by Michael Moore, in his 2004 documentary, *Fahrenheit 9/11*. Michigan congressman John Conyers makes an incredible statement in the movie, on the matter of those who did or did not read the act before passing it. In Conyers's very own words: "We don't read most of the bills: do you really know what that would entail if we read every bill that we passed?"

Faced with such an extraordinary and mind-numbing statement—that major, congressional figures do not read the bills they may be asked to pass—bills that can have significant bearing on the entire American population—it's hardly surprising that the Patriot Act made an almost effortless transition from concept to reality. The passing of the law did not, however, stop numerous attempts to have the act modified and curtailed. At the same time that critics of the act were trying to reign in its abilities, however, government personnel were trying to make it even more powerful.

The Benjamin Franklin True Patriot Act and the Protecting the Rights of Individuals Act were among the bills that sought to cap the capability of the Patriot Act to intrude into, and limit, the rights of U.S. citizens and residents. It's a sign of the power that those who wanted the act passed yielded, since neither bill had any bearing on the power of the Patriot Act—they both failed. The government responded in 2003 by creating what was known as the Domestic Security Enhancement Act, which, in essence, was an outgrowth of, and an amendment to, the original Patriot Act. When copies were leaked to the media, it caused a sensation, despite assertions from officialdom that it was nothing more than a concept for change, rather than a literal, soon-to-be-in-place plan.

It was specifically thanks to the Center for Public Integrity that the document (draft or otherwise) surfaced. The CPI noted (see "About the Center for Public Integrity"):

The Center for Public Integrity was founded in 1989 by Charles Lewis. We are one of the country's oldest and largest nonpartisan, nonprofit investigative news organizations. Our mission: To serve democracy by revealing abuses of power, corruption, and betrayal of public trust by powerful public and private institutions, using the tools of investigative journalism.

In the first week of February 2003 the CPI acquired the document that contained two key amendments: the government planned to (a) increase its ability to intrude into the lives of American citizens, and (b) make it more and more difficult for courts to deny the instigation of the amendments. It is, almost certainly due to the actions of the CPI—who quickly posted the document to its website—that the "draft" was pulled.

Had it gone through, in its original form, it would have allowed for (a) the collection of DNA from people suspected of having terrorist links— even if wholly unproven, (b) the legal ability to

Film director Michael Moore questioned the wisdom of the U.S. government's actions after the terrorist attacks in his film *Fahrenheit 9/11*.

undertake so-called search-and-surveillance overseas, and without any kind of court-order needed, and (c) extensions and modifications to the death penalty.

Without doubt the creepiest part of the Patriot Act was alluded to earlier— namely, the government's legal and wide-reaching ability to monitor the reading habits of every single American citizen. This relates to what are termed National Security Letters, or NSLs. They are, essentially, subpoenas that are used "to protect against international terrorism or clandestine intelligence activities."

Such NSLs can permit agencies to demand access to—and with potential imprisonment for those who do not comply—bank account data, email history and address-books, telephone numbers (both called and received), and books bought, borrowed, and read. All of this falls under Section 215 of the Patriot Act. In a decidedly hazy fashion—that conveniently allows for widespread interpretation on the part of those who employ it—the act notes that certain "tangible things" may be accessed, such as "books, records, papers, documents, and other items."

Four years after the Patriot Act was passed, Library Connection—a Connecticut-based body—joined forces with the ACLU to highlight and curtail the government's ability to monitor the average reading matter of the average American:

> Librarians need to understand their country's legal balance between the
> protection of freedom of expression and the protection of national secu-
> rity. Many librarians believe that the interests of national security, im-

portant as they are, have become an excuse for chilling the freedom to read.

The American Civil Liberties Union (ACLU) elaborated on this in "Surveillance Under the USA PATRIOT Act":

> One of the most significant provisions of the Patriot Act makes it far easier for the authorities to gain access to records of citizens' activities being held by a third party. At a time when computerization is leading to the creation of more and more such records, Section 215 of the Patriot Act allows the FBI to force anyone at all—including doctors, libraries, bookstores, universities, and Internet service providers—to turn over records on their clients or customers.

The ACLU also revealed that the judicial oversight of the new powers that the Patriot Act allows for is "essentially non-existent." It continued:

> The government must only certify to a judge—with no need for evidence or proof—that such a search meets the statute's broad criteria, and the judge does not even have the authority to reject the application.

Surveillance orders, noted the ACLU, "can be based in part on a person's First Amendment activities, such as the books they read, the Web sites they visit, or a letter to the editor they have written."

Slate.com aired its concerns on the matter of the Patriot Act, too: "Post-Patriot Act, third-party holders of your financial, library, travel, video rental, phone, medical, church, synagogue, and mosque records can be searched without your knowledge or consent, providing the government said it's trying to protect against terrorism."

As for the situation in more recent years, in May 2011 Spencer Ackerman said in "There's a Secret Patriot Act, Senator Says," which was written for *Wired*:

> You think you understand how the Patriot Act allows the government to spy on its citizens. Sen. Ron Wyden said it's worse than you know. Congress is set to reauthorize three controversial provisions of the surveillance law as early as Thursday. Wyden (D-Oregon) said that powers they grant the government on their face, the government applies a far broader legal interpretation—an interpretation that the government has conveniently classified, so it cannot be publicly assessed or challenged. But one prominent Patriot-watcher asserts that the secret interpretation empowers the government to deploy "dragnets" for massive amounts of information on private citizens; the government portrays its data-collection efforts much differently.

In Senator Wyden's own words, quoted by *Wired*: "We're getting to a gap between what the public thinks the law said and what the American government secretly thinks the law said. When you've got that kind of a gap, you're going to have a problem on your hands."

[National Security Letters are] subpoenas that are used "to protect against international terrorism or clandestine intelligence activities."

Slate.com has also demonstrated that the change in presidency—from George W. Bush to Barack Obama—made very little difference to the power of the Patriot Act. Emma Roller, in "This Is What Section 215 of the Patriot Act Does," noted:

> Sen. Obama voted to reauthorize the Patriot Act in 2005, a decision he defended on the campaign trail in 2008 with the caveat that some provisions contained in Section 215, like allowing the government to go through citizens' library records, "went way overboard." But in 2011 President Obama signed a bill to extend the Patriot Act's sunset clause to June 1, 2015—with Section 215 intact in its 2005 form.

Today, the Patriot Act continues to stand just as it has since 2001. Coming soon to a library near you.

//Sen. Obama voted to reauthorize the Patriot Act in 2005, a decision he defended on the campaign trail in 2008...."

WEAPONS OF MASS DESTRUCTION: MISSING IN ACTION

There is absolutely no doubt, whatsoever, that one of the primary reasons why the war in Iraq went ahead when it did, and on the scale it did, is because of the claims that Saddam Hussein possessed huge amounts of what became known famously as weapons of mass destruction, or WMDs. We were told by our leaders that it was practically imperative that the WMDs be found, lest the entire western world might find itself in the midst of a near-Armageddon-like disaster. The following quotes on the WMD issue come from CounterPunch Wire's "Weapons of Mass Destruction: Who Said What When."

On August 26, 2002, Vice President Dick Cheney said: "Simply stated, there is no doubt that Saddam Hussein now has weapons of mass destruction."

One month later, Senator Joseph Lieberman told the American people: "Every day Saddam remains in power with chemical weapons, biological weapons, and the development of nuclear weapons is a day of danger for the United States."

In February 2003, Colin Powell stated: "We know that Saddam Hussein was determined to keep his weapons of mass destruction, and determined to make more."

Then, on March 18, 2003, President George W. Bush warned America: "Intelligence gathered by this and other governments leaves no doubt that the Iraq regime continues to possess and conceal some of the most lethal weapons ever devised."

Four days later, General Tommy Franks announced:

There is no doubt that the regime of Saddam Hussein possesses weapons of mass destruction. As this operation continues, those weapons will be identified, found, along with the people who have produced them and who guard them.

Meanwhile, on the other side of the pond, and in the same time frame, the British prime minister, Tony Blair, made some very vocal statements, ones that left very little room for misinterpretation. Blair told the British public (see "In Quotes: Blair and Iraq Weapons"):

Saddam Hussein's regime is despicable, he is developing weapons of mass destruction, and we cannot leave him doing so unchecked. He is a threat to his own people and to the region and, if allowed to develop these weapons, a threat to us also. [British Intelligence] concludes that Iraq has chemical and biological weapons that Saddam has continued to produce them, that he has existing and active military plans for the use of chemical and biological weapons, which could be activated within 45 minutes, including against his own Shia population; and that he is actively trying to acquire nuclear weapons capability.

There are literally thousands of sites. As I was told in Iraq, information is coming in the entire time, but it is only now that the Iraq survey group has been put together that a dedicated team of people, which includes former UN inspectors, scientists and experts, will be able to go in and do the job properly. As I have said throughout, I have no doubt that they will find the clearest possible evidence of Saddam's weapons of mass destruction.

No one doubts that Saddam Hussein was a murderous dictator, one that the world is much better off without. His ousting and death were very rightly welcomed by millions. But that does not take away an important question: Was Hussein really the major threat to the West he was said to be? Did the WMDs really exist? Were the claims surrounding Hussein's capabilities exaggerated to ensure that both the United States and the United Kingdom would receive the support of their respective populations, media, and politicians?

Saddam Hussein was a ruthless killer, one who had no qualms about using chemical weapons on the battlefield. They were used by the Iraqi regime in the 1980s (when Iran was in Hussein's sights) and during the first Gulf War of 1990, against Kuwaiti forces. There is good evidence, too, that Hussein was doing his utmost to develop and build atomic weapons.

Unlike the situation in the 2000s, when the first Gulf War of 1990 ended and when United Nations inspectors toured Iraq, they actually found weapons of mass destruction—and in mass numbers, too. They were carefully contained and then completely obliterated. Nevertheless, the reluctance of the Iraqi regime to assist in the quest to find all the WMDs in this period led to nagging and worrying suspicions on the part of the U.N. that, even though significant amounts of deadly, chemical weapons were found and destroyed, a certain amount might still have remained hidden by Hussein's military.

The only saving grace in all of this was that the U.N. concluded that as long as its personnel carefully, and diligently, kept watch on Iraq, it was unlikely—to the point of being near impossible—that Hussein would be able to resurrect his WMD programs without the world's major intelligence services noticing. That still left the

U.S. secretary of state Colin Powell, along with other top U.S. officials, asserted to the world in a bid to justify going to war that Iraq defintely possessed weapons of mass destruction.

ones that might be hidden away to worry about, however. Those specific worries revolved around the likes of anthrax, sarin, and botulinim.

Time and again checks were made, and time and again, nothing was found that was truly incriminating, as the 1990s became the 2000s. Either the WMDs were *really* well hidden, or the U.N. had succeeded in destroying all of Iraq's WMDs that survived the first Gulf War. That situation radically changed in 2002—and even more so in 2003—when the world was told that new intelligence data had confirmed that Hussein had been secretly creating more and more WMDs behind the world's back. And, unless something was done about it—and done quickly—each and every one of us would be in grave, mortal danger. Elements of the United Nations expressed deep puzzlement, since they were the ones with their boots on the ground, yet they were not receiving any such intelligence.

There was a sharp contrast between what happened after the first Gulf War of 1990 and the events that erupted in 2002–2003. In the wake of the former, the WMDs were found and destroyed. In the latter, the alleged existence of the weapons of mass destruction was all based on hazy, and hardly ever expanded on, references to "intelligence data" and "expert sources."

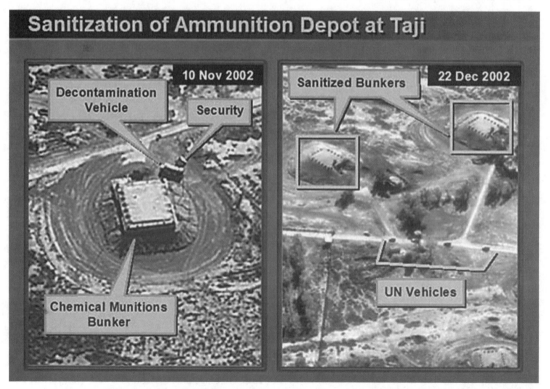

This image from U.S. spy satellites was used by the government to argue before the U.N. Security Council that Iraq had secret facilities developing chemical and other weapons of mass destruction.

Whether the new weapons of mass destruction actually existed or not, a case was aggressively made that an invasion of Iraq was needed. And it was needed right now. Unless he wished to see his country attacked and overrun, Hussein was to provide "immediate, unconditional and active cooperation" to the United Nations' weapons inspectors.

Colin Powell, in February 2003, added to the claims that we were all in major danger. He did so at a meeting of the United Nations Security Council. Powell came straight to the point (see "Transcript of Powell's U.N. presentation"):

> One of the most worrisome things that emerges from the thick intelligence file we have on Iraq's biological weapons is the existence of mobile production facilities used to make biological agents. Let me take you inside that intelligence file and share with you what we know from eyewitness accounts. We have firsthand descriptions of biological weapons factories on wheels and on rails. The trucks and train cars are easily moved and are designed to evade detection by inspectors.
>
> In a matter of months, they can produce a quantity of biological poison equal to the entire amount that Iraq claimed to have produced in the years prior to the Gulf War. Although Iraq's mobile production program began in the mid-1990s, U.N. inspectors at the time only had vague hints of such programs. Confirmation came later in the year 2000. The source was an eyewitness, an Iraqi chemical engineer who supervised one of these facilities. He actually was present during biological agent production runs. He was also at the site when an accident occurred in 1998. Twelve technicians died from exposure to biological agents.

On the other hand, there are the words of a certain Hans Blix.

From 2000 to 2003, Hans Blix was the head of the United Nations Monitoring, Verification and Inspection Commission that oversaw the search for Saddam Hussein's elusive WMDs. His view on the situation was not welcomed by the governments of the United States and the United Kingdom. Blix certainly had no love, whatsoever, for Hussein, but, at the start of 2003, he did admit that the Iraqis were cooperating—albeit slowly—in the operation to figure out whether the WMDs really existed and, if so, where they were housed. The Bush administration was outraged and demanded the United Nations allow the use of military action against Iraq. It was denied.

U.N. weapons inspector William Scott Ritter said in his book with William Rivers Pitt, *War on Iraq*:

> There's no doubt Iraq hasn't fully complied with its disarmament obligations as set forth by the Security Council in its resolution. But on the other hand, since 1998 Iraq has been fundamentally disarmed: 90–95% of Iraq's weapons of mass destruction capacity has been verifiably eliminated. We have to remember that this missing 5–10% doesn't necessarily constitute a threat. It constitutes bits and pieces of a weapons program which in its totality doesn't amount to much, but which is still prohibited. We can't give Iraq a clean bill of health; therefore we can't close the book on

their weapons of mass destruction. But simultaneously, we can't reasonably talk about Iraqi non-compliance as representing a de-facto retention of a prohibited capacity worthy of war.

Ritter made an important observation that was overlooked, or not even realized, by those who demanded an immediate invasion of Iraq: chemical weapons, such as sarin, anthrax, and botulinim only retain their deadly potency for between three and five years. After that, they degrade to the point where they are, essentially, harmless. So, even if Hussein did possess chemical weaponry that was a hangover from the Gulf War of 1990, it would have been useless by 2002/2003. And, that the U.N. was pretty sure Iraq had not created any substantial new amounts of such weaponry in subsequent years was a good indicator that the grave situation was massively exaggerated.

None of this was of any concern to President Bush, who took the proverbial bull by the proverbial horns: the war on Iraq began in earnest in March 2003. On the nineteenth of the month, Bush told the American people:

> My fellow citizens. At this hour, American and coalition forces are in the early stages of military operations to disarm Iraq, to free its people and to defend the world from grave danger.
>
> On my orders, coalition forces have begun striking selected targets of military importance to undermine Saddam Hussein's ability to wage war. These are opening stages of what will be a broad and concerted campaign.
>
> More than 35 countries are giving crucial support from the use of naval and air bases to help with intelligence and logistics to deployment of combat units.
>
> Every nation in this coalition has chosen to bear the duty and share the honor of serving in our common defense.
>
> To all the men and women of the United States armed forces now in the Middle East, the peace of a troubled world and the hopes of an oppressed people now depend on you. That trust is well placed.
>
> The enemies you confront will come to know your skill and bravery. The people you liberate will witness the honorable and decent spirit of the American military.
>
> Now that conflict has come, the only way to limit its duration is to apply decisive force and I assure you this will not be a campaign of half measures and we will accept no outcome but victory.
>
> My fellow citizens, the dangers to our country and the world will be overcome. We will pass through this time of peril and carry on the work of peace. We will defend our freedom. We will bring freedom to others and we will prevail.
>
> May God bless our country and all who defend her.

There is no doubt that the one issue that unified the entirety of the coalition forces was the threat posed by the theo-

// [S]ince 1998 Iraq has been fundamentally disarmed: 90–95% of Iraq's weapons of mass destruction capacity has been verifiably eliminated."

retical weapons of mass destruction. This was made very clear by Paul Wolfowitz, who was deputy secretary of defense when the Iraq war began. His words follow (see "Wolfowitz Comments Revive Doubts over Iraq's WMD"):

> The truth is that for reasons that have a lot to do with the U.S. government bureaucracy, we settled on the one issue that everyone could agree on, which was weapons of mass destruction as the core reason, but, there have always been three fundamental concerns. One is weapons of mass destruction, the second is support for terrorism, the third is the criminal treatment of the Iraqi people. Actually I guess you could say there's a fourth overriding one which is the connection between the first two.

This was in sharp contrast to the words of a man named David Kay, which are reproduced in a BBC article of June 2004, "US Expert Slams WMD 'Delusions.'" The former head of the Iraq Survey Group, he told the BBC that: "Anyone out there holding—as I gather Prime Minister Blair has recently said—the prospect that, in fact, the Iraq Survey Group is going to unmask actual weapons of mass destruction, is really delusional."

A major, damning dent in the claim that the Iraqis were hiding WMDs surfaced in late May 2003, when the Iraq war was well underway. On the twenty-seventh of the month, analysts from the Defense Intelligence Agency revealed to the White House that a pair of trailers that had been captured by Kurdish military personnel, and which the then secretary of state, Colin Powell, in the buildup to war, was saying were connected to Iraq's plans to deploy deadly chemical weaponry, were actually nothing of the sort.

//The truth is that for reasons that have a lot to do with the U.S. government bureaucracy, we settled on the one issue that everyone could agree on...."

In words that came back to haunt him, Powell said: "We have firsthand descriptions of biological weapons factories on wheels and on rails. We know what the fermenters look like. We know what the tanks, pumps, compressors and other parts look like."

Despite the fact that the DIA made it very clear that the trailers had zero "connection to anything biological," the White House refused to acknowledge that fact, and the DIA continued to loudly assert that the trailers were being used in "mobile biological weapons production."

In 2006 the *Washington Post* finally got to the heart of at least part of the story (see "Lacking Biolabs, Trailer Carried Case for War"):

> A spokesman for the DIA asserted that the team's findings were neither ignored nor suppressed, but were incorporated in the work of the Iraqi Survey Group, which led the official search for Iraqi weapons of mass destruction. The survey group's final report in September 2004—15 months after the technical report was written—said the trailers were "impractical" for biological weapons production and were "almost certainly intended" for manufacturing hydrogen for weather balloons.

U.S. general Tommy Franks, who had commanded forces in Iraq, stated that he was surprised that the Iraqis had never used WMDs against his troops.

As the war progressed, it became increasingly obvious that Saddam Hussein did not have an arsenal of weapons of mass destruction that he could fall back on to save both himself and his government. Even General Tommy Franks, who led the invasion of Iraq, was moved to state: "No one in this country probably was more surprised than I when weapons of mass destruction were not used against our troops as they moved toward Baghdad."

Ultimately, no WMDs were ever found. All of the blunders, whether in the United States or the United Kingdom, were down to faulty intelligence data. The leaders of both nations were at pains to stress that the stories of the WMDs had not been created, out of whole cloth, to deceive the public into thinking that war—and war *right now*—was the only option.

The one saving grace of the Iraq war was that it resulted in the ousting and death of Saddam Hussein. That the war yielded absolutely no evidence of weapons of mass destruction, however, left a bad taste in the mouths of both the American and British public and suspicions that the populace and the media had been lied to, all as a part of a concerted effort to invade, and seize control of, Iraq for reasons more likely connected to oil than western safety.

President George W. Bush admitted that "the intelligence" suggesting the WMDs were real "was wrong," but added that "Saddam Hussein had invaded a country, he had used weapons of mass destruction, he had the capability of making weapons of mass destruction, he was firing at our pilots. He was a state sponsor of terror. Removing Saddam Hussein was the right thing for world peace and the security of our country."

In February 2004—in the face of the criticism that the Iraq war was all for nothing, and that Hussein could have been gotten rid of without a huge war, one that was costly in both lives and money—President Bush established a body, the Iraq Intelligence Commission, to address the huge errors, or as some saw it, deliberate mistakes, on the matter of Hussein's WMDs. Its conclusions mirrored those of what just about everyone else was saying.

The U.K.'s prime minister, Tony Blair, said (see "In Quotes: Blair and Iraq Weapons"):

> What you can say is that we received that intelligence about Saddam's programs and about his weapons that we acted on that, it's the case throughout the whole of the conflict.

I remember having conversations with the chief of defense staff and other people were saying well, we think we might have potential WMD find here or there. Now these things didn't actually come to anything in the end, but I don't know is the answer.

We expected, I expected to find actual usable, chemical or biological weapons after we entered Iraq.

But I have to accept, as the months have passed, it seems increasingly clear that at the time of invasion, Saddam did not have stockpiles of chemical or biological weapons ready to deploy.

The evidence about Saddam having actual biological and chemical weapons, as opposed to the capability to develop them, has turned out to be wrong. I acknowledge that and accept it. I simply point out, such evidence was agreed by the whole international community, not least because Saddam had used such weapons against his own people and neighboring countries.

And the problem is, I can apologize for the information that turned out to be wrong, but I can't, sincerely at least, apologize for removing Saddam.

The world is a better place with Saddam in prison not in power.

I can apologize for the information being wrong but I can never apologize, sincerely at least, for removing Saddam.

Blair concluded that the world was better off with Hussein in prison.

It's true; but did we need to be deceived into thinking that war was the only option, lest we would all find ourselves dying from the effects of sarin and anthrax that wasn't there in the first place?

MICROBIOLOGY DEATHS: SCIENTISTS DROP LIKE FLIES

From the final months of 2001 to mid-2005, many people employed in the elite field of microbiology—which is defined as the study of organisms that are too small to be seen with the naked eye, such as bacteria and viruses—died under circumstances that some within the media and government came to view as highly suspicious and deeply disturbing in nature. Many of the deaths appeared, at first glance at least, to have down-to-earth explanations. But, even those who were skeptical of the notion that the deaths were suspicious in nature could not deny one overriding and important factor: many of those dead microbiologists had secret links to worldwide intelligence services, including the United States' CIA, Britain's MI5 and MI6, and Israel's Mossad.

Inevitably, this mysterious collection of deaths, in such a tightly knit area of cutting-edge research, has led to a proliferation of theories in an attempt to resolve the matter. Some believe that a cell of deep-cover terrorists, from the Middle East, wiped out the leading names within the field of microbiology as part of a plot to prevent Western nations from developing the ultimate bio-weapon. A darker theory suggests that this same weapon has *already* been developed, and, with their work complete, the microbiologists were systematically killed, one by one, by Western intelligence in an effort to prevent them from being kidnapped by terrorists who may then have forced them to work for the other side.

The controversy largely began on November 12, 2001, when Dr. Benito Que, a cell biologist working on infectious diseases, including HIV, was found dead outside of his laboratory at the Miami Medical School, Florida. The *Miami Herald* stated that his death occurred as he headed for his car, a white Ford Explorer, parked on Northwest Tenth Avenue. Police said that he was possibly the victim of a mugger.

According to later developments uncovered by the media, however, the new word on the street was that Dr. Que had been attacked by four men equipped with baseball bats. This was later recanted, however, and it was stated by officialdom that Que had died of nothing stranger than cardiac arrest. And with that final statement in the public domain, police refused to comment any further on Que's death, rather intriguingly.

Eleven days later, Dr. Vladimir Pasechnik, a former microbiologist for Bioreparat, a bio-weapons production facility that existed in Russia prior to the collapse of the Soviet Union, was found dead near his home in the county of Wiltshire, England. His defection to Britain in 1989 revealed to the West for the very first time the incredible scale of the Soviet Union's clandestine biological warfare program.

And his revelations about the scale of the Soviet Union's production of biological agents, including anthrax, bubonic plague, tularemia, and smallpox, provided an inside account of one of the best kept secrets of the Cold War. According to British Intelligence, Pasechnik passed away from effects of a massive stroke and nothing more.

Then, on November 24, 2001, the FBI announced that it was monitoring an investigation into the disappearance of a Harvard biologist because of "his research into potentially lethal viruses," including Ebola. Dr. Don C. Wiley, aged fifty-seven, had last been seen in Memphis, Tennessee, where he attended the annual meeting of the Scientific Advisory Board of the St. Jude Children's Research Hospital. His rented car was found at 4:00 A.M. on November 16 on a bridge over the Mississippi River, with a full fuel tank, and the key still in the ignition.

Wiley had left the Peabody Hotel just four hours previously. He was due to meet his wife and two children later that same day in Cambridge, Massachusetts. FBI agents took an interest in Wiley's disappearance because of his expertise and as a direct result of "our state of affairs post-September 11," said Memphis-based FBI agent William Woerne.

Wiley was a Harvard biochemistry and biophysics professor and was considered a national expert on Ebola, HIV, herpes, and influenza. In 1999, Wiley and another Harvard professor, Dr. Jack Strominger, won the Japan Prize for their discoveries of how the immune system protects humans from infection.

Notably, on the same day that authorities were diligently searching for Wiley, three more microbiologists were killed when a Swissair flight from Berlin to Zurich crashed during its landing approach. Altogether, twenty-two people died and nine survived. Among the dead were Dr. Yaakov Matzner (fifty-four years old), Dean of the Hebrew University School of Medicine; Amiramp Eldor (fifty-nine), who ran the Hematology Department at Ichilov Hospital in Tel Aviv and a man who was a world-recognized expert in blood clotting; and Avishai Berkman (fifty), director of the Tel Aviv Public Health Department. And the bodies continued to pile up.

On December 12, 2001, it was revealed in the media that a leading researcher on DNA sequencing analysis had been found dead in the secluded northern Virginian farmhouse where he lived alone. The body of Robert M. Schwartz was discovered by neighbors, two days earlier, after co-workers at his place of employment reported he had seemingly skipped work and had missed a meeting.

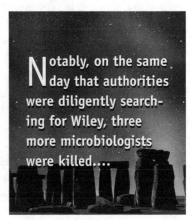

Notably, on the same day that authorities were diligently searching for Wiley, three more microbiologists were killed....

"We're all stunned," said Anne Armstrong, president of the Virginia Center for Innovative Technology, a nonprofit

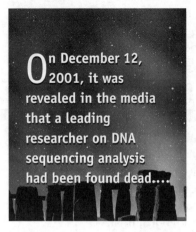

On December 12, 2001, it was revealed in the media that a leading researcher on DNA sequencing analysis had been found dead....

agency where Schwartz worked. "We don't know anything. What we're assuming is maybe he walked in on something." Schwartz was a founding member of the Virginia Biotechnology Association, worked at the center for almost fifteen years, and served as the executive director of research and development and university relations. He also worked on the first national online database of DNA sequence information.

On the other side of the world, forty-eight hours later, equally disturbing events were occurring. Set Van Nguyen was a microbiologist at the Commonwealth Scientific and Industrial Research Organization's Animal Diseases Establishment at Geelong, Australia. He had been employed there for fifteen years when his end came far too suspiciously soon.

Police in Victoria, Australia, stated (and are quoted in Ian Gurney's "The Mystery of the Dead Scientists: Coincidence or Conspiracy?"):

> Set Van Nguyen, 44, appeared to have died after entering an airlock into a storage laboratory filled with nitrogen. His body was found when his wife became worried after he failed to return from work. He was killed after entering a low temperature storage area where biological samples were kept. He did not know the room was full of deadly gas which had leaked from a liquid nitrogen cooling system. Unable to breathe, Mr. Nguyen collapsed and died.

Also on the same day, much publicity was given to a story that appeared in the London *Times* newspaper, which discussed how Israel was working on a biological weapon designed to kill specific types of people. The *Times* reported: "The intention is to use the ability of viruses and certain bacteria to alter the DNA inside their host's living cells. The scientists are trying to engineer deadly microorganisms that attack only those bearing the distinctive genes." In other words, it was a highly controversial plan to provoke death by racial profiling.

On December 15, 2001, a formal announcement was made that three people had been charged with murder in the case of the scientist Robert M. Schwartz. Police revealed that he had been killed with a two-foot sword in a "planned assassination" and that an "X" had been carved into his back. "I have no idea what this means," said the prosecutor, Robert Anderson. Police in Maryland arrested three young suspects: eighteen-year-old Kyle Hulbert, twenty-one-year-old Michael Pfohl, and nineteen-year-old Katherine Inglis.

The next day, an intriguing revelation surfaced to the effect that Inglis, in January 2001, had reported to the Naval Recruit Training Command Center in Great Lakes, Illinois. Navy officials stated that she had been trained to work "in aviation" but had suddenly, and inexplicably, left on May 28. One of the other suspects, Michael Pfohl, had, very shortly before Schwartz's death, expressed an interest in joining nothing less than the elite, deadly, and covert world of Special Forces.

Four days on, police announced they had located the remains of missing Harvard University scientist Don C. Wiley. A body carrying identification was found on December 18 near a hydroelectric plant in the Mississippi River, and about 300 miles from where Wiley was last seen. Police Lt. Joe Scott said that a positive identification was planned when the body was returned to Memphis for an autopsy.

A number of scientific organizations, including St. Jude's Children's Research Hospital where Wiley worked, put up rewards totaling $26,000 for information leading to the arrest and charge of anyone responsible for Wiley's disappearance. "As soon as the body gets in our morgue, the medical examiner will begin the autopsy to help answer a lot of questions," said Memphis Police director Walter Crews.

Interestingly, Reuters news service stated that Wiley's death had "triggered alarm bells," due to the "current bio-warfare fears" and the nature of his work, but did not elaborate as to who, exactly, the alarm bells had been triggered with. The FBI stated that it was leaving the investigation of Wiley's death in the hands of the police. Friends and family of Wiley, meanwhile, stated vocally and publicly that he would not commit suicide under any circumstances.

Wiley's death had "triggered alarm bells," due to the "current bio-warfare fears" and the nature of his work....

And still controversial deaths continued to occur, this time in Russia. On January 28, 2002, a microbiologist, and a member of the Russian Academy of Science, Alexi Brushlinski, died as the result of what was blamed on a "bandit attack" in Moscow. Then, two weeks later, Victor Korshunov (fifty-six) also a noted microbiologist, was hit over the head and killed at the entrance of his home in Moscow, Russia. He just happened to be the head of the microbiology sub-faculty at the Russian State Medical University.

Four days after that revelation, a similar story surfaced out of England. Detectives were busily trying to unravel the circumstances that led to the death of a leading university research scientist, Ian Langford, a senior Fellow at the University of East Anglia's Center for Social and Economic Research. His work began in 1993 after he gained his Ph.D. in childhood leukemia and infection following a first-class honors degree in environmental sciences. He had worked most recently as a senior researcher assessing risk to the environment.

Professor Kerry Turner, director of the center, said that all of Langford's colleagues were devastated and praised Langford for his groundbreaking work in the field of environmental risks to human health.

On March 24, 2002, Denver car dealer Kent Rickenbaugh, his wife, Caroline, and their son Bart were killed in a plane crash near Centennial Airport. The pilot, Dr. Steven Mostow, was also killed. It transpired that Mostow was one of the United States' leading infectious disease experts and the associate dean at the University of Colorado's Health Sciences Center. Mostow was a crusader for better

[David Wynn-Williams] was studying how microbes of a potentially hostile nature adapt to living in extreme environments.

health, an early advocate for widespread flu vaccinations, and more recently had been deep in talks with U.S. Intelligence officials on the threat of bioterrorism.

And on the same day that Dr. Mostow was killed, another life ended—in England again—when microbiologist David Wynn-Williams was hit by a car while jogging near his home in Cambridge. He was an astrobiologist with the Antarctic Astrobiology Project and the NASA Ames Research Center and was studying how microbes of a potentially hostile nature adapt to living in extreme environments.

On July 18, 2003, it was reported in the British press that David Kelly, a British biological weapons expert, had slashed his own wrists while walking in woods near his home. Kelly was the British Ministry of Defense's chief scientific officer, the senior adviser to the Proliferation and Arms Control Secretariat and to the Foreign Office's Non-Proliferation Department. The senior adviser on biological weapons to the UN biological weapons inspections teams (Unscom) from 1994 to 1999, Kelly was also, in the opinion of his peers, pre-eminent in his field, not only in the U.K., but in the world, too. Almost four months later to the day, forty-five-year-old scientist Robert Leslie Burghoff was killed by a hit-and-run driver who jumped the sidewalk and ploughed into him in the 1600 block of South Braeswood, Texas. At the time, he was studying outbreaks of viruses on board cruise ships and their potential links to terrorist activity.

Moving into 2004, during the first week of May a Russian scientist at a former Soviet biological weapons laboratory in Siberia died after an alleged accident with a needle laced with Ebola. Officials said the incident raised concerns about safety and secrecy at the State Research Center of Virology and Biotechnology, known as Vector, which in Soviet times specialized in turning deadly viruses into biological weapons.

Two months later, on July 3, 2004, Dr. Paul Norman of Salisbury, Wiltshire, England, was killed when the single-engine Cessna 206 aircraft he was piloting crashed in the county of Devon. He was married with a fourteen-year-old son and a twenty-year-old daughter. But that's not all—Norman was the chief scientist for chemical and biological defense at the British Ministry of Defense's laboratory at Porton Down, Wiltshire. The crash site was sealed off, and examined by officials from the Air Accidents Investigation Branch, and the wreckage of the aircraft was moved from the site to the AAIB base at Farnborough, England. The tragedy was firmly ruled accidental and nothing else.

In August 2004, six weeks after the death of Dr. Paul Norman, Professor John Clark, head of the science laboratory that created Dolly the "cloned" sheep, was found hanging in his holiday home. Clark led the Roslin Institute in Midlothian, Scotland, one of the world's leading animal biotechnology research centers, and played a crucial role in creating the transgenic sheep that earned the institute worldwide fame. Professor Clark also founded three spin-off firms from Roslin: PPL Therapeutics; Rosgen; and Roslin BioMed.

As a new year dawned, still the deaths continued to increase. On January 7, 2005, Korean Jeong H. Im, a retired research assistant professor at the University of Missouri and primarily a protein chemist, died of multiple stab wounds to the chest before firefighters found his body in the trunk of a burning car on the third level of the Maryland Avenue Garage. A person of interest, described as a male around six feet tall and wearing some type of mask, was seen acting in a suspicious fashion in the garage. He was never caught.

Then, in May 2005, Australian scientist David Banks, a fifty-five-year old who was the principal scientist with Biosecurity Australia, a company described as being a "quarantine authority," was killed in an aircraft crash at Queensland. At the time, he was undertaking a "survey for the Northern Australia quarantine strategy." It was all just a tragic accident, maintained officialdom, to anyone who cared to poke their nose in.

Were the deaths of so many microbiologists in such a clearly delineated period simply a bizarre and collective coincidence? Or was something stranger afoot? In today's climate of near-surreal uncertainty, it should, of course, be recognized that any suspicious deaths in the fields of microbiology, bacteriological warfare, and lethal viruses—and specifically where many of the victims had links to the covert intelligence services of a number of countries—might be an indication that powerful figures were at work in at least *some* of the deaths, if not indeed all of them. Microbiology is a dangerous game during the best of times. Between 2001 and 2005, however, it became downright deadly.

7/7 BOMBINGS: TERROR IN LONDON

On the morning of July 7, 2005, the United Kingdom's capital city of London was plunged into a state of overwhelming chaos the likes of which had not been seen since the 1970s and 1980s, when the Irish Republican Army (IRA) regularly launched terrorist attacks on British soil. It was a morning that began just like any other in the bustling city, but which ended with fifty-six people dead, including four individuals believed to have been the crazed and deluded masterminds behind the attack. On top of that, in excess of 700 people received injuries that ranged from minor to severe. It was an event that quickly became known as 7/7. It's also an event that has since become steeped in conspiracy theories.

The perpetrators chose their locations and times coldly, calculatingly, and carefully: the busy streets and packed London Underground rail system at the height of the early morning rush hour. Not only that, the date of the attacks was just one day after the U.K. had secured the contract to host the 2012 Olympic Games. Clearly, creating terror and intimidation—at a time that should have been one of overriding celebration and national pride—was the name of the deadly game.

July 7 was a day very much like any other—that is, until 8:50 A.M. In less than one minute three huge explosions rocked the London Underground. Unsurprisingly, confusion reigned. Initial reports suggested the explosions had been caused by power surges on the tracks. Other rumors flew around to the effect that two trains had catastrophically collided. It quickly became clear, however, that neither scenario was correct. London was under attack.

The first event involved a train that left the Kings Cross St. Pancras tube station, heading east. Barely three hundred feet from Liverpool Street station, there was an ear-splitting explosion. It was followed only seconds later by a second blast, this one on a train that was making its way to London Paddington Station, after having left the station at Edgware Road. In near-rapid-fire fashion, a third explosion occurred: on the Piccadilly Line, shortly after the train in question had exited Kings Cross-St. Pancras. All three trains were packed with commuters whose lives were either wiped out or forever changed and scarred—both physically and psychologically.

Less than sixty minutes later, yet another bomb detonated. It did not, however, occur on a speeding train on the Underground. Rather, the target was a Lon-

Ambulances flood Russell Square in London, England, soon after the bombing of July 7, 2005.

don double-decker bus. As it reached Tavistock Square, the bus was violently torn apart, as if by some giant can-opener. Four events across the course of one hour, dozens dead, the emergency services doing their utmost to control the situation, the government in a state of emergency, and a condition of quickly growing panic all across London were the immediate effects of that terrible, fateful day.

The country's media—led by the BBC, ITV and Sky News—ran continuous coverage, updating the British people on every aspect of what, it soon became clear, was a major disaster of deadly proportions. The country was outraged, the government pledged that the guilty parties would pay, and the security services launched an immediate investigation. In the days that followed, things became clearer. Or did they?

The British government did not look to the Middle East for the answers to who was responsible for the nightmarish events of July 7, 2005. Certainly, in the aftermath of 9/11, Britain's MI5 and MI6—the U.K.'s equivalents of the FBI and the CIA—began to fear and suspect that any similar attack on mainland Britain would likely be undertaken by homegrown terrorists, rather than those operating out of a cave in the mountains of Afghanistan. They appear to have been correct.

//We are at war and I am a soldier," said Khan, as he targeted his rage against the West.

It did not take long for officialdom to identify the guilty parties. Careful and widespread study of literally hundreds of closed-circuit cameras across London, coupled with intelligence-based leads, revealed the chief suspects as Germaine Lindsay, Mohammad Sidique Khan, Hasib Hussain, and Shehzad Tanweer. Hussein, Tanweer, and Khan lived in the English city of Leeds, while Lindsay was from the Buckinghamshire town of Aylesbury.

All four men were recorded on CCTV cameras—together, as a group—at Luton Station, on the morning of the attacks. They were also variously filmed on the London Underground, or as they made their way towards it. Explosives were found in Tanweer's vehicle, which was parked at Luton Railway Station. Lindsay, Tanweer, and Khan died in the Underground explosions, while Hussain met his end on the double-decker.

Khan and Tanweer had made video recordings that leave no room for doubt when it came to their mindset. "We are at war and I am a soldier," said Khan, as he targeted his rage against the West. In a pre-recorded statement, Janweer chillingly stated: "What you have witnessed now is only the beginning."

In addition, leads that developed from digging into the lives and backgrounds of all four men allowed both the police and the security services to make a number of arrests, and also uncover quantities of explosives at a variety of locations across the country. In other words, there seems to be little doubt regarding who was responsible for the shocking events: home-grown terrorists who felt the need to take out their deranged fury on the people of London. So, with that being the case, why have so many questioned the official version of events? Let's take a look.

In an article titled *Coincidence of Bomb Exercises?*—which was prepared for Britain's Channel 4—writer Nicholas Glass wrote of the conspiracy theories surrounding 7/7:

> It began when Peter Power, one time high ranking employee of Scotland Yard and member of its Anti-Terrorist Branch, reported in two major UK media outlets that his company Visor Consulting had on the morning of the seventh of July been conducting "crisis exercises" whose scenarios uncannily mirrored those of the actual attack.

Glass also noted that during the course of interviews with elements of the British media—specifically *Radio 5 Live* and *ITV News*—Power "appeared" to assert that the exercises in question involved "a thousand people," along with a "dedicated crisis team," one whose total number was never revealed. More astonishing, as Glass noted, Power described "the simulation of 'simultaneous attacks on an underground and mainline station' and 'bombs going off *precisely* at the railway stations' at which the actual bombings occurred."

Part of the exercise involved Visor Consulting planning to practice switching from a "slow time thinking" to a "quick time thinking" of the kind required by a situation dominated by crisis. As it transpired, said Glass, "they were forced to do so for real." And the story is not quite over.

Glass continued:

> Three days after the London bombings, Power was in Toronto for the *15th World Conference on Disaster Management*. There, he took part in a discussion panel for the Canadian Broadcasting Corporation's news discussion program *CBS: Sunday Night*, in which he was quizzed again about what the host called the "extraordinary" conjunction of his company's planned scenarios and the actual events. Power dismissed this as "spooky coincidence."

> Power added: "Our scenario was very similar, but it wasn't totally identical. It was based on bombs going off—the time, the locations, all this sort of stuff."

In response, Glass wrote that this undeniably odd development was

> … ignored by the mainstream media. Online publishers stepped in to add fuel to the fires of indignation. Colman Jones, an Associate Producer on *CBS: Sunday Night*, claimed in his blog that, while escorting participants from the building, he enquired of Power "why there had not been more media coverage of this." "They were trying to keep it quiet," Power purportedly responded, with what Jones called "a knowing smile."

As Channel 4 also demonstrated, the world of conspiracy theorizing quickly sat up and took notice of this admittedly odd state of affairs. Particularly quick off the mark was the website *Prison Planet*. In an article titled *London Underground Bombing "Exercises" Took Place at Same Time as Real Attack*, a writer for the site noted:

> Whether Mr. Power and Visor Consultants were "in on the bombing" is not that important…. The British government or one of their private company offshoots could have hired Visor to run the exercise for a number of purposes. This is precisely what happened on the morning of September 11, 2001, with the CIA conducting drills of flying hijacked planes into the WTC and Pentagon at 8:30 in the morning.

In June 2007 the following was revealed by Channel 4 (in Darshna Soni's article, "Survey: Government Hasn't Told Truth about 7/7"):

> Channel 4 News, with GFK NOP, has commissioned a survey to reveal the Muslim community's attitudes towards the "official narrative" surrounding the 7/7 bombings revealing that: 59% of the 500 people polled believe that the government has not told the public the whole truth about the 7th July bombings. 52% believe that the British security services have "made up" evidence to convict terrorist suspects. 24% believe the four men identified as the July 7th bombers were not actually responsible for the attacks.

Of course, a good argument can be made to the effect the Muslims *would* say that!

On May 2, 2007, the Manchester *Guardian* newspaper revealed the sheer and extraordinary extent to which the highly suspicious actions of the four key players in the London bombings were overlooked by British intelligence—something that conspiracy theorists find equally suspicious. According to the newspaper's article, titled "7/7 Leader: More Evidence Reveals What Police Knew," and that was written by Vikram Dodd, Ian Cobain, and Helen Carter:

> Police were investigating the ringleader of the July 7 bombings just five months before he led the suicide attacks on London that killed 52 people, the *Guardian* has learned. In what appears to have been a renewed investigation, a witness gave detectives in January 2005 part of Mohammad Sidique Khan's name, his mobile telephone number and the name and the address of his mother-in-law. The revelation suggests Khan was being investigated much nearer to the London bombings than has been officially admitted.

> Details of how Khan and a second bomber, Shehzad Tanweer, came repeatedly under surveillance in 2004 were disclosed this week after five of their associates were jailed for life for planning attacks around southeast England.

The revelation that Khan was reinvestigated the following year, said newspaper staff, appeared to contradict claims from MI5 that inquiries about him ceased in 2004, after it was concluded that—from a national security perspective—other terrorism suspects were perceived as being of greater importance. Staff added: "It is also likely to lead to scrutiny of MI5's assertion that its officers, who had followed, photographed, and secretly recorded Khan, and made other inquiries about him, did not know who he was."

Guardian reporters also discovered that on January 27, 2005, police took a statement from the manager of a garage in Leeds that had loaned Khan a courtesy car while his vehicle was being repaired. MI5 had followed Khan and Tanweer as they drove the courtesy car across London, in March of the previous year. The garage manager told police that the car had been loaned to a "Mr. S. Khan," who gave his mobile telephone number and an address on Gregory Street, Batley, which is located in the county of West Yorkshire.

//It is becoming more and more clear that the story presented to the public and parliament is at odds with the facts."

Khan, the police were told, had asked for his repaired car to be delivered to another address, in nearby Dewsbury, which happened to be his mother-in-law's home. Almost a year earlier, MI5 officers had followed Khan to the same address after watching him meet a number of suspected terrorists.

That was not the end of police interest in Khan in 2005. On the afternoon of February 3, an officer from Scotland Yard's anti-terrorism branch carried out inquiries with the company that had insured a car in which Khan was seen driving almost a year earlier. He discovered that Khan had insured a five-door silver Honda Accord in his own name. Inquiries also showed that the car was registered in the name of Khan's mother-in-law.

The *Guardian* told its readers: "Nothing about these inquiries appeared in the report by parliament's intelligence and security committee after it investigated the July 7 attacks. The shadow home secretary, David Davis, said: 'It is becoming more and more clear that the story presented to the public and parliament is at odds with the facts.'"

Scotland Yard, after being contacted for comment, merely commented that everything was "routine." Hardly routine, however, was the next revelation that the *Guardian* brought to light:

> There was more confusion over evidence that Shehzad Tanweer was surfing the internet for bomb-making tips in June 2005, two weeks before the suicide attacks. According to a document which prosecution lawyers … disclosed to the defense before the trial began, Tanweer was heard to be discussing bombings and using the internet to make such a bomb.

Rather intriguingly, the very same document noted:

> Tanweer told the same person he had entered Afghanistan and met people from around the world who had got into his head. MI5 said this information is "false." But the Crown Prosecution Service told the Guardian the information was passed to it by Scotland Yard. The Yard does not deny this but said its officers in the case had "no recollection" of the information.

To a degree, this dove tails with the words of journalist Mark Honigsbaum, who wrote, in a 2006 article, "Seeing Isn't Believing," that

> … a computer technician who helped to encrypt emails at an Islamic bookshop in Leeds where Khan and Tanweer used to hang out became so alarmed by their calls for jihad that in October 2003 he delivered a dossier to West Yorkshire anti-terrorist police. Martin Gilbertson's claims have not been denied. West Yorkshire police simply admitted it couldn't say whether or not his dossier had "made its way into the intelligence system."

Clearly, someone within officialdom had put together a great deal of data on the bombers, but was evidently failing to do anything meaningful with it—something that led conspiracy theorists to believe a decision had been taken by shadowy, Machiavellian figures in government to allow the 7/7 attack to go ahead, as justification for the continued and escalating annexing of the Middle East.

Then there is the matter of the official inquiry—or, rather, the lack of an inquiry into what happened on July 7, 2005. On August 1, 2011, journalist Esther Addley, in an article for the *Guardian* newspaper titled "7/7 Survivors End Battle for Public Inquiry into Bombings," revealed the following:

> Survivors and relatives of those who died in the 7 July bombings have abandoned their legal attempt to force the government to hold a public inquiry into the attacks, acknowledging that proceedings would be likely to be unsuccessful and would cause "further unnecessary distress."

> Fifty-two people were killed and more than 700 injured by four suicide bombers on the London transport network in 2005. An inquest into the murders, presided over by the high court judge Lady Justice Hallett, found

This memorial in Hyde Park is dedicated to the victims of the 2005 London bombing.

in May that the attacks could not be blamed on failures by MI5 and that it was unlikely that any of those who died would have survived had the emergency service response been swifter.

After the verdicts a number of bereaved relatives said important questions remained unanswered. They called for an independent public inquiry to examine, in particular, the question of whether the attacks could have been prevented.

To date, there has been no such inquiry.

It is issues such as those above that ensure the conspiracy theorists continue to suggest there is more to 7/7 than meets the eye. One of those conspiracy theorists is a man named John Hill. He hails from Sheffield, England, and—under the alias of Muad Dib (a character in the movie *Dune*)—made a documentary in 2007 titled *7/7 Ripple Effect*. It took no prisoners and suggested the guilty parties in 7/7 were former British prime minister Tony Blair, Israel's security service—Mossad—elements of the British Police Force, and shadowy sources buried deep within the world of officialdom. Hill further asserted that the four presumed bombers (that Hill perceived were definitive patsies) were executed *prior* to the detonations, by the British Police Force. It scarcely needs mentioning that the highly controversial production quickly gained a cult-following and became an Internet hit.

The furor surrounding Hill's film reached stratospheric proportions when, rather incredibly, he was arrested and extradited back to England from Ireland.

The charge: perverting the cause of justice by mailing copies of *7/7 Ripple Effect* to the judge and jury foreman in a trial that had links to the attacks. Although Hill was acquitted, his followers asserted that this was nothing less than a blatant tactic to try and silence him. Perhaps they were right.

As for where things stand today, the official verdict—that 7/7 was the work of a group of domestic terrorists—remains precisely that.

The final word goes to Rachel North, a survivor of the July 7 bombings, whose comments journalist Mike Rudin noted in a June 2009 article for the BBC titled "The Conspiracy Files: 7/7":

> If people in mosques think that the government is so antagonistic towards them that they're actually willing to frame them for a monstrous crime they didn't commit, what does that do to levels of trust? That is a problem for the government and for everybody in this country.

REDUCING THE POPULATION: A MODERN HOLOCAUST

In 2010, the website *Fourwinds10* stated in an article titled "22 Shocking Population Control Quotes from the Global Elite":

> There are now large numbers of global leaders that are convinced that the exploding population of the world has become like a virus or a plague, and that it must be combated as such. In fact, it would be very difficult to understate just how obsessed many members of the global elite are with population control. The United Nations puts out position papers about it, universities have entire courses dedicated to it, radical population control advocates have been appointed to some of the highest political positions in the world, and some of the wealthiest people on the planet get together just to talk about it.

Can it be true? Are nefarious and deadly forces hard at work to reduce the world's population—and to reduce it quickly, drastically, and to levels that will amount to nothing less than full-blown decimation? Certainly, one only has to take a look at the case of Adolf Hitler. He waged a determined war of extermination against the Jews during the Second World War. And, as a result, and with phenomenal, horrific speed, an entire race of people can come close to being systematically wiped off the face of the planet. Could such a thing, one day, happen again? If it does, will it be due to the actions of a future Hitler, a madman with lunatic delusions of grandeur? Maybe not: conspiracy theorists maintain that the death knell for not just millions, but for *billions*, might come from none other than the United Nations.

That planet Earth cannot adequately house an ever-growing population indefinitely is not a matter of any doubt. That the world's weather is changing—in ways that are seen as both hostile and suspicious—has given rise to the likelihood that global warming is the culprit. Humankind's ever-growing need for dwindling fossil fuels, combined with its near-exponentially increasing polluting of the planet's eco-system, has almost irreversibly altered our future and has raised fears that our most precious commodity—water—will soon become scarce.

In 2012, the Manchester *Guardian* reported in "How Will Climate Change Impact on Fresh Water Security?":

> Fresh water is crucial to human society—not just for drinking, but also for farming, washing, and many other activities. It is expected to become increas-

ingly scarce in the future, and this is partly due to climate change."

The newspaper added:

Especially little is known about future declines in regional groundwater resources because of lack of research on this topic, even though around 50% of global domestic water supply comes from groundwater. Although scientists are making progress in reducing uncertainty about fresh water scarcity, these kinds of unknowns mean that water supply strategies must be adaptable so that they can be effective under different scenarios.

In May 2013 Melanie McDonagh of the *Spectator* noted in her article "Dan Brown's Latest Conspiracy Theory—and the Powerful People Who Believe It" that the Royal Society had published a paper by Paul and Anne Ehrlich titled *Can a Collapse of Global Civilization Be Avoided?*

Of the question that the title of the report asked, McDonagh said: "No, is the short answer, unless we adopt 'dramatic cultural change.'"

The Ehrlichs noted:

During World War II, the German exterminated millions of people, including Jews and other minorities, in concentration camps like the one at Dachau (a watchtower at the camp is shown here). Might today's elite be planning a mass extermination, too?

Today, for the first time, humanity's global civilization ... is threatened with collapse by an array of environmental problems. Humankind finds itself engaged in what Prince Charles described as "an act of suicide on a grand scale." The human predicament is driven by overpopulation, overconsumption of natural resources and the use of unnecessarily environmentally damaging technologies.

McDonagh added: "The authors assume an increase in population to 9.5 billion by 2050. Result: 'global collapse.'"

It could be argued that a radically smaller, worldwide population would help allay—and perhaps even successfully keep at bay—dwindling supplies of water, as noted by the *Guardian* in 2012. But there are other things that have certain people worried, such as fuel. In 2014, *USA Today* reported that the planet's entire oil reserves may be gone by 2065. It was *USA Today*'s juddering and shuddering revelation that led *Gas 2* (champions of so-called "green cars") to state in "BP Estimates the World Has Just 53.3 Years of Oil Left":

These estimates are actually 1.1% more than last year, thanks in part to growing estimates of American shale oil. Of course keep in mind that the oil industry is regularly growing or shrinking estimated energy reserves, with California's Monterey Shale having its reserves downgraded some

96%. There's also suspicion that countries like Saudi Arabia are outright lying about how much crude they actually have left. So yeah. Skepticism.

Gas 2 cautioned, however: "53 years sounds like awhile, right? Well not really, but the bigger problem is that, as humanity reaches the last of its oil reserves, without an adequate energy transition in place, some countries could be caught flat-footed."

"Flat-footed" may very well prove to be an understatement of mammoth proportions. Worldwide panic, chaos, anarchy, and disaster might actually be far closer to the truth of what awaits us. And it's this issue—of potential, planetary collapse—that has led to dark and disturbing theories that powerful figures have decided the only way to save the future of humanity is to shrink it, and to shrink it *soon*. Does evidence of such a nightmarish program exist? Astonishingly, yes it does. Make no mistake, the issue of over-population—and how to deal with it—is a major issue.

The speed at which the human race is infesting the planet (which is not unjustified terminology) is as alarming as it is amazing. It was in the very earliest years of the nineteenth century that the world's population finally reached one billion. It was not until around 1930 that the population was doubled to two billion. By the dawning of the sixties, there were three billion of us, four billion by the mid-seventies, and five billion by the late eighties. As the twenty-first century began, the number was six billion. In 2013 we hit seven billion. You may not like—or even be prepared for—what is to come next. Current estimates are that 2024 will roughly be when the Earth finds itself buckling under the weight of eight billion people. By 2040, we'll be at nine billion.

As the world's population increases exponentially, the planet's resources will become increasingly scarce, resulting in famine, disease, and resource wars.

The United Nations has offered several different scenarios for what might be in store in the decades ahead of us. In a 2003 report titled *Long-range World Population Projections* (prepared by the Department of Economic and Social Affairs), various scenarios were detailed for the years to come. One such scenario was truly nightmarish. The DESA recorded: "If the fertility of major areas is kept constant at 1995 levels, the world population soars to 256 billion by 2150."

To put that figure in to an understandable context, we would be talking about a worldwide population of more than *thirty times* its current figure. Of course, all of this could be averted by encouraging smaller families, via a greater promotion of birth-control. The conspiracy rumor-mill suggests this is not enough for the world's most powerful figures. They want the figures down sooner than later. And by just about any means possible. We're talking wipeout. For all intents and purposes, we're talking *holocaust*. And it's something that dates back decades.

Many conspiracy theorists believe that things began in 1974, specifically on December 10 of that year, when a highly controversial report was prepared for the United States' National Security Council. It was a report, and attendant project and study, overseen by one of the most powerful figures in global politics, Henry Kissinger, who held such positions as U.S. secretary of state and national security advisor to the presidential office. The report was titled *Implications of Worldwide Population Growth for U.S. Security and Overseas Interests.* (See "National Security Study Memorandum 200 (NSSM 200)—April 1974.")

//If the fertility of major areas is kept constant at 1995 levels, the world population soars to 256 billion by 2150."

Rather disturbingly, while the document noted that a growing, worldwide population was undeniably a problem—and one destined to only get worse—much of its attention was focused on targeting specific nations, instead of the planet and its people as a whole. In other words, rather than encourage a united Earth to address the issue, the scenario was of lowering the population levels in the least advanced parts of the world. The countries that Kissinger's team felt posed the biggest "problems" were India, Bangladesh, Pakistan, Indonesia, Thailand, the Philippines, Turkey, Nigeria, Egypt, Ethiopia, Mexico, Colombia, and Brazil. It was estimated that these particular countries would account for close to fifty percent of the future increases in the world's population. And such increases, combined with the attendant, localized possibilities for societal collapse, should not be allowed to come to pass.

As the authors noted, in those particular countries—where growth and development were far from being on par with the rest of the planet—there was a distinct possibility that with falling food supplies, dwindling water and fuel, and more and more people, demands from the relevant populations for action to combat famine would soon become civil unrest, and then uncontrollable anarchy. There was another worry for Kissinger's people. If the economies of countries with exploding populations collapsed, the result might be that the United States would be unable to import from those same countries things that were essential to its own economy. In that scenario, everyone suffers. Or, maybe not: Kissinger was determined that the U.S. would not fall, even if other nations did. It was up to the United Nations and the United States to solve the problem.

Clearly, as the following extracts show, a great deal of thought had gone into how the rise of populations in the underdeveloped world could possibly bring the United States to its knees:

> The U.S. economy will require large and increasing amounts of minerals from abroad, especially from less developed countries. That fact gives the U.S. enhanced interest in the political, economic, and social stability of the supplying countries. Wherever a lessening of population pressures through reduced birth rates can increase the prospects for such stability,

New York City's Mayor Bill de Blasio attends an anti-fracking protest. Many feel fracking is an environmentally hazardous way to extract oil that is now used because many easier-to-reach oil reserves are drying up.

population policy becomes relevant to resource supplies and to the economic interests of the United States.

The document continued:

The location of known reserves of higher grade ores of most minerals favors increasing dependence of all industrialized regions on imports from less developed countries. The real problems of mineral supplies lie not in basic physical sufficiency, but in the politico-economic issues of access, terms for exploration and exploitation, and division of the benefits among producers, consumers, and host country governments.

Anticipating how things could turn very bad for the U.S., there is the following:

Whether through government action, labor conflicts, sabotage, or civil disturbance, the smooth flow of needed materials will be jeopardized. Although population pressure is obviously not the only factor involved, these types of frustrations are much less likely under conditions of slow or zero population growth.

The brains behind the report then targeted the people themselves, their collective mindset, and how to get around increasing issues of concern. In a section titled *Populations with a High Proportion of Growth*, it was noted:

The young people, who are in much higher proportions in many LDCs, are likely to be more volatile, unstable, prone to extremes, alienation, and violence than an older population. These young people can more readily be persuaded to attack the legal institutions of the government or real property of the "establishment," "imperialists," multinational corporations, or other-often foreign-influences blamed for their troubles.

There were words of warning in the report, too:

We must take care that our activities should not give the appearance to the LDCs of an industrialized country policy directed against the LDCs. Caution must be taken that in any approaches in this field we support in the LDCs are ones we can support within this country. "Third World" leaders should be in the forefront and obtain the credit for successful programs. In this context it is important to demonstrate to LDC leaders that such family planning programs have worked and can work within a reasonable period of time.

The authors of the report make an interesting statement: "In these sensitive relations, however, it is important in style as well as substance to avoid the appearance of coercion."

In other words, the report does not deny that nations might be coerced, only that there is a concerted effort to "avoid the appearance" of such.

So much for the 1970s—when the program of planetary extermination, on an obscene scale, is reported to have begun—but what of today? According to some, today it's downright out of control.

Although the *Implications of Worldwide Population Growth for U.S. Security and Overseas Interests* document was prepared in the 1970s, there is evidence the world of officialdom has taken its position on population control down some controversial and dark directions. Take, for example, President Obama's science advisor, John P. Holdren, who said (see "John Holdren, Obama's Science Czar, Says: Forced Abortions and Mass Sterilization Needed to Save the Planet"):

A program of sterilizing women after their second or third child, despite the relatively greater difficulty of the operation than vasectomy, might be easier to implement than trying to sterilize men. The development of a long-term sterilizing capsule that could be implanted under the skin and removed when pregnancy is desired opens additional possibilities for coercive fertility control. The capsule could be implanted at puberty and might be removable, with official permission, for a limited number of births.

President George W. Bush's science advisor, Paul Ehrlich, came straight to the point: "Each person we add now disproportionately impacts on the environment and life-support systems of the planet." He also said, in downright chilling fashion: "A cancer is an uncontrolled multiplication of cells. The population ex-

Dr. John P. Holdren, who has served as President Barack Obama's science advisor, suggested that human populations could be controlled by sterilizing women after they have given birth to one or two children.

plosion is an uncontrolled multiplication of people. We must shift our efforts from the treatment of the symptoms to the cutting out of the cancer. The operation will demand many apparently brutal and heartless decisions."

Prince Philip, the Duke of Edinburgh, has a very novel and unique answer to the problem: "If I were reincarnated I would wish to be returned to earth as a killer virus to lower human population levels."

Then there is Ted Turner, the brains behind CNN: "A total population of 250–300 million people, a 95% decline from present levels, would be ideal."

"A reasonable estimate for an industrialized world society at the present North American material standard of living would be 1 billion. At the more frugal European standard of living, 2 to 3 billion would be possible," stated the United Nations' Global Diversity Assessment, in shockingly matter-of-fact fashion.

All of the above quotes can be found at "22 Shocking Population Control Quotes from the Global Elite That Will Make You Want to Lose Your Lunch."

Prison Planet correspondent Paul Joseph Watson said in a 2009 article, "The Population Reduction Agenda for Dummies":

> There are still large numbers of people amongst the general public, in academia, and especially those who work for the corporate media, who are still in denial about the on-the-record stated agenda for global population reduction, as well as the consequences of this program that we already see unfolding.

He continued with his warning: "In China, the one child policy is enforced by means of taxes on each subsequent child, allied to an intimidation program which includes secret police and 'family planning' authorities kidnapping pregnant women from their homes and performing forced abortions."

Two years later—and specifically in October 2011—Michael Snyder of *The American Dream* stated in "From 7 Billion People to 500 Million People—The Sick Population Control Agenda of the Global Elite":

> In recent years, the UN and other international organizations have become bolder about trying to push the sick population control agenda of the global elite. Most of the time organizations such as the UN will simply talk about "stabilizing" the global population, but … there are many

among the global elite that are not afraid to openly talk about a goal of reducing the population of the world to 500 million (or less).

And, as Snyder also noted, and in a fashion that we would all be wise to remember: "To you and I it may seem like insanity to want to get rid of more than 90 percent of the global population, but there is a growing consensus among the global elite that this is absolutely necessary for the good of the planet."

MICRO-CHIPPING THE WORLD: CONSTANT SPYING

Back in 1994, David Icke, the well-known and controversial author on all manner of conspiracy theories, said in his book, *The Robots' Rebellion*:

> The Brotherhood of the New World Order … want us bar-coded so we can be "read" at supermarkets and banks, like a checkout assistant now reads a tin of beans. A man at IBM who invented the laser-bar reader for supermarkets has also developed a method of putting the same type of device under human skin in one billionth of a second. It is invisible to the naked eye and could carry all the information anyone needed to know about us. We could be permanently linked to a computer, and who is to say that signals could not be sent both ways?

Icke added, in *And The Truth Shall Set You Free*:

> … the game plan is known as the Great Work of Ages or the New World Order, and it seeks to introduce a world government to which all nations would be colonies; a world central bank and currency; a world army; and a microchipped population connected to a global computer. What is happening today is the culmination of the manipulation which has been unfolding for thousands of years.

At the time, the mainstream media scoffed loudly and derisively, and the public largely dismissed what was perceived as nothing more than arrant nonsense. It appears, however, and with the benefit of hindsight and time, that Icke was not only on the right track, but that, incredibly, he may actually have *underestimated* the dire future ahead of us all. Today, more than two decades after Icke warned of what was to come, his words are looking less and less like science fiction and scaremongering. They are looking far more like chilling prophecies of a terrifying world that is almost upon us, one that goes far beyond anything that even George Orwell could ever have imagined.

To understand how and why such a future might actually come to pass, it's first important to note what, precisely, microchips are. Essentially, they are integrated circuits that can be placed under the surface of the skin and which contain certain, specific data on the implanted individual. Extremely small, they utilize what is termed Radio Frequency Identification (RFID) to ensure that all relevant data is collected, stored, and available to those that require it.

The perfect example is the widespread chipping of pet dogs and cats. Of course, this is a case of the technology being utilized for wholly positive reasons: when man's best friends get lost, such wireless-based devices very often prove invaluable in identifying their owners—and quickly, too. The result is an overjoyed reunion between owner and pet. There is, however, a world of difference between micro-chipping a dog and a human. Not in terms of the physical procedure of implanting the chip, but from the perspectives of personal privacy, ethics, and morals.

Let's first focus on the research and findings of author Brad Steiger, who has dug deeply into this particular topic. What he has uncovered may shock you. If it doesn't, it should. Steiger said in 2014's *The Zombie Book*:

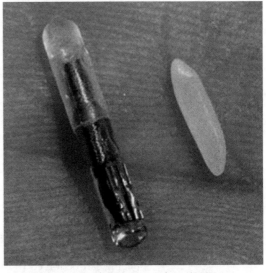

Radio Frequency Identification chips (RFID, shown next to a grain of rice at right) like this one could some day soon be implanted in all citizens, who could then be tracked by the government. Some fear, too, they might be used for mind control.

> In the 1950s and 60s, a large number of experiments in behavior modification were conducted in the United States, and it is well known that electrical implants were inserted into the brains of animals and humans. Later, when new techniques in influencing brain functions became a priority to military and intelligence services, secret experiments were conducted with such unwilling guinea pigs as inmates of prisons, soldiers, mental patients, handicapped children, the elderly, and any group of people considered expendable.

Steiger continued:

> Rauni-Leena Luukanen-Kilde, M.D., Former Chief Medical Officer of Finland, has stated that mysterious brain implants the size of one centimeter began showing up in X-rays in the 1980s. In a few years, implants were found the size of a grain of rice. Dr. Luukanen-Kilde stated that the implants were made of silicon, later of gallium arsenide. Today such implants are small enough that it is nearly impossible to detect or remove them. They can easily be inserted into the neck or back during surgical operations, with or without the consent of the subject.

> It has been stated that within a few years all Americans will be forced to receive a programmable biochip implant somewhere in their body. The biochip is most likely to be implanted on the back of the right or the left hand so it will be easy to scan at stores. The biochip implant will also be used as a universal type of identification card. A number will be assigned at birth and will follow that person throughout life. Eventually, every newborn will be injected with a microchip, which will identify the person for the rest of his or her life.

Initially, said Steiger:

//The technology exists right now to create a New World Order served by the zombie-like masses."

People will be informed that the biochip will be used largely for purposes of identification. The reality is that the implant will be linked to a massive supercomputer system that will make it possible for government agencies to maintain a surveillance of all citizens by ground sensors and satellites. Today's microchips operate by means of low-frequency radio waves that target them.

With the help of satellites, the implanted person can be followed anywhere. Their brain functions can be remotely monitored by supercomputers and even altered through the changing of frequencies. Even worse, say the alarmists, once the surveillance system is in place, the biochips will be implemented to transform every man, woman, and child into a controlled slave, for these devices will make it possible for outside intelligences to influence a person's brain cell conversations and to talk directly with the individual's brain neurons. Through cybernetic biochip brain implants, people can be forced to think and to act exactly as government intelligence agencies have preprogrammed them to think and behave.

Steiger continues to warn us:

The technology exists right now to create a New World Order served by the zombie-like masses. Secret government agencies could easily utilize covert neurological communication systems in order to subvert independent thinking and to control social and political activity.

The National Security Agency's (NSA) electronic surveillance system can simultaneously follow the unique bioelectrical resonance brain frequency of millions of people. NSA's Signals Intelligence group can remotely monitor information from human brains by decoding the evoked potentials (3.50 hertz, 5 milliwatts) emitted by the brain. Electromagnetic frequency (EMF) brain stimulation signals can be sent to the brains of specific individuals, causing the desired effects to be experienced by the target.

A U.S. Naval research laboratory, funded by intelligence agencies, has achieved the incredible breakthrough of uniting living brain cells with microchips. When such a chip is injected into a man's or a woman's brain, he or she instantly becomes a living vegetable and a subservient slave. And once this device is perfected, the biochip implant could easily be converted by the Defense Department into an army of killer zombies.

Experts have said that a micromillimeter microchip may be placed into the optical nerve of the eye and draw neuro-impulses from the brain which embody the experiences, smells, sights, and voice of the implanted subject. These neuro-impulses may be stored in a computer and may be projected back to the person's brain via the microchip to be re-experienced. A computer operator can send electromagnetic messages to the target's nervous system, thereby inducing hallucinations.

If you think that the words of Brad Steiger are nothing but science-fiction-style fantasy, you're very wrong, as you'll now see.

In May 2002 it was revealed that American doctors had successfully implanted chips into the arms of an entire Florida family that contained their complete medical histories. The Jacobs family—husband and wife, Jeffrey and Leslie, and their son, Derek—agreed to undergo the controversial procedure that, rather chillingly, their doctors stated they hoped would soon become "standard practice" all across the United States. Collectively, it took less than forty seconds—in a Boca Raton, Florida, clinic—to transform father, mother, and son into walking, talking human barcodes. It was all "thanks" to the VeriChip, the brainchild of a Florida-based company called Applied Digital Solutions.

Certain elements of the world's corporate media praised this groundbreaking procedure. They cited the fact that such implants would do away with the need for medical-alert bracelets, would prove to be vital in terms of identifying diseases and conditions when time was of the essence, and would allow for continual updating of a person's medical history as and when deemed necessary.

Other elements of the media were less than enamored by this creepy, creeping technology, including the BBC, who noted when the story surfaced: "The chips could also be used to contain personal information and even a global positioning device which could track a person's whereabouts, leading to fears the chip could be used for more sinister purposes."

Two years later, in 2006, the pros and cons of the micro-chipping technology were still being hotly debated. And it was still the VeriChip that was under the microscope, so to speak. Champions of the chips noted that crucial data—on such issues as blood type and potentially life-threatening allergies—could be stored and accessed by medical professionals and lives would be saved as a direct result. Applied Digital Solutions expressed its hopes that, in terms of sales of the chip, it would be a case of today the United States and tomorrow the United Kingdom. After that it was anyone's guess, or bad dream.

Also in 2006, the British media waded in on the controversy. In an article titled "Britons 'Could Be Microchipped Like Dogs in a Decade,'" *Daily Mail* journalist Dan Newling noted that in the near future, "human beings may be forced to be 'micro-chipped' like pet dogs, a shocking official report into the rise of the Big Brother state has warned."

The report to which the press was referring was edited by two highly respected sources, Dr. David Murakami Wood, the managing editor of the journal *Surveillance and Society*, and Dr. Kirstie Ball, who was an Open University lecturer on organization studies. Their report made

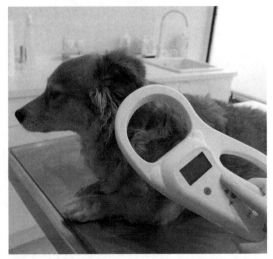

It's fairly common practice to put microchips in dogs and cats so that pets can be located and returned home to their owners. Doing the same thing to human beings is a much different matter.

[B]y 2016 "our almost every movement, purchase and communication could be monitored by a complex network of interlinking surveillance technologies."

the shocking claim that by 2016 "our almost every movement, purchase and communication could be monitored by a complex network of interlinking surveillance technologies."

It was a report written by noted academics and for the specific attention of the U.K.'s information commissioner, Richard Thomas. The *Daily Mail* warned its readers that the chips "could be used by companies who want to keep tabs on an employee's movements or by governments who want a foolproof way of identifying their citizens—and storing information about them."

Moving on to 2012, Michael Snyder of *The American Dream*, asked (in his article, "After the Government Microchips Our Soldiers, How Long Will It Be Before They Want to Put a Microchip in YOU"), on May 9, two important, yet very disturbing, questions: "What would you do if someday the government made it mandatory for everyone to receive an implantable microchip for identification purposes? Would you take it?"

Snyder noted, correctly, that microchips are increasingly being used to monitor the health of troops on the battlefield. It was something that led him to pose another question:

> Once the government has microchips implanted in all of our soldiers, how long will it be before they want to put a microchip in all government employees for the sake of national security? Once the government has microchips in all government employees, how long will it be before they want to put a microchip in you?

He foresaw a situation where the technology would not be forced on us overnight, by jackbooted minions of the New World Order. Rather, it would work its way into our lives, bit by bit, piece by piece: "For now, it will creep into our lives at an incremental pace. But after enough people have voluntarily accepted the 'benefits' of implantable microchips, it will only be a matter of time before they become mandatory. Are you ready for that?"

Well, are you?

As 2013 rolled around, matters became even more surreal and disturbing. That was when news surfaced that a former director of the Defense Advanced Research Projects Agency (DARPA), Regina Dugan, was championing something that definitely raised both eyebrows and anxiety levels. It was what was described (in Paul Joseph Watson's article for *Infowars*, "Ex-DARPA Head Wants You to Swallow ID Microchips") as nothing less than "an edible authentication microchip," one designed to "contain a minute chip that transmits an individual's personal data."

Each chip is able to read a unique signal, one that, if fully embraced, will spell the death knell for online passwords, passports, drivers' licenses, and just about any and all private data. Rather than being implanted into a person's body on a one-time basis, it is inserted into a pill—a pill that a person will be required to swallow every day and that will be "designed to move through the body at the normal process of digestion, and according to engineers working on the device, it can be taken every day for up to a month."

Rather incredibly, the device—which, at the time I write these words has already been officially approved by the Food and Drug Administration—is fueled by a battery that uses nothing less than the acid created in the stomach of the individual. When the chip and the acid interact, the former emits a minute signal that can be read by mobile devices, thereby determining and verifying the identity of the person.

//Would you swallow a Google microchip every day simply to access your cellphone?"

As for Regina Dugan, the head of advanced technology at Motorola, Watson's article notes she revealed that the company was "working on a microchip inside a pill that users would swallow daily in order obtain the 'superpower' of having their entire body act as a biological authentication system for cellphones, cars, doors and other devices."

In stark terms, the whole human body becomes, as Dugan worded it, "your authentication token."

Infowars, which followed the story closely, noted: "Privacy advocates will wince at the thought, especially given Dugan's former role as head of DARPA, the Pentagon agency that many see as being at the top of the pyramid when it comes to the Big Brother technocracy."

Infowars also considered that Dugan's claim that just such a pill could be taken an astonishing thirty times a day, every day, for the rest of one's natural life, was "seemingly dubious." They also asked the question: "Would you swallow a Google microchip every day simply to access your cellphone?"

Some might actually do that and much more, too. Dugan, in a fashion that must surely send chills up and down the spines of sane people everywhere, revealed that Motorola was working to develop a "wearable tattoo," one that could essentially read the human mind by "detecting the unvocalized words in their throat."

John Hewitt, of Extreme Tech, explained the science behind this: "It has been known for decades that when you speak to yourself in your inner voice, your brain still sends neural spike volleys to your vocal apparatus, in a similar fashion to when you actually speak aloud."

Dugan apparently already had a method in place that would ensure a sizeable number of young people would eagerly sign up for the "e-tattoo." If it was designed in a fashion that was cool and rebellious, teenagers would quickly be on board, "if only to piss off their parents."

As *Infowars'* Paul Joseph Watson noted:

The edible microchip and the wearable e-tattoo are prime examples of how transhumanism is being made "trendy" in an effort to convince the next generation to completely sacrifice whatever privacy they have left in the name of faux rebellion (which is actually cultural conformism) and convenience.

Thankfully, there are others who have warned of the growing threat: "The technology exists to create a totalitarian New World Order," notes Rauni-Leena Luukanen-Kilde, MD, a former Finnish chief medical officer. She added (and is quoted in Greg Szymanski's "Plans to Microchip Every Newborn in US and Europe Underway"):

Covert neurological communication systems are in place to counteract independent thinking and to control social and political activity on behalf of self-serving private and military interests. When our brain functions are already connected to supercomputers by means of radio implants and microchips, it will be too late for protest. This threat can be defeated only by educating the public, using available literature on biotelemetry and information exchanged at international congresses.

Greg Szymanski, who has followed the micro-chipping scandal, asks:

Are you ready for a total elimination of privacy and a robotizing of mankind, as well as an invasion of every thought going through your head? Are you prepared to live in a world in which every newborn baby is micro-chipped? And finally are you ready to have your every move tracked, recorded and placed in Big Brother's data bank?

Let's hope each and every one of us has the common sense to answer those questions with a decisive and unswerving "No!"

BIRD FLU: A BIOLOGICAL WEAPON

In 2005, President George W. Bush stated that with regard to the fears of bird flu erupting in the United States, and erupting big time (see "Bush Wants Right to Use Military if Bird Flu Hits"):

> If we had an outbreak somewhere in the United States, do we not then quarantine that part of the country? And how do you, then, enforce a quarantine? It's one thing to shut down airplanes. It's another thing to prevent people from coming in to get exposed to the avian flu. And who best to be able to effect a quarantine? One option is the use of a military that's able to plan and move.

Bush's words raised eyebrows in both the mainstream media and the domain of conspiracy theorizing. For the former, it was a case of the media suggesting Bush was overreacting by making semi-veiled allusions to martial law and military occupations of infected zones. For the latter, suspicions rose to the effect that the Bush administration was planning on using fears of avian flu breaking out all across America as a means to invoke martial law at a whim and possibly even keep it in place for an extensive time, maybe even near-permanently. Before we get to the conspiracy angles, let's first take a look at what avian flu actually is.

There is no better source to turn to for information on bird flu than the Centers for Disease Control and Prevention, which has its headquarters in Atlanta, Georgia. The CDC is at the forefront of helping to lessen, and ultimately stop, any and all threats posed by deadly viruses. "Category A" viruses are considered by the CDC to be the most serious ones of all.

They are those specific viruses that, said the CDC, "can be easily spread or transmitted from person to person," that "result in high death rates and have the potential for major public health impact," that "might cause panic and social disruption," and that would "require special action for public health preparedness."

Moreover, and by the CDC's very own admission, its work is "a critical component of overall U.S. national security." The U.S. government most assuredly recognizes the profound importance of the CDC from that very same national security perspective. Currently, the CDC receives yearly funding of around $1.3 billion to "build and strengthen national preparedness for public health emergencies caused by natural, accidental, or intentional events." It also works closely with the

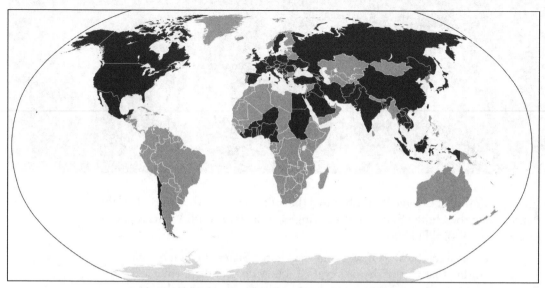

The above map indicates countries (in dark gray) infected with avian flu by 2009. The rapid spread of the disease engendered considerable alarm worldwide.

Department of Homeland Security, and with FEMA, the Federal Emergency Management Agency.

On the matter of bird flu, the CDC noted in an online article at its website, "Key Facts About Avian Influenza (Bird Flu) and Highly Pathogenic Avian Influenza A (H5N1) Virus":

Avian influenza is an infection caused by avian (bird) influenza (flu) A viruses. These influenza A viruses occur naturally among birds. Wild birds worldwide get flu A infections in their intestines, but usually do not get sick from flu infections. However, avian influenza is very contagious among birds and some of these viruses can make certain domesticated bird species, including chickens, ducks, and turkeys, very sick and kill them.

The agency continued:

Infected birds can shed influenza virus in their saliva, nasal secretions, and feces. Susceptible birds become infected when they have contact with contaminated secretions or excretions or with surfaces that are contaminated with secretions or excretions from infected birds. Domesticated birds may become infected with avian influenza virus through direct contact with infected waterfowl or other infected poultry, or through contact with surfaces (such as dirt or cages) or materials (such as water or feed) that have been contaminated with the virus.

Infection with avian influenza viruses in domestic poultry, said the CDC,

… causes two main forms of disease that are distinguished by low and high extremes of virulence. The "low pathogenic" form may go undetected and usually causes only mild symptoms (such as ruffled feathers and a drop in egg production). However, the highly pathogenic form spreads more rapidly through flocks of poultry. This form may cause disease that affects multiple internal organs and has a mortality rate that can reach 90–100% often within 48 hours.

So much for the lethal effects that the viruses can have on birds: But what about when avian flu jumps species? What about when it reaches the human population? This is a matter of deep and critical concern to the CDC, as its staff notes:

Usually, "avian influenza virus" refers to influenza A viruses found chiefly in birds, but infections with these viruses can occur in humans. The risk from avian influenza is generally low to most people, because the viruses do not usually infect humans. However, confirmed cases of human infection from several subtypes of avian influenza infection have been reported since 1997. Most cases of avian influenza infection in humans have resulted from contact with infected poultry (e.g., domesticated chicken, ducks, and turkeys) or surfaces contaminated with secretion/excretions from infected birds. The spread of avian influenza viruses from one ill person to another person has been reported very rarely, and has been limited, inefficient and unsustained.

//The spread of avian influenza viruses from one ill person to another person has been reported very rarely...."

The CDC expands on the dangers posed to the human race:

Currently, H3N2 and H1N1 influenza A subtypes are circulating among humans and H2N2 influenza A circulated from about 1957–1968. Some genetic parts of current human influenza A viruses had their origin in bird flu viruses originally. Influenza A viruses are constantly changing, and they might adapt over time to infect and spread among humans.

And what, precisely, are the physical effects that can surface when avian flu hits the human population? They are many, varied, and sometimes lethal:

Symptoms of avian influenza in humans have ranged from typical human influenza-like symptoms (e.g., fever, cough, sore throat, and muscle aches) to eye infections, pneumonia, severe respiratory diseases (such as acute respiratory distress), and other severe and life-threatening complications. The symptoms of avian influenza may depend on which virus caused the infection.

In view of the fact that avian flu has the ability to not just make a person acutely ill, but to actually kill them, a great deal of research has been undertaken to try and keep bird flu outbreaks in the human population to a minimum, as the CDC demonstrates. Nevertheless, the CDC admits that a great deal more research needs to be done in this specific area:

Studies done in laboratories suggest that some of the antiviral drugs approved in the United States for human influenza viruses should work in treating avian influenza infection in humans. However, influenza viruses can become resistant to these drugs, so these medications may not always work. Additional studies are needed to demonstrate the effectiveness of these medicines. When avian influenza A viruses are identified to cause illness in humans, the viruses should be tested for susceptibility to influenza antiviral medications.

The CDC then turned its attentions to what is termed highly pathogenic Influenza A (H5N1) virus, or, as it's also known, HPAI H5N1 virus. It's particularly notable for its deadly ability to jump from species to species. That's to say, from bird to human. Of the HPAI H5N1 virus, the CDC reveals:

Of the few avian influenza viruses that have crossed the species barrier to infect humans, HPAI H5N1 has caused the largest number of detected cases of severe disease and death in humans. However, it is possible that those cases in the most severely ill people are more likely to be diagnosed and reported, while milder cases are less likely to be detected and reported.

And the seriousness of the virus, and its potential ability to kill on a large scale, should not be underestimated. The CDC has been careful to warn people of the potentially deadly effects of exposure to this particular strain:

//Of the few avian influenza viruses that have crossed the species barrier to infect humans, HPAI H5N1 has caused the largest number of detected cases of severe disease and death in humans."

Of the human cases associated with the ongoing HPAI H5N1 outbreaks in poultry and wild birds in Asia and parts of Europe, the Near East and Africa, about 60% of those people reported infected with the virus have died. Most cases have occurred in previously healthy children and young adults and have resulted from direct or close contact with H5N1-infected poultry or H5N1-contaminated surfaces. In general, HPAI H5N1 remains a very rare disease in people. The HPAI H5N1 virus does not infect humans easily, and if a person is infected, it is very difficult for the virus to spread to another person.

The CDC has words of warning with regard to what the future may bring, when it comes to the matter of avian flu:

Because all influenza viruses have the ability to change and because the HPAI H5N1 known ability to cause human infections, scientists remain concerned that HPAI H5N1 viruses have the potential to possibly change into a form of the virus that is able to spread easily from person to person. Because these viruses do not commonly infect humans, there is little or no immune protection against them in the human population. If HPAI H5N1 virus were to gain the capacity to spread easily from person to person, an influenza pandemic (worldwide outbreak of disease) could begin.

Although the current number of people who, on a worldwide basis, have died from avian flu is only in the hundreds, as the CDC's words above show, that situation could change both significantly and drastically—something that brings us to the world of bird flu-based conspiracies.

In February 2008, an extraordinary story surfaced out of Indonesia. The nation's health minister, Dr. Siti Fadilah Supari, hit the headlines with her then new book, *It's Time for the World to Change: The Divine Hand behind Avian Influenza*. One particular part of the book made the world's media sit up and take notice. It was the allegation that the U.S. government was secretly working to transform bird flu into a deadly, biological weapon. It was an allegation fully endorsed by Indonesia's president, Susilo Bambang Yudhoyono.

Supari became deeply worried by the fact that the World Health Organization shared samples with the United States national laboratory in Los Alamos, New Mexico, where nuclear weapons are developed.

Supari additionally commented (her words can be found in Geoff Thompson's article for ABC.net.au, "US Involved in Bird Flu Conspiracy"):

> Whether they use is it to make vaccine or develop chemical weapons, would depend on the need and interest of the US government. It is indeed a very dangerous situation for the destiny of humanity. It is a matter of choice whether to use the material for vaccines or biological weapon development.

One year later, an Austrian journalist named Jane Bürgermeister filed criminal charges against a wealth of official bodies and agencies, including the FBI, the United Nations, the World Health Organization, and even President Obama, himself.

It was Bürgermeister's conclusion that a vast conspiracy was in the making, one that involved the development of a form of bird flu that (a) was designed to spread all across the planet, and (b) would kill billions in no time at all. In other words, Bürgermeister believed she had uncovered a plot to, in stark essence, cull the herd—chiefly, to keep populations low and under manageable control by a martial law-obsessed New World Order.

In Bürgermeister's very own words (available for inspection at David Icke's article, "Flu Is Not the Biggest Danger … It's The Vaccine!":

> There is evidence that an international corporate criminal syndicate, which has annexed high government office at Federal and State level, is intent on carrying out a mass genocide against the people of the United States by using an artificial (genetic) flu pandemic virus and forced vaccine program to cause mass death and injury and depopulate America in order to transfer control of the United States to the United Nations and affiliated security forces (UN troops from countries such as China, Canada, the UK and Mexico).

She added:

> There is proof many organizations—World Health Organization, UN as well as vaccine companies such as Baxter and Novartis—are part of a single system under the control of a core criminal group, who give the strategic leadership, and who have also funded the development, manufacturing and release of artificial viruses in order to justify mass vaccinations with a bioweapon substance in order to eliminate the people of the USA, and so gain control of the assets, resources etc., of North America.

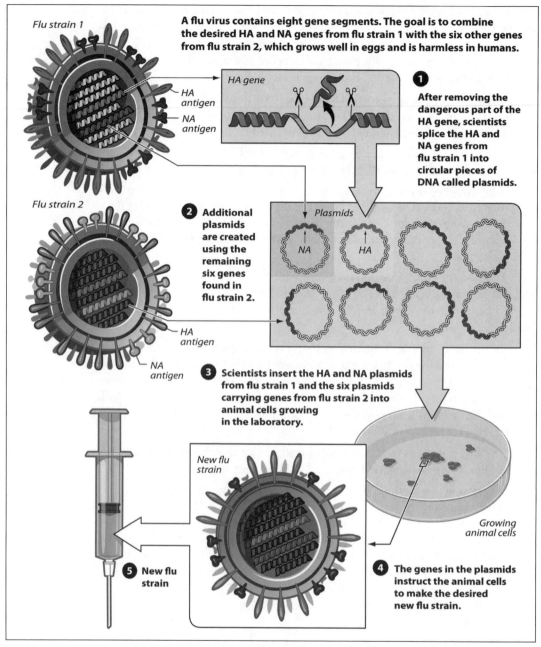

Flu strain 1

A flu virus contains eight gene segments. The goal is to combine the desired HA and NA genes from flu strain 1 with the six other genes from flu strain 2, which grows well in eggs and is harmless in humans.

HA gene

HA antigen

NA antigen

1 After removing the dangerous part of the HA gene, scientists splice the HA and NA genes from flu strain 1 into circular pieces of DNA called plasmids.

Flu strain 2

2 Additional plasmids are created using the remaining six genes found in flu strain 2.

Plasmids

NA

HA

HA antigen

NA antigen

3 Scientists insert the HA and NA plasmids from flu strain 1 and the six plasmids carrying genes from flu strain 2 into animal cells growing in the laboratory.

New flu strain

Growing animal cells

5 New flu strain

4 The genes in the plasmids instruct the animal cells to make the desired new flu strain.

A technique for creating an avian flu vaccine explained in this graphic uses reverse genetics. Similar techniques could be used to create new viruses to commit genocide.

The motivation for the crime is classical robbery followed by murder although the scale and method are new in history. The core group sets its strategic goals and operative priorities in secret using committees such as the Trilateral Commission, and in person to person contact in the annual Bilderberg meeting.

Although Bürgermeister's suit proved unsuccessful in terms of bringing to justice what she perceived to be the guilty parties, she continues her work to expose what she believes is a malignant, worldwide plot to drastically change the face of human civilization.

In 2012, Joseph Kim, the head of Inovio Pharmaceuticals, a company that is striving to develop what would amount to a universal flu vaccine, said (see Jason Koebler's 2012 feature, "Global Flu Pandemic 'Inevitable,' Expert Warns"): "I really believe we were lucky in 2009 because the strain that won out was not particularly lethal. Bird flu kills over 60 percent of people that it infects, regardless of health or age. It is a phenomenal killing machine."

Echoing the words of Kim are those of Ron Fouchier, a Dutch researcher who, in 2011, succeeded in genetically modifying a strain of H5N1 to make it transmissible between ferrets, which are often used to test human-to-human transmissibility. Fouchier openly acknowledged he had just created what was almost certainly one of the "most dangerous viruses you can make."

Paul Keim, an expert in genetics with the U.S. National Science Advisory Board for Biosecurity, had his say on the matter (and is also referenced by Koebler): "I can't think of another pathogenic organism that is as scary as this one. I don't think anthrax is scary at all compared to this."

Then, in April 2013, a Chinese Air Force officer, Colonel Dai Xu, of the People's Liberation Army, said that the then current outbreak of H7N9 bird flu amounted to a deliberate spreading of the virus by U.S. forces. In response, former Department of State intelligence analyst John Tkacik, branded Xu "a shameless liar."

Today, the world waits, wondering when and where the next outbreak of avian flu will occur. Wherever it may be, and whether the result of Mother Nature or a secret, government lab, of only one thing can we be sure: there will be human deaths.

BIN LADEN'S BODY: WHERE'S THE EVIDENCE?

It was, and to this day remains, one of the most controversial and mystery-filled killings of all time. It is a saga filled with conspiracy theories, with intense doubts about the official version of events, and with shadowy and powerful players with even more shadowy and powerful agendas. We are talking about the May 2011 killing of Osama bin Laden. Or, as many conspiracy theorists prefer it: the *alleged* killing of Osama bin Laden. Before we get to matters shrouded in cover-up and chicanery, let's take a look at the official story of bin Laden's final hours. It goes like this....

Osama bin Laden—the brains behind al-Qaeda and the events of September 11, 2001—was shot and killed on May 2, 2011, by U.S. Navy Seals attached to the U.S. Naval Special Warfare Development Group. Or, as they are far better known: Team Six. Shrouded in overwhelming secrecy, the goal of the project—which was controlled by the CIA and designated the title of *Operation Neptune Spear*—was to launch a team from Afghanistan and have it make its stealthy way into neighboring Pakistan.

Upon crossing the border, the project called for the Seals to take out bin Laden in his fortified base of operations—at Abbottabad, Pakistan. The operation was apparently a complete success: bin Laden was quickly located and salvo upon salvo of bullets ensured he would no longer pose a threat to the free world. The body of bin Laden was then carefully examined to confirm it really was him, after which the corpse was hastily, and secretly, buried at sea.

It wasn't long afterwards that President Obama told the world that one of the most feared men on the planet was no more. In part, Obama's statement to the nation and the world went as follows (see "President Obama's Speech on Osama bin Laden's Death"):

> Good evening. Tonight, I can report to the American people and to the world that the United States has conducted an operation that killed Osama bin Laden, the leader of al Qaeda, and a terrorist who's responsible for the murder of thousands of innocent men, women, and children.
>
> It was nearly ten years ago that a bright September day was darkened by the worst attack on the American people in our history. The images of 9/11 are seared into our national memory—hijacked planes cutting

through a cloudless September sky; the Twin Towers collapsing to the ground; black smoke billowing up from the Pentagon; the wreckage of Flight 93 in Shanksville, Pennsylvania, where the actions of heroic citizens saved even more heartbreak and destruction.

The president added:

Shortly after taking office, I directed Leon Panetta, the director of the CIA, to make the killing or capture of bin Laden the top priority of our war against al Qaeda, even as we continued our broader efforts to disrupt, dismantle, and defeat his network.

Then, last August, after years of painstaking work by our intelligence community, I was briefed on a possible lead to bin Laden. It was far from certain, and it took many months to run this thread to ground. I met repeatedly with my national security team as we developed more information about the possibility that we had located bin Laden hiding within a compound deep inside of Pakistan. And finally, last week, I determined that we had enough intelligence to take action, and authorized an operation to get Osama bin Laden and bring him to justice.

The logo designed by the military for Operation Neptune Spear includes (left to right) seals for the CIA, the Naval Special Warfare Command, the Joint Special Operation Command, and the Night Stalkers (160th Special Operations Aviation Regiment), all of which participated in the operation to track down and capture or kill Osama bin Laden.

Today, at my direction, the United States launched a targeted operation against that compound in Abbottabad, Pakistan. A small team of Americans carried out the operation with extraordinary courage and capability. No Americans were harmed. They took care to avoid civilian casualties. After a firefight, they killed Osama bin Laden and took custody of his body.

For over two decades, bin Laden has been al Qaeda's leader and symbol, and has continued to plot attacks against our country and our friends and allies. The death of bin Laden marks the most significant achievement to date in our nation's effort to defeat al Qaeda.

Yet his death does not mark the end of our effort. There's no doubt that al Qaeda will continue to pursue attacks against us. We must—and we will—remain vigilant at home and abroad.

As we do, we must also reaffirm that the United States is not—and never will be—at war with Islam. I've made clear, just as President Bush did shortly after 9/11, that our war is not against Islam. Bin Laden was not a Muslim leader; he was a mass murderer of Muslims. Indeed, al Qaeda has slaughtered scores of Muslims in many countries, including our own. So his demise should be welcomed by all who believe in peace and human dignity.

On May 1, 2011, U.S. leaders sat in the White House Situation Room to hear news about the mission to finally find Osama bin Laden. Seated around the table (left to right) are Vice President Joe Biden, President Barack Obama, Brigadier General Marshall B. Webb of the U.S. Air Force (Assistant Commanding General, Joint Special Operations Command), Deputy National Security Adviser Denis McDonough, Secretary of State Hilary Clinton, and Secretary of Defense Robert Gates.

The statement made by the president, that bin Laden was indeed killed in his Abbottabad compound, was reinforced by senior members of al-Qaeda—four days later and across the Internet. Those same senior members made no bones about the fact that they would have their revenge on the West—and on Pakistan, too, for helping the operation come to fruition. The response to bin Laden's passing was, very understandably, a positive and welcome one. The European Union, the United Nations, and both the U.S. Senate and Congress were suitably satisfied and relieved at the outcome. It wasn't long, however, before people—and *lots* of people—began asking questions about the official line, with some even accusing President Obama, the CIA, and the military of outright lying about what really happened—or what didn't happen.

It's abundantly obvious why so many conspiracy theorists expressed deep doubts and cynicism about bin Laden's alleged killing. Absolutely no solid evidence—in terms of photographs of bin Laden's corpse, film footage taken at the scene, DNA, audio recordings, documents, images shot at the funeral at sea, or statements from the team involved—was ever presented to the world to see and scrutinize, not even in the slightest. Was this because of fears of bin Laden being turned into a martyr? Or, incredibly, was it because the official story was nothing less than a bald-faced lie?

It's important to be aware it wasn't just conspiracy theorists that noted certain inconsistencies in the version of events we are told was the truth. Even the United States' media expressed puzzlement as it sought to uncover something, *anything*, to try and confirm the story. The likes of Fox News, CBS News, Reuters, Citizens United, and Associated Press all did their very best to use the Freedom of Information Act to force open the doors of secrecy. Each and every one of them spectacularly failed. Then, when it was revealed that close to half-an-hour of the live feed that recorded the raid on bin Laden's compound was mysteriously missing, people *really* began to wonder what the truth was.

The government knew that it had to make a statement and it did. The official line was that the decision not to reveal any photographs showing the body of bin Laden was simply because they were overly graphic, displayed him riddled with bullets, and were perceived as too shocking for mainstream audiences. This was a scenario that received a degree of backing and support from Jim Inhofe; he was both a senator (with the Republican Party) and a member of the Senate Armed Services Committee. Inhofe went on record as saying he had seen certain images of bin Laden after his death. He came straight to the point and said the photos were "gruesome." Inhofe had no doubt about the authenticity of the pictures, which he had viewed at some point before May 11.

Since the government admitted that imagery did exist and Inhofe confirmed he had seen it, further steps were taken by the media to try and secure the priceless data. One of the most interesting developments came in April 2012. That was when Judicial Watch—a group that was determined to get to the bottom of the puzzle—had its case against the Department of Defense thrown out of court. The U.S. Federal Court tossed out Judicial Watch's argument that the terms of the Freedom of Information Act should allow for the release of evidence of bin Laden's death. The court disagreed. Judicial Watch was far from happy: "The court got it terribly wrong. There is no provision under the Freedom of Information Act that allows documents to be kept secret because their release might offend our terrorist enemies. We will appeal."

Most people, by now, will not be surprised to know that appealing made absolutely no difference whatsoever.

So much for the overwhelmingly unsuccessful attempts to get hard evidence of Osama bin Laden's death, but what about that burial at sea? Simply an attempt to ensure that one of the world's most hated men never had a grave that his followers were able to turn into a shrine? Or, was the story merely that—a story? And, if so, was it a tale created as a convenient way to explain why there *was* no corpse? Maybe there never had been a corpse. Certainly, that was the view of many within conspiracy-themed domains.

As with the matter of the photographs, let's first begin with the government's position—and statements—on the sunken body of bin Laden. The Obama

The U.S. Federal Court tossed out Judicial Watch's argument that the terms of the Freedom of Information Act should allow for the release of evidence of bin Laden's death.

administration has explained its position on why the body of the notorious terrorist was buried at sea. It relates to Muslim traditions. Within Muslim culture, the dead must be buried inside one day, that's to say, twenty-four hours. The problem with bin Laden, the White House said, was that given the unique circumstances it became clear there would not be sufficient time to (a) raid bin Laden's compound, (b) kill him, (c) have his DNA confirmed, (d) prepare the body, and (e) then bury it according to Muslim traditions, all within one day. So, the only option was to quickly have bin Laden's corpse taken out to sea and dumped as soon as possible.

That particular scenario is not out of the question. But, doubt has been cast upon it for one specific reason. On July 22, 2003, U.S. military personnel—in the Iraqi city of Mosul—shot and killed Saddam Hussein's sons Uday and Qusay, who were hiding out in a villa in the city. Almost two weeks went by before the bodies of both men were relinquished by the military for a burial. In view of this, conspiracy theorists ask: Why was there a pressing need to get rid of bin Laden's body in one day, when the circumstances surrounding the deaths and burials of Uday and Qusay Hussein were very different? All three were Muslims. Therefore, if the government was so intent on ensuring that bin Laden was buried within twenty-four hours, why did that rule not apply to Saddam Hussein's sons?

It wasn't just conspiracy theorists who questioned the reasons why bin Laden was dumped at sea. Peter Romaniuk, a respected professor at John Jay College, gave his opinion on the curious state of affairs (an opinion referenced in Alison Bowen's "Osama bin Laden: Conspiracy Theories Thrive on Lack of Proof"): "Obviously they're going to be under pressure to show a body or produce further evidence, but this was a way of taking that issue off the table."

A further development in the story suggested that the entire angle of the shoot-out at Abbottabad, Pakistan, was completely fictitious. One person who was extremely vocal on this particular matter was Hamid Gul, the former head of Pakistan's Inter-Services Intelligence (ISI), who believed that bin Laden actually passed away a number of years earlier. Commenting on the U.S. government, Gul said (see "In the Arena," May 5, 2011):

They must have known that he had died some years ago so they were waiting. They were keeping this story on ice and they were looking for an appropriate moment. And it couldn't be a better moment because President Obama had to fight off his first salvo in his next year's election as he runs for the presidential and for the White House. And I think it is a very appropriate time to come out, bring this out of the closet.

A somewhat similar scenario was suggested by staff on the Urdu newspaper *Ausaf.* Patrick Kingsley and Sam Jones note this in 2011, in "Osama bin Laden Death: The Conspiracy Theories"): "Bin Laden has been killed somewhere else. But since the U.S. intends to extend the Afghan war into Pakistan, and accuse

Pakistan, and obtain a permit for its military's entry into the country, it has devised the scenario."

And the theories and assertions that bin Laden did not die under the circumstances—or even in the same time frame or location—as the Obama administration suggested, continued at a steady and controversial pace. An Iranian Member of Parliament, Javad Jahangirzadeh, said that he had information suggesting the United States was behind the 9/11 atrocities and that bin Laden had played a dutiful, witting, and helpful role in the events. Kingsley and Jones quoted his words: "The West has been very pleased with bin Laden's operations in recent years. Now the West was forced to kill him in order to prevent a possible leak of information he had, information more precious than gold."

Iran's President Mahmoud Ahmadinejad had his say, too: "I have exact information that bin Laden was held by the American military for sometime [and] until the day they killed him he was a prisoner held by them."

Of course, one can make the highly justifiable observation that the Iranians have no love for the United States, so they *would* say that—and much worse, too. But, it was not just the Iranians who maintained that what the world was told was not what actually happened. A famous and controversial radio host made his thoughts very clear. It was Alex Jones, host of the Austin, Texas-based *The Alex Jones Show*, and someone whose YouTube page has been viewed on an astonishing *400 million-plus* occasions.

When he was interviewed on *Russia Today*, Jones revealed that a contact in the White House—unnamed, unfortunately; although some might say predictably—had told him that bin Laden died more than a decade earlier. The story continued that the body of the terrorist had been carefully preserved—in liquid nitrogen, no less—until such a time when he would be "rolled out" and his death announced.

Even respected politicians were determined to have their say. The Canadian deputy Leader of the Opposition and MP, Thomas Mulcair, was careful and tactful in his words, but they left very little room for doubt with regard to his views on the matter (see: "Conspiracy Theory: NDP Deputy Leader Mulcair Doubts U.S. Has bin Laden Photos"): "I don't think from what I've heard that those pictures exist."

Finally, we have a story that surfaced in March 2014, one which suggests a down to earth explanation, after all, for why no photos or footage were released to confirm bin Laden's death, and why normal burial procedures were not adhered to for the notorious terrorist. On March 14 Britain's *Daily Mail* newspaper reported (in "Navy SEALs 'Took Turns Dumping HUNDREDS of Bullets' into Osama bin Laden's

On July 22, 2003, troops from the 101st Airborne Division surrounded a house in Mosul, Iraq, in which Saddam Hussein's sons Uday and Qusay were hiding. The two men were killed during the ensuing gun battle.

J ones revealed that a contact in the White House ... had told him that bin Laden died more than a decade earlier.

Dead Body, a New Report Reveals") that a new story had surfaced that could put to rest the conspiracy theories. Citing an account that came from, as the newspaper described it, "a website known within the intelligence and armed services community," *Daily Mail* staff revealed that bin Laden's face and body had been horrifically mutilated by the effects of having more than one hundred bullets pumped into his body by U.S. troops.

The *Daily Mail* said: "Citing two confidential sources, *The Special Operations Forces Situation Report* tells how 'operator after operator took turns dumping magazines-worth of ammunition into Bin Laden's body.'"

The author of the online report to which the *Daily Mail* referred was Jack Murphy, who said: "What happened on the Bin Laden raid is beyond excessive. The level of excess shown was not about making sure that Bin Laden was no longer a threat. The excess was pure self-indulgence."

The *Daily Mail* concluded:

At the time of the assassination, President Obama and his administration argued that they were justified in never releasing the photos of the dead body or the burial at sea because they could be used as propaganda for al-Qaeda. The new theories, however, suggest that they are just trying to avoid retribution for allegedly being excessive.

It's unlikely that—even if true—*The Special Operations Forces Situation Report's* story will successfully lay to rest the conspiracy theories that suggest the official story of bin Laden's final hours amounted to nothing but lies and deceit. In all likelihood, the shooting of bin Laden will become the JFK assassination of the Age of Terror, yet another controversial death filled with conflicting stories, numerous theories, but very few hard facts anywhere in sight.

SNOWDEN AND SURVEILLANCE: BIG BROTHER REALITY

Nineteen Eighty Four is a satirical novel of a definitively political nature, written by George Orwell in 1949. The story takes place in a nightmarish society in which not only does the state demand one hundred percent conformity via indoctrination, punishment, fear, and propaganda, it also intrudes into the lives of one and all via constant surveillance and spying. Such a thing couldn't happen in the real world, could it? Wake up, world: it already has. Welcome to the revelations of the planet's most notorious whistleblower since Watergate's Deep Throat. We're talking about Edward Snowden. Up until the summer of 2013, he was a man unknown to just about everyone except his family, friends, and work colleagues. Specifically after the summer of 2013, practically everyone knew his name.

It was not so much who Snowden was that caught the world's attention but what he had to say. As an employee of the National Security Agency (NSA), Snowden blew the whistle just about as loudly as he possibly could on the alarming and near-unbelievable extent to which the NSA was spying not just on foreign nations but on U.S. citizens too—as in just about each and every one of them. Landlines, cell-phones, email, Facebook, Twitter, and Skype: they had all been penetrated by the NSA, very often with the witting, subservient, and unforgivable help of those same companies. The data collection process was so mind-bogglingly huge that it would likely have had even George Orwell himself shaking his head in disbelief, except for just one thing: this was all too real.

To some, Snowden is an outright national hero, one who succeeded in demonstrating to the world that the NSA is an agency run riot in its goal to place the entire United States under electronic surveillance. To others, he is a man who has jeopardized U.S. national security and placed our troops in danger. To many people, Snowden falls somewhere between both. Before we get to the matter of what, precisely, Snowden revealed, let us take a look at the man's background.

Born in 1983, in North Carolina, Edward Snowden has had an interesting, albeit turbulent, life. Despite the fact that he is constantly and near-consistently referred to as an "NSA whistleblower," Snowden has proved, in his thirty-something years, to have been much more than that. It's interesting to note that practically the entire Snowden family has had significant links to officialdom. Snowden's mother works for the U.S. District Court. His grandfather, Edward J. Barrett, held a senior position in the Federal Bureau of Investigation. And his father served in the Coast

Edward Snowden fled to Russia after leaking information about the U.S. National Security Agency to the American public.

Guard. It was, then, perhaps, inevitable that Edward Snowden would also gravitate to a government job—and he did, several of them, actually.

From May to September 2004, Snowden was with the United States Navy Reserve, that is, until a serious accident, in which his legs were broken, prompted his exit. One year later, Snowden held a position of sensitivity at the Center for Advanced Study of Language. Evidently, Snowden was seen as a potentially valuable asset to U.S. intelligence, as in the following year, 2006, he signed up with none other than the CIA, where he was employed in the agency's Global Communications Division. He stayed with the CIA until 2009.

It was in that year Snowden took a job with Dell, Inc. This was no normal job, however. Dell has contracts with numerous U.S. government, military, and intelligence agencies, meaning that it wasn't long before Snowden was working for Dell at an NSA installation in Fussa, Japan, where much of his daily work revolved around combating the threats posed by computer hackers.

Two years later, Snowden was back in the United States, working on Dell-CIA programs. Then, in early 2012, Snowden was reassigned to Hawaii, where he not only held a senior position with the NSA, but began to see how the NSA was increasingly violating the constitution of the United States, engaging in widespread surveillance of the American people, and watching an untold number of individuals whose daily activities had no bearing upon national security or the defense of the nation and the free world. So, disillusioned and outraged by what he had seen, Snowden decided to do something about it: he went public in just about the biggest way possible.

The story of the process by which revealed Snowden to the world the nature of the information he was in possession of, and how he came to be in possession of it, surfaced bit by bit, piece by piece. So far as can be ascertained, it was around one month after he started working in Hawaii that Snowden started to download massive amounts of documentation that detailed the many shocking, violations of law that Snowden wished to expose. The actual number of documents that Snowden accessed, downloaded, released to the press, and others that are yet to surface, was estimated in some media quarters and government quarters to be close to a quarter of a million.

On May 20, 2013, Snowden took a flight to Hong Kong. He knew it would not be long before the authorities were to his tail, and so, the very last place he needed to be was Hawaii. It was while in Hong Kong that Snowden briefed journalist Glenn Greenwald (of *Guardian US*) and film producer-director Laura Poitras on what was going down deep in the heart of the National Security Agency. On June 5, the Snowden revelations began to surface in the press; as did, several days later, Snowden's name.

> **W**ithout doubt the biggest and most shocking revelations centered upon something that is called PRISM.

The U.S. government took immediate steps to try and curtail Snowden's actions: He faced a three-decades-long jail term for breaking the terms of the Espionage Act, and his passport was revoked. Snowden was very quickly a man on the run. Where, exactly, he ran to—or, rather, flew to—was Moscow, Russia's Sheremetyevo International Airport. Despite initial concerns on Snowden's part that he would not be allowed to stay—because of certain visa issues—his fears were soon eased when he was given a 365-day period of asylum. That has since been extended to a three-year period of asylum. At the time of writing, Snowden remains in Russia, living in secret, and doing his utmost to be allowed to live out his life somewhere in Europe.

So, what was it that caused so much consternation for the United States government, and specifically for the NSA? A great deal, that's what.

Without doubt the biggest and most shocking revelations centered upon something that is called PRISM. Essentially, PRISM is a program that both collects and stores electronic data—and on a massive scale. We have to "thank" President George W. Bush for pushing PRISM through, via the terms of (a) the Protect America Act of 2007, which was implemented on August 5 of that year; and (b) the FISA Amendments Act of 2008—FISA standing for Foreign Intelligence Surveillance Act. Collectively, the acts permit the gathering of electronic data from countless sources—and, in the process, protects those same sources from prosecution.

What outraged so many was who, precisely, the sources were that Snowden knew of and blew the whistle on. They included Sprint, Yahoo, AT&T, Facebook, YouTube, Verizon, Google, Skype, Microsoft, Apple, and Paltalk—and that was just the top of the long list. In no time at all, the world realized the implications of all this: the National Security Agency practically had carte blanche to wade through the emails, photos, instant messages, Skype conversations (both audio and video), texts, file-transfers, voice-mail messages, and live conversations by phone and Net, of every U.S. citizen and resident—and without hardly a concern for the law or matters relative to personal privacy.

If all the NSA was doing was carefully watching the activities of potential or known terrorists, others who wish to do us harm, and those who are possible threats to the security of the nation, very few people would likely have any complaints. But, as the Snowden revelations showed, that's not what was, or still is, going on. Hospitals, universities, private corporations, and even libraries were targeted, as were bank records, doctor-patient files, and more.

Glenn Greenwald said (and is quoted in Kari Rea's "Glenn Greenwald: Low-Level NSA Analysts Have 'Powerful and Invasive' Search Tool") that the NSA's employees "listen to whatever emails they want, whatever telephone calls, browsing histories, Microsoft Word documents. And it's all done with no need to go to a court, with no need to even get supervisor approval on the part of the analyst."

It wasn't long after the Snowden revelations stunned the world that the National Security Agency hit back, and hit back majorly. On June 7, 2013, the director of National Intelligence, James Clapper, confirmed that, yes, the NSA was working with the likes of Facebook and Google. But, he clarified this by stating that the program only targeted overseas individuals and groups that were potentially threatening to the United States.

Clapper added ("Reports about PRISM Contain 'Numerous Inaccuracies,'" 2013):

> *The Guardian* and *The Washington Post* articles refer to collection of communications pursuant to Section 702 of the Foreign Intelligence Surveillance Act. They contain numerous inaccuracies. Section 702 is a provision of FISA that is designed to facilitate the acquisition of foreign intelligence information concerning non-U.S. persons located outside the United States. It cannot be used to intentionally target any U.S. citizen, any other U.S. person, or anyone located within the United States. The unauthorized disclosure of information about this important and entirely

The National Security Operations Center in Washington, D.C., has been a hub of activity in snooping on the American public.

legal program is reprehensible and risks important protections for the security of Americans.

This statement was made on the back of another statement from Clapper—on March 13, 2013, when he said the NSA wasn't "wittingly" collecting data on hundreds of millions of Americans. It turned out this was all nothing but a bald-faced lie; the Snowden files showed the NSA was doing exactly that. Clapper said, when caught (see Olivier Knox's "Intelligence Chief Clapper: I Gave 'Least Untruthful' Answer on U.S. Spying"): "I responded in what I thought was the most truthful, or least untruthful manner by saying no."

June 7 was also the day on which President Obama weighed in on the increasingly incendiary situation (see "Transcript: Obama's Remarks on NSA Controversy"):

> What you've got is two programs that were originally authorized by Congress, have been repeatedly authorized by Congress. Congress is continually briefed on how these are conducted. Bipartisan majorities have approved them. There are a whole range of safeguards involved. And federal judges are overseeing the entire program throughout. You can't have 100 percent security and then also have 100 percent privacy and zero inconvenience. You know, we're going to have to make some choices as a society.

And the revelations kept on coming. In March 2014, in an article penned by Glenn Greenwald and Ryan Gallagher ("How the NSA Plans to Infect 'Millions' of Computers with Malware"), it was stated:

> Top-secret documents reveal that the National Security Agency is dramatically expanding its ability to covertly hack into computers on a mass scale by using automated systems that reduce the level of human oversight in the process.

> The classified files—provided previously by NSA whistleblower Edward Snowden—contain new details about groundbreaking surveillance technology the agency has developed to infect potentially millions of computers worldwide with malware "implants." The clandestine initiative enables the NSA to break into targeted computers and to siphon out data from foreign Internet and phone networks.

> The covert infrastructure that supports the hacking efforts operates from the agency's headquarters in Fort Meade, Maryland, and from eavesdropping bases in the United Kingdom and Japan. GCHQ, the British intelligence agency, appears to have played an integral role in helping to develop the implants tactic.

What was, almost certainly, the biggest and most disturbing revelation surfaced in July 2014. *The Washington Post* discovered that, from information provided by Snowden, around ninety percent of those secretly watched by the NSA had no ties to matters of a national security nature—at all. They were, as the newspaper simply put it, "ordinary Americans."

It was reported (in the *Louisiana State News*'s article "Vast Majority of NSA Spy Targets Are Mistakenly Monitored"):

> Some 160,000 emails and instant-messages and 7,900 documents from 11,000 online accounts, gathered by the NSA between 2009 and 2012, have been examined by the *Washington Post*, which alleges that nine out of ten of the account holders were not the intended targets.

The story continued that the information gathered provides a startling insight into the lives of ordinary Americans, but is not of any intelligence value. For the most part, the electronic data that was under the scrutiny of the NSA revolved around "love and heartbreak, illicit sexual liaisons, mental-health crises, political and religious conversions, financial anxieties and disappointed hopes."

This chapter started with George Orwell of *Nineteen Eighty Four* fame. It will end with him, too. Orwell said (see "George Orwell Quotes") something memorable that could easily apply to Edward Snowden and his decision to blow the whistle on the National Security Agency: "In a time of universal deceit, telling the truth becomes a revolutionary act."

THE MYSTERY OF MH370: A VANISHING PLANE

The March 8, 2014, disappearance of Malaysia Airlines's Flight MH370 captured the attention of conspiracy theorists everywhere; it was an event that the world's media latched onto and would not let go of (for very understandable reasons), and that deeply worried the governments of numerous nations. For the crew and passengers of the ultimately doomed plane, the day began just like any other. It most assuredly did not stay that way, however.

The plane, a Boeing 777, took to the skies from Malaysia's Kuala Lumpur International Airport, situated in the state of Selangor. The time was 12:41 A.M. Its destination was Beijing Capital International Airport, China, where it was due to arrive at 6:30 A.M. On board were a dozen crew and more than 200 passengers. What should have been a routine flight turned out to be the exact opposite when the aircraft vanished—as in, it *literally* vanished. Indeed, since that fateful day, when MH370 soared into the air, neither it, nor anyone aboard, has ever been seen again. Hardly surprisingly, a multitude of conspiracy theories surfaced in the immediate aftermath of the disappearance of aircraft, crew, and passengers.

The only things that can be confirmed thus far are those that occurred *prior* to the disappearance of MH370; everything else is wide open to question and interpretation. The takeoff from Kuala Lumpur was a smooth and uneventful one. All was good until some point after 1:19 A.M. That was when the very last verbal contact was made with the crew. Their final words: "Goodnight, Malaysian three-seven-zero." Only three minutes later, something deeply disturbing happened: the aircraft's transponder ceased working.

Then, as the 777 flew over the Gulf of Thailand, it vanished from secondary radars. While it's not certain, investigators believe that the aircraft then turned in a westerly direction. At 2:22 A.M., military radar made a definite lock-on with MH370 over the Malacca Strait. From there, it's anyone's guess. The most prevailing theory is that the aircraft continued to fly for around six hours, at which point it plunged into the depths of the southern section of the Indian Ocean. The biggest mystery of all was: Why, exactly, did the crew choose to change its flight plan? Were they forced to do so by terrorists? Was it all due to the actions of the pilot? Whatever the answer, Malaysian authorities considered—and *still* consider—the change in course to have been a "deliberate event."

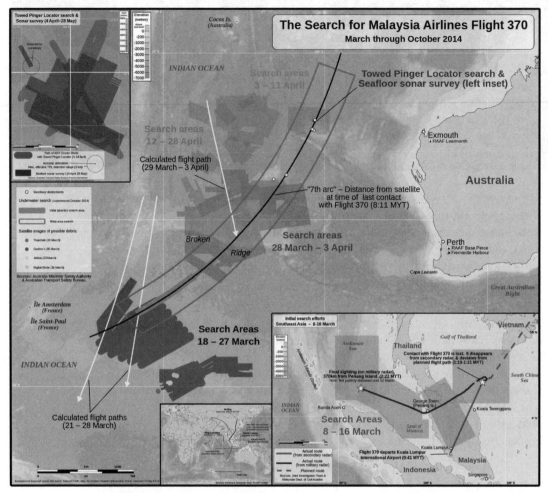

The massive search for Flight MH370 covered large swathes of the Indian Ocean without luck.

When it became clear that MH370 was lost, a huge search was quickly launched to try and find the aircraft and, hopefully, at least some survivors of whatever it was that had caused the loss of the aircraft. Such was the sheer scale of the search—which, ultimately, involved the cooperation of numerous nations—it became the most costly one in the history of aviation-based disasters.

Although initial searches were focused on the China Sea and the Gulf of Thailand, eventually the quest became more and more directed towards the Indian Ocean, specifically west of Australia. The likelihood was that since this particular area was far from land, the 777 slammed into the ocean, killing all those aboard, and sinking to the ocean floor, whether utterly shattered or semi-intact. The biggest puzzle in this scenario, however, is why—despite initial searches that proved promising—no signal from the aircraft's black boxes was ever found. Also, why was no tell-tale wreckage from MH370 ever seen floating on, or even recovered from, the surface of the ocean? Who was piloting the plane at the time? Did they have a covert agenda?

Malaysian authorities recognized not just the tragedy in all this, but the profound weirdness too. Three days after the disappearance, Dato' Azharuddin Abrul Rahman, the director general of the Department of Civil Aviation (DCA), said:

> Our heart goes to the next of kin of the passengers and all of us would like to know what actually happened on the ill-fated flight MAS Boeing 777 flight number MH370 registration 9MMRO. The DCA with all the assisting agencies have conducted a thorough rescue and search operation over a very wide area—South China Sea that covered the 50 nautical mile radius.
>
> On the point of where the last aircraft was reported in the morning of Saturday, 8th March, 2014, we also conducted search[es] in the areas of north Straits of Malacca, as we do not want to discount possibilities of the aircraft air turn back to the Straits of Malacca.
>
> And we also receive cooperation, a very good cooperation from neighboring countries to assist DCA in our effort to locate the missing aircraft. And so to date we use a large number of assets comprising of 34 aircrafts, 40 ships, hundred over men, thousand over man hours, as we deployed.
>
> And countries that assisted us include Vietnam, China, Singapore, Indonesia, USA, Thailand, Australia and Philippines. The air search was conducted daily from 7 am to 7 pm. And the search by the ships continue throughout the night and unfortunately ladies and gentlemen, we have not found anything that appears to be objects from the aircraft, let alone the aircraft.

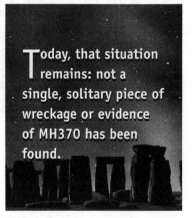

Today, that situation remains: not a single, solitary piece of wreckage or evidence of MH370 has been found.

Today, that situation remains: not a single, solitary piece of wreckage or evidence of MH370 has been found. For all intents and purposes it is gone. As to where and why, they are the issues that have provoked so many conspiracy theories.

Perhaps inevitably, and maybe with just cause, a great deal of suspicion fell on the crew. The pilot was fifty-three-year-old Zaharie Ahmad Shah, and the co-pilot was Fariq Abdul Hamid, who was twenty-seven. It turns out that on at least a couple of occasions, Hamid—in direct violation of aviation safety rules—had allowed non-cleared people into the cockpit, to have their photos taken with him, *during* flights, no less. He apparently smoked on flights, too. None of this, of course, is evidence of wrongdoing on a massive scale. But, a question was asked, in light of this: might Hamid's propensity to bend the rules have inadvertently allowed terrorists to gain access to the cockpit and overwhelm the crew?

Far more suspicious than the actions of Hamid were those of the pilot, Zaharie Ahmad Shah, who had worked for Malaysian Airlines since 1981. In the aftermath of the disappearance of MH370, police raided the home of Shah. In doing so they discovered something deeply troubling. Shah had, in his home, a flight

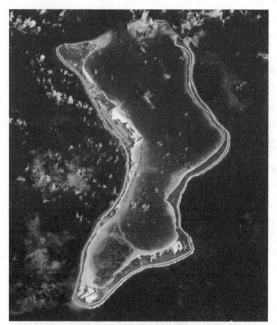

The remote island of Diego Garcia is owned by the British but is home to the U.S. Navy's Naval Support Facility. Conspiracy theorist He Xin believes Flight MH370 landed there in secret because it carried a secret.

simulator. It was one he had used to plot a course to an island in the Indian Ocean. Even more suspicious, Shah had later deleted the data from the simulator—although it was recovered by computer specialists who were tasked with studying the simulator's contents.

Attention has also been focused on the passengers: 153 were Chinese. The rest was a mixture of French, Australian, Canadian, Dutch, Iranian, Indonesian, and Ukrainian citizens. Particular attention was given to two Iranian men who were traveling with stolen passports. Initially, this lead seemed promising, until it was quickly determined that both men were simply trying to make their way to Germany and leave the hostile, Iranian regime behind them. Their actions, then, were born out of desperation, rather than out of anything more sinister.

Another theory suggests that the plane was flown to, and landed on, the island of Diego Garcia. It's an island owned by the United Kingdom that is home to a U.S. military base. Supposedly the United States had a deep and vested interest in securing a "special person" or "special object" allegedly on the plane. One of those who have promoted this theory is a Chinese blogger in the field of conspiracy theories, He Xin. Quite who this person or what this object might be has never been made clear, although Xin maintains that the aircraft was systematically taken apart at a hangar at the base, and then dumped in deep, ocean waters. Despite the fantastic and unlikely nature of the theory, it must be noted that such was the speed with which this theory took hold—and continues to have numerous supporters—U.S. officials from the American Embassy in Malaysia felt obliged to make an official denial of its validity.

Very quickly, in the aftermath of the disappearance of Flight MH370, a book was written titled *Flight MH370: The Mystery*. The author was a man named Nigel Cawthorne. He claimed that the aircraft may have been accidentally shot down by personnel involved in a joint U.S.–Thailand military exercise in the South China Sea. Cawthorne noted (see: Adam Withnall's "Missing Malaysia Airlines Flight MH370 Was 'Shot Down in Military Training Excercise' Claims First Book Released about Lost Jet"): "The drill was to involve mock warfare on land, in water, and in the air, and would include live-fire exercises." Of course, there is a significant problem with this theory: A sudden, explosive impact that brought down the plane would still not explain why the aircraft went mysteriously off-course.

A deeply alternative scenario was offered by Christopher Green, of the appropriately named Alternative Media Television. Green's theory was that the aircraft had been hijacked by terrorists and that those same terrorists, right now, might be "retrofitting this plane, arming it with a nuclear bomb for a later attack that could literally destroy and blow up an entire American city."

A long-time investigator of conspiracies, Mike Adams, was hot on the trail of the truth, practically immediately after the disappearance occurred. He said (and is quoted in Tom Philips's September 2014 article for the *Telegraph* newspaper, "MH370: Six 'Reasons' Why Plane Vanished"): "There are some astonishing things you're not being told about Malaysia Airlines Flight 370." One of those "things," said Adams, was "some entirely new, mysterious and powerful force" that had the ability to pull "airplanes out of the sky without leaving behind even a shred of evidence. If there does exist a weapon with such capabilities, whoever controls it already has the ability to dominate all of Earth's nations with a fearsome military weapon of unimaginable Power. That thought is a lot more scary than the idea of an aircraft suffering a fatal mechanical failure."

And the theories continue—with varying degrees of credibility.

One scenario that has gained a fair amount of traction offers that MH370 was taken over by Chinese Uighur Muslim separatists. It is a fact that more than fifty percent of the passengers were Chinese. The theory suggests the aircraft was flown to China's Taklamakan Desert—for reasons that remain tantalizingly unknown. Despite the unlikely nature of this version of events, the BBC's Jonah Fisher reported (see: Tom de Castella's article "Missing Malaysia Plane: 10 Theories Examined"): "Being briefed by Malaysia officials they believe most likely location for MH370 is on land somewhere near Chinese/Kyrgyz border."

While such a possibility is not entirely out of the question, it is let down by one critical issue: to reach the location, whoever was flying the plane would have had to take it into the airspace of several nations. That none of those same nations reported an out-of-place aircraft in their skies, or any kind of suspicious activity from a plane refusing to identify itself, is a strong indicator the theory lacks validity.

Diego Garcia was not the only island identified as a potential landing site for MH370. India's Nicobar and Andaman Islands—which amount to the most eastern parts of India, and which are situated between the coasts of Thailand, Burma, and Indonesia—have also been suggested as possible candidates. The editor of the *Andaman Chronicle* newspaper poured complete and utter scorn on the story. Although it's a fact that the island has four runways, the newspaper noted that to have such an aircraft land there, and not be noticed, was absurd. On the other side of the coin, conspiracy theorists noted that of the 570 islands that comprise the Andamans, only three-dozen are inhabited.

Steve Buzdygan, who flew 777s, said that, in theory, a skilled pilot could have landed the plane on one of the islands, providing there was at least a stretch of around 5,000 feet on which to land, slow down, and, finally, stop the plane. Buzdygan suggested that the best way to achieve this would be by keeping the wheels up and landing the plane on its belly—which, given the fuel contained in the wings, would have been a decidedly hazardous maneuver to attempt.

Keith Ledgerwood, an expert in the field of aviation and a blogger too, has offered an ingenious, and perhaps not overly unlikely, scenario that whoever was flying the plane essentially camouflaged it by using the radar signature of another aircraft in the area: Flight SIA 68. Ledgerwood said in de Castella's article: "It became apparent as I inspected SIA68's flight path history that MH370 had maneuvered itself directly behind SIA68 at approximately 18:00UTC and over the next 15 minutes had been following SIA68."

Ledgerwood continued to outline his theory:

It is my belief that MH370 likely flew in the shadow of SIA68 through India and Afghanistan airspace. As MH370 was flying "dark" without a transponder, SIA68 would have had no knowledge that MH370 was anywhere around, and as it entered Indian airspace, it would have shown up as one single blip on the radar with only the transponder information of SIA68 lighting up ATC and military radar screens.

As for the final destination of Flight 370, Ledgerwood said: "There are several locations along the flight path of SIA68 where it could have easily broken contact and flown and landed in Xinjiang, Kyrgyzstan, or Turkmenistan."

Rupert Murdoch, who is one of the world's most powerful media moguls, said in a tweet (see: Dylan Stableford's article "Rupert Murdoch Tweets His Theory on Malaysian Plane Disappearance"): "World seems transfixed by 777 disappearance. Maybe no crash but stolen, effectively hidden, perhaps in northern Pakistan, like Bin Laden."

Hardly surprisingly, Murdoch's comments generated a flurry of comments. Also not surprisingly, many of the comments came out of Pakistan, which firmly denied any involvement in the affair. Indeed, Pakistan's assistant to the prime minister on aviation, Shujaat Azeem, hit back at Murdoch's tweet. He said in de Castella's article: "Pakistan's civil aviation radars never spotted this jet, so how it could be hidden somewhere in Pakistan?"

Azeem had a good point.

> [W]hoever was flying the plane essentially camouflaged it by using the radar signature of another aircraft in the area....

An aviation expert named Chris Goodfellow offered the theory that an on-board fire broke out, something that caused the pilot to take drastic measures, as he sought to save his aircraft, passengers, and crew, as well as preventing a disaster on the ground, if the plane were to crash in a major, built-up area. Goodfellow commented in de Castella's article: "This pilot did all the right things. He was confronted by some major event on-board that made him make that immediate turn back to the closest safe airport."

He continued: "Actually he was taking a direct route to Palau Langkawi, a 13,000-foot strip with an approach over water at night with no obstacles. He did not turn back to Kuala Lumpur because he knew he had 8,000 foot ridges to cross. He knew the terrain was friendlier towards Langkawi and also a shorter distance."

In such a scenario, however, the pilot was unable to make it to Langkawi and plunged into the ocean. As plausible as this theory might seem it does suffer from one, particular flaw. Aviation experts suggested that if there had been an on-board emergency, the crew would almost certainly have tried to correct things by taking Flight 370 out of its auto-pilot mode and flying the aircraft manually. As the *New York Times* noted, however (de Castella), someone in the cockpit had typed "seven or eight keystrokes into a computer on a knee-high pedestal between the captain and the first officer, according to officials," something that "has reinforced the belief of investigators—first voiced by Malaysian officials—that the plane was deliberately diverted and that foul play was involved."

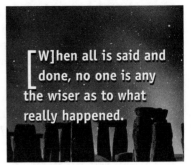

[W]hen all is said and done, no one is any the wiser as to what really happened.

On August 28, 2014, the Malaysian Minister of Transport, YB Dato' Sri Liow Tiong Lai, released a statement, one that offered thanks to those who had helped in the quest to locate the remains of MH370, and that outlined the plans for the future (see "Media Statement and Information on Flight MH370"):

On behalf of Prime Minister Dato' Sri Mohd Najib Bin Tun Haji Abdul Razak, the Malaysian government and the people of Malaysia, I want to express my profound gratitude for the leadership role the Australian government has played in this complex and challenging exercise, and to the Chinese government for their ongoing support and resources dedicated to our efforts. The discussion during the tripartite meeting today was productive and allowed us to discuss the progress in the search for MH370 and to chart the way forward.

I have been heartened by the openness and willingness of these nations who have provided us with immediate and ongoing assistance.

Today, Malaysia signed an MOU with Australia which provides the framework and broad parameters for cooperation in the search for MH370. This forms an important part of our existing cooperation with Australia and reaffirms Malaysia's commitment towards the search.

In this regard Malaysia will provide the necessary financial contribution towards the search effort and match Australia's commitment. The combination of undersea search equipment, world-class experts and cutting edge technology that is being used will be our best chance of finding MH370 and we are hopeful in our prospects of doing so.

I want to assure the loved ones of the passengers and crew on-board MH370 that we are resolute in our efforts to search for this aircraft. I have been touched by many of the stories I have heard and we will do our best to engage the next of kin and help them find closure. To that end we will be providing more regular updates and information related to the search as it becomes available.

Again, today Malaysia pledges its continued and unwavering support in response to the unprecedented nature and scale of this event through our financial commitment, technical expertise, equipment and stamina in our search for answers.

While the March 8, 2014, disappearance of MH370 continues to fascinate conspiracy theorists, still attracts major media coverage, has clearly caused concern amongst numerous nations, and has resulted in numerous searches for the missing Boeing 777, when all is said and done, no one is any the wiser as to what really happened.

Former Royal Air Force navigator Sean Maffett sums things up in brief, yet undeniably, accurate fashion in de Castella's article: "We are now at the stage where very, very difficult things have to be considered as all sensible options seem to have dropped off."

BIBLIOGRAPHY

"1953 Hunrath and Wilkinson Disappearance." *UFO*BC*. Accessed January 13, 2015. http://www.ufobc.ca/kinross/planeMishaps/hunrathAndWilkinson.html.

"1977 Senate Hearings on MKULTRA." *DRC Net Online Library of Drug Policy*. Accessed January 12, 2015. http://www.druglibrary.org/Schaffer/history/e1950/mkultra/index.htm/.

"1980: John Lennon Shot Dead." *BBC News*. Accessed January 13, 2015. http://news.bbc.co.uk/onthisday/hi/dates/stories/december/8/newsid_2536000/2536321.stm.

"2003 Looting of the Iraq National Museum." Stanford University. October 20, 2008. https://web.stanford.edu/group/chr/drupal/ref/the-2003-looting-of-the-iraq-national-museum.

"22 Shocking Population Control Quotes from the Global Elite." *Fourwinds10*. Accessed January 14, 2015. http://www.fourwinds10.net/siterun_data/health/intentional_death/news.php?q=1291600521.

"25 Marconi Scientists, 1982-88." *Project Camelot*. Accessed February 2, 2015. http://projectcamelot.org/marconi.html.

"9/11 Attacks." *History*. Accessed February 13, 2015. http://www.history.com/topics/9-11-attacks.

"9/11 Conspiracy Theorist to Leave Brigham Young." *Washington Post*. October 22, 2006. http://www.washingtonpost.com/wp-dyn/content/article/2006/10/21/AR2006102100635.html

Ackerman, Spencer. "There's a Secret Patriot Act, Senator Says." *Wired*. May 25, 2014. http://www.wired.com/2011/05/secret-patriot-act/.

Adachi, Ken. "Chemtrails." *Educate-Yourself*. Accessed January 2, 2015. http://educate-yourself.org/ct/.

Adams, Tom. *The Choppers and the Choppers*. Paris, TX: Project Stigma, 1991.

Addley, Esther. "7/7 Survivors End Battle for Public Inquiry into Bombings." *The Guardian*. August 1, 2011. http://www.theguardian.com/uk/2011/aug/01/7-july-bombings-public-inquiry.

"Adolf Hitler." *FBI: The Federal Bureau of Investigation*. Accessed February 2, 2015. http://vault.fbi.gov/adolf-hitler/.

"Adolf Hitler Biography." *Biography*. Accessed November 6, 2014. http://www.biography.com/people/adolf-hitler-9340144#death-and-legacy.

"Adolf Hitler Escaped to Argentina after the War." *Liberty Voice*. February 24, 2014. http://guardianlv.com/2014/02/adolf-hitler-escaped-to-argentina-after-the-war/.

Advisory Committee on Human Radiation Experiments. Pittsburgh, PA: U.S. Government Printing Office, October 1995.

"Advisory Committee on Pesticides." *Parliament.uk*. November 8, 2005. http://www.publications.parliament.uk/pa/cm200506/cmhansrd/vo051108/text/51108w11.htm.

Aho, Jim. "Ezekiel's Wheel." *UFO Evidence*. Accessed January 22, 2015. http://www.ufoevidence.org/cases/case493.htm.

"Air Force 2025—Final Report." *Biblioteca Pleyades*. Accessed October 11, 2014. http://www.bibliotecapleyades.net/sociopolitica/sociopol_weatherwar08.htm.

"Alleged Unauthorized Helicopter Flights in Derbyshire and Cheshire." File number HO/371/74/94. March 1974.

Allen, Joseph. "The White God Quetzalcoatl." *Nephi Project*. Accessed February 2, 2015. https://www.nephiproject.com/white_god_quetzalcoatl.htm.

Allen-Block, Irene. *The Psychic Spy*. Vernon, NJ: Glannant Ty, 2013.

Alten, Steve. *The Shell Game*. Springville, UT: Sweetwater Books, 2009.

"Amerithrax or Anthrax Investigation." *FBI: The Federal Bureau of Investigation*. Accessed December 21, 2014. www.fbi.gov/about-us/history/famous-cases/anthrax-amerithrax/amerithrax-investigation.

"The Ancient Secrets of Levitation." *Pegasus Research Consortium*. Accessed January 8, 2015. http://www.thelivingmoon.com/44cosmic_wisdom/02files/Levitation02.html.

Anderson, Neil T. *Victory over the Darkness*. Ventura, CA: Regal, 2000.

Anderson, Porter. "Witnesses to the Moments." *CNN*. September 11, 2001. http://edition.cnn.com/2001/US/09/11/witnesses/.

Anderson, Vicki. "Goddess, the Divine Feminine." *The Awakening*. September 30, 2011. https://hiddenlighthouse.wordpress.com/2011/09/30/goddess-the-divine-feminine-2/.

"Animal Mutilation." *FBI: The Federal Bureau of Investigation*. Accessed November 21, 2015. http://vault.fbi.gov/Animal%20Mutilation.

"Another Dead Scientist: Composite Released in Fatal Hit and Run." *Houston Chronicle*, December 12, 2003.

"Anunnaki." *Library of Halexandria*. February 5, 2009. http://www.halexandria.org/dward185.htm.

"The Anunnaki: Ancient Gods." *ZetaTalk*. Accessed December 5., 2014. http://zetatalk.com/index/blog0926.htm.

"Arizona Militia Figure Is Shot to Death." *Los Angeles Times*. November 7, 2001. http://articles.latimes.com/2001/nov/07/news/mn-1182.

"Assassination of Martin Luther King, Jr. (4 April 1968)." *The Martin Luther King, Jr. Research and Education Institute*. Accessed November 25, 2014. http://mlk-kpp01.stanford.edu/index.php/encyclopedia/encyclopedia/enc_kings_assassination_4_april_1968/.

"Assassination of President Abraham Lincoln." *The Library of Congress: American Memory*. Accessed December 11, 2014. http://memory.loc.gov/ammem/alhtml/alrintr.html.

"The Assassination of the President." *U.S. History*. Accessed January 3, 2015. http://www.ushistory.org/us/34f.asp.

Atkinson, Nancy. "Scientist Claims UFO Collided with Tunguska Meteorite to Save Earth." *Universe Today*. May 26, 2009. http://www.universetoday.com/31438/scientist-claims-ufo-collided-with-tunguska-meteorite-to-save-earth/.

"Attack at Pearl Harbor." *EyeWitness to History*. Accessed January 2, 2015. http://www.eyewitnesstohistory.com/pearl.htm.

Baxter, John, and Thomas Atkins. *The Fire Came By*. London: Macdonald & Jane's, 1975.

Begg, Paul. *Jack the Ripper: The Uncensored Facts*. London: Robson Books, 1993.

———, Martin Fido, and Keith Skinner. *The Jack the Ripper A to Z*. London: Headline Book Publishing, 1991.

Bell, Rachel. "The Death of Marilyn." *crimelibrary*. Accessed February 2, 2015. http://www.crimelibrary.com/notorious_murders/celebrity/marilyn_monroe/index.html.

Bergier, Jacques. *Mysteries of the Earth*. London, U.K.: Sidgwick & Jackson, 1974.

Bernstein, Carl, and Bob Woodward. *All the President's Men*. London: Quartet Books, 1974.

Bethurum, Truman. *Aboard a Flying Saucer*. Los Angeles: DeVorss & Co., 1954.

"Bill Uhouse on the Kingman Crash." *Honk If You Know Townsend*. February 7, 2013. http://jansrose.blogspot.com/2013/02/bill-uhouse-on-kingman-crash.html.

Bishop, Greg. *Wake Up Down There!* Kempton, IL: Adventures Unlimited Press, 2000.

Black, John. "The Story of Jonah." *Ancient Origins*. February 16, 2013. http://www.ancient-origins.net/myths-legends/story-jonah-00160.

Blackburn, Michael, and Mark Bennett. "Re-Engineering the Ark." *Fortean Times*. March, 2006. http://www.forteantimes.com/features/articles/106/reengineering_the_ark.html.

Blumrich, Josef F. *The Spaceships of Ezekiel*. London: Corgi Books, 1974.

———. "The Spaceships of the Prophet Ezekiel." Impact of Science on Society, *UNESCO XXIV*, no. 4 (October-December 1974).

Bogdanos, Michael. *Thieves of Baghdad*. New York: Bloomsbury, 2005.

Bollyn, Christopher. "Did Rupert Murdoch Have Prior Knowledge of 9-11?" *Christopher Bollyn: Journaliste sans Frontière*. October 3, 2003. http://www.bollyn.com/did-rupert-murdoch-have-prior-knowledge-of-9-11-2.

———. "Eyewitnesses Saw Military Aircraft at Scene of Flight 93." *Christopher Bollyn: Journaliste sans Frontière*. July 15, 2005. http://www.bollyn.com/eyewitnesses-saw-military-aircraft-at-scene-of-flight-93-2.

Booth, Billy. "UFO Visits New Jersey in 1966." *About Entertainment*. Accessed February 3, 2015. http://ufos.about.com/od/ufosjan2012/a/Ufo-Visits-New-Jersey-In-1966.htm.

Bowart, Walter. *Operation Mind Control*. New York: Dell Publishing, 1978.

Bowen, Alison. "Osama bin Laden: Conspiracy Theories Thrive on Lack of Proof." *Metro*. May 2, 2011. http://www.metro.us/newyork/news/international/2011/05/02/osama-bin-laden-conspiracy-theories-thrive-on-lack-of-proof/.

"BP Estimates the World Has Just 53.3 Years of Oil Left." *Gas2*. Accessed May 7, 2014. http://gas2.org/2014/07/03/bp-estimates-world-just-53-3-years-oil-left/.

Bragalia, Anthony. "Book Exposed: Jacobsen's Secret Source Revealed with Interview." *Project Avalon*. May 27, 2011. http://projectavalon.net/forum4/archive/index.php/t-22275.html?s=205b9ef9a34779a958b46ca9728d1ad2.

Brewda, Joseph. "Kissinger's 1974 Plan for Food Control Genocide." *Executive Intelligence Review*. December 8, 1995. http://www.larouchepub.com/other/1995/2249_kissinger_food.html.

Broden, L. "The Bob Lazar Story." *UFO Evidence*. Accessed October 30, 2014. http://www.ufoevidence.org/documents/doc1249.htm.

Buchan, James. "Miss Bell's Lines in the Sand." *The Guardian*. March 11, 2003. http://www.theguardian.com/world/2003/mar/12/iraq.jamesbuchan.

Buchanan, Lyn. *The Seventh Sense: The Secrets of Remote Viewing as Told by a "Psychic Spy" for the U.S. Military*. New York: Gallery Books, 2003.

Bunch, William. "Flight 93: We Know It Crashed But Not Why." *What Really Happened*. November 15, 2001. http://whatreallyhappened.com/WRHARTICLES/flight_93_crash.html.

"Bush Declares War." *CNN*. March 19, 2003. http://www.cnn.com/2003/US/03/19/sprj.irq.int.bush.transcript/.

"Bush 'Disappointed' Data on Prewar Iraq Were Wrong." *The Washington Times*. April 6, 2006. http://www.washingtontimes.com/news/2006/apr/6/20060406-112119-5897r/?page=all.

"Bush Wants Right to Use Military If Bird Flu Hits." *Free Republican*. Accessed January 28, 2015. http://www.freerepublic.com/focus/news/1497126/posts?page=152.

Cameron, Grant. "The Disney UFO Connection." *The Presidents UFO Website*. August 6, 2009. http://www.presidentialufo.com/disney-ufo-connection/151-the-disney-ufo-connection.

Carlisle, Frank E. "Solving the Riddle of Ezekiel's Wheels." *UFO Evidence*. December 4, 2004. http://www.ufoevidence.org/Cases/CaseSubarticle.asp?ID=496.

Carrasco, David. *Quetzalcoatl and the Irony of Empire: Myths and Prophecies in the Aztec Tradition*. Boulder, CO: University Press of Colorado, 2001.

Cayce, Edgar Evans. *Edgar Cayce on Atlantis*. New York: Paperback Library, 1969.

"Chariots of the Gods." *Peru-Facts*. Accessed February 2, 2015. http://peru-facts.co.uk/chariots-of-the-gods.html.

"Chemtrails." *Stop the Sheep Killers before It's Too Late*. Accessed January 14, 2015. http://www.sheepkillers.com/chemtrails.html.

"Chemtrail Conspiracy Theory." *Moon Conspiracy*. Accessed December 15, 2014. http://moonconspiracy.wordpress.com/chemtrail-conspiracy-theory/.

"Chemtrails—Spraying in Our Sky." *Chemtrails—Spraying in Our Skies*. February 2, 2015. http://www.holmestead.ca/chemtrails/response-en.html.

Cheshire Police Force. Press release. January 14, 1974.

"CIA Killed Lennon." *CIA Killed Lennon*. December 2005. http://ciakilledlennon.blogspot.com/2005/12/q-who-killed-john-lennon-the-cia-or.html.

Clapp, Ann Lee. "The Egyptian Heritage." *Edgar Cayce's A.R.E.* Accessed November 13, 2014. http://www.edgarcayce.org/are/ancient_mysteries.aspx?id=4139.

Coleman, Loren. *Bigfoot! The True Story of Apes in America*. New York: Paraview-Pocket Books, 2003.

Collins, Michael S. "An Interview with Duncan Lunan—Part Two—Unabridged Version." *Winterwind Productions*. Accessed September 20, 2014. http://www.winterwind-productions.com/feature_articles/duncan_lunan_unabridged_pt2/pg2/.

Collins, Tony. *Open Verdict: An Account of 25 Mysterious Deaths in the Defense Industry*. London: Sphere Books, Ltd., 1990.

Committee on Biological Warfare. (Documents declassified under the terms of the Freedom of Information Act). March 28, October 16, October 19, and October 22, 1947.

A Concise Compendium of the Warren Commission Report on the Assassination of John F. Kennedy. New York: Popular Library, 1964.

"Conspiracy Theory: NDP Deputy Leader Mulcair Doubts U.S. Has bin Laden Photos." *The Star*. May 4, 2011. http://www.thestar.com/news/canada/2011/05/04/conspiracy_theory_ndp_deputy_leader_mulcair_doubts_us_has_bin_laden_photos.html.

"Conspiracy Theory: NDP Deputy Leader Mulcair Doubts U.S. Has bin Laden Photos." *The Star*. May 4, 2011. http://www.thestar.com/news/canada/2011/05/04/conspiracy_theory_ndp_deputy_leader_mulcair_doubts_us_has_bin_laden_photos.html.

Controlled Offensive Behavior—USSR. Defense Intelligence Agency, 1972.

"A Conversation with Matthew F. Bogdanos." *Archaeology Archive*. October 16, 2003. http://archive.archaeology.org/online/interviews/bogdanos/.

Coppens, Philip. "Ancient Atomic Wars: Best Evidence." *Biblioteca Pleyades*. January 2005. http://www.bibliotecapleyades.net/ancientatomicwar/esp_ancient_atomic_07.htm.

———. "Nazca: Airport of the Gods?" *Frontier*. March-April, 1999.

Corbett, James. "Lone Gunmen Producer Questions Government on 9/11." *Corbett Report*. February 25, 2008. http://www.corbettreport.com/articles/20080225_gunmen_911.htm.

Cowan, Alison Leigh. "Four Librarians Finally Break Silence in Records Case." *New York Times*. May 31, 2006. http://www.nytimes.com/2006/05/31/nyregion/31library.html?_r=0.

Dakss, Brian. "John Lennon Remembered." *CBS News*. December 8, 2005. http://www.cbsnews.com/news/john-lennon-remembered-08-12-2005/.

Daniel, John. "Scarlet and the Beast." *The Knights of the Golden Circle*. April 21, 2011. http://knights-of-the-golden-circle.blogspot.com/2011/04/scarlet-and-beast.html.

Darling, David. "Tunguska Phenomenon." *The Words of David Darling*. Accessed February 2, 2015. http://www.daviddarling.info/encyclopedia/T/Tunguska.html.

"Daughter Charged in Slaying of Scientist." *Washington Post*, February 2, 2002.

Davidson, Michael. "A Career in Microbiology Can Be Harmful to Your Health—Especially since 9-11." *Rense*. February 15, 2002. http://www.rense.com/general20/car.htm.

———, and Michael C. Ruppert. "Microbiologist Death Toll Mounts as Connections to Dynocorp, Hadron, Promis Software & Disease Research Emerge." *Rense*. March 3, 2002. http://www.rense.com/general20/mic.htm.

De Castella, Tom. "Missing Malaysia Plane: 10 Theories Examined." *BBC*. March 18, 2014. http://www.bbc.com/news/magazine-26609687.

Deschamps, Michel M. "My Personal Belief System (and Wow It's Been Affected by UFOs)." *NOUFOURS: Northern Ontario UFO Research and Study*. Accessed February 2, 2015. http://www.noufors.com/my_personal_belief_system.htm.

Dione, R.L. *God Drives a Flying Saucer*. London: Corgi Books, 1969.

Documentary Update on Project Sunshine "Body Snatching." Memorandum. Advisory Committee on Human Radiation Experiments. Advisory Committee Staff, June 9, 1995.

Dodd, Vikram, Ian Cobain, and Helen Carter. "7/7 Leader: More Evidence Reveals What Police Knew." *The Guardian*. May 2, 2007. http://www.theguardian.com/uk/2007/may/03/july7.topstories3.

Donnelly, Ignatius. *Atlantis: The Antediluvian World*. Teddington, UK: Echo Library, 2006.

Doyle, Aidan. "When Books Kill." *Salon*. December 15, 2003. http://www.salon.com/2003/12/15/books_kill/.

Drake, W. Raymond. *Gods or Spacemen?* New York: Signet, 1964.

Durante, Thomas. "Bin Laden WAS NOT Buried at Sea, But Flown to the U.S. for Cremation at Secret Location, Claims Intelligence Boss in Leaked Email." *Daily Mail*. March 7, 2012. http://www.dailymail.co.uk/news/article-2111001/Osama-bin-Laden-WAS-NOT-buried-sea-flown-US-cremation-leaked-emails-reveal.html.

"Edward Snowden: Timeline." *BBC*. August 20, 2013. http://www.bbc.com/news/world-us-canada-23768248.

Edwards, Anna. "New Book Claims THIS Picture Proves Hitler Escaped His Berlin Bunker and Died in South America in 1984 Aged 95." *Daily Mail*. January 25, 2014. http://www.dailymail.co.uk/news/article-2545770/New-book-claims-THIS-picture-proves-Hitler-escaped-Berlin-bunker-died-South-America-1984-aged-95.html.

Eldritch, Tristan. "The Green Children of Woolpit." *A Few Years in the Absolute Elsewhere*. December 29, 2011. http://2012diaries.blogspot.com/2011/12/green-children-of-woolpit.html.

Enserink, Martin. "Scientists Brace for Media Storm Around Controversial Flu Studies." *Science Magazine*. November 23, 2011. http://news.sciencemag.org/2011/11/scientists-brace-media-storm-around-controversial-flu-studies.

"Environment, Food and Rural Affairs Advisory Committee on Pesticides." *Parliament.uk*. November 8, 2005. http://www.publications.parliament.uk/pa/cm200506/cmhansrd/vo051108/text/51108w11.htm.

Estabrooks, G.H. "Hypnosis Comes of Age." *Science Digest*, April 1971.

"Even If Iraq Managed to Hide These Weapons, What They Are Now Hiding Is Harmless Goo." *The Guardian*. September 18, 2002. http://www.theguardian.com/world/2002/sep/19/iraq.features11.

"Everything You Need to Know about PRISM." *The Verge*. July 17, 2013. http://www.theverge.com/2013/7/17/4517480/nsa-spying-prism-surveillance-cheat-sheet.

"The Evolution of a Conspiracy Theory." *BBC*. July 4, 2008. http://news.bbc.co.uk/2/mobile/uk_news/magazine/7488159.stm.

Examples of Ground Markings Investigated. File reference: WO 199/1982. National Archives, Kew, England.

"Explosion and Crash." *9-11 Research*. March 21, 2013. http://911research.wtc7.net/pentagon/evidence/witnesses/crash.html.

"Fahrenheit 9/11 Quotes." *International Movie Database*. http://www.imdb.com/title/tt0361596/quotes. Accessed June 1, 2014.

Fairclough, Melvin. *The Ripper and the Royals*. London: Gerald Duckworth & Co., 1992.

"Family Implanted with Computer Chips." *USA Today*. May 10, 2002. http://usatoday30.usatoday.com/tech/news/2002/05/10/implantable-chip.htm.

Fawcett, Lawrence & Greenwood, Barry, *Clear Intent: The Government Cover Up of the UFO Experience*. Englewood Cliffs, NJ: Spectrum Books, 1984.

"FBI Does Not Rule Out Shootdown Of Hijacked 757 Over Pennsylvania." *Rense*. September 13, 2001. http://www.rense.com/general13/penn.htm.

"FBI Looks into Missing Biologist Case". *Los Angeles Times*. November 25, 2001. http://articles.latimes.com/2001/nov/25/news/mn-8183.

"Featured Author: Paul Devereux." *The Megalithic Portal*. Accessed June 1, 2014. http://www.megalithic.co.uk/mm/book/devereux1trans.htm.

Federal Bureau of Investigation files on George Van Tassel, declassified under the terms of the Freedom of Information Act, 1988.

Fido, Martin. *The Crimes, Detection & Death of Jack the Ripper*. London: Weidenfeld & Nicolson, Ltd., 1987.

Firestone, Richard B., and William Topping. "Terrestrial Evidence of a Nuclear Catastrophe in Paleoindian Times." *The Mammoth Trumpet*, March 2001.

Fisher, Max. "Chinese Army Colonel Says Avian Flu Is an American Plot against China." *Washington Post*. April 9, 2013. http://www.washingtonpost.com/blogs/worldviews/wp/2013/04/09/chinese-army-colonel- says-avian-flu-is-an-american-plot-against-china/.

Flem-Ath, Rand and Rose. *Atlantis Beneath the Ice*. Rochester, VT: Bear & Company, 2012.

"Flight 93." *History*. Accessed June 15, 2014. http://www.history.com/topics/flight-93.

"Flight 93 Hijacker: 'Shall We Finish It Off?'" *CNN*. July 23, 2004. http://www.cnn.com/2004/US/07/22/911.flight.93/.

"Food for Thought—Several Dozen Microbiologists & Scientists Dead under "Suspicious Circumstances." *Organic Consumers Association*. January 27, 2005. http://www.organicconsumers.org/corp/suspicious012805.cfm.

"Fred Crisman." *The Majestic Documents*. Accessed June 15, 2014. http://majesticdocuments.com/personnel/crisman.php.

Friedman, Stanton T. "UFO Propulsion Systems." *Stanton Friedman*. February 3, 2009. http://www.stantonfriedman.com/index.php?ptp=articles&fdt=2009.02.03.

Galanopoulos, Angelos Georgiou. *Atlantis: The Truth behind the Legend*. Indianapolis, IN: Bobbs-Merrill Co., 1969.

Gallagher, Ryan, and Glenn Greenwald. "How the NSA Plans to Infect 'Millions' of Computers with Malware." *First Look Media*. March 12, 2013. https://firstlook.org/theintercept/2014/03/12/nsa-plans-infect-millions-computers-malware/.

Gardner, Laurence. *Genesis of the Grail Kings*. New York: Bantam Press, 1999.

"George Orwell Quotes." *BrainyQuote*. Accessed February 2, 2015. http://www.brainyquote.com/quotes/authors/g/george_orwell.html.

Gardner, Zen. "Hidden History: Monoatomic Gold and Human Origins—Jim Marrs." *ZenGardner.* July 25, 2013. http://www.zengardner.com/hidden-history-monoatomic-gold-and-human-origins-jim-marrs/.

Garrison, Jim. *On the Trail of the Assassins.* London: Penguin Books, 1988.

Geerhart, Bill. "Red Scare: The Best of Kenneth Goff." *Conelrad Adjacent.* September 11, 2010. http://conelrad.blogspot.com/2010/09/red-scare-best-of-kenneth-goff.html.

Gentleman, Amelia, and Robin McKie. "Red Rain Could Prove That Aliens Have Landed." *Observer,* March 5, 2006.

"George Wingfield." *Noufors: Northern Ontario Research and Study.* Accessed September 1, 2014. http://www.noufors.com/George_Wingfield.htm.

Gibbons, Gavin. *They Rode in Space Ships.* New York: Citadel Press, 1957.

Gidda, Mirren. "Edward Snowden and the NSA Files—Timeline." *The Guardian.* July 25, 2013. http://www.theguardian.com/world/2013/jun/23/edward-snowden-nsa-files-timeline.

Gill, N.S. "Atlantis—Plato's Atlantis from the Timaeus." *About Education.* July 25, 2007. http://ancienthistory.about.com/od/lostcontinent/qt/072507Atlantis.htm.

Glass, Nicholas. "Coincidence of Bomb Exercises?" *Channel 4.* July 17, 2005. http://www.channel4.com/news/articles/uk/coincidence+of+bomb+exercises/109010.html.

Global Research. "9/11 Theologian Says Controlled Demolition of World Trade Center Is Now a Fact, Not a Theory/" *Global Research.* October 21, 2005. http://www.globalresearch.ca/9-11-theologian-says-controlled-demolition-of-world-trade-center-is-now-a-fact-not-a-theory/1129?print=1.

Glod, Maria. "Scientist Found Slain in His Loudoun Home." *Washington Post,* December 12, 2001.

———, and Josh White. "Va. Scientist Was Killed with Sword: Three Friends Interested in Occult and Witchcraft, Friends Say." *Washington Post,* December 14, 2001.

Godfrey, Linda. *Real Wolfmen.* New York: Tarcher, 2012.

Godwin, Jocelyn. *Atlantis and the Cycles of Time.* Rochester, VT: Inner Traditions, 2011.

Goff, Kenneth. *Red Shadows.* Englewood, CO: privately printed, 1959.

Goodfellow, Chris. "A Startlingly Simple Theory about the Missing Malaysia Airlines Jet." *Wired.* March 18, 2014. http://www.wired.com/2014/03/mh370-electrical-fire/.

Gordon, Stan. *Silent Invasion: The Pennsylvania UFO-Bigfoot Casebook.* Greensburg, PA: privately printed, 2010.

Goss, Jennifer L. "Hitler Commits Suicide." *About Education.* Accessed August 1, 2014. http://history1900s.about.com/od/1940s/a/Hitler-Suicide.htm.

Graham, Anne E., and Carol Emmas. *The Last Victim.* London: Headline Book Publishing, 1999.

Graham, Robbie. "UFOs and Disney." *Silver Screen Saucers.* July 29, 2011. http://silver-screensaucers.blogspot.com/2011/07/ufos-and-disney-behind-magic-kingdom.html.

Gray, L. Patrick, and Ed Gray. *In Nixon's Web: A Year in the Crosshairs of Watergate.* New York: St. Martin's Griffin, 2009.

"The Green Children of Woolpit." *Mysterious Britain and Ireland.* Accessed January 4, 2015. http://www.mysteriousbritain.co.uk/england/suffolk/folklore/the-green-children-of-woolpit.html.

"Green Children of Woolpit: Mysterious Visitors from an Unknown Land." Accessed January 28, 2015. http://laymwe01.hubpages.com/hub/Green-Children-of-Woolpit-Mysterious-visitors-from-an-unknown-land.

Grisales, Carolina Manosca. "Men and Apes." *Fortean Times*. Accessed September 4, 2014. http://www.forteantimes.com/strangedays/ghostwatch/5710/men_and_apes.html.

Gurney, Ian. "The Mystery of the Dead Scientists: Coincidence or Conspiracy?" *Rense*. July 20, 2003. http://www.rense.com/general39/death.htm.

Gurney, Mark. "SARS Virus First Discovered in 1998." *Rense*. Accessed March 18, 2003. http://www.rense.com/general35/sarrs.htm.

Hamre, Bonnie. "Nazca Lines, Peru: Who Drew the Lines in the Sand? How?" *About Travel*. Accessed September 12, 2014. http://gosouthamerica.about.com/cs/southamerica/a/PerNazca.htm.

Hanks, Micah. "The Ancient Nukes Question: Were There WMDs in Prehistoric Times?" *Mysterioud Universe*. December 19, 2011. http://mysteriousuniverse.org/2011/12/the-ancient-nukes-question-were-there-wmds-in-prehistoric-times/.

———. "Curious Cryptohominids: A Link between Aliens and Bigfoot?" *Mysterious Universe*. September 9, 2010. http://mysteriousuniverse.org/2010/09/curious-cryptohominids-a-link-between-aliens-and- bigfoot/.

———. "Secrets of the Past: Early Evidence of Nuclear Weapons?" *New Page Books*. March 26, 2012. http://newpagebooks.blogspot.com/2012/03/secrets-of-past.html.

Harper, Mark J. "Dead Scientists and Microbiologists—Master List." *Rense*. Accessed November 2, 2014. http://rense.com/general62/list.htm.

Harpur, Merrily. "The ABC X-Files." *Fortean Times*, No. 278, October 2011.

Hatcher-Childress, David. "Giant Unexplained Crater Near Bombay." *Biblioteca Pleyades*. Accessed December 20, 2014. http://www.bibliotecapleyades.net/ancientatomicwar/esp_ancient_atomic_12.htm.

Haughton, Brian. "The Green Children of Woolpit." *Brian Haughton*. Accessed August 10, 2014. http://brian-haughton.com/articles/green-children-of-woolpit/.

Havill, Adrian. *Deep Truth: The Lives of Bob Woodward and Carl Bernstein*. New York: Birch Lane Press, 1993.

Hayakawa, Norio. "My Recollections of the Enigmatic Bob Lazar…. Alleged Former Area 51 'Scientist.'" *Rense*. July 8, 2006. http://www.rense.com/general72/rec-oll.htm.

Head, Tom. "5 Reasons Aaron Kosminski Might Not Have Been Jack the Ripper." *Mysterious Universe*. January 15, 2014. http://mysteriousuniverse.org/2014/09/5-reasons-aaron-kosminski-might-not-have-been-jack-the-ripper/.

Helmore, Edward. "Human Consumption: Flying in the Face of Logic." *The Guardian*. July 15, 2008. http://www.theguardian.com/environment/2008/jul/16/human consumption.

"Hindu Wisdom—Vimanas." *Hindu Wisdom*. October 28, 2008. http://www.hindu wisdom.info/Vimanas.htm.

Hodal, Kate. "Malaysian MH370 Co-pilot Entertained Teenagers in Cabin on Earlier Flight." *The Guardian*. March 11, 2014. http://www.theguardian.com/world/2014/mar/11/malaysian-flight-mh370-copilot-teenagers- fariq-abdul-hamid.

Hodges, Dave. "Will Humanity Survive the Depopulation Agenda of the Global Elite?" *The Common Sense Show*. April 26, 2014. http://www.thecommonsenseshow

.com/2014/04/26/will-humanity-survive-the-depopulation- agenda-of-the-global-elite/.

Hoeck, Kenneth M. "The Jesuit Connection to the Assassination of Abraham Lincoln." *Truth on the Web*. November 1999. http://www.truthontheweb.org/abe.htm.

Holland, Max. "The Assassination Tapes." *The Atlantic*. June 2004. http://www.the atlantic.com/past/docs/issues/2004/06/holland.htm.

Holy Bible: Contemporary English Version. New York: American Bible Society, 1995.

Honigsbaum, Mark. "Seeing Isn't Believing." *The Guardian*. June 26, 2006. http://www .theguardian.com/uk/2006/jun/27/july7.uksecurity.

"How Will Climate Change Impact on Fresh Water Security?" *The Guardian*. December 21, 2012. http://www.theguardian.com/environment/2012/nov/30/climate-change-water.

Howells, Martin, and Keith Skinner. *The Ripper Legacy*. London: Sphere Books, Ltd., 1988.

"Hyperchromic Anemia." *The Free Dictionary*. Accessed January 28, 2015. http://medical-dictionary.thefreedictionary.com/hyperchromic+anemia.

Icke, David. *And the Truth Shall Set You Free*. Isle of Wight, UK: David Icke Books, 2004.

———. *Children of the Matrix*. Isle of Wight, UK: David Icke Books, 2001.

———. "Flu Is Not the Biggest Danger…. It's the Vaccine!" *Biblioteca Pleyades*. Accessed January 15, 2015. http://www.bibliotecapleyades.net/ciencia/ciencia_influenza32.htm.

———. *The Robots' Rebellion*. Isle of Wight, UK: Gateway Books, 1994.

"If I Were Reincarnated I Would Wish to Be Returned to Earth as a Killer Virus to Lower Human Population Levels." *Before It's News*. August 9, 2014. http:// beforeitsnews.com/politics/2014/08/if-i-were-reincarnated-i-would-wish-to-be-returned- to-earth-as-a-killer-virus-to-lower-human-population-levels-2643598.html.

"In Quotes: Blair and Iraq Weapons." *BBC Newes*. September 29, 2004. http://news.bbc .co.uk/2/hi/uk_news/politics/3054991.stm.

"In the Arena." *CNN*. May 5, 2011. http://transcripts.cnn.com/TRANSCRIPTS/1105/ 05/ita.01.html.

"Interview with Zecharia Sitchin." *Biblioteca Pleyades*. Accessed December 20, 2014. http://www.bibliotecapleyades.net/sitchin/esp_sitchin_3a.htm.

"Interview with Zecharia Sitchin: An Introduction." *Connecting Link* 17 (2014).

Introvigne, Massimo. "L. Ron Hubbard, Kenneth Goff, and the 'Brain-Washing Manual' of 1955." *CESNUR: Center for Studies on New Religions*. Accessed December 1, 2014. http://www.cesnur.org/2005/brainwash_13.htm.

"Intrusive Alien Abduction at Night from Bedroom." *CureZone*. Accessed January 28, 2015. http://curezone.org/forums/am.asp?i=2123567.

"Irish Supreme Court OKs Extradition of DVD Mailer to British Courts." *Educate-Yourself*. November 10, 2010. http://educate-yourself.org/lte/irishsupremecourt decision16nov10.shtml.

"Is Catcher in the Rye an Assassination Trigger?" *atomicpoet*. January 31, 2012. http:// atomicpoet.wordpress.com/2012/01/31/is-catcher-in-the-rye-an-assassination-trigger/.

Isaacs, Roger D. *Talking with God*. Chicago: Sacred Closet Books, 2010.

"J. Robert Oppenheimer Now I Am Become Death…." *Atomic Archive*. Accessed January 28, 2015. http://www.atomicarchive.com/Movies/Movie8.shtml.

"Jack the Ripper Was Polish Immigrant Aaron Kosminski, Book Claims." *The Guardian*. September 7, 2014. http://www.theguardian.com/uk-news/2014/sep/08/jack-the-ripper-polish-aaron-kosminski-dna.

Jacobsen, Annie. *Area 51: An Uncensored History of America's Top Secret Military Base*. New York: Little, Brown & Co., 2012.

"James Earl Ray Biography. Murderer (1928–1998)." *Biography*. Accessed January 14, 2015. http://www.biography.com/people/james-earl-ray-20903161.

"John Holdren, Obama's Science Czar, Says: Forced Abortions and Mass Sterilization Needed to Save the Planet." *zombietime*. Accessed January 11, 2015. http://zombietime.com/john_holdren/.

"The John Lennon FBI Files." *The John Lennon FBI Files*. Accessed February 2, 2015. http://www.lennonfbifiles.com/.

Johnston, Grahame. "Nazca Lines and the Nazca Culture." *Archaeology Expert*. November 29, 2014. http://www.archaeologyexpert.co.uk/nazca.html.

Jones, Alex. "A Brief Analysis of the Domestic Security Enhancement Act 2003." *Rickie Lee Jones*. Accessed February 3, 2015. http://www.rickieleejones.com/political/patriotact.htm.

Jones, Barbara M. "Librarians Shushed No More: The USA Patriot Act, the 'Connecticut Four,' and Professional Ethics." *Newsletter on Intellectual Freedom* 58, no. 6 (2009).

Jones, Marie, and Larry Flaxman. *The Resonance Key*. Pompton Plains, NJ: New Page Books, 2009.

Jordan, Debbie. *Abducted! The Story of the Intruders Continues*. New York: Dell Publishing, 1995.

Jordan, Lara Jakes. "Senator: Anthrax Not 1 Man's Work." *Denver Post*. September 18, 2008. http://www.denverpost.com/ci_10492103?source=pkg.

"Judicial Watch Sues Department of Defense for Records of Communications Relating to May 2011 FOIA Request for bin Laden Death Photos." *Judicial Watch*. July 24, 2014. http://www.judicialwatch.org/press-room/press-releases/judicial-watch-sues-department-defense-records-communications-relating-may-2011-foia-request-bin-laden-death-photos/.

Keith, Jim. *Black Helicopters II*. Lilburn, GA: IllumiNet Press, 1997.

———. *Black Helicopters Over America*. Lilburn, GA: IllumiNet Press, 1994.

———. *Mind Control, World Control*. Kempton, IL: Adventures Unlimited Press, 1998.

———. "Roswell UFO Bombshell." *Llewellyn*. Accessed January 28, 2015. http://www.llewellyn.com/journal/print.php?id=69.

"Kenneth Goff." Federal Bureau of Investigation file, declassified under the terms of the Freedom of Information Act.

"Key Facts about Avian Influenza (Bird Flu) and Highly Pathogenic Avian Influenza A (H5N1) Virus." *Center for Disease Control*. Accessed October 12, 2014. http://www.cdc.gov/flu/avian/gen-info/facts.htm.

"Kim Johnson's Chemtrail Analysis—Updated." *New Mexicans for Science and Reason*. October 31, 1999. http://www.nmsr.org/mkjrept.htm.

King, Jeffrey. "The Lone Gunmen Episode 1: Pilot." *Plague Puppy.* Accessed November 5, 2014. http://www.plaguepuppy.net/public_html/Lone%20Gunmen/The_Lone_Gunmen_Episode_1.htm.

King, Jon. "Did the CIA Murder John Lennon?" *Conscious Ape.* October 8, 2012. http://www.consciousape.com/2012/10/08/did-the-cia-murder-john-lennon/.

"The Kingman, Arizona UFO Crash." *PRUFON (Puerto Rican UFO Network).* December 30, 2012. http://www.prufon.net/2012/12/the-kingman-arizona-ufo-crash.html.

Kingsley, Patrick, and Sam Jones. "Osama bin Laden Death: The Conspiracy Theories." *The Guardian.* May 5, 2011. http://www.theguardian.com/world/2011/may/05/osama-bin-laden-conspiracy-theories.

Knight, Stephen. *Jack the Ripper: The Final Solution.* London: Grafton Books, 1989.

Knox, Olivier. "Intelligence Chief Clapper: I Gave 'Least Untruthful' Answer on U.S. Spying." *Yahoo! News.* June 10, 2013. http://news.yahoo.com/blogs/the-ticket/intel-chief-clapper-gave-least-untruthful-answer-u-164742798.html.

Koebler, Jason. "Global Flu Pandemic 'Inevitable,' Expert Warns." *U.S. News & World Report.* December 24, 2012. http://www.usnews.com/news/articles/2012/12/24/global-flu-pandemic-inevitable-expert- warns.

Korkis, Jim. "Ward Kimball and UFOs." *Mouse Planet.* August 24, 2011. http://www.mouseplanet.com/9720/Ward_Kimball_and_UFOs.

Koslovic, Melanie. "Green Children of Woolpit." *Prezi.* July 16, 2014. http://prezi.com/re8juu0kv0eb/green-children-of-woolpit/.

Kress, Kenneth A. *Studies in Intelligence.* Central Intelligence Agency, 1977.

Krystek, Lee. "The Lines of Nazca Peru." *The Museum of Unnatural History.* Accessed January 28, 2015. http://www.unmuseum.org/nazca.htm.

Lammer, Helmut. "New Evidence of Military Involvement in Abductions." *Rense.* Accessed December 23, 2014. http://rense.com/ufo/newevabduct.htm.

Lardinois, Frederic. "U.S. Government: Reports about PRISM Contain 'Numerous Inaccuracies.'" *TC: TechCrunch.* June 6, 2013. http://techcrunch.com/2013/06/06/u-s-government-reports-about-prism-contain-numerous-inaccuracies/.

Lashmar, Paul. "Pearl Harbor Conspiracy Is Bunk." *The Independent.* August 24, 1998. http://www.independent.co.uk/news/pearl-harbor-conspiracy-is-bunk-1173728.html.

"Lee Harvey Oswald." *Kennedy Assassination Home Page.* Accessed January 28, 2015. http://jfkassassination.net/russ/jfkinfo4/jfk12/defector.htm#OSWALD.

Lee, Timothy B. "Here's Everything We Know about PRISM to Date." *Washington Post.* June 12, 2013. http://www.washingtonpost.com/blogs/wonkblog/wp/2013/06/12/heres-everything-we-know- about-prism-to-date/.

"Long-range World Population Projections." *United Nations.* Accessed January 14, 2015. http://www.un.org/esa/population/publications/longrange/longrange.htm.

Lucero, Lisa J., and Jed Panganiban. "The Ideology of the Absent: The Feathered Serpent and Classic Maya Rulership." University of Illinois at Urbana-Champaign Department of Anthropology. Accessed January 28, 2015. http://www.anthro.illinois.edu/faculty/lucero/documents/12-luceropanganiban.pdf.

Maestri, Nicoletta. "Quetzalcoatl—Pan-Mesoamerican Deity." *About Education.* http://archaeology.about.com/od/Aztec-Religion/a/Queztalcoatl.htm.

"The Mahabharata." *Internet Sacred Text Archive*. Accessed January 30, 2015. http://www.sacred-texts.com/hin/maha/.

"Malaysia Airlines Flight 370: FBI Analyzing Deleted Data from Pilot's Home Flight Simulator." *CBS News*. March 19, 2014. http://www.cbsnews.com/news/malaysia-airlines-flight-370-pilot-zaharie-ahmad-shah-deleted-files-from-simulator-police/.

Malone, Nicole. "The Bible, Physics, and the Abilities of Fallen Angels". *A Modern Guide to Demons and Fallen Angels*. Accessed November 1, 2014. http://paradoxbrown.com/biblephysicsfallenangels.htm/2009.

Mandelbaum, W. Adam. *The Psychic Battlefield*. New York: Thomas Dunne Books, 2000.

Mark, Joshua J. "Gilgamesh." October 13, 2010. *Ancient History Encyclopedia*. http://www.ancient.eu/gilgamesh/.

"Mark Chapman: The Assassination of John Lennon." *Crime and Investigation*. Accessed October 22, 2014. http://www.crimeandinvestigation.co.uk/crime-files/ mark-chapman—the-assassination-of-john-lennon.

Martin, Patrick. "The Sacking of Iraq's Museums: US Wages War against Culture and History." *World Socialist Web Site*. April 16, 2003. http://www.wsws.org/en/articles/2003/04/muse-a16.html.

McClellan, Jason. "Bob Lazar Still Defends Area 51 UFO info 25 Years Later." *Open Minds*. May 14, 2014. http://www.openminds.tv/bob-lazar-still-defends-area-51-ufo-info-25-years-later/27560.

McDonagh, Melanie. "Dan Brown's Latest Conspiracy Theory—and the Powerful People Who Believe It." *The Spectator*. May 25, 2013. http://www.spectator.co.uk/features/8915171/dan-browns-demography/.

McDonald, Hugh. *Appointment in Dallas*. New York: Zebra, 1975.

McGreal, Chris. "September 11 Conspiracy Theories Continue to Abound." *The Guardian*. September 5, 2011. http://www.theguardian.com/world/2011/sep/05/september-11-conspiracy-theories.

Meacher, Michael. "This War on Terrorism Is Bogus." *The Guardian*. September 6, 2003. http://www.theguardian.com/politics/2003/sep/06/september11.iraq.

Meek, James Gordon. "FBI Was Told to Blame Anthrax Scare on Al Qaeda by White House Officials." *New York Daily News*. August 2, 2008. http://www.nydailynews.com/news/national/2008/08/02/2008-08-02_fbi_was_told_to_blame_anthrax_scare_on_a.html.

"Media Statement and Information on Flight MH370." *Malaysia Airlines*. November 10, 2014. http://www.malaysiaairlines.com/mh370.

Medina, David. *The Ark of the Covenant*. New Brunswick, NJ: Inner Light, 2014.

Mendo, Alberto. "Quetzalcoatl: Beyond the Feathered Serpent." *UC Berkeley Academic Achievements Program*. Accessed January 28, 2015. http://www.aap.berkeley.edu/journals/2003Journal/AMendo.html.

Meyer, David. "Ark of the Covenant: Lost Technology." *Guerilla Explorer*. July 23, 2011. http://www.guerrillaexplorer.com/strange-science/ark-of-the-covenant-lost-technology/.

"Microchip Mind Control, Implants and Cybernetics." *Rense*. December 6, 2001. http://www.rense.com/general17/imp.htm.

"A Microchipped Population—David Said This Was Coming 12 Years Ago and Here It Is Folks!" *Red Ice Creations*. October 23, 2004. http://www.redicecreations.com/news/2004/microicke.html.

Miller Judith. "Russian Scientist Dies in Ebola Accident at Former Weapons Lab." *New York Times*. May 25, 2004.

Mitchell, Alanna, Simon Cooper, and Carolyn Abraham. "Strange Cluster of Microbiologists' Deaths under the Microscope." *Globe and Mail*. May 4, 2002.

Montgomery, John Warwick. *Principalities and Powers*. Calgary, AB, Canada: Canadian Institute for Law, Theology & Public Policy, Inc. 2001.

Mooney, Richard. *Colony Earth*. New York: Stein & Day, 1974.

Morgan, Bill. "Will Iraq Be World's First Electromagnetic 'Scalar' War?" *Rense*. October 10, 2002. http://www.rense.com/general30/mager.htm.

Morton, Ella. "Unholy Trinity: Visiting the Site of the First Nuclear Weapon Test." *Slate*. March 18, 2014. http://www.slate.com/blogs/atlas_obscura/2014/03/18/the _trinity_site_in_new_mexico_where_the_first_nuclear_weapon_was_tested.html.

Murdock, D.M., and S. Acharya. "Who Are the Anunnaki?" *Truth Be Known*. September 2014. http://www.truthbeknown.com/anunnaki.htm.

Myers, Dale K. "The Assassination of William Greer." *Secrets of a Homicide*. July 17, 2008. http://jfkfiles.blogspot.com/2008/07/assassination-of-william-greer.html.

Nance, Rahkia. "James Earl Ray's Brother Claims Federal Government Killed Martin Luther King." *Birmingham News*, April 1, 2008.

National Archive File: AIR 2/17526. 1964.

"National Security Study Memorandum 200 (NSSM 200)—April 1974." *The Center for Research on Population and Security*. Accessed February 2, 2015. http://www .population-security.org/28-APP2.html.

"Native American Bigfoot Figures of Myth and Legend." *Native Languages of America*. Accessed January 29, 2015. http://www.native-languages.org/legends-bigfoot.htm.

"Navy SEALs 'Took Turns Dumping HUNDREDS of Bullets'into Osama bin Laden's Dead Body, a New Report Reveals." *Daily Mail*. March 14, 2014. http://www.dailymail.co.uk/news/article-2581354/Navy-SEALs-took-turns-dumping-HUNDREDS-bullets-Osama-bin-Ladens-dead-body-new-report-reveals.html.

"Nazca Lines and Cahuachi Culture." *Crystalinks*. Accessed January 14, 2015. http:// www.crystalinks.com/nazca.html.

"The Nazca Lines Discoverer Paul Kosok." *Mystical Locations*. Accessed February 5, 2015. http://www.mystical-locations.info/pictures_nazca_kosok.html.

"Nazca Lines, Peru." *Sacred Destinations*. Accessed December 11, 2014. http://www. sacred-destinations.com/peru/nazca-lines.

"The Nephilim—Giants in the Bible." *Beginning and End*. May 23, 2011. http:// beginningandend.com/nephilim-giants-bible/.

Newling, Dan. "Britons 'Could Be Microchipped Like Dogs in a Decade.'" *Daily Mail*. October 30, 2006. http://www.dailymail.co.uk/news/article-413345/Britons-microchipped-like-dogs-decade.html.

"News Gathering Is Illegal under New Patriot Act II." *Democratic Underground*. September 27, 2005. http://www.democraticunderground.com/discuss/duboard.php?az =view_all&address=132x1403815.

Nichelson, Oliver. "Tesla's Wireless Power Transmitter." *Biblioteca Pleyades*. Accessed January 4, 2015. http://www.bibliotecapleyades.net/ciencia/esp_ciencia_tunguska 02.htm.

Nickell, Joe. "The Nazca Lines Revisited: Creation of a Full-sized Duplicate." *Onagocag Publishing Co.* Accessed November 22, 2014. http://www.onagocag.com/nazca.html. 2014.

"NSSM 200: Understanding National Security Study Memorandum 200." *Population Research Institute*. Accessed January 11, 2015. http://www.pop.org/content/nssm-200-understanding-national-security-1478.

"Operation Clambake Present: FBI the H-Files: An Archive of Documents Released by FBI about L. Ron Hubbard, the Founder of Scientology. Sorted by Date as Received from FBI Archives." *Operation Clambake*. Accessed December 2, 2014. http://www.xenu.net/archive/FBI/table.html.

Pacheco, Nelson S., and Tommy Blann. *Unmasking the Enemy*. Bendan Press, Inc. 1993.

"Pearl Harbor, 7 December, 1941." *Bytes*. December 6, 2010. http://bytesdaily.blogspot.com/2010/12/pearl-harbour-7-december-1941.html.

"Pearl Harbor Conspiracy." *Mystic Order of Noble Knowledge*. Accessed January 4, 2015. http://www.ancientmonks.com/mystical-order-of-neglected-knowledge/ 6th-degree-master-bishop-of-the-arcane-secret/pearl- harbor-conspiracy.

"Pearl Harbor, Oahu—The Attack: Facts and Information." *Pearl Harbor*. Accessed January 24, 2015. https://www.pearlharboroahu.com/attack.htm.

Peabody, David. "Exploding the Ripper Masonic Link." *MQ Magazine*, July 2002.

Peebles, Curtis. *Dark Eagles*. Novato, CA: Presidio Press, 1999.

Perloff, James. "Pearl Harbor: Hawaii Was Surprised; FDR Was Not." *The New American*. December 7, 2013. http://www.thenewamerican.com/culture/history/item/4740-pearl-harbor-hawaii-was-surprised-fdr-was-not.

Philips, Tom. "MH370: Six 'Reasons' Why Plane Vanished." *The Telegraph*. September 8, 2014. http://www.telegraph.co.uk/news/worldnews/asia/malaysia/11078770/MH370-Six-reasons-why-plane-vanished.html.

"Physical Evidence of Ancient Atomic Wars Can Be Found World-Wide." *Message to Eagle*. June 3, 2014. http://www.messagetoeagle.com/nuclearwarsgods.php#.VClKhWOEeSo.

Pilkington, Mark. "Ancient Electricity." *The Guardian*. April 21, 2004. http://www.theguardian.com/science/2004/apr/22/science.research.

———. "Plane Truth on the Conspiracy Trail." *archive.today*. Accessed January 28, 2015. http://archive.today/NFCOW.

Pitt, William Rivers, and Scott Ritter. *War on Iraq*. New York: Context Books, 2002.

Pittman, Ross. "9/11 Must See." *Consciouse Life News*. September 11, 2014. http://consciouslifenews.com/911-prove-airplane-hit-pentagon-major-general-albert-stubblebine/.

"Plato's Atlantis." *Ascending Passage*. Accessed December 4, 2015. http://ascendingpassage.com/plato-atlantis-critias.htm.

Popko, Rick. "Mythology/quetzalcoatl." *AllExperts*. March 3, 2010. http://en.allexperts.com/q/Mythology-658/2009/4/f/quetzalcoatl.htm.

"President Obama's Speech on Osama bin Laden's Death." *L. A. Times*. May 2, 2011. http://articles.latimes.com/2011/may/02/nation/la-na-bin-laden-obama-text-20110502.

"Proposed Studies on the Implications of Peaceful Space Activities for Human Affairs." *rr0*. Accessed January 29, 2015. http://rr0.org/time/1/9/6/1/04/18/Brookings_ ProposedStudiesOnTheImplicationsOfPeacefulSpaceActivitiesForHuman Affairs_NASA/index.html.

Prothero, Donald. "Area 51: Myth and Reality." *skepticblog*. January 8, 2014. http://www.skepticblog.org/2014/01/08/area-51-myth-and-reality/.

"Purple (cipher machine)." *Princeton University*. January 15, 2015. https://www.princeton.edu/~achaney/tmve/wiki100k/docs/Purple_%28cipher_machine%29.html.

Quayle, Steve. "Dead Scientists 2004–2014." *Steve Quayle*. January 2, 2015. http://www.stevequayle.com/?s=146.

"Quetzalcoatl." *Aztec and Maya Calendar*. December 20, 2015. http://www.azteccalendar.com/god/quetzalcoatl.html.

"Quetzalcoatl." *Crystalinks*. Accessed November 20, 2014. http://www.crystalinks.com/quetzalcoatl.html.

Radford, Ben. "Curious Contrails: Death from the Sky?" *Skeptical Inquirer*. March/April 2009.

Radford, Benjamin. "Viral Video Claims to Prove 'Chemtrails' Conspiracy." *Discovery News*. May 1, 2014. http://news.discovery.com/human/psychology/viral-video-claims-to-prove-chemtrails-conspiracy-140501.htm.

"Radioactive Remains from 8-12,000 Years Ago." *Forbidden History*. Accessed January 5, 2015. https://www.forbiddenhistory.info/?q=node/130.

Randle, Kevin. "New Roswell UFO Document?" *Kevin Randle*. October 23, 2009. http://kevinrandle.blogspot.com/2009/10/new-roswell-ufo-document.html.

———. "Philip Corso and the Day after Roswell, Again." *Kevin Randle*. January 22, 2014. http://kevinrandle.blogspot.com/2014/01/philip-corso-and-day-after-roswell-again.html.

Rea, Kari. "Glenn Greenwald: Low-Level NSA Analysts Have 'Powerful and Invasive' Search Tool." *ABC News*. July 28, 2013. http://abcnews.go.com/blogs/politics/2013/07/glenn-greenwald-low-level-nsa-analysts-have-powerful-and-invasive-search-tool/.

"Red Shadows." *Conelrad*. Accessed January 1, 2015. http://conelrad.com/books/spine.php?id=388_0_1_0_C. 2014.

Redfern, Nick. *Contactees*. Pompton Plains, NJ: New Page Books, 2009.

———. "Did Japan Invade Roswell?" *Mysterioud Universe*. December 13, 2013. http://mysteriousuniverse.org/2013/12/did-japan-invade-roswell/.

———. *Final Events*. San Antonio, TX: Anomalist Books, 2010.

———. Interview with Joe Jordan, February 4, 2010.

———. Interviews with Mac Tonnies, March 14, 2004 and September 9, 2006.

———. Interview with Neil Arnold, January 14, 2012.

———. Interview with Nick Pope, January 22, 1997.

———. Interview with Ray Boeche, January 22, 2007.

———. Interview with Ronan Coghlan, September 12, 2012.

———. *Wildman!* Woolsery, UK: CFZ Press, 2012.

———, and Brad Steiger. *The Zombie Book*. Detroit, MI: Visible Ink Press, 2014.

Reece, Katherine. "Grounding the Nasca Balloon." *In the Hall of Ma'at*. Accessed December 4, 2014. http://www.hallofmaat.com/modules.php?name=Articles&file=article&sid=96.

"Reform the Patriot Act." *ACLU*. Accessed January 14, 2015. https://www.aclu.org/reform-patriot-act.

"Report of Air Force Research Regarding the Roswell Incident." *Strange Magazine*. Accessed December 12, 2014. http://www.strangemag.com/reviews/reportofairforceresearch.html.

"Report of Scientific Advisory Panel on Unidentified Flying Objects Convened by Office of Scientific Intelligence, CIA January 14—18, 1953." *CUFON: The Computer UFO Network*. Accessed January 29, 2015. http://www.cufon.org/cufon/robert.htm.

Report of the Presidential Commission on the Space Shuttle Challenger Accident. Washington, DC: U.S. Government Printing Office, 1986.

"Report of the Select Committee on Assassinations of the U.S. House of Representatives." *National Archives*. Accessed January 23, 2015. http://www.archives.gov/research/jfk/select-committee-report/.

"Reptilians and Aztec." *Arcturi: Extra-terrestrial Database*. Accessed October 12, 2014. http://arcturi.com/ReptilianArchives/AztecMythology.html.

"Retired Agent Paid Undisclosed Amount in JFK Shooting Case." *Google News*. Accessed November 12, 2014. http://news.google.com/newspapers?id=dUsxAAAAIBAJ&sjid=gOYFAAAAIBAJ&pg =4654%2C213971.

"Retired General 'Surprised' No WMD Found." *ABC*. August 16, 2004. http://www.abc.net.au/news/2004-08-16/retired-general-surprised-no-wmd-found/2026360.

"RFK Assassination Witness Nina Rhodes-Hughes Says Sirhan Sirhan Didn't Act Alone." *Huffington Post*. April 30, 2012. http://www.huffingtonpost.com/2012/04/30/rfk-assassination-nina-rhodes-hughes_n_1464439.html.

Rifat, Tim. *Remote Viewing*. London: Vision Paperback, 2001.

Ritter, Steve. "Wiley's Death Caused by an Accidental Fall." *Chemical and Engineering News*. 80, no. 3 (January 21, 2002).

"The Robert Kennedy Assassination." *Mary Ferrell Foundation*. Accessed February 2, 2015. https://www.maryferrell.org/wiki/index.php/Robert_Kennedy_Assassination.

"Robert Wadlow, World's Tallest Man." *Roadside America*. Accessed December 3, 2014. http://www.roadsideamerica.com/story/2086.

Roberts, Paul Dale. "In Search of Quetzalcoatl." *Unexplained Mysteries*. February 26, 2009. http://www.unexplained-mysteries.com/column.php?id=147918.

Roberts, Sam. "In Archive, New Light on Eisenhower Speech." *The New York Times*. December 10, 2010. http://www.nytimes.com/2010/12/11/us/politics/11eisenhower.html?_r=1&.

Roberts, Scott Alan. *The Rise and Fall of the Nephilim*. Pompton Plains, NJ: New Page Books, 2012.

———. *The Secret History of the Reptilians*. Pompton Plains, NJ: New Page Books, 2013.

Roddy, Dennis B. "Looting of Baghdad Treasures Shines Light on a 'Dirty Business.'" *Pittsburgh Post-Gazette*. April 27, 2003. http://old.post-gazette.com/World/20030427lootingworld3p3.asp.

Roller, Emma. "This Is What Section 215 of the Patriot Act Does." *Slate*. June 7, 2013. http://www.slate.com/blogs/weigel/2013/06/07/nsa_prism_scandal_what_patriot_act_section_215_does.html.

"The Rollright Stones." *The Rollright Stones*. Access February 2, 2015. http://www.rollrightstones.co.uk/

Rosenberg, Jennifer. "Robert Kennedy Assassination." *About Education*. Accessed January 12, 2015. http://history1900s.about.com/od/1960s/a/Robert-Kennedy-Assassination.htm.

"Roswell and the Reich: The Nazi Connection." *ExoHuman*. February 2012. http://www.exohuman.com/wordpress/2012/02/roswell-and-the-reich-the-nazi-connection/.

Rubtsov, Vladimir V. "The Unknown Tunguska—What We Know and What We Do Not Know about the Great Explosion of 1908." *Fate*, May 2001.

Rudin, Mike. "The Conspiracy Files: 7/7." *BBC*. June 24, 2009. http://www.bbc.co.uk/blogs/legacy/theeditors/2009/06/the_conspiracy_files_77.html.

Rumbelow, Donald. *The Complete Jack the Ripper*. London: Penguin Books, 1988.

"Saddam Hussein's Weapons of Mass Destruction." *PBS*. Accessed January 12, 2015. http://www.pbs.org/wgbh/pages/frontline/shows/gunning/etc/arsenal.html.

Salla, Michael. "An Exopolitical Perspective on the Preemptive War against Iraq." *Exopolitics*. February 3, 2003. http://exopolitics.org/Study-Paper2.htm.

Sanderson, Ivan T. *Invisible Residents*. Cleveland, OH: The World Publishing Company, 1970.

Sangster, Angela. "Who Were the Anunnaki?" *True Ghost Tales*. Accessed October 14, 2014. http://www.trueghosttales.com/who-were-the-annunaki.php.

Satellite Accidents with Radiation Hazards. Home Office. March 2, 1979.

Schneweis, Emil. *Angels and Demons According to Lactantius*. Washington, DC: Catholic University of America Press, 1944.

Schoch, Robert M. "The Great Sphinx." *Robert Schoch*. Accessed January 3, 2015. http://www.robertschoch.com/sphinxcontent.html.

Schroeder, Paul. "Ancient Aliens and the Ark of the Covenant." *Before It's News*. September 1, 2010. http://beforeitsnews.com/paranormal/2010/09/ancient-aliens-and-the-ark-of-the-covenant-by-paul-schroeder-158206.html.

"The Secret History of the U-2—and Area 51." *The National Security Archive at George Washington University*. August 15, 2013. http://www2.gwu.edu/~nsarchiv /NSAEBB/NSAEBB434/.

"Shamanic Order to be Established Here." *Los Angeles Times*, April 1934.

Shannan, Pat. "Former CIA Participant Says He Was Part Of It—Raoul Identified as FBI Agent." *Rense*. January 12, 2002. http://www.rense.com/general19/part.htm.

Shuker, Karl. "The Green Children of Woolpit: Investigating a Medieval Mystery." *The Electarium of Dr. Shuker*. November 29, 2012. http://eclectariumshuker.blogspot.com/2012/11/the-green-children-of-woolpit.html.

Sibir, July 2, 1908.

"Sirhan Sirhan and His Account of Delta Programming Mind Control." *Vigilant Citizen*. May 5, 2011. http://vigilantcitizen.com/latestnews/sirhan-sirhan-and-his-account-of-delta-programming-mind-control/.

Sitchin, Zecharia. *The 12th Planet*. New York: Harper-Collins, 2007.

———. *Divine Encounters*. New York: Avon Books, 1996.

———. *Genesis Revisited*. New York: Avon Books, 1990.

———. "The Case of the Evil Wind." *The Official Website of Zecharia Sitchin*. November 2001. http://www.sitchin.com/evilwind.htm.

———. *When Time Began*. New York: Avon Books, 1993.

Snyder, Michael. "After the Government Microchips Our Soldiers, How Long Will It Be before They Want to Put a Microchip in YOU." *End of the American Dream*. May 8, 2012. http://endoftheamericandream.com/archives/after-the-government -microchips-our-soldiers-how-long-will-it-be-before-they-want-to-put-a-micro chip-in-you.

———. "From 7 Billion People to 500 Million People—The Sick Population Control Agenda of the Global Elite." *End of the American Dream*. October 27, 2011. http://end oftheamericandream.com/archives/from-7-billion-people-to-500-million-people -the-sick-population-control- agenda-of-the-global-elite.

Soni, Darshna. "Survey: 'Government Hasn't Told Truth about 7/7.'" *Channel 4*. June 4, 2007. http://www.channel4.com/news/articles/society/religion/survey+govern ment+hasnt+told+truth+about+77/545847.html.

"Space-Life Report Could Be Shock." *NICAP UFO Investigator*. December 1960/January 1961.

"Space Shuttle Challenger." *FBI*. Accessed December 5, 2014. http://vault.fbi.gov/Space %20Shuttle%20Challenger%20/.

Sperber, A.M. *Murrow: His Life and Times*. Bronx, NY: Fordham University Press, 1999.

Stableford, Dylan. "Rupert Murdoch Tweets His Theory on Malaysian Plane Disappearance." *Yahoo! News*. March 16, 2014. http://news.yahoo.com/rupert-mur doch-malaysian-plane-tweet-152052211.html.

Stebner, Beth. "Bobby Kennedy Assassin Still Claims He Was 'Victim of Mind Control and His Gun Didn't Fire Fatal Shot' in New Appeal after Parole Is Denied." *The Daily Mail*. December 15, 2011. http://www.dailymail.co.uk/news/article-2066883 /Robert-F-Kennedy-assassin-Sirhan-Sirhan-claims-victim-mind-control.html.

Steiger, Brad. "Who Really Killed Abraham Lincoln?" *Rense*. February 11, 2008. http:// www.rense.com/general80/slin.htm.

Steiger, Brad. *Real Monsters, Gruesome Critters, and Beasts from the Darkside*. Detroit, MI: Visible Ink Press, 2011.

———, and Sherry Steiger. *Conspiracies and Secret Societies: The Complete Dossier*. Detroit, MI: Visible Ink Press, 2012.

Stinnett, Robert B. "The Pearl Harbor Deceit." *World War II History Info*. Accessed January 29, 2015. http://worldwar2history.info/Pearl-Harbor/deceit.html.

Strickler, Lon. "The Bigfoot Paradox." *Phantoms and Monsters*. Accessed January 3, 2015. http://www.phantomsandmonsters.com/p/near-end-of-overnight-appearance- of.html.

Stringfield, Leonard. *Situation Red: The UFO Siege*. London: Sphere Books, 1978.

———. *UFO Crash/Retrievals: Amassing the Evidence*. Cincinnati, OH: privately printed, 1982.

Stuster, J. Dana. "Declassified: The CIA Secret History of Area 51." *FP*. August 15, 2013. http://blog.foreignpolicy.com/posts/2013/08/15/declassified_the_cias_secret_ history_of_area_51.

"Surveillance Under the USA PATRIOT Act." *ACLU*. December 10, 2010. https:// www.aclu.org/national-security/surveillance-under-usa-patriot-act.

Szymanksi, Greg. "Plans to Microchip Every Newborn in US and Europe Underway— Former Chief Medical Officer of Finland." *Rense*. May 11. 2006. http://www .rense.com/general71/under.htm.

Taylor, Philip. "The Mystic and the Spy: Two Early British UFO Writers." *Magonia*, No. 61, 1997.

Taylor, III, Porcher. "Ararat Anomaly." *NoahsArkSearch*. January 9, 1996. http://www .noahsarksearch.com/porcher.htm.

Thomas, Gordon. "The Secret World of Dr. David Kelly." *The Rumor Mills News Reading Room*. August 21, 2003. http://www.rumormillnews.com/cgi-bin/archive.cgi ?noframes;read=35765.

Thomas, William. "Stolen Skies: The Chemtrail Mystery." *Earth Island Institute*. Accessed December 3, 2015. http://www.earthisland.org/journal/index.php/eij/ article/stolen_skies_the_chemtrail_mystery/.

Thompson, Geoff. "US Involved in Bird Flu Conspiracy: Indonesia." *ABNC*. February 20, 2008. http://www.abc.net.au/am/content/2008/s2167325.htm.

Thompson, Reginald Campbell. *Devils and Evil Spirits of Babylonia*. Whitefish, MT: Kessinger Publishing, 2003.

"Timeline for American Airlines Flight 77." *NPR*. June 17, 2004. http://www.npr.org/ templates/story/story.php?storyId=1962742.

"TIMELINE—How Malaysia's Flight MH370 Went Missing." *Reuters*. March 17, 2014. http://www.reuters.com/article/2014/03/17/malaysia-airlines-idUSL3N0ME0RL 20140317.

"Timeline of Flight MH370." *CNBC*. April 7, 2014. http://www.cnbc.com/id/101559060#.

"Timeline of the 7 July Attacks." *BBC*. July 11, 2006. http://news.bbc.co.uk/2/hi/uk_ news/5032756.stm.

Tonnies, Mac. *After the Martian Apocalypse*. New York: Paraview-Pocket Books, 2004.

———. *The Cryptoterrestials*. San Antonio, TX: Anomalist Books, 2010.

"Transcript: Obama's Remarks on NSA Controversy." *WSJ Blogs*. June 7, 2013. http://blogs.wsj.com/washwire/2013/06/07/transcript-what-obama-said-on-nsa-controversy/.

"Transcript of Powell's U.N. presentation." *CNN*. February 5, 2003. http://www.cnn .com/2003/US/02/05/sprj.irq.powell.transcript.05/.

"The Travels of Pedro de Cieza de Léon, A.D. 1532–50, Contained in the First Part of His Chronicle of Peru (1864)." *Internet Archive*. March 10, 2001. https:// archive.org/details/travelsofpedrode33ciez.

Treiman, Daniel. "A 9/11 Conspiracy? 'I Would Not Be Surprised,' Says Tikkun Editor." *Forward: The Jewish Daily*. February 6, 2007. http://forward.com/articles/ 10024/a-govt-conspiracy-i-wouldnt-be-surprised-sa/.

"A True Account of Alien Abduction." *UFO Casebook*. Accessed February 2, 2015. http://www.ufocasebook.com/trueaccountofalienabduction.html.

"The Tunguska Impact—100 Years Later." *NASA Science: Science News*. June 30, 2008. http://science.nasa.gov/science-news/science-at-nasa/2008/30jun_tunguska/.

Unger, Merrill F. *Demons in the World Today*. Northumberland, UK: Tynedale House, 1995.

———. *What Demons Can Do to Saints*. Chicago, IL: Moody Press, 1977.

"United States Department of Justice Investigation of Recent Allegations Regarding the Assassination of Dr. Martin Luther King, Jr." *The United States Department of Justice*. June 2000. http://www.justice.gov/crt/about/crm/mlk/part1.php.

"Unusual Option Market Activity and the Terrorist Attacks of September 11, 2001." *Reddit*. Accessed November 8, 2014. http://www.reddit.com/r/investing/comments/2g43y5/unusual_option_market_activity_and_the_terrorist/.

"U.S. Department of Defense, DoD News Briefing: Secretary of Defense William S. Cohen." *U.S. Department of Defense*. April 28, 1997. www.defense.gov/transcripts/transcript.aspx?transcriptid=674.

"US Expert Slams WMD 'Delusions.'" *BBC*. June 5, 2004. http://news.bbc.co.uk/2/hi/middle_east/3778987.stm.

"US Family Gets Health Implants." *BBC*. May 11, 2002. http://news.bbc.co.uk/2/hi/health/1981026.stm.

Valiunis, Algis. "The Agony of Atomic Genius." *The New Atlantis*, Number 14, Fall 2006.

Van Woerkom, Barbara. "Timeline: The Raid on Osama Bin Laden's Hideout." *NPR*. May 3, 2011. http://www.npr.org/2011/05/03/135951504/timeline-the-raid-on-osama-bin-ladens-hideout.

"Vast Majority of NSA Spy Targets Are Mistakenly Monitored." *Louisiana State News*. July 6, 2014. http://www.louisiana.statenews.net/index.php/sid/223558101/scat/b8de8e630faf3631/ht/Vast-majority-of-NSA-spy-targets-are-mistakenly-monitored.

Velikovsky, Immanuel. *Earth in Upheaval*. London: Paradigma, 2009.

"Vimanas." *Hindu Wisdom*. October 28, 2008. http://www.hinduwisdom.info/Vimanas.htm.

Vintini, Leonardo. "Desert Glass Formed by Ancient Atomic Bombs?" *Epoch Times*. April 30, 2013. http://m.theepochtimes.com/n3/23630-ancient-atomic-bombs/.

Vorhees, Josh. "Obama Defends NSA Surveillance: 'Nobody Is Listening to Your Telephone Calls.'" *Slate*. June 7, 2013. http://www.slate.com/blogs/the_slatest/2013/06/07/obama_defends_nsa_surveillance.html.

Wald, Matthew L., and Michael S. Schmidt. "Lost Jet's Path Seen as Altered via Computer." *The New York Times*. March 17, 2014. http://www.nytimes.com/2014/03/18/world/asia/malaysia-airlines-flight.html.

Warrick, Joby. "Lacking Biolabs, Trailer Carried Case for War." *The Washington Post*. April 12, 2006. http://www.washingtonpost.com/wp-dyn/content/article/2006/04/11/AR2006041101888.html.

"Watergate: The Scandal That Brought Down Richard Nixon." *Watergate.info*. Accessed January 30, 2015. http://watergate.info/.

Watson, Paul Joseph. "Ex-DARPA Head Wants You to Swallow ID Microchips." *InfoWars*. January 7, 2014. http://www.infowars.com/ex-darpa-head-wants-you-to-swallow-id-microchips/.

———. "Military Whistleblower Claims She Witnessed Flight 93 Shootdown Order." *Alex Jones' Prison Planet*. April 8, 2009. http://www.prisonplanet.com/military-whistleblower-claims-she-witnessed-flight-93-shootdown-order.html.

———. "The Population Reduction Agenda for Dummies." *Alex Jones' Prison Planet*. June 26, 2009. http://www.prisonplanet.com/the-population-reduction-agenda-for-dummies.html.

———, and Alex Jones. "London Underground Bombing 'Exercises' Took Place at Same Time as Real Attack." *Alex Jones' Prison Planet*. July 13, 2005. http://www.prison planet.com/articles/july2005/090705bombingexercises.htm.

Watson, Traci. "Conspiracy Theories Find Menace in Contrails." *USA Today*. March 7, 2001. http://usatoday30.usatoday.com/weather/science/2001-03-07-contrails.htm.

"Weapons of Mass Destruction: Who Said What When." *Counterpunch*. May 29, 2003. http://www.counterpunch.org/2003/05/29/weapons-of-mass-destruction-who-said-what-when/.

Weaver, Sandra. "Quetzalcoatl Is Deeper Than Just a Mayan Story or Myth." *Spiritual Growth Prophecies*. Accessed February 2, 2015. http://www.2012-spiritual-growth-prophecies.com/quetzalcoatl.html.

Webby, Sean, and Lisa Krieger. "Pizza Delivery May Have Been Ambush: Suspect Later Found Dead." *San Jose Mercury News*, February, 28, 2002.

"Welcome to Woolpit Village." *Woolpit Village*. http://www.woolpit.org/. Accessed January 30, 2015.

"What Hit the Pentagon?" *9-11 Review*. December 21, 2012. http://911review.com/attack/pentagon/hypothesis.html.

"When Was Pearl Harbor, December 7, 1941, a Day That Will Live in Infamy!" *Before It's News*. December 6, 2012. http://beforeitsnews.com/alternative/2012/12/when-was-pearl-harbor-december-7-1941-a-day-that-will-live-in-infamy-2509294.html.

"Who Killed Off Star Wars Scientists?" *UFO Evidence*. Accessed January 30, 2015. http://www.ufoevidence.org/documents/doc826.htm.

"Why Was John Lennon's Doorman on CIA Payroll?" *The Rumor Mill News Reading Room*. May 27, 2006. http://www.rumormillnews.com/cgi-bin/archive.cgi/noframes/read/86959.

Wilkinson, Sophie. "Harvard Biochemist Don C. Wiley Disappears in Memphis." *Chemical and Engineering News*, 79, no. 49 (December 3, 2001).

"William Mark Felt Biography." *Biography*. Accessed January 30, 2015. http://www.biography.com/people/william-mark-felt-396780.

Wilmut, Ian. "John Clark: Pioneering Scientist Whose Entrepreneurial Skills Paved the Way for Dolly the Sheep." *Guardian*, August 25, 2004.

Wilson, Lawrence. "Hypnosis." *Dr. L. Wilson*. June 2013. http://www.drlwilson.com/Articles/HYPNOSIS.htm.

Wingate, Richard. *Atlantis in the Amazon*. Rochester, VT: Bear & Company, 2011.

"The Winterwind Papers." *Winterwind Productions*. Accessed January 15, 2015. http://www.winterwind-productions.com/issue18/duncan_lunan3.htm.

Withnall, Adam. "Missing Malaysia Airlines Flight MH370 Was 'Shot Down in Military Training Exercise' Claims First Book Released about Lost Jet." *The Independent*. May 18, 2014. http://www.independent.co.uk/news/world/asia/missing-malaysia-airlines-flight-mh370-was-shot-down-in-military-training-exercise-claims-first-book-released-about-lost-jet-9391964.html.

Wittnebel, Matthew, and Andrew Mann. "The Tunguska Event." *The Lone Conspirators*. Accessed January 6, 2015. http://theloneconspirators.com/tunguska.htm.

"Wolfowitz Comments Revive Doubts over Iraq's WMD." *USA Today*. June 1, 2003. http://usatoday30.usatoday.com/news/world/iraq/2003-05-30-wolfowitz-iraq_x.htm.

Woodman, Jim. *Nazca: Journey to the Sun*. New York: Pocket Books, 1977.

Woodward, Bob. "How Mark Felt Became 'Deep Throat.'" *Washington Post*. June 2, 2005. http://www.washingtonpost.com/wp-dyn/articles/A40105-2005Jun2.html?nav=E8.

———. *The Secret Man: The Story of Watergate's Deep Throat*. New York: Simon & Schuster, 2006.

INDEX

Note: (ill.) indicates photos and illustrations.

U

U-2, 258–59

Uecker, Karl, 211

UFO Crash/Retrievals: Amassing the Evidence (Stringfield), 305

UFO Reports and Classified Projects, 147

UFOs

alien demons, 54–55, 57

alien parallels to the Ten Commandments, 5–10

Anunnaki, 47

Area 51 conspiracy, 256, 260–66

Bigfoot and, 81–86

black helicopter conspiracy, 301–3, 305

Brookings Report conspiracy, 183–84, 187

cattle mutilation conspiracy, 222, 229

crop circle conspiracy, 269, 271

Ezekiel's wheel, 24, 26–29

fake alien conspiracy, 178–182

government secrets, 60, 63–64

green children of Woolpit, 87–88

illustration, 84 (ill.)

John F. Kennedy conspiracy, 197

Jonah and the whale, 102–6

Marilyn Monroe conspiracy, 189

photo, 302 (ill.)

plagues of Egypt, 73

Quetzalcoatl, 66–67

Roswell crash conspiracy, 145–151

secrets of the museum, 40

stealthy aircraft vs. aliens conspiracy, 277–282, 284–85

Tunguska conspiracy, 125

Walt Disney conspiracy, 162, 164–68

UFOs: Friend, Foe, or Fantasy? 167

Uhouse, Bill, 263–64

Ulfketel, Earl, 88

UN (United Nations), 337–340, 348, 358, 360–61, 364, 377, 382

UN Security Council, 338–39

UNESCO (United Nations Educational, Scientific and Cultural Organization), 75–76

Unger, Merrill F., 56

Unidentified Submerged Objects (USOs), 103–4

United Airlines, 309, 311, 316–18

United Grand Lodge of England, 115

United Kingdom Atomic Energy Authority, 233

United Nations Educational, Scientific and Cultural Organization (UNESCO), 75–76

United Nations Monitoring, Verification and Inspection Commission, 339

United Nations (UN), 337–340, 348, 358, 360–61, 364, 377, 382

United States Army Intelligence and Security Command, 320

United States Army Medical Research Institute of Infectious Diseases (USAMRIID), 325–27, 329

Unmasking the Enemy (Pacheco and Blann), 57

Unusual Martian Surface Features (DiPietro and Molenaar), 93

U.S. Army Health Services Command (HSC), 325

U.S. Army Material Command, 325

U.S. Army Medical Command, 325

U.S. Biological Warfare Program, 325

U.S. National Science Advisory Board for Biosecurity, 379

U.S. Naval Special Warfare Development Group, 380

USAF 2025, 286, 288–89, 291–92, 294–95

USAMRIID (United States Army Medical Research Institute of Infectious Diseases), 325–27, 329

USOs (Unidentified Submerged Objects), 103–4

USS *Shaw*, 127 (ill.)

Utopia (More), 13

Uxmal, 60, 61 (ill.)

V

Valdez, Gabe, 223–28, 303

Valley of Elah, 51

Van Arsdale, Peter, 229

Van Flandern, Tom, 95

Van Nguyen, Set, 346

Van Tassel, George, 9–11

Vanavara Factory, 123

Vancouver Island, 298

vanishing plane, 393–400

Varandal, Jean, 89

Vasilyev, N. V., 125

The Vault, 135, 164, 222, 238, 246, 303

Vector, 348

Velikovsky, Immanuel, 32, 32 (ill.)

VeriChip, 369

Verizon, 389

Victoria, Queen, 115

Victoria International Airport, 297–98

Victory Over the Darkness (Anderson), 56

Vietnam War, 210

Vigilant Guardian, 311

Viking 1, 92–93

Vimanas, 35

Vintini, Leonardo, 32

Virginia Biotechnology Association, 346

Virginia Center for Innovative Technology, 345

viruses, alien, 69–74

Vishnu, 36

Visor Consulting, 352–53

von Braun, Werner, 142–43, 143 (ill.), 168 (ill.)

von Daniken, Erich, 28–29, 68, 78–79

Vrishnis, 35

W

Wadlow, Robert, 53, 53 (ill.)

Wainwright, Milton, 72

Wake Up Down There! (Bishop), 7

Wald, Jerry, 192

Walker, John, 55

Wallace Jr., George, 219

Walt Disney Corporation, 162

Walt Disney, Inc., 167

Walter, Mike, 320

Wanaque Reservoir, 301

war, ancient nuclear, 30–37

War of the Worlds (Wells), 147, 181, 264

War on Iraq (Ritter and Pitt), 339

War on Terror, 276, 328

War Serpent, 67

Warka Vase, 39

Warren, Earl, 195

Warren, Larry, 84

Warren, Shani, 252

Warren, Shields, 172

Warren, Sir Charles, 115–16

Warren Commission, 195

The Wars of Gods and Men (Sitchin), 46

Wash, Jonathan, 251

Washington Dulles International Airport, 319

Washington National Airport, 162–63

Watergate, 216–221, 238, 387

Watergate Complex, 216, 220 (ill.)

Watson, Paul Joseph, 318, 364, 370–71

Watson, Traci, 297

weapons, biological, 373–79

Weapons of Mass Destruction (WMDs), 336–343, 338 (ill.)

Weather as a Force Multiplier: Owning the Weather in 2025, 286

Weaver, Sandra, 67

Webb, Brigadier General Marshall B., 382 (ill.)

Webster, William H., 246

Weijerman, F. G., 130

Weimar Republic, 132

Weisel, William, 212

Welles, Orson, 167, 180–81, 181 (ill.)

Wells, Alice, 7

Wells, H. G., 181

West Bank, 51

Western Airlines, 193

Westwood Village Memorial Park Cemetery, 191, 191 (ill.)